THE TRADIT

OF THE

WESTERN WORLD

GENERAL EDITOR, J. H. HEXTER
Yale University

Volume 1

ANTIQUITY AND

THE MIDDLE AGES

CONTRIBUTING EDITORS: JOHN W. SNYDER
Indiana University

PETER RIESENBERG
Washington University

Rand McNally & Company
Chicago

RAND McNALLY HISTORY SERIES

FRED HARVEY HARRINGTON, *Advisory Editor*

THE TRADITIONS OF THE WESTERN WORLD

General Editor: J. H. HEXTER

Volume I   *Antiquity and the Middle Ages*
Contributing Editors: JOHN W. SNYDER
PETER RIESENBERG

Volume II   *Renaissance, Reformation, and the Early Modern Period*
Contributing Editors: PETER RIESENBERG
FRANKLIN L. FORD

Volume III   *The Recent Period, 1815 to the Present*
Contributing Editor: KLAUS EPSTEIN

FOR THE READER:
HOW TO GET THE MOST OUT OF
THIS WORK

In issuing multivolume paperback editions of *The Traditions of the Western World,* the publisher's purpose is to preserve the unique useful features of the successful one volume edition, and also to produce books adapted to the wide variety of courses on Western Civilization. These paperback volumes can be used separately in the study of single eras in the history of the Western World, or as a series for a comprehensive study of the development of Western civilization.

The publisher wishes again to stress the care and thorough planning that went into the development of this excellent work and to restate the editors' aim and design:

1. To broaden the scope of the book as it approaches the present. This proportioning does not stand as a measure or estimate of worth of the men of earlier ages; it merely recognizes that the recent past has more directly molded our present thoughts and patterns.

2. To provide relevant background material in short introductions that do not impose on the reader the editors' interpretations of the documents.

3. To choose documents that will help readers understand the varied traditions of Western civilization, and will render those traditions intelligible without elaborate pre-commentary by the editors. Sometimes the editors have grouped several documents into a "source cluster." In such instances the significance of a particular document is revealed by considering it in the context provided by the other documents in the cluster.

4. To precede the documents or source clusters with questions which bring into focus the significant points in the material that follows, without providing the reader with a prepackaged interpretation. This will give the student a frame of reference for each selection but will still require him to study it carefully to arrive at his own conclusion about its significance and meaning.

5. To supply in footnotes background on unfamiliar material or events that students may find necessary to understanding. The back-references in footnotes refer the reader to documents included earlier in the

entire work. Such references suggest some sort of relationship with the earlier source, but do not necessarily indicate that the relationship is one of *derivation;* on the contrary, the relationship may be one of *deviation.* Such references will distinguish continuities and discontinuities in the development of the traditions of our civilization.

6. To indicate kinds of abridgment in the documents by the use of three forms: (1) the ellipses (. . .) where the omission does not break into the flow of the document; (2) linear asterisks (* * *) where there is a major disjunction of thought; and (3) italic editor's comments that summarize the omitted material where the omission could cause confusion.

7. "Translations" from English to English, where Middle, and even sixteenth- and seventeenth-century, English would obscure the authors' meanings to modern-English-speaking students.

The editors have, in this work, produced a better and more useful text than any other of its kind. It is a work that enables the reader who has not done so before to familiarize himself with many of the traditions of the Western world, and to do so in a convenient and efficient manner.

THE COLLEGE DEPARTMENT
RAND McNALLY & COMPANY

Fall, 1969

TABLE OF CONTENTS

Antiquity

Edited by *JOHN W. SNYDER*

CONTENTS

The Middle Ages

Edited by PETER RIESENBERG

THE TRADITIONS OF
THE WESTERN WORLD

Volume 1

THE SOURCES OF
WESTERN TRADITIONS

*Since the Renaissance and, even more, since the early nineteenth century,
Western men have grown increasingly conscious of their historic past, increasingly aware of the complex of traditions that have formed them. Before launch-
ing into a study of this selection of documents, chosen because they embody
and represent many of those traditions, the student may do well to gain some
sense of the terrain he is traversing. This source book therefore begins with a
survey of that terrain by an articulate and intelligent present-day Protestant
theologian, Reinhold Niebuhr (1892–   ). Many of his fellow Christians would
disagree in part with Niebuhr's appraisals of some features of the terrain, while
some non-Christians would agree in part. As the reader reads the documents
in this book, he may find himself agreeing or disagreeing on the whole or in
part. Niebuhr's survey is presented here not to instruct the reader about what he
should see en route, but to provide him with some sense of the direction in
which he is heading. When he has gone the course, he may wish to return to
Niebuhr's summary and evaluate it on the basis of his own experience.*

THE NATURE AND DESTINY OF MAN*

Reinhold Niebuhr

Man has always been his own most vexing problem. How shall he
think of himself? Every affirmation which he may make about his stature,
virtue, or place in the cosmos becomes involved in contradictions when fully
analysed. The analysis reveals some presupposition or implication which seems
to deny what the proposition intended to affirm.

If man insists that he is a child of nature and that he ought not to pre-
tend to be more than the animal, which he obviously is, he tacitly admits that
he is, at any rate, a curious kind of animal who has both the inclination and

---

* Reprinted with permission of Charles Scribner's Sons from *Human Nature*, Volume I of
The Nature and Destiny of Man, pages 1–25, by Reinhold Niebuhr. Copyright 1941 Charles
Scribner's Sons.

the capacity to make such pretensions. If on the other hand he insists upon his unique and distinctive place in nature and points to his rational faculties as proof of his special eminence, there is usually an anxious note in his avowals of uniqueness which betrays his unconscious sense of kinship with the brutes. This note of anxiety gives poignant significance to the heat and animus in which the Darwinian controversy was conducted and the Darwinian thesis was resisted by the traditionalists. Furthermore the very effort to estimate the significance of his rational faculties implies a degree of transcendence over himself which is not fully defined or explained in what is usually connoted by "reason." For the man who weighs the importance of his rational faculties is in some sense more than "reason" and has capacities which transcend the ability to form general concepts.

If man takes his uniqueness for granted he is immediately involved in questions and contradictions on the problem of his virtue. If he believes himself to be essentially good and attributes the admitted evils of human history to specific social and historical causes he involves himself in begging the question; for all these specific historical causes of evil are revealed, upon close analysis, to be no more than particular consequences and historical configurations of evil tendencies in man himself. They cannot be understood at all if a capacity for, and inclination toward, evil in man himself is not presupposed. If, on the other hand, man comes to pessimistic conclusions about himself, his capacity for such judgments would seem to negate the content of the judgments. How can man be "essentially" evil if he knows himself to be so? What is the character of the ultimate subject, the quintessential "I," which passes such devastating judgments upon itself as object?

If one turns to the question of the value of human life and asks whether life is worth living, the very character of the question reveals that the questioner must in some sense be able to stand outside of, and to transcend the life which is thus judged and estimated. Man can reveal this transcendence more explicitly not only by actually committing suicide but by elaborating religions and philosophies which negate life and regard a "lifeless" eternity, such as Nirvana, as the only possible end of life.

Have those who inveigh so violently against otherworldliness in religion, justified as their criticisms may be, ever fully realized what the error of denying life implies in regard to the stature of man? The man who can negate "life" must be something other than mere vitality. Every effort to dissuade him from the neglect of natural vitality and historic existence implies a vantage point in him above natural vitality and history; otherwise he would not be tempted to the error from which he is to be dissuaded.

Man's place in the universe is subject to the same antinomies. Men have been assailed periodically by qualms of conscience and fits of dizziness for pretending to occupy the center of the universe. Every philosophy of life is touched with anthropocentric tendencies. Even theocentric religions believe that the Creator of the world is interested in saving man from his unique predicament. But periodically man is advised and advises himself to moderate his pretensions and admit that he is only a little animal living a precarious existence on a second-rate planet, attached to a second-rate sun. There are moderns who believe that this modesty is the characteristic genius of modern man and the fruit of his discovery of the vastness of interstellar spaces; but it was no modern astronomer who confessed, "When I consider thy heavens, the work of thy fingers, the moon and the stars, which thou hast ordained; What is man that thou art mindful of him?" (Ps. 8:4). Yet the vantage point from which man judges his insignificance is a rather significant vantage point. This fact has not been lost on the moderns whose modesty before the cosmic immensity was modified considerably by pride in their discovery of this immensity. It was a modern, the poet Swinburne,[1] who sang triumphantly:

> The seal of his knowledge is sure, the truth and his spirit are wed; . . .
> Glory to Man in the highest! for man is the master of things,

thereby proving that the advance of human knowledge about the world does not abate the pride of man.

While these paradoxes of human self-knowledge are not easily reduced to simpler formulae, they all point to two facts about man: one of them obvious and the other not quite so obvious. The two are not usually appreciated with equal sympathy. The obvious fact is that man is a child of nature, subject to its vicissitudes, compelled by its necessities, driven by its impulses, and confined within the brevity of the years which nature permits its varied organic form, allowing them some, but not too much, latitude. The other less obvious fact is that man is a spirit who stands outside of nature, life, himself, his reason and the world. This latter fact is appreciated in one or the other of its aspects by various philosophies. But it is not frequently appreciated in its total import. That man stands outside of nature in some sense is admitted even by naturalists who are intent upon keeping him as close to nature as possible. They must at least admit that he is *homo faber*, a tool-making animal. That man stands outside the world is admitted by rationalists who, with Aristotle, define man as a rational animal and interpret reason as the capacity for making general concepts. But the rationalists do not always understand that man's rational capacity involves a further ability to stand outside himself, a capacity for self-transcendence, the ability to make himself his own object, a quality of spirit which is usually not fully comprehended or connoted in *"ratio"* or "nous" or "reason" or any of the concepts which philosophers usually use to describe the uniqueness of man.

How difficult it is to do justice to both the uniqueness of man and his affinities with the world of nature below him is proved by the almost unvarying tendency of those philosophies, which describe and emphasize the rational faculties of man or his capacity for self-transcendence to forget his relation to nature and to identify him, prematurely and unqualifiedly, with the divine and the eternal; and of naturalistic philosophies to obscure the uniqueness of man.

THE CLASSICAL VIEW OF MAN

Though man has always been a problem to himself, modern man has aggravated that problem by his too simple and premature solutions. Modern man, whether idealist or naturalist, whether rationalist or romantic, is char-

---

[1] Algernon Charles Swinburne (1837–1909), English lyrical poet.

acterized by his simple certainties about himself. He has aggravated the problem of understanding himself because these certainties are either in contradiction with each other or in contradiction with the obvious facts of history, more particularly of contemporary history; and either they have been controverted by that history or they are held in defiance of its known facts. It is not unfair to affirm that modern culture, that is, our culture since the Renaissance, is to be credited with the greatest advances in the understanding of nature and with the greatest confusion in the understanding of man. Perhaps this credit and debit are logically related to each other.

Fully to appreciate the modern conflicts in regard to human nature, it is necessary to place the characteristically modern doctrines of man in their historic relation to the traditional view of human nature which have informed western culture. All modern views of human nature are adaptations, transformations and varying compounds of primarily two distinctive views of man: (*a*) The view of classical antiquity, that is of the Graeco-Roman world, and (*b*) the Biblical view. It is important to remember that while these two views are distinct and partly incompatible, they were actually merged in the thought of medieval Catholicism. (The perfect expression of this union is to be found in the Thomistic synthesis of Augustinian and Aristotelian thought.) The history of modern culture really begins with the destruction of this synthesis, foreshadowed in nominalism, and completed in the Renaissance and Reformation. In the dissolution of the synthesis, the Renaissance distilled the classical elements out of the synthesis, and the Reformation sought to free the Biblical from the classical elements. Liberal Protestantism is an effort (on the whole an abortive one) to reunite the two elements. There is, in fact, little that is common between them. What was common in the two views was almost completely lost after modern thought had reinterpreted and transmuted the classical view of man in the direction of a greater naturalism. Modern culture has thus been a battleground of two opposing views of human nature. This conflict could not be resolved. It ended in the more or less complete triumph of the modernized classical view of man, a triumph which in this latter day is imperilled not by any external foe but by confusion within its own household. To validate this analysis of the matter requires at least a brief preliminary analysis of the classical and the Christian views of human nature.

The classical view of man, comprised primarily of Platonic, Aristotelian and Stoic conceptions of human nature, contains, of course, varying emphases but it may be regarded as one in its common conviction that man is to be understood primarily from the standpoint of the uniqueness of his rational faculties. What is unique in man is his *nous*. *Nous* may be translated as "spirit" but the primary emphasis lies upon the capacity for thought and reason. In Aristotle[2] the *nous* is the vehicle of purely intellectual activity and is a universal and immortal principle which enters man from without. Only one element in it, the "passive" in distinction to the "active" *nous* becomes involved in, and subject to, the individuality of a particular physical organism. How completely the Aristotelian *nous* is intellectual may best be understood by Aristotle's explicit denial of its capacity for self-consciousness. It does not

---

[2] The reader will become more closely acquainted later with Aristotle and others named in this selection.

make itself its own object except in making things known the object of consciousness: "No mind knows itself by participation in the known; it becomes known by touching and knowing, so that the same thing is mind and object of mind." This definition is the more significant when contrasted with Aristotle's conception of divine consciousness which expresses itself only in terms of self-knowledge.

In Plato the *nous* or *logistikon* is not as sharply distinguished from the soul as in Aristotle. It is, rather, the highest element in the soul, the other two being the spirited element and the appetitive element. In both Plato and Aristotle "mind" is sharply distinguished from the body. It is the unifying and ordering principle, the organ of *logos,* which brings harmony into the life of the soul, as *logos* is the creative and forming principle of the world. Greek metaphysical presuppositions are naturally determinative for the doctrine of man; and since Parmenides Greek philosophy had assumed an identity between being and reason on the one hand and on the other hand presupposed that reason works upon some formless or unformed stuff which is never completely tractable. In the thought of Aristotle matter is "a remnant, the non-existent in itself unknowable and alien to reason, that remains after the process of clarifying the thing into form and conception. This non-existent neither is nor is not; it is 'not yet,' that is to say it attains reality only insofar as it becomes the vehicle of some conceptual determination."

Plato and Aristotle share a common rationalism; and also a common dualism which is explicit in the case of Plato and implicit and covert in the case of Aristotle. The effect of this rationalism and dualism has been determinative for the classical doctrine of man and for all modern doctrines which are borrowed from it. The consequences are: (*a*) The rationalism practically identifies rational man (who is essential man) with the divine; for reason is, as the creative principle, identical with God. Individuality is no significant concept, for it rests only upon the particularity of the body. In the thought of Aristotle only the active *nous,* precisely the mind which is not involved in the soul, is immortal; and for Plato the immutability of ideas is regarded as a proof of the immortality of the spirit. (*b*) The dualism has the consequence for the doctrine of man of identifying the body with evil and of assuming the essential goodness of mind or spirit. This body-mind dualism and the value judgments passed upon both body and mind stand in sharpest contrast to the Biblical view of man and achieve a fateful influence in all subsequent theories of human nature. The Bible knows nothing of a good mind and an evil body.

While Stoicism, as a monistic and pantheistic philosophy, sharply diverges from the Aristotelian and Platonic concepts in many respects, its view of human nature betrays more similarities than differences. The similarities are great enough, at any rate, to constitute it a part of the general "classical" picture of man. The Stoic reason is more immanent in both the world process and in the soul and body of man than in Platonism; yet man is essentially reason. Even the dualism is not completely lacking. For while Stoicism is not always certain whether the reason which governs man must persuade him to emulate nature as he finds it outside of his reason or whether it, being a special spark of the divine reason, must set him against the impulses of nature, it arrives on the whole at convictions which do not qualify the classical concepts essentially. The emphasis upon human freedom in its psychology overcomes the pantheistic naturalism of its metaphysics; and its completely negative attitude toward the passions and the whole impulsive life of man set reason in contrast to the impulses of the body, however much it conceives reason as basically the principle of harmony within the body.

Obviously, the Platonic, Aristotelian and Stoic conceptions which define the "classical" view of man do not exhaust Greek speculations about human nature. Modern vitalism and romanticism have their antecedents in the earlier Dionysian religion, in Heraclitus' conception of ultimate reality as Flux and Fire and more particularly in the development of the Dionysian theme in Greek tragedy. Subsequent mysticism is anticipated in Orphism and Pythagoreanism. Even more significant for developments in contemporary culture, Democritus and Epicurus interpreted man, in accordance with their naturalism and materialism, not as standing outside of nature by the quality of his unique reason, but as wholly a part of nature. This Greek materialism was no less rationalistic than Platonism or Aristotelianism but it reduced the immanental reason in the world to mechanical necessity and sought to understand man in terms of this mechanism. It was by combining Stoic with Democritan and Epicurean naturalism that modern culture arrived at concepts which were to express some of its most characteristic interpretations of man, as primarily a child of nature.

It must be observed that while the classical view of human virtue is optimistic when compared with the Christian view (for it finds no defect in the centre of human personality) and while it has perfect confidence in the virtue of the rational man, it does not share the confidence of the moderns in the ability of all men to be either virtuous or happy. Thus an air of melancholy hangs over Greek life which stands in sharpest contrast to the all-pervasive optimism of the now dying bourgeois culture, despite the assumption of the latter that it had merely restored the classical world view and the Greek view of man. "There is nothing, methinks, more piteous than a man, of all things that creep and breathe upon the earth," declares Zeus in the *Iliad,* and that note runs as a consistent strain through Greek thought from Homer to the Hellenistic age. Primarily it was the brevity of life and the mortality of man which tempted the Greeks to melancholy. They were not dissuaded from this mood either by Plato's assurance of immortality nor yet by Epicurus' counsel that death need not be feared, since there was nothing on the other side of the grave.

Aristotle confessed that "not to be born is the best thing and death is better than life," and gave it as his opinion that melancholy was a concomitant of genius. The philosophers were optimistic in their confidence that the wise man would be virtuous; but, alas, they had no confidence that the many could be wise. The Stoic Chryssipus could conceive happiness only for the wise and was certain that most men were fools. The Stoics tended on the one hand to include all men in the brotherhood of man on the ground that they all had the spark of divine reason; but on the other hand they pitied the multitude for having no obvious graces of rationality. Thus their equalitarianism rapidly degenerated into an aristocratic condescension not very different from Aristotle's contempt for the slave as a "living tool." Seneca, despite his pious universalism, prays "forgive the world: they are all fools."

*   *   *

THE CHRISTIAN VIEW OF MAN

The Christian view of man, which modern culture ostensibly rejects in its entirety but by which its estimate of human nature is influenced more than it realizes, will be more fully analysed in this book. At this point we must anticipate subsequent elaborations briefly by distinguishing the Christian view from the classical doctrine of man. As the classical view is determined by Greek metaphysical presuppositions, so the Christian view is determined by the ultimate presuppositions of Christian faith. The Christian faith in God as Creator of the world transcends the canons and antinomies of rationality, particularly the antinomy between mind and matter, between consciousness and extension. God is not merely mind who forms a previously given formless stuff. God is both vitality and form and the source of all existence. He creates the world. This world is not God; but it is not evil because it is not God. Being God's creation, it is good.

The consequences of this conception of the world upon the view of human nature in Christian thought is to allow an appreciation of the unity of body and soul in human personality which idealists and naturalists have sought in vain. Furthermore it prevents the idealistic error of regarding the mind as essentially good or essentially eternal and the body as essentially evil. But it also obviates the romantic error of seeking for the good in man-as-nature and for evil in man-as-spirit or as reason. Man is, according to the Biblical view, a created and finite existence in both body and spirit. Obviously a view which depends upon an ultra-rational presupposition is immediately endangered when rationally explicated; for reason which seeks to bring all things into terms of rational coherence is tempted to make one known thing the principle of explanation and to derive all other things from it. Its most natural inclination is to make itself that ultimate principle, and thus in effect to declare itself God. Christian psychology and philosophy have never completely freed themselves from this fault, which explains why naturalists plausibly though erroneously regard Christian faith as the very fountain source of idealism. . . .

The second important characteristic of the Christian view of man is that he is understood primarily from the standpoint of God, rather than the uniqueness of his rational faculties or his relation to nature. He is made in the "image of God." It has been the mistake of many Christian rationalists to assume that this term is no more than a religious-pictorial expression of what philosophy intends when it defines man as a rational animal. We have previously alluded to the fact that the human spirit has the special capacity of standing continually outside itself in terms of indefinite regression. Consciousness is a capacity for surveying the world and determining action from a governing centre. Self-consciousness represents a further degree of transcendence in which the self makes itself its own object in such a way that the ego is finally always subject and not object. The rational capacity of surveying the world, of forming general concepts and analysing the order of the world is thus but one aspect of what Christianity knows as "spirit." The self knows the world, insofar as it knows the world, because it stands outside both itself and the world, which means that it cannot understand itself except as it is understood from beyond itself and the world.

This essential homelessness of the human spirit is the ground of all religion; for the self which stands outside itself and the world cannot find the meaning of life in itself or the world. It cannot identify meaning with causality in nature; for its freedom is obviously something different from the necessary causal links of nature. Nor can it identify the principle of meaning with rationality, since it transcends its own rational processes, so that it may, for instance, ask the question whether there is a relevance between its rational forms and the recurrences and forms of nature. It is this capacity of freedom which finally prompts great cultures and philosophies to transcend rationalism and to seek for the meaning of life in an unconditional ground of existence. But from the standpoint of human thought this unconditioned ground of existence, this God, can be defined only negatively. This is why mystic religions in general, and particularly the neo-Platonic tradition in western culture, have one interesting similarity with Christianity and one important difference in their estimate of human nature. In common with Christianity they measure the depth of the human spirit in terms of its capacity of self-transcendence. Thus Plotinus defines *nous* not as Aristotle defines it. For him it is primarily the capacity for self-knowledge and it has no limit short of the eternal. Mysticism and Christianity agree in understanding man from the standpoint of the eternal. But since mysticism leads to an undifferentiated ultimate reality, it is bound to regard particularity, including individuality, as essentially evil. All mystic religions therefore have the characteristic of accentuating individuality in as far as individuality is inherent in the capacity for self-consciousness emphasized in mysticism and is something more than mere bodily particularity; but all mystic philosophies ultimately lose the very individuality which they first emphasize, because they sink finite particularity in a distinctionless divine ground of existence. . . .

This conception of man's stature is not, however, the complete picture of man. The high estimate of the human stature implied in the concept of "image of God" stands in paradoxical juxtaposition to the low estimate of human virtue in Christian thought. Man is a sinner. His sin is defined as rebellion against God. The Christian estimate of human evil is so serious precisely because it places evil at the very centre of human personality: in the will. This evil cannot be regarded complacently as the inevitable consequence of his finiteness or the fruit of his involvement in the contingencies and necessities of nature. Sin is occasioned precisely by the fact that man refuses to admit his "creatureliness" and to acknowledge himself as merely a member of a total unity of life. He pretends to be more than he is. Nor can he, as in both rationalistic and mystic dualism, dismiss his sins as residing in that part of himself which is not his true self, that is, that part of himself which is involved in physical necessity. In Christianity it is not the eternal man who judges the finite man; but the eternal and holy God who judges sinful man. Nor is redemption in the power of the eternal man who gradually sloughs off finite man. Man is not divided against himself so that the essential man can be extricated from the nonessential. Man contradicts himself within the terms of his true essence. His essence is free self-determination. His sin is the wrong use of his freedom and its consequent destruction. . . .

Christianity, therefore, issues inevitably in the religious expression of an uneasy conscience. Only within terms of the Christian faith can man not only understand the reality of the evil in himself but escape the error of attributing that evil to any one but himself. It is possible of course to point out that man is tempted by the situation in which he stands. He stands at the juncture of nature and spirit. The freedom of his spirit causes him to break the harmonies of nature and the pride of his spirit prevents him from establishing a new harmony. The freedom of his spirit enables him to use the forces and processes of nature creatively; but his failure to observe the limits of his finite existence causes him to defy the forms and restraints of both nature and reason. Human self-consciousness is a high tower looking upon a large and inclusive world. It vainly imagines that it is the large world which it beholds and not a narrow tower insecurely erected amidst the shifting sands of the world.

* * *

THE MODERN VIEW OF MAN

The modern view of man is informed partly by classical, partly by Christian and partly by distinctively modern motifs. The classical element tends to slip from the typical classical, Platonic and Aristotelian rationalism to a more naturalistic rationalism. That is, the Epicurean and Democritan naturalism, which remained subordinate in the classical period of Greek thought, becomes dominant in the modern period. This modern naturalism is in accord with the Christian concept of man as "creature" but it contradicts the Christian concept of man as "image of God" which the early Renaissance emphasized in opposition to the Christian idea of man as creature and man as sinner. The curious compound of classical, Christian and distinctively modern conceptions of human nature, involved in modern anthropology, leads to various difficulties and confusions which may be briefly summarized as follows: (a) The inner contradictions in modern conceptions of human nature between idealistic and naturalistic rationalists; and between rationalists, whether idealistic or naturalistic, and vitalists and romanticists. (b) The certainties about human nature in modern culture which modern history dissipates, particularly the certainty about individuality. (c) The certainties about human nature, particularly the certainty about the goodness of man, which stands in contradiction to the known facts of history.

(a) One of the unresolved antinomies in modern culture is the contradictory emphasis of the idealists and the naturalists. The former are inclined to protest against Christian humility and to disavow both the doctrine of man's creatureliness and the doctrine of his sinfulness. This was the mood of the Renaissance, the thought of which upon this issue was determined by Platonic, neo-Platonic and Stoic conceptions. Bruno[3] is concerned to establish the in-

---

[3] Giordano Bruno (c. 1548–1600), Italian philosopher.

finity of human self-consciousness; and the infinity of space is merely an interesting analogue of this infinity of spirit in his pantheistic system. He prizes the achievements of Copernican astronomy because Copernicus "emancipated our knowledge from the prison house in which, as it were, it saw stars only through small windows." In the same manner Leonardo da Vinci[4] is more concerned to prove that the mathematical method which unlocks nature's mysteries and discloses her regularities and dependable recurrences is a fruit and symbol of the greatness of the human mind, than that it is a tool of nature's mastery. Petrarch sees nature as a mirror in which man beholds his true greatness.

Yet there was a minor note in the Renaissance which finally led to the naturalistic rationalism of the eighteenth century. It expresses itself in Francis Bacon's primary interest in nature, and in Montaigne's effort to understand man in the variety of his natural differentiations. Bacon is afraid lest the "unquietness of the human spirit," that is the very hankering after infinity which Bruno praises as the true mark of humanity, will "interfere most mischievously in the discovery of causes," that is, with the sober inductive processes of science. Thus modern culture slips from the essential Platonism of the early Renaissance to the Stoicism of Descartes and Spinoza and the seventeenth century generally and then to the more radical, materialistic and Democritan naturalism of the eighteenth century. Modern man ends by seeking to understand himself in terms of his relation to nature, but he remains even more confused about the relation of reason in nature and reason in man than the Stoics were. The thought of the French enlightenment is a perfect exposition of this confusion. The idealistic reaction to this naturalism is to be found in German idealism, where, with the exception of Kant, reason and being are more unqualifiedly equated than in Platonism. Descartes, the fountain source of modern cu⸍ ᴊre, manages to conceive of man purely in terms of thought, nature in terms ⸌f mechanics and to find no organic unity between the two, thus bearing witᴊ in himself both the contradictions and the extravagances of modernity.

In terms of social history, this course of modern thought from an idealistic protest against the Christian conception of man as creature and as sinner to the naturalistic protest against man as the "image of God" may be interpreted as the anticlimactic history of bourgeois man. The middle-class world begins with a tremendous sense of the power of the human mind over nature. But having destroyed the ultimate reference by which medieval man transcended nature spiritually, even while acknowledging his dependence practically, the bourgeois and technical world ends by seeking asylum in nature's dependabilities and serenities. Modern capitalism really expresses both attitudes at the same time. The spirit of capitalism is the spirit of an irreverent exploitation of nature, conceived as a treasure-house of riches which will guarantee everything which might be regarded as the good life. Man masters nature. But the social organization of capitalism at least theoretically rests upon the naive faith that nature masters man and that her pre-established

---

[4] Leonardo da Vinci (1452–1519), Italian painter, sculptor, architect, and engineer.

harmonies will prevent the human enterprise from involving itself in any serious catastrophes (physiocratic theory).

The conflict between idealistic and naturalistic rationalists is complicated by a further factor; the protest of the romantic naturalists who interpret man as primarily vitality and who find neither a pale reason nor a mechanical nature an adequate key to man's true essence. This romantic interpretation of man is in some respects the newest element in modern anthropological doctrines, for it is only partially foreshadowed in either classical or Christian thought. Its bitterest fruit is modern fascism. Marxist thought complicates the pattern further; for it interprets man, as he is, primarily in vitalistic terms and rightly discounts the pretenses of rational man who does not know his own finiteness; but the man who is to be will build a society which will be governed by the most remarkable rational coherence of life with life and interest with interest. The conflict between rationalists and romanticists has become one of the most fateful issues of our day, with every possible religious and political implication. Modern man, in short, cannot determine whether he shall understand himself primarily from the standpoint of the uniqueness of his reason or from the standpoint of his affinity with nature; and if the latter whether it is the harmless order and peace of nature or her vitality which is the real clue to his essence. Thus some of the certainties of modern man are in contradiction with one another; and it may be questioned whether the conflict can be resolved within terms of the presuppositions with which modern culture approaches the issues.

(b) The concept of individuality in modern culture belongs to that class of certainties of modern man about himself which his own history has gradually dissipated. The tremendous emphasis upon individuality in the Renaissance is clearly a flower which could have grown only on Christian soil, since the classical culture, to which the Renaissance is an ostensible return, lacked this emphasis completely. The Italian Renaissance avails itself primarily of neo-Platonic conceptions to establish its idea of the dignity and the liberty of man. But these conceptions would not yield the idea of individuality if Christian ideas were not presupposed. The Renaissance is particularly intent upon establishing the freedom of the human spirit in opposition to Christian doctrines of divine predestination.

Pico della Mirandola extols the freedom of the human spirit in concepts drawn from Platonism. God said to man, according to Pico: "You alone are not bound by any restraint, unless you will adopt it by the will which we have given you. I have placed you in the centre of the world that you may the easier look about and behold all that is in it. I created you a creature, neither earthly nor heavenly, neither mortal nor immortal, so that you could be your own creator and choose whatever form you may assume for yourself."

While classical thought was used by the Renaissance to challenge the Christian idea of man's dependence and weakness, by emphasis upon his uniqueness and the freedom of his spirit, classicism was obviously not able to suggest the concept of individuality which the Renaissance held so dear. This idea must be regarded partly a Christian inheritance and partly a consequence of the emergence of the bourgeois individual from the historical and traditional cohesions, patterns and restraints of the medieval world. This bourgeois individual felt himself the master of his own destiny and was impatient with both classical and medieval life. Speaking in social terms one may say that he lost this individuality immediately after establishing it by his destruction of the medieval solidarities. He found himself the artificer of a technical civilization which creates more enslaving mechanical interdependencies and collectivities than anything known in an agrarian world. Furthermore no one can be as completely and discreetly an individual as bourgeois individualism supposes, whether in the organic forms of an agrarian or the more mechanical forms of a technical society.

Considered in terms of philosophical issues bourgeois individualism had an insecure foundation, not only in the Platonism and neo-Platonism in which it first expressed itself but also in the later naturalism of the eighteenth and nineteenth centuries. Idealism begins by emphasizing man's freedom and transcendence over nature but ends by losing the individual in the universalities of rational concepts and ultimately in the undifferentiated totality of the divine. Naturalism begins by emphasizing natural variety and particularity. Thus it was Montaigne's interest to picture the multifarious forms of social and moral custom under the influence of the diversities of geography. But variety in nature comes short of individuality. There is no place for individuality in either pure mind or pure nature. As the idealists lose individuality in the absolute mind, so the naturalists lose it in "streams of consciousness" when dealing with the matter psychologically, and in "laws of motion" when thinking sociologically. Thus the individualism of the Renaissance and of the eighteenth century is dissipated culturally, just as bourgeois libertarian idealism disintegrates politically and succumbs to fascist and Marxist collectivism. A genuine individuality can be maintained only in terms of religious presuppositions which can do justice to the immediate involvement of human individuality in all the organic forms and social tensions of history, while yet appreciating its ultimate transcendence over every social and historical situation in the highest reaches of its self-transcendence. The paradox of man as creature and man as child of God is a necessary presupposition of a concept of individuality, strong enough to maintain itself against the pressures of history, and realistic enough to do justice to the organic cohesions of social life.

(c) The final certainty of modern anthropology is its optimistic treatment of the problem of evil. Modern man has an essentially easy conscience; and nothing gives the diverse and discordant notes of modern culture so much harmony as the unanimous opposition of modern man to Christian conceptions of the sinfulness of man. The idea that man is sinful at the very centre of his personality, that is in his will, is universally rejected. It is this rejection which has seemed to make the Christian gospel simply irrelevant to modern man, a fact which is of much more importance than any conviction about its incredibility. If modern culture conceives man primarily in terms of the uniqueness of his rational faculties, it finds the root of his evil in his involvement in natural impulses and natural necessities from which it hopes to free him by the increase of his rational faculties. This essentially Platonic idea manages to creep into many social and educational theories, even when they are ostensibly naturalistic and not Platonic. On the other hand, if it conceives of man primarily in terms of his relation to nature, it hopes to rescue man from the daemonic chaos in which his spiritual life is involved by beguiling him back to the harmony, serenity and harmless unity of nature. In this the mechanistic rationalist and the Rousseauistic romantic of the French enlightenment seem to stand on common ground. Either the rational man or the natural man is conceived as essentially good, and it is only necessary for man either to rise from the chaos of nature to the harmony of mind or to descend from the chaos of spirit to the harmony of nature in order to be saved. The very fact that the strategies of redemption are in such complete contradiction to each other proves how far modern man is from solving the problem of evil in his life.

A further consequence of modern optimism is a philosophy of history expressed in the idea of progress. Either by a force immanent in nature itself, or by the gradual extension of rationality, or by the elimination of specific sources of evil, such as priesthoods, tyrannical government and class divisions in society, modern man expects to move toward some kind of perfect society. The idea of progress is compounded of many elements. It is particularly important to consider one element of which modern culture is itself completely oblivious. The idea of progress is possible only upon the ground of a Christian culture. It is a secularized version of Biblical apocalypse and of the Hebraic sense of a meaningful history, in contrast to the meaningless history of the Greeks. But since the Christian doctrine of the sinfulness of man is eliminated, a complicating factor in the Christian philospohy is removed and the way is open for simple interpretations of history, which relate historical process as closely as possible to biological process and which fail to do justice either to the unique freedom of man or to the daemonic misuse which he may make of that freedom.

There are of course pessimistic reactions to this optimism about both the individual and the total human enterprise. In the mechanistic naturalism of Hobbes and the romantic naturalism of Nietzsche a thoroughgoing pessimism is elaborated. One of the modern fruits of Nietzschean thought is Freudian pessimism. Here we have no good opinion about human nature; yet there is no uneasy conscience in this pessimism. The egotism and the will-to-power which Christian thought regards as the quintessence of sin and which, in the view of bourgeois liberalism, is a defect to be sloughed off by a new education or a new social organization, is regarded as normal and normative. Hobbes accepts and Nietzsche glorifies the will-to-power. In Hobbes a political vantage point against individual egotism is gained but none against the collective egotism, embodied in the state. In Nietzsche's transvaluation of values, the characteristics of human life which make for conflict between life and life are raised to the eminence of the ideal. The fateful consequences in contemporary political life of Hobbes's cynicism and Nietzsche's nihilism are everywhere apparent. . . .

ANTIQUITY

Edited by John W. Snyder

I

THE JUDEO-CHRISTIAN SOURCE
OF WESTERN TRADITIONS

The principal sources of the traditions of the Western world are two—Judeo-Christian and Greco-Roman or Classical. Not many years ago, historians might have been inclined to add a third main source—Germanic. Now, however, it seems unlikely that the backward illiterate folk that overran the West beginning in the fourth century after Christ left on the civilization that emerged in that area imprints comparable in depth and durability to the traditions present there when the barbarians poured across the frontiers of the Roman Empire. As a consequence of the depth and durability of the Judeo-Christian and the Greco-Roman elements in the traditions of the West, even today, in complex and subtle ways, the habits of thinking and doing still current in the Western world are permeated by the intellectual and spiritual discoveries of men who died from fifteen hundred to three thousand years ago. The materials of the following three sections of this book illustrate the Western heritage from Antiquity as it relates to the two major religions of the West, Judaism and Christianity, and to cultural, philosophical, and political conceptions for which we are indebted to the civilization of Greece and Rome.

Religion seems to have been a necessity for most men of all past ages. In ancient days, a vast variety were practiced. There were peculiar combinations of superstition and occultism, fire worship, sun worship, and animal worship; and there were also efforts to order and make sense of these practices.

Most ancient religions are dead, but two of them, Judaism and Christianity, have survived in the West from the ancient world into our own times. From its beginning, Christianity was closely related to Judaism. Although the Christians believed that they had a new revelation, they still deemed their faith a direct continuation of the religion of the people of Israel, the beliefs of the Jewish peoples of southern Syria. Christians insisted that the coming of their Christ had been foretold centuries earlier by the prophets of Israel, that he was the culmination of the revelation of God to the Jews that had begun with the calling of the patriarch Abraham out of Ur of the Chaldees nearly two thousand years before.

A. The Jews

The origin of the Jewish people is not altogether clear. Some time within the period from 1400 B.C. to 1200 B.C., a group of nomadic tribes entered southern Syria, an area which they knew as Canaan. These people identified themselves by the name of the patriarch Israel (also called Jacob), who was the grandson of Abraham, and they traced their descent from the twelve sons of Jacob. Peoples with whom they later came in contact called them Jews, from the name of one of the twelve sons of Israel, Judah. The Jews came to Canaan with a tradition that said they had been in Egypt for several centuries. Some of their earliest lore insisted that by miraculous intervention God had led them out of Egypt and into Canaan, which He had personally promised to Abraham and all his legitimate descendants as a homeland.

The Jewish state in Canaan, established in the mountain regions around Jerusalem, became wealthy and influential in the years immediately after 1000 B.C. Under the direction of the kings David and Solomon, it gained by the weaknesses of its neighbors and the commerce of the wealthy Phoenician trading cities on the nearby Mediterranean coast. With the renewed struggle of the great powers of the Near East in the ninth and eighth centuries B.C., however, the Jews found themselves squeezed between the Babylonians and Assyrians of Mesopotamia and the Egyptians of the Nile Valley. The rulers of those powerful realms fought each other for control of the area between them, of which Canaan was an important part. Caught up in the swirl of Near Eastern politics, the Jews frequently were tempted to form alliances with one or the other of these competitors for Palestine. Internal troubles demanded attention as well. After the reign of Solomon, the original kingdom divided into Israel in the north and the smaller kingdom of Judah in the south. The two kingdoms often pursued policies independent of each other. Their troubles increased until the Assyrians carried off the chief Israelites in 722 B.C., and the Babylonians captured the kingdom of Judah in 586 B.C. Except for the poorer people left behind by the Assyrians, the Jews of the northern kingdom, or Israel, disappeared from history. But after the Persians conquered the Babylonians in 539 B.C., many of the people of Judah returned to Palestine, where they found it very difficult to maintain independence. The revived Jewish state bowed to a succession of conquerors, from the Persians to the Greeks (333–63 B.C.) to the Romans (63 B.C.–A.D. 70). Except for a brief period under the Maccabees in the middle of the second century B.C., Jewish history became that of a subject and tributary people. With the destruction of the great temple in Jerusalem, the Romans brought the ancient Jewish state to an end in A.D. 70.

1. What Was the Beginning of Things, of Man, and of His Troubles?

The Scriptures, or Holy Writings, of the Jews are contained in the collection of documents now known as the Old Testament, the first part of the Christian Bible. The main concern of the Old Testament is with the God of the Jews and the relation of the Jewish people and of all men to Him. The very first chapters of the first book of Scriptures, Genesis, offer answers to questions which have puzzled men in all ages.

GENESIS*

In the beginning God created the heavens and the earth. And the earth was waste and void; and darkness was upon the face of the deep: and the Spirit of God moved upon the face of the waters. And God said, Let there be light: and there was light. And God saw the light, that it was good: and God divided the light from the darkness. And God called the light Day, and the darkness he called Night. And there was evening and there was morning, one day.

And God said, Let there be a firmament in the midst of the waters, and let it divide the waters from the waters. And God made the firmament, and divided the waters which were under the firmament from the waters which were above the firmament: and it was so. And God called the firmament Heaven. And there was evening and there was morning, a second day.

And God said, Let the waters under the heavens be gathered together unto one place, and let the dry land appear: and it was so. And God called the dry land Earth; and the gathering together of the waters called he Seas: and God saw that it was good. And God said, Let the earth put forth grass, herbs yielding seed, *and* fruit-trees bearing fruit after their kind, wherein is the seed thereof, upon the earth: and it was so. And the earth brought forth grass, herbs yielding seed after their kind, and trees bearing fruit, wherein is the seed thereof, upon the earth: and it was so. And the earth brought forth grass, herbs yielding seed after their kind, and trees bearing fruit, wherein is the seed thereof, after their kind: and God saw that it was good. And there was evening and there was morning, a third day.

And God said, Let there be lights in the firmament of heaven to divide the day from the night: and let them be for signs, and for seasons, and for days and years: and let them be for lights in the firmament of heaven to give light upon the earth: and it was so. And God made the two great lights; the greater light to rule the day, and the lesser light to rule the night: *he made* the stars also. And God set them in the firmament of heaven to give light upon the earth, and to rule over the day and over the night, and to divide the light from the darkness: and God saw that it was good. And there was evening and there was morning, a fourth day.

And God said, Let the waters swarm with swarms of living creatures, and let birds fly above the earth in the open firmament of heaven. And God created the great sea-monsters, and every living creature that moveth, wherewith the waters swarmed, after their kind, and every winged bird after its kind: and God saw that it was good. And God blessed them, saying, Be

---

*Genesis 1–3. Chapter and verse numbers have been omitted in all selections from the Old Testament, which are taken from the American Standard Version (New York: Thomas Nelson & Sons, 1901).

fruitful, and multiply, and fill the waters in the seas, and let birds multiply on the earth. And there was evening and there was morning, a fifth day.

And God said, Let the earth bring forth living creatures after their kind, cattle, and creeping things, and beasts of the earth after their kind: and it was so. And God made the beasts of the earth after their kind, and the cattle after their kind, and everything that creepeth upon the ground after its kind: and God saw that it was good. And God said, Let us make man in our image, after our likeness: and let them have dominion over the fish of the sea, and over the birds of the heavens, and over the cattle, and over all the earth, and over every creeping thing that creepeth upon the earth. And God created man in his own image, in the image of God created he him; male and female created he them. And God blessed them: and God said unto them, Be fruitful, and multiply, and replenish the earth, and subdue it; and have dominion over the fish of the sea, and over the birds of the heavens, and over every living thing that moveth upon the earth. And God said, Behold, I have given you every herb yielding seed, which is upon the face of all the earth, and every tree, in which is the fruit of a tree yielding seed; to you it shall be for food: and to every beast of the earth, and to every bird of the heavens, and to every-thing that creepeth upon the earth, wherein there is life, *I have given* every green herb for food: and it was so. And God saw everything that he had made, and, behold, it was very good. And there was evening and there was morning, the sixth day.

And the heavens and the earth were finished, and all the host of them. And on the seventh day God finished his work which he had made; and he rested on the seventh day from all his work which he had made. And God blessed the seventh day, and hallowed it; because that in it he rested from all his work which God had created and made.

These are the generations of the heavens and of the earth when they were created, in the day that Jehovah God made earth and heaven. And no plant of the field was yet in the earth, and no herb of the field had yet sprung up; for Jehovah God had not caused it to rain upon the earth: and there was not a man to till the ground; but there went up a mist from the earth, and watered the whole face of the ground. And Jehovah God formed man of the dust of the ground, and breathed into his nostrils the breath of life; and man became a living soul. And Jehovah God planted a garden eastward, in Eden; and there he put the man whom he had formed. And out of the ground made Jehovah God to grow every tree that is pleasant to the sight, and good for food; the tree of life also in the midst of the garden, and the tree of the knowl-edge of good and evil. And a river went out of Eden to water the garden; and from thence it was parted, and became four heads. The name of the first is Pishon: that is it which compasseth the whole land of Havilah, where there is gold; and the gold of that land is good: there is bdellium and the onyx stone. And the name of the second river is Gihon: the same is it that compasseth the whole land of Cush. And the name of the third river is Hiddekel: that is it which goeth in front of Assyria. And the fourth river is the Euphrates. And Jehovah God took the man, and put him into the garden of Eden to dress it and to keep it. And Jehovah God commanded the man, saying, Of every tree of the garden thou mayest freely eat: but of the tree of the knowledge of good and evil, thou shalt not eat of it: for in the day that thou eatest thereof thou shalt surely die.

And Jehovah God said, It is not good that the man should be alone; I will make him a help meet for him. And out of the ground Jehovah formed every beast of the field, and every bird of the heavens; and brought them unto the man to see what he would call them: and whatsoever the man called every living creature, that was the name thereof. And the man gave names to all cattle, and to the birds of the heavens, and to every beast of the field; but for man there wast not found a help meet for him. And Jehovah God caused a deep sleep to fall upon the man and he slept; and he took one of his ribs, and closed up the flesh instead thereof: and the rib which Jehovah God had taken from the man, made he a woman and brought her unto the man. And the man said, This is now bone of my bones, and flesh of my flesh: she shall be called Woman, because she was taken out of Man. Therefore shall a man leave his father and his mother, and shall cleave unto his wife: and they shall be one flesh. And they were both naked, the man and his wife, and were not ashamed.

Now the serpent was more subtle than any beast of the field which Jehovah God had made. And he said unto the woman, Yea, hath God said, Ye shall not eat of any tree of the garden? And the woman said unto the serpent, Of the fruit of the trees of the garden we may eat: but of the fruit of the tree which is in the midst of the garden, God hath said, Ye shall not eat of it, neither shall ye touch it, lest ye die. And the serpent said unto the woman, Ye shall not surely die: for God doth know that in the day ye eat thereof, then your eyes shall be opened, and ye shall be as God, knowing good and evil. And when the woman saw that the tree was good for food, and that it was a delight to the eyes, and that the tree was to be desired to make one wise, she took of the fruit thereof, and did eat; and she gave also unto her husband with her, and he did eat. And the eyes of them both were opened, and they knew that they were naked; and they sewed fig-leaves together, and made themselves aprons. And they heard the voice of Jehovah God walking in the garden in the cool of the day: and the man and his wife hid themselves from the presence of Jehovah God amongst the trees of the garden.

And Jehovah God called unto the man, and said unto him, Where art thou? And he said, I heard thy voice in the garden, and I was afraid, because I was naked; and I hid myself. And he said, Who told thee that thou wast naked? Hast thou eaten of the tree, whereof I commanded thee that thou shouldest not eat? And the man said, The woman whom thou gavest to be with me, she gave me of the tree, and I did eat. And Jehovah God said unto the woman, What is this thou hast done? And the woman said, The serpent beguiled me, and I did eat. And Jehovah God said unto the serpent, Because thou hast done this, cursed art thou above all cattle, and above every beast of the field; upon thy belly shalt thou go, and dust shalt thou eat all the days of thy life: and I will put enmity between thee and the woman, and between thy seed and her seed: he shall bruise thy head, and thou shalt bruise his heel. Unto the woman he said, I will greatly multiply thy pain and thy conception; in pain thou shalt bring forth children; and thy desire shall be to thy husband, and he shall rule over thee. And unto Adam he said, Because thou hast hearkened unto the voice of thy wife, and hast eaten of the tree, of which I commanded thee, saying, Thou shalt not eat of it: cursed is the ground for thy sake; in toil shalt thou eat of it all the days of thy life; thorns also and thistles shall it bring forth to thee; and thou shalt eat the herb of the field; in the sweat of thy face shalt thou eat bread, till thou return unto the ground; for out of it wast thou taken: for dust thou art, and unto dust shalt thou return. And the man called his wife's name Eve; because she was the mother of all living. And Jehovah God made for Adam and for his wife coats of skins, and clothed them.

And Jehovah God said, Behold, the man is become as one of us, to know good and evil; and now, lest he put forth his hand, and take also of the tree of life, and eat, and live for ever—therefore Jehovah God sent him forth from the garden of Eden, to till the ground from whence he was taken. So he drove out the man; and he placed at the east of the garden of Eden the Cherubim, and the flame of a sword which turned every way, to keep the way of the tree of life.

2. What Was the Basis of the Relation of the Jewish People to God?

The book of Genesis also tells us that when He called Abraham out of Ur of the Chaldees in Mesopotamia to come to a distant country, God promised His servant not only the land, but also a mighty and numerous people as his descendants. The land was Canaan, and in due course Abraham appeared there with his relatives and servants. But as yet he had no son by his rightful wife, Sarah, and both were very old. In the story of Abraham, the Jews, and later the Christians, found in part the explanation of God's choice of them among all the peoples of the world to receive the special revelation of His will and purpose with respect to all men.

GENESIS*

And Jehovah visited Sarah as he had said, and Jehovah did unto Sarah as he had spoken. And Sarah conceived, and bare Abraham a son in his old age, at the set time of which God had spoken to him. And Abraham called the name of his son that was born unto him, whom Sarah bare to him, Isaac. And Abraham circumcised his son Isaac when he was eight days old, as God had commanded him. And Abraham was a hundred years old, when his son Isaac was born unto him. And Sarah said, God hath made me to laugh; every one that heareth will laugh with me. And she said, Who would have said unto Abraham, that Sarah should give children suck? for I have borne him a son in his old age.

And the child grew, and was weaned: and Abraham made a great feast on the day that Isaac was weaned.

*   *   *

And it came to pass after these things, that God did prove Abraham, and said unto him, Abraham; and he said, Here am I. And he said, Take

---

*Genesis 21:1–8; 22:1–18.

now thy son, thine only son, whom thou lovest, even Isaac, and get thee unto the land of Moriah;[1] and offer him there for a burnt-offering upon one of the mountains which I will tell thee of. And Abraham rose early in the morning, and saddled his ass, and took two of his young men with him, and Isaac his son; and he cut the wood for the burnt-offering, and rose up, and went unto the place of which God had told him. On the third day Abraham lifted up his eyes, and saw the place afar off. And Abraham said unto his young men, Abide ye here with the ass, and I and the lad will go yonder; and we will worship, and come again to you. And Abraham took the wood of the burnt-offering, and laid it upon Isaac his son; and he took in his hand the fire and the knife; and they went both of them together. And Isaac spake unto Abraham his father, and said, My father: and he said, Here am I, my son. And he said, Behold, the fire and the wood: but where is the lamb for a burnt-offering? And Abraham said, God will provide himself the lamb for a burnt-offering, my son: so they went both of them together.

And they came to the place which God had told him of; and Abraham built the altar there, and laid the wood in order, and bound Isaac his son, and laid him on the altar, upon the wood. And Abraham stretched forth his hand, and took the knife to slay his son. And the angel of Jehovah called unto him out of heaven, and said, Abraham, Abraham: and he said, Here am I. And he said, Lay not thy hand upon the lad, neither do thou anything unto him; for now I know that thou fearest God, seeing thou hast not withheld thy son, thine only son, from me. And Abraham lifted up his eyes, and looked, and, behold, behind him a ram caught in the thicket by his horns: and Abraham went and took the ram, and offered him up for a burnt-offering in the stead of his son. And Abraham called the name of that place Jehovah jireh:[2] as it is said to this day, In the mount of Jehovah it shall be provided. And the angel of Jehovah called unto Abraham a second time out of heaven, and said, By myself have I sworn, saith Jehovah, because thou hast done this thing, and hast not withheld thy son, thine only son, that in blessing I will bless thee, and in multiplying I will multiply thy seed as the stars of the heavens, and as the sand which is upon the sea-shore; and thy seed shall possess the gate of his enemies; and in thy seed shall all the nations of the earth be blessed; because thou hast obeyed my voice.

3. What Does God Command His Followers To Do?

According to tradition, Jacob, the son of Isaac, the grandson of Abraham, left Canaan for Egypt during a period of famine. He took eleven of his sons with him; the twelfth, Joseph, had already made his fortune there as administrator to the ruler. Jacob died soon after arriving in Egypt. For a time, things went well for his twelve sons, and they settled down in the region near the Nile, far from the land Jehovah had promised to them and their children. The descendants of the sons of Jacob remained in Egypt for several centuries and increased in number to a vast host, as God had said they would.

---

[1] A hilly district which some scholars believe was later part of the city of Jerusalem.
[2] That is, "Jehovah will provide."

Later, however, a king "who knew not Joseph" arose and began to oppress the Jews. So God brought them out of Egyptian bondage under the leadership of Moses, whom He had called for that work. Then one terrifying day, on a mountain in the desolate peninsula of Sinai, God forged a new link between Himself and the people He had chosen by telling Moses what He expected of them.

EXODUS*

And Moses went up unto God, and Jehovah called unto him out of the mountain, saying, Thus shalt thou say to the house of Jacob, and tell the children of Israel: Ye have seen what I did unto the Egyptians, and how I bare you on eagles' wings, and brought you unto myself. Now therefore, if ye will obey my voice indeed, and keep my covenant, then ye shall be mine own possession from among all peoples: for all the earth is mine: and ye shall be unto me a kingdom of priests, and a holy nation. These are the words which thou shalt speak unto the children of Israel.

And Moses came and called for the elders of the people, and set before them all these words which Jehovah had commanded him. And all the people answered together, and said, All that Jehovah hath spoken we will do. And Moses reported the words of the people unto Jehovah. And Jehovah said unto Moses, Lo, I come unto thee in a thick cloud, that the people may hear when I speak with thee, and may also believe thee for ever. And Moses told the words of the people unto Jehovah. And Jehovah said unto Moses, Go unto the people, and sanctify[1] them to-day and to-morrow, and let them wash their garments, and be ready against the third day; for the third day Jehovah will come down in the sight of all the people upon mount Sinai.[2] And thou shalt set bounds unto the people round about, saying, Take heed to yourselves, that ye go not up into the mount, or touch the border of it: whosoever toucheth the mount shall be surely put to death: no hand shall touch it, but he shall surely be stoned, or shot through; whether it be beast or man, he shall not live: when the trumpet soundeth long, they shall come up to the mount. And Moses went down from the mount unto the people, and sanctified the people; and they washed their garments. And he said unto the people, Be ready against the third day: come not near a woman.

And it came to pass on the third day, when it was morning, that there were thunders and lightnings, and a thick cloud upon the mount, and the voice of a trumpet exceeding loud; and all the people that were in the camp trembled. And Moses brought forth the people out of the camp to meet God; and they stood at the nether part of the mount. And mount Sinai, the whole of it, smoked, because Jehovah descended upon it in fire; and the smoke thereof ascended as the smoke of a furnace, and the whole mount quaked greatly. And when the voice of the trumpet waxed louder and louder, Moses spake, and God answered him by a voice. And Jehovah came down upon

---

*Exodus 19:3–20:22.

[1] The word "sanctify" here probably means that Moses was to set the people apart from their usual daily activities and sins by having them confess their sins and wash themselves.

[2] Mount Sinai's exact location is still a matter of some dispute, but clearly it is one of the many sharply rising peaks in the area between Canaan and Egypt, the modern Sinai Peninsula.

mount Sinai, to the top of the mount: and Jehovah called Moses to the top of the mount; and Moses went up. And Jehovah said unto Moses, Go down, charge the people, lest they break through unto Jehovah to gaze, and many of them perish. And let the priests also, that come near to Jehovah, sanctify themselves, lest Jehovah break forth upon them. And Moses said unto Jehovah, Thy people cannot come up to mount Sinai: for thou didst charge us, saying, Set bounds about the mount, and sanctify it. And Jehovah said unto him, Go, get thee down; and thou shalt come up, thou and Aaron[3] with thee: but let not the priests and the people break through to come up unto Jehovah, lest he break forth upon them. So Moses went down unto the people and told them.

And God spake all these words, saying, I am Jehovah thy God, who brought thee out of the land of Egypt, out of the house of bondage.

THOU SHALT HAVE NO OTHER GODS BEFORE ME.

THOU SHALT NOT MAKE UNTO THEE A GRAVEN IMAGE, NOR ANY LIKENESS OF ANY THING THAT IS IN HEAVEN ABOVE, OR THAT IS IN THE EARTH BENEATH, OR THAT IS IN THE WATER UNDER THE EARTH: THOU SHALT NOT BOW DOWN THYSELF UNTO THEM, NOR SERVE THEM; FOR I JEHOVAH THY GOD AM A JEALOUS GOD, VISITING THE INIQUITY OF THE FATHERS UPON THE CHILDREN, UPON THE THIRD AND UPON THE FOURTH GENERATION OF THEM THAT HATE ME, AND SHOWING LOVING KINDNESS UNTO THOUSANDS OF THEM THAT LOVE ME AND KEEP MY COMMANDMENTS.

THOU SHALT NOT TAKE THE NAME OF JEHOVAH THY GOD IN VAIN:[4] FOR JEHOVAH WILL NOT HOLD HIM GUILTLESS THAT TAKETH HIS NAME IN VAIN.

REMEMBER THE SABBATH DAY, TO KEEP IT HOLY. SIX DAYS SHALT THOU LABOR, AND DO ALL THY WORK; BUT THE SEVENTH DAY IS A SABBATH UNTO JEHOVAH THY GOD: IN IT THOU SHALT NOT DO ANY WORK, THOU, NOR THY SON, NOR THY DAUGHTER, NOR THY MAN-SERVANT, NOR THY MAID-SERVANT, NOR THY CATTLE, NOR THY STRANGER THAT IS WITHIN THY GATES: FOR IN SIX DAYS JEHOVAH MADE HEAVEN AND EARTH, THE SEA, AND ALL THAT IN THEM IS, AND RESTED THE SEVENTH DAY: WHEREFORE JEHOVAH BLESSED THE SABBATH DAY, AND HALLOWED IT.

HONOR THY FATHER AND THY MOTHER, THAT THY DAYS MAY BE LONG IN THE LAND WHICH JEHOVAH THY GOD GIVETH THEE.

THOU SHALT NOT KILL.

THOU SHALT NOT COMMIT ADULTERY.

THOU SHALT NOT STEAL.

THOU SHALT NOT BEAR FALSE WITNESS AGAINST THY NEIGHBOR.

THOU SHALT NOT COVET THY NEIGHBOR'S HOUSE, THOU SHALT NOT COVET THY NEIGHBOR'S WIFE, NOR HIS MAN-SERVANT, NOR HIS MAID-SERVANT, NOR HIS OX, NOR HIS ASS, NOR ANYTHING THAT IS THY NEIGHBOR'S.

And all the people perceived the thunderings, and the lightnings, and the voice of the trumpet, and the mountain smoking: and when the people saw it, they trembled, and stood afar off. And they said unto Moses, Speak thou with us, and we will hear; but let not God speak with us, lest we die. And Moses said unto the people, Fear not: for God is come to prove you, and that his fear may be before you, that ye sin not. And the people stood afar off, and Moses drew near unto the thick darkness where God was.

---

[3] Aaron was the brother of Moses. God had chosen him to assist his brother in the leading of the Jews.

[4] That is, not use Jehovah's name lightly or frivolously.

And Jehovah said unto Moses, Thus thou shalt say unto the children of Israel, Ye yourselves have seen that I have talked with you from heaven. . . .

Besides the Ten Commandments, the first five books of the Bible contain a mass of other injunctions which the Jews believed God called on them to obey. Some of those laws affect the religious observances of Orthodox Jews to this day.

GENESIS*

And God said unto Abraham, And as for thee, thou shalt keep my covenant, thou, and thy seed after thee throughout their generations. This is my covenant, which ye shall keep, between me and you and thy seed after thee: every male among you shall be circumcised. And ye shall be circumcised in the flesh of your foreskin; and it shall be a token of a covenant betwixt me and you. And he that is eight days old shall be circumcised among you, every male throughout your generations, he that is born in the house, or bought with money of any foreigner that is not of thy seed. He that is born in thy house, and he that is bought with thy money, must needs be circumcised: and my covenant shall be in your flesh for an everlasting covenant. And the uncircumcised male who is not circumcised in the flesh of his foreskin, that soul shall be cut off from his people; he hath broken my covenant.

A hitherto unknown book of the law called Deuteronomy turned up mysteriously in the midst of a crisis of the late seventh century B.C., when the existence of the Jews as a people was in grave jeopardy. It emphasized a dimension of the relation between the children of Israel and their God not so clearly represented in the other books of the law.

DEUTERONOMY†

Now this is the commandment, the statutes, and the ordinances, which Jehovah your God commanded to teach you, that ye might do them in the land whither ye go over to possess it; that thou mightest fear Jehovah thy God, to keep all his statutes and his commandments, which I command thee, thou, and thy son, and thy son's son, all the days of thy life; and that thy days may be prolonged. Hear therefore, O Israel, and observe to do it; that it may be well with thee, and that ye may increase mightily, as Jehovah, the God of thy fathers, hath promised unto thee, in a land flowing with milk and honey. Hear, O Israel: Jehovah our God is one Jehovah: and thou shalt love Jehovah thy God with all thy heart, and with all thy soul, and with all thy might. And these words, which I command thee this day, shall be upon thy

*Genesis 17:9-14.
† Deuteronomy 6:1-15.

heart; and thou shalt teach them diligently unto thy children, and shalt talk of them when thou sittest in thy house, and when thou walkest by the way, and when thou liest down, and when thou risest up. And thou shalt bind them for a sign upon thy hand, and they shall be for frontlets between thine eyes. And thou shalt write them upon the door-posts of thy house, and upon thy gates.[1]

And it shall be, when Jehovah thy God shall bring thee into the land which he sware unto thy fathers, to Abraham, to Isaac, and to Jacob, to give thee, great and goodly cities, which thou buildedst not, and houses full of all good things, which thou filledst not, and cisterns hewn out, which thou hewedst not, vineyards and olive-trees, which thou plantedst not, and thou shalt eat and be full; then beware lest thou forget Jehovah, who brought thee forth out of the land of Egypt, out of the house of bondage. Thou shalt fear Jehovah thy God; and him shalt thou serve, and shalt swear by his name. Ye shall not go after other gods, of the gods of the peoples that are round about you; for Jehovah thy God in the midst of thee is a jealous God; lest the anger of Jehovah thy God be kindled against thee, and he destroy thee from off the face of the earth.

4. What Are the Full Dimensions and Implications of God's Relation to His Chosen People?

Prophecy and soothsaying are ancient professions among many peoples, and the kingdoms of Israel and Judah had their share of both. Most of the prophets are forgotten, but three clusters who appeared among the children of Jacob are remembered. For one thing, they appeared in crises in the history of the Jews—before the fall of Israel, before the fall of Judah, and among the people of Judah during their exile. Second, in the first two crises, these prophets proclaimed an incredible message—that God was so angered with the chosen people that He was about to destroy what they deemed the very basis of their existence as a people, their link with the land He had promised them; and what the prophets foresaw actually happened. Third, in exile, the third cluster of prophets found ways to restore the heart, courage, and faith of the Jews despite the apparently irreparable disaster which had overtaken them. Finally, these prophets wrote down their prophecies, and they survive in the Old Testament. In the course of their meditations on the relations of the chosen people to their God, the prophets proclaimed a new and profound vision of the ways in which the Divine Creator was related to His creation, to men, and especially to the people of Israel.

---

[1] From the beginning, the commandment of Deuteronomy 6:8, that the words of God should be bound as a sign upon the worshipper's hand and as a frontlet between his eyes, was implemented by the use of devices now known as *phylacteries,* from the Greek; *tefillin* in Hebrew. The *tefillin* are small leather cases containing four biblical passages (Deuteronomy 6:4–9, 11:13–21; Exodus 13:1–10, 11–16) written on parchment. These originally were worn constantly, bound by light leather straps to left hand and forehead, but now they are used only on special occasions by Orthodox Jews. Their use is taken to symbolize the direction of all that is done, seen, and thought to the will of God, and their presence is considered to be a protection against sin and evil. In this last probably lies the explanation of the two separate ideas in the Greek *phylassein* "to guard," and the Hebrew *tefillah* "prayer," which are the sources of the modern terms *phylacteries* and *tefillin.* Similar devices were nailed to the door-posts of Jewish homes.

Amos was the earliest of the "writing" prophets who foresaw the fall of the northern kingdom of Ephraim, or Israel.

AMOS*

Hear ye this word which I take up for a lamentation over you, O house of Israel. The virgin of Israel is fallen; she shall no more rise: she is cast down upon her land; there is none to raise her up. For thus saith the Lord Jehovah: The city that went forth a thousand shall have a hundred left, and that which went forth a hundred shall have ten left, to the house of Israel.

For thus saith Jehovah unto the house of Israel, Seek ye me, and ye shall live; . . . Seek Jehovah, and ye shall live; lest he break out like fire in the house of Joseph, and it devour, and there be none to quench it. . . . Ye who turn justice to wormwood, and cast down righteousness to the earth, *seek him* that maketh the Pleiades and Orion,[1] and turneth the shadow of death into the morning, and maketh the day dark with night; that calleth for the waters of the sea, and poureth them out upon the face of the earth (Jehovah is his name); that bringeth sudden destruction upon the strong, so that destruction cometh upon the fortress.

They hate him that reproveth in the gate, and they abhor him that speaketh uprightly. Forasmuch therefore as ye trample upon the poor, and take exactions from him of wheat: ye have built houses of hewn stone, but ye shall not dwell in them; ye have planted pleasant vineyards, but ye shall not drink the wine thereof. For I know how manifold are your transgressions, and how mighty are your sins—ye that afflict the just, that take a bribe, and that turn aside the needy in the gate *from their right*. Therefore he that is prudent shall keep silence in such a time; for it is an evil time.

Seek good, and not evil, that ye may live; and so Jehovah, the God of hosts, will be with you, as ye say. Hate the evil, and love the good, and establish justice in the gate: it may be that Jehovah, the God of hosts, will be gracious unto the remnant of Joseph.

Therefore thus saith Jehovah, the God of hosts, the Lord: Wailing shall be in all the broad ways; and they shall say in all the streets, Alas! alas! and they shall call the husbandman to mourning, and such as are skilful in lamentation to wailing. And in all vineyards shall be wailing; for I will pass through the midst of thee, saith Jehovah.

Woe unto you that desire the day of Jehovah! Wherefore would ye have the day of Jehovah? It is darkness and not light. As if a man did flee from a lion, and a bear met him; or went into the house and leaned his hand on the wall, and a serpent bit him. Shall not the day of Jehovah be darkness, and not light? even very dark, and no brightness in it?

I hate, I despise your feasts, and I will take no delight in your solemn assemblies. Yea, though ye offer me your burnt-offerings and meal-offerings, I will not accept them; neither will I regard the peace-offerings of your fat beasts. Take thou away from me the noise of thy songs; for I will not hear the

---

*Amos 5.

[1] The prophet here was referring to two well-known constellations as evidence for the creative power of the God his readers were spurning by their rejection.

melody of thy viols. But let justice roll down as waters, and righteousness as a mighty stream.

Did ye bring unto me sacrifices and offerings in the wilderness forty years, O house of Israel? Yea, ye have borne the tabernacle of your king and the shrine of your images, the star of your god, which ye made to yourselves. Therefore will I cause you to go into captivity beyond Damascus, saith Jehovah, whose name is the God of hosts.

Later Isaiah foresaw the fall of the kingdom of Judah and of Jerusalem, where the only temple of Israel's God was.

ISAIAH*

The vision of Isaiah the son of Amoz, which he saw concerning Judah and Jerusalem, in the days of Uzziah, Jotham, Ahaz, and Hezekiah, kings of Judah.

Hear, O heavens, and give ear, O earth; for Jehovah hath spoken: I have nourished and brought up children, and they have rebelled against me. The ox knoweth his owner, and the ass his master's crib; *but* Israel doth not know, my people doth not consider. Ah sinful nation, a people laden with iniquity, a seed of evil-doers, children that deal corruptly! they have forsaken Jehovah, they have despised the Holy One of Israel, they have estranged *and gone* backward. Why will ye be still stricken, that ye revolt more and more? the whole head is sick, and the whole heart faint. From the sole of the foot even unto the head there is no soundness in it; *but* wounds, and bruises, and fresh stripes: they have not been closed, neither bound up, neither mollified with oil. Your country is desolate; your cities are burned with fire; your land, strangers devour it in your presence, and it is desolate, as overthrown by strangers. And the daughter of Zion is left as a booth in a vineyard, as a lodge in a garden of cucumbers, as a besieged city. Except Jehovah of hosts had left unto us a very small remnant, we should have been as Sodom, we should have been like unto Gomorrah.[1]

Hear the word of Jehovah, ye rulers of Sodom; give ear unto the law of our God, ye people of Gomorrah. What unto me is the multitude of your sacrifices? saith Jehovah: I have had enough of the burnt-offerings of rams, and the fat of fed beasts; and I delight not in the blood of bullocks, or of lambs, or of he-goats. When ye come to appear before me, who hath required this at your hand, to trample my courts? Bring no more vain oblations; incense is an abomination unto me; new moon and sabbath, the calling of assemblies,— I cannot away with iniquity and the solemn meeting. Your new moons and your appointed feasts my soul hateth; they are a trouble unto me; I am weary of bearing them. And when ye spread forth your hands, I will hide mine eyes from you; yea, when ye make many prayers, I will not hear: your hands are

---

*Isaiah 1–2.

[1] Sodom and Gomorrah were the two cities upon which the judgment of God fell in the form of fire and brimstone in the time of Abraham (Genesis 19:24).

full of blood. Wash you, make you clean; put away the evil of your doings from before mine eyes; cease to do evil; learn to do well; seek justice, relieve the oppressed, judge the fatherless, plead for the widow.

Come now, and let us reason together, saith Jehovah: though your sins be as scarlet, they shall be as white as snow; though they be red like crimson, they shall be as wool. If ye be willing and obedient, ye shall eat the good of the land: but if ye refuse and rebel, ye shall be devoured with the sword; for the mouth of Jehovah hath spoken it.

How is the faithful city become a harlot! she that was full of justice! righteousness lodged in her, but now murderers. Thy silver is become dross, thy wine mixed with water. Thy princes are rebellious, and companions of thieves; every one loveth bribes, and followeth after rewards: they judge not the fatherless, neither doth the cause of the widow come unto them.

Therefore saith the Lord, Jehovah of hosts, the Mighty One of Israel, Ah, I will ease me of mine adversaries, and avenge me of mine enemies; and I will turn my hand upon thee, and thoroughly purge away thy dross, and will take away all thy tin; and I will restore thy judges as at the first, and thy counsellors as at the beginning: afterward thou shalt be called The city of righteousness a faithful town. Zion shall be redeemed with justice, and her converts with righteousness. But the destruction of transgressors and sinners shall be together, and they that forsake Jehovah shall be consumed. For they shall be ashamed of the oaks which ye have desired, and ye shall be confounded for the gardens that ye have chosen. For ye shall be as an oak whose leaf fadeth, and as a garden that hath no water. And the strong shall be as tow, and his work as a spark; and they shall both burn together, and none shall quench them.

The word that Isaiah the son of Amoz saw concerning Judah and Jerusalem.

And it shall come to pass in the latter days, that the mountain of Jehovah's house shall be established on the top of the mountains, and shall be exalted above the hills; and all nations shall flow unto it. And many peoples shall go and say, Come ye, and let us go up to the mountain of Jehovah, to the house of the God of Jacob; and he will teach us of his ways, and we will walk in his paths: for out of Zion shall go forth the law, and the word of Jehovah from Jerusalem. And he will judge between the nations, and will decide concerning many peoples; and they shall beat their swords into plowshares, and their spears into pruning-hooks; nation shall not lift up sword against nation, neither shall they learn war any more.

O house of Jacob, come ye, and let us walk in the light of Jehovah. For thou hast forsaken thy people the house of Jacob, because they are filled *with customs* from the east, and *are* soothsayers like the Philistines, and they strike hands with the children of foreigners. And their land is full of silver and gold, neither is there any end of their treasures; their land also is full of horses, neither is there any end of their chariots. Their land also is full of idols; they worship the work of their own hands, that which their own fingers have made. And the mean man is bowed down, and the great man is brought low: therefore forgive them not. Enter into the rock, and hide thee in the dust, from before the terror of Jehovah, and from the glory of his majesty. The lofty looks of man shall be brought low, and the haughtiness of men shall be bowed down, and Jehovah alone shall be exalted in that day.

For there shall be a day of Jehovah of hosts upon all that is proud and haughty, and upon all that is lifted up; and it shall be brought low; and upon all the cedars of Lebanon, that are high and lifted up, and upon all the oaks of Bashan, and upon all the high mountains, and upon all the hills that are lifted up, and upon every lofty tower, and upon every fortified wall, and upon all the ships of Tarshish, and upon all pleasant imagery. And the loftiness of man shall be bowed down, and the haughtiness of men shall be brought low; and Jehovah alone shall be exalted in that day. And the idols shall utterly pass away. And men shall go into the caves of the rocks, and into the holes of the earth, from before the terror of Jehovah, and from the glory of his majesty, when he ariseth to shake mightily the earth. In that day men shall cast away their idols of silver, and their idols of gold, which have been made for them to worship, to the moles and to the bats; to go into the caverns of the rocks, and into the clefts of the ragged rocks, from before the terror of Jehovah, and from the glory of his majesty, when he ariseth to shake mightily the earth. Cease ye from man, whose breath is in his nostrils; for wherein is he to be accounted of?

Micah also spoke in the name of Israel's God, reproaching the Judaeans for defecting from His word.

MICAH*

Hear ye now what Jehovah saith: Arise, contend thou before the mountains, and let the hills hear thy voice. Hear, O ye mountains, Jehovah's controversy, and ye enduring foundations of the earth; for Jehovah hath a controversy with his people, and he will contend with Israel. O my people, what have I done unto thee? and wherein have I wearied thee? testify against me. For I brought thee up out of the land of Egypt, and redeemed thee out of the house of bondage . . . that ye may know the righteous acts of Jehovah.

Wherewith shall I come before Jehovah, and bow myself before the high God? shall I come before him with burnt-offerings, with calves a year old? will Jehovah be pleased with thousands of rams, *or* with ten thousands of rivers of oil? shall I give my first-born for my transgression, the fruit of my body for the sin of my soul? He hath showed thee, O man, what is good; and what doth Jehovah require of thee, but to do justly, and to love kindness, and to walk humbly with thy God?

The voice of Jehovah crieth unto the city, and *the man of* wisdom will see thy name: hear ye the rod, and who hath appointed it. Are there yet treasures of wickedness in the house of the wicked, and a scant measure that is abominable? Shall I be pure with wicked balances, and with a bag of deceitful weights? For the rich men thereof are full of violence, and the inhabitants thereof have spoken lies, and their tongue is deceitful in their mouth.

---

*Micah 6.

Therefore I also have smitten thee with a grievous wound; I have made thee desolate because of thy sins. Thou shalt eat, but not be satisfied; and thy humiliation shall be in the midst of thee: and thou shalt put away, but shalt not save; and that which thou savest will I give up to the sword. Thou shalt sow, but shalt not reap; thou shalt tread the olives, but shalt not anoint thee with oil; and the vintage, but shalt not drink the wine. For the statues of Omri are kept, and all the works of the house of Ahab,[1] and ye walk in their counsels; that I may make thee a desolation, and the inhabitants thereof a hissing: and ye shall bear the reproach of my people.

Finally, the great prophet of the exile spoke words of consolation and hope to a people in desperate straits.

ISAIAH*

But now thus saith Jehovah that created thee, O Jacob, and he that formed thee, O Israel: Fear not, for I have redeemed thee; I have called thee by thy name, thou art mine. When thou passest through the waters, I will be with thee; and through the rivers, they shall not overflow thee: when thou walkest through the fire, thou shalt not be burned, neither shall the flame kindle upon thee. For I am Jehovah thy God, the Holy One of Israel, thy Saviour; I have given Egypt as thy ransom, Ethiopia and Seba in thy stead. Since thou hast been precious in my sight, *and* honorable, and I have loved thee; therefore will I give men in thy stead, and peoples instead of thy life. Fear not; for I am with thee: I will bring thy seed from the east, and gather thee from the west; I will say to the north, Give up; and to the south, Keep not back; bring my sons from far, and my daughters from the end of the earth; every one that is called by my name, and whom I have created for my glory, whom I have formed, yea, whom I have made.

Bring forth the blind people that have eyes, and the deaf that have ears. Let all the nations be gathered together, and let the peoples be assembled: who among them can declare this, and show us former things? let them bring their witnesses, that they may be justified; or let them hear, and say, It is truth. Ye are my witnesses, saith Jehovah, and my servant whom I have chosen; that ye may know and believe me, and understand that I am he: before me there was no God formed, neither shall there be after me. I, even I, am Jehovah; and besides me there is no saviour. I have declared, and I have saved, and I have showed; and there was no strange *god* among you: therefore ye are

---

[1] Ahab, son of Omri, was king of the northern kingdom of Israel before its captivity by Assyria in 722 B.C. Ahab's career of opposition to the prophet Elijah, culminating in the famous contest with the prophets of Baal and the death of Jezebel, is narrated in I Kings 16 and following. Micah's reference to those stirring events is a distinct warning to any who may think of imitating Ahab's behavior.

*Isaiah 43:1–13, 52:7–53:12. Although this passage appears in the book of Isaiah, it is often thought to have been written by a later prophet than the author of the first forty chapters. Isaiah 40–66 are usually ascribed by scholars to one or more such later prophets and are called deutero-Isaiah.

my witnesses, saith Jehovah, and I am God. Yea, since the day was I am he; and there is none that can deliver out of my hand: I will work, and who can hinder it?

*　　*　　*

How beautiful upon the mountains are the feet of him that bringeth good tidings, that publisheth peace, that bringeth good tidings of good, that publisheth salvation, that saith unto Zion,[1] Thy God reigneth! The voice of thy watchmen! they lift up the voice, together do they sing; for they shall see eye to eye, how Jehovah returneth to Zion. Break forth unto joy, sing together, ye waste places of Jerusalem; for Jehovah hath comforted his people, he hath redeemed Jerusalem. Jehovah hath made bare his holy arm in the eyes of all the nations; and all the ends of the earth have seen the salvation of our God. . . .

Behold, my servant shall deal wisely, he shall be exalted and lifted up, and shall be very high. Like as many were astonished at thee (his visage was so marred more than any man, and his form more than the sons of men), so shall he startle many nations; kings shall shut their mouths because of him: for that which had not been told them shall they see; and that which they had not heard shall they consider.

Who hath believed our message? and to whom hath the arm of Jehovah been revealed? For he[2] grew up before him as a tender plant, as a root out of a dry ground: he hath no form nor comeliness that we should look upon him; nor beauty that we should desire him. He was despised, and forsaken by men; a man of sorrows, and acquainted with sickness:[3] and he hid as it were his face from us; and we esteemed him not.

Surely he hath borne our sicknesses, and carried our sorrows; yet we did esteem him stricken, smitten of God, and afflicted. But he was wounded for our transgressions, he was bruised for our iniquities; the chastisement of our peace was upon him; and with his stripes we are healed. All we like sheep have gone astray; we have turned every one to his own way; and Jehovah hath laid on him the iniquity of us all.

He was oppressed, yet when he was afflicted he opened not his mouth; as a lamb that is led to the slaughter, and as a sheep that before its shearers is dumb, so he opened not his mouth. By oppression and judgment he was taken away; and as for his generation, who among them considered that he was cut off out of the land of the living? for the transgression of my people was he stricken. And they made his grave with the wicked, and with a rich man in his death; although he had done no violence, neither was any deceit in his mouth.

Yet it pleased Jehovah to bruise him; he hath put him to grief: when thou shalt make his soul an offering for sin, he shall see his seed, he shall prolong his days, and the pleasure of Jehovah shall prosper in his hand. He shall see of the travail of his soul, and shall be satisfied: by his knowledge shall my righteous servant make many righteous; and he shall bear their

---

[1] Zion was originally one of the hills upon which Jerusalem was built. Later it came to mean the city itself, and through it symbolically to mean the people of Jerusalem, the Jews.

[2] Jehovah's servant of the preceding paragraph, whom Christians identify as Christ, but Jews see as the Jewish nation, God's Suffering Servant.

[3] The "sickness" here is often translated as "grief."

iniquities. Therefore will I divide him a portion with the great, and he shall divide the spoil with the strong; because he poured out his soul unto death, and was numbered with the transgressors: yet he bare the sin of many, and made intercession for the transgressors.

B. Christianity

Unlike many other peoples of the ancient Near East, the Jews did not altogether disappear when their territories fell into the hands of conquerors— Babylonians, Persians, Greeks, Romans. A firm religious bond held the Jews together, and they survive to this day as a people, many of whom still practice their ancient religion. Moreover, all the founders of Christianity—Jesus and his disciples and the apostle Paul—were Jews, and so Jewish religious tradition also continued, greatly modified, in Christianity.

From 336 through 333 B.C., Alexander the Great, a Greek-educated Macedonian, conquered the Persian overlords of the Jews and succeeded to the vast Persian Empire. His death bequeathed to the world a long history of international intrigue, diplomacy, and war. The states into which Alexander's empire split fought each other for the same territories over which Egyptians and Mesopotamians had struggled earlier. The Jews found themselves again embroiled in international conflict. After a series of bloody skirmishes, some of the Jews appealed for help to Rome, and in 63 B.C. the Romans acquired Palestine. The liberators brought with them their tax collectors, however, and soon turned from being friends to being lords of Galilee and Judea (two of the territories into which Rome divided southern Syria). Ultimately, the Romans controlled Galilee through their client Herod, while Judea was under direct Roman administration.

In such conditions Jesus, born in 4 B.C.,[1] *grew up. We know little of his early life. When he began to preach, he acquired a following so large he made the Jewish leaders fear for their position. They were concerned lest his ability to stir crowds call down upon them and their puppet government the strong hand of further Roman "pacification." Seizing upon Jesus' admission that he deemed himself the Messiah, chosen by God to redeem Israel, they secured his condemnation before the Roman procurator or governor of Judea, Pontius Pilate.*[2] *His death on the cross in A.D. 30 ended any political threat by his followers to Roman rule or to the dominant group of Jerusalem's Jews.*

What his followers came to believe about Jesus' birth, words, deeds, suffering, death, and resurrection and their meaning for man became the basis of a new religion. The world was ready for the new faith when Christianity came upon the scene. Many Jews expected the advent of some sort of leader who would enable them to fulfill their hopes as Jehovah's chosen people.

---

[1] Although our present calendar is based upon the birth of Christ as its year one, modern scholarship has tended to support the assertion that earlier calculations of the precise time of his birth were inaccurate. Most now agree that Jesus was born during the last days of the reign of Herod the Great, which ended in 4 B.C. by the Julian Calendar. Therefore, the birth of Christ must have also been in 4 B.C.

[2] Pontius Pilate was the fifth in the line of Roman procurators sent out as governors of Judea. He remained there from A.D. 26 to 36.

They expected that leader also to solve their serious political problems with the Romans, but Jesus did not fulfill such political expectations. It was those Jews who believed that the life and death of Jesus fulfilled their religious rather than political hopes who became the first Christians.

Outside Israel as well, conditions were ripe for Christianity. While after Alexander's conquest the culture of the Greeks only slowly permeated the Near East, their language spread more rapidly. It provided a common tongue for preaching Christianity. Moreover, at the time of Jesus, the Roman Empire had acquired the entire Mediterranean basin and at some points had penetrated deep inland from its shores. Within this huge area, it was possible for missionaries to travel under the protection of Roman law and to enjoy the ease of communication provided by a single government. In such a world, at least partly unified by language and political institutions, the apostle Paul and other early missionaries spread Christianity with a speed that would have been impossible a century earlier.

Christianity, however, was to have difficulties with its Jewish heritage. By the beginning of the New Testament period, the Jews had settled the old problem concerning the clear and general acceptance of Jehovah and His Law; but there had arisen the more subtle issue of how to keep the Law. Was the Law a matter of formal observance of certain prescribed rules? Was it a matter of spirit and principle, with no limits to its ethical and spiritual growth, adaptation, and interpretation?

1. How Ought a Follower of Jesus Live?

Jesus believed that he had a mission from God, and that part of his mission was to teach his fellow Jews what God expected of them. Jesus taught by preaching sermons, by telling stories called parables, and by his own example. Some of the things he preached have come to us in the form of the Sermon on the Mount, which contains some of his judgments on the relation of his followers to the Jewish Law and on the sort of life they should strive to lead. This sermon ultimately found its way into a record of the life and deeds of Jesus called the Gospel according to St. Matthew, after one of the inner circle of Jesus' personal followers.

ST. MATTHEW*

When he [Jesus] saw the crowds he went up the hill. There he took his seat, and when his disciples had gathered round him he began to address them. And this is the teaching he gave:

'How blest are those who know that they are poor;
    the kingdom of Heaven is theirs.

---

* Matthew 5–7. From: *The New English Bible;* New Testament. © The Delegates of the Oxford University Press and the Syndics of Cambridge University Press, 1961. Reprinted by permission, as are all subsequent passages used here from the New Testament.

How blest are the sorrowful;
 they shall find consolation.
How blest are those of a gentle spirit;
 they shall have the earth for their possession.
How blest are those who hunger and thirst to see right prevail;
 they shall be satisfied.
How blest are those who show mercy;
 mercy shall be shown to them.
How blest are those whose hearts are pure;
 they shall see God.
How blest are the peacemakers;
 God shall call them his sons.
How blest are those who have suffered persecution for the cause of right;
 the kingdom of Heaven is theirs.

'How blest you are, when you suffer insults and persecution and every kind of calumny for my sake. Accept it with gladness and exultation, for you have a rich reward in heaven; in the same way they persecuted the prophets before you.

'You are salt to the world. And if salt becomes tasteless, how is its saltness to be restored? It is now good for nothing but to be thrown away and trodden underfoot.

'You are light for all the world. A town that stands on a hill cannot be hidden. When a lamp is lit, it is not put under the mealtub, but on the lampstand, where it gives light to everyone in the house. And you, like the lamp, must shed light among your fellows, so that, when they see the good you do, they may give praise to your Father in Heaven.

'Do not suppose that I have come to abolish the Law and the prophets; I did not come to abolish, but to complete. I tell you this: so long as heaven and earth endure, not a letter, not a stroke, will disappear from the Law until all that must happen has happened. If any man therefore sets aside even the least of the Law's demands, and teaches others to do the same, he will have the lowest place in the kingdom of Heaven, whereas anyone who keeps the Law and teaches others so will stand high in the kingdom of Heaven. I tell you, unless you show yourselves far better men than the Pharisees and the doctors of the law, you can never enter the kingdom of Heaven.

'You have learned that our forefathers were told, "Do not commit murder; anyone who commits murder must be brought to judgement." But what I tell you is this: Anyone who nurses anger against his brother must be brought to judgement. If he abuses his brother he must answer for it to the court; if he sneers at him he will have to answer for it in the fires of hell.

'If, when you are bringing your gift to the altar, you suddenly remember that your brother has a grievance against you, leave your gift where it is before the altar. First go and make your peace with your brother, and only then come back and offer your gift.

'If someone sues you, come to terms with him promptly while you are both on your way to court; otherwise he may hand you over to the judge, and the judge to the constable, and you will be put in jail. I tell you, once you are there you will not be let out till you have paid the last farthing.

'You have learned that they were told, "Do not commit adultery." But what I tell you is this: If a man looks on a woman with a lustful eye, he has already committed adultery with her in his heart.

'If your right eye leads you astray, tear it out and fling it away; it is better for you to lose one part of your body than for the whole of it to be thrown into hell. And if your right hand is your undoing, cut it off and fling it away; it is better for you to lose one part of your body than for the whole of it to go to hell.

'They were told, "A man who divorces his wife must give her a note of dismissal." But what I tell you is this: If a man divorces his wife for any cause other than unchastity he involves her in adultery; and anyone who marries a woman so divorced commits adultery.

'Again, you have learned that they were told, "Do not break your oath," and, "Oaths sworn to the Lord must be kept." But what I tell you is this: You are not to swear at all—not by heaven, for it is God's throne, nor by earth, for it is his footstool, nor by Jerusalem, for it is the city of the great King, nor by your own head, because you cannot turn one hair of it white or black. Plain "Yes" or "No" is all you need to say; anything beyond that comes from the devil.

'You have learned that they were told, "An eye for an eye, and a tooth for a tooth." But what I tell you is this: Do not set yourself against the man who wrongs you. If someone slaps you on the right cheek, turn and offer him your left. If a man wants to sue you for your shirt, let him have your coat as well. If a man in authority makes you go one mile, go with him two. Give when you are asked to give; and do not turn your back on a man who wants to borrow.

'You have learned that they were told, "Love your neighbour, hate your enemy." But what I tell you is this: Love your enemies and pray for your persecutors, only so can you be children of your heavenly Father, who makes his sun rise on good and bad alike, and sends the rain on the honest and the dishonest. If you love only those who love you, what reward can you expect? Surely the taxgatherers do as much as that. And if you greet only your brothers, what is there extraordinary about that? Even the heathen do as much. You must therefore be all goodness, just as your heavenly Father is all good.'

2. What Was the End of Jesus' Life on Earth and What Did It Mean?

By his teaching and his healing of the sick, Jesus won many followers, some of whom believed he was especially sent by God to deliver the Jews from the Roman yoke. It was disturbing, therefore, to the Roman authorities, but even more so to the Jewish leaders who were trying to get along with them, that Jesus should decide to come to Jerusalem, the Holy City, to celebrate the Passover. This was the feast on which the Jews rejoiced in their deliverance by another man especially sent by God, Moses, from another oppressor of His chosen people, Egypt. The events which followed marked the climax and the end of Jesus' life on earth. They are recorded in the Gospel according to St.

Mark, the shortest of the four surviving accounts of the words and deeds of Jesus. It may provide the narrative base of two others, Matthew and Luke. Because of their similarities, these three Gospels are called synoptic, that is, written from a common point of view.

ST. MARK*

Now the festival of Passover and Unleavened Bread was only two days off; and the chief priests and the doctors of the law were trying to devise some cunning plan to seize him and put him to death. 'It must not be during the festival,' they said, 'or we should have rioting among the people.' . . .

Then Judas Iscariot, one of the Twelve,[1] went to the chief priests to betray him to them. When they heard what he had come for, they were greatly pleased, and promised him money; and he began to look for a good opportunity to betray him.

Now on the first day of Unleavened Bread, when the Passover lambs were being slaughtered, his disciples said to him, 'Where would you like us to go and prepare for your Passover supper?' So he sent out two of his disciples with these instructions: 'Go into the city, and a man will meet you carrying a jar of water. Follow him and when he enters a house give this message to the householder: "The Master says, 'Where is the room reserved for me to eat the Passover with my disciples?'"" He will show you a large room upstairs, set out in readiness. Make the preparations for us there.' Then the disciples went off, and when they came into the city they found everything just as he had told them. So they prepared for Passover.

In the evening he came to the house with the Twelve. As they sat at supper Jesus said, 'I tell you this: one of you will betray me—one who is eating with me.' At this they were dismayed; and one by one they said to him, 'Not I, surely?' 'It is one of the Twelve,' he said, 'who is dipping into the same bowl with me. The Son of Man is going the way appointed for him in the scriptures; but alas for that man by whom the Son of Man is betrayed! It would be better for that man if he had never been born.'

During supper he took bread, and having said the blessing he broke it and gave it to them, with the words: 'Take this; this is my body.' Then he took a cup, and having offered thanks to God he gave it to them; and they all drank from it. And he said, 'This is my blood of the covenant, shed for many. I tell you this: never again shall I drink from the fruit of the vine until that day when I drink it new in the kingdom of God.'

After singing the Passover Hymn, they went out to the Mount of Olives.[2] And Jesus said, 'You will all fall from your faith; for it stands written: "I will strike the shepherd down and the sheep will be scattered." Nevertheless, after I am raised again I will go on before you into Galilee.' Peter answered,

---

* Mark 14–6.

[1] That is, one of the original twelve apostles chosen by Jesus and sent out to preach.

[2] A rise situated about three-fifths of a mile east of Jerusalem, on the other side of the valley of the Kidron.

'Everyone else may fall away, but I will not.' Jesus said, 'I tell you this: today, this very night, before the cock crows twice, you yourself will disown me three times.' But he insisted and repeated: 'Even if I must die with you, I will never disown you.' And they all said the same.

When they reached a place called Gethsemane, he said to his disciples, 'Sit here while I pray.' And he took Peter and James and John with him. Horror and dismay came over him, and he said to them, 'My heart is ready to break with grief; stop here, and stay awake.' Then he went forward a little, threw himself on the ground, and prayed that, if it were possible, this hour might pass him by. 'Abba, Father,' he said, 'all things are possible to thee; take this cup away from me. Yet not what I will, but what thou wilt.'

He came back and found them asleep; and he said to Peter, 'Asleep, Simon?[3] Were you not able to keep awake for one hour? Stay awake, all of you; and pray that you may be spared the test: the spirit is willing, but the flesh is weak.' Once more he went away and prayed. On his return he found them asleep again, for their eyes were heavy; and they did not know how to answer him.

The third time he came and said to them, 'Still sleeping? Still taking your ease? Enough! The hour has come. The Son of Man is betrayed to sinful men. Up, let us go forward! My betrayer is upon us.'

Suddenly, while he was still speaking, Judas, one of the Twelve, appeared, and with him was a crowd armed with swords and cudgels, sent by the chief priests, lawyers, and elders. Now the traitor had agreed with them upon a signal: 'The one I kiss is your man; seize him and get him safely away.' When he reached the spot, he stepped forward at once and said to Jesus, 'Rabbi,' and kissed him. Then they seized him and held him fast.

One of the party drew his sword, and struck at the High Priest's servant, cutting off his ear. Then Jesus spoke: 'Do you take me for a bandit, that you have come out with swords and cudgels to arrest me? Day after day I was within your reach as I taught in the temple, and you did not lay hands on me. But let the scriptures be fulfilled.' Then the disciples all deserted him and ran away.

Among those following was a young man with nothing on but a linen cloth. They tried to seize him; but he slipped out of the linen cloth and ran away naked.

Then they led Jesus away to the High Priest's house, where the chief priests, elders, and doctors of the law were all assembling. Peter followed him at a distance right into the High Priest's courtyard; and there he remained, sitting among the attendants, warming himself at the fire.

The chief priests and the whole Council[4] tried to find some evidence against Jesus to warrant a death-sentence, but failed to find any. Many gave false evidence against him, but their statements did not tally. Some stood up and gave this false evidence against him: 'We heard him say, "I will throw down this temple, made with human hands, and in three days I will build

---

[3] Simon was the name of the man originally; Christ had changed that name to Peter (the "Rock") at their first meeting. The Aramaic translation of the Greek word *Petros* is Cephas, which also appears in the New Testament as a name for Peter.

[4] This was the Sanhedrin, the ruling council of Jewish elders.

another, not made with hands."' But even on this point their evidence did not agree.

Then the High Priest stood up in his place and questioned Jesus: 'Have you no answer to the charges that these witnesses bring against you?' But he kept silence; he made no reply.

Again the Hight Priest questioned him: 'Are you the Messiah, the Son of the Blessed One?' Jesus said, 'I am; and you will see the Son of Man seated on the right hand of God and coming with the clouds of heaven.' Then the High Priest tore his robes and said, 'Need we call further witnesses? You have heard the blasphemy. What is your opinion?' Their judgment was unanimous: that he was guilty and should be put to death.

Some began to spit on him, blindfolded him, and struck him with their fists, crying out, 'Prophesy!' And the High Priest's men set upon him with blows.

Meanwhile Peter was still in the courtyard downstairs. One of the High Priest's serving-maids came by and saw him there warming himself. She looked into his face and said, 'You were there too, with this man from Nazareth, this Jesus.' But he denied it: 'I know nothing,' he said; 'I do not understand what you mean.' Then he went outside into the porch; and the maid saw him there again and began to say to the bystanders, 'He is one of them'; and again he denied it.

Again, a little later, the bystanders said to Peter, 'Surely you are one of them. You must be; you are a Galilean.' At this he broke out into curses, and with an oath he said, 'I do not know this man you speak of.' Then the cock crew a second time; and Peter remembered how Jesus had said to him, 'Before the cock crows twice you will disown me three times.' And he burst into tears.

When morning came the chief priests, having made their plan with the elders and lawyers and all the Council, put Jesus in chains; then they led him away and handed him over to Pilate. Pilate asked him, 'Are you the king of the Jews?' He replied, 'The words are yours.' And the chief priests brought many charges against him. Pilate questioned him again: 'Have you nothing to say in your defence? You see how many charges they are bringing against you.' But to Pilate's astonishment, Jesus made no further reply.

At the festival season the Governor used to release one prisoner at the people's request. As it happened, the man known as Barabbas was then in custody with the rebels who had committed murder in the rising.[5] When the crowd appeared asking for the usual favour, Pilate replied, 'Do you wish me to release for you the king of the Jews?' For he knew it was out of spite that they had brought Jesus before him. But the chief priests incited the crowd to ask him to release Barabbas rather than Jesus. Pilate spoke to them again: 'Then what shall I do with the man you call king of the Jews?' They shouted back, 'Crucify him!' 'Why, what harm has he done?' Pilate asked. They shouted all the louder, 'Crucify him!' So Pilate, in his desire to satisfy the mob, released Barabbas to them; and he had Jesus flogged and handed him over to be crucified.

---

[5] That is, during the uprising he had led against the established authority.

Then the soldiers took him inside the courtyard (the Governor's head-quarters) and called together the whole company. They dressed him in purple, and having plaited a crown of thorns, placed it on his head. Then they began to salute him with , 'Hail, King of the Jews!' They beat him about the head with a cane and spat upon him, and then knelt and paid mock homage to him. When they had finished their mockery, they stripped him of the purple and dressed him in his own clothes.

Then they took him out to crucify him. A man called Simon from Cyrene, the father of Alexander and Rufus, was passing by on his way in from the country, and they pressed him into service to carry his cross.

They brought him to the place called Golgotha, which means 'Place of a skull.' He was offered drugged wine, but he would not take it. Then they fastened him to the cross. They divided his clothes among them, casting lots to decide what each should have.

The hour of the crucifixion was nine in the morning, and the inscription giving the charge against him read, 'The king of the Jews.' Two bandits were crucified with him, one on his right and the other on his left.

The passers-by hurled abuse at him: 'Aha!' they cried, wagging their heads, 'you would pull the temple down, would you, and build it in three days? Come down from the cross and save yourself!' So too the chief priests and the doctors of the law jested with one another: 'He saved others,' they said, 'but he cannot save himself. Let the Messiah, the king of Israel, come down now from the cross. If we see that, we shall believe.' Even those who were crucified with him taunted him.

At midday darkness fell over the whole land, which lasted till three in the afternoon; and at three Jesus cried aloud, *'Eli, Eli, lema sabachthani?'* which means, 'My God, my God, why hast thou forsaken me?' Some of the passers-by, on hearing this, said, 'Hark, he is calling Elijah.'[6] A man came running with a sponge, soaked in sour wine, on the end of a cane, and held it to his lips. 'Let us see,' he said, 'if Elijah is coming to take him down.' Then Jesus gave a loud cry and died. And the curtain of the temple was torn in two from top to bottom. And when the centurion who was standing opposite him saw how he died, he said, 'Truly this man was a son of God.' . . .'[7]

By this time evening had come; and as it was Preparation-day (that is, the day before the Sabbath), Joseph of Arimathaea, a respected member of the Council, a man who was eagerly awaiting the kingdom of God, bravely went in to Pilate and asked for the body of Jesus. Pilate was surprised to hear that he was already dead; so he sent for the centurion and asked him whether it was long since he died. And when he heard the centurion's report, he gave Joseph leave to take the dead body. So Joseph bought a linen sheet, took him down from the cross, and wrapped him in the sheet. Then he laid him in a tomb cut out of the rock, and rolled a stone against the entrance. And Mary of Magdala and Mary the mother of Joseph were watching and saw where he was laid.

When the Sabbath was over, Mary of Magdala, Mary the mother of James, and Salome bought aromatic oils intending to go and anoint him;

---

[6] They mistook Jesus' "Eli" for the name of the Old Testament prophet Elijah.
[7] Compare the account of Christ's suffering with the prophecy of Isaiah, above, p. 33.

and very early on the Sunday morning, just after sunrise, they came to the tomb. They were wondering among themselves who would roll away the stone for them from the entrance to the tomb, when they looked up and saw that the stone, huge as it was, had been rolled back already. They went into the tomb, where they saw a youth sitting on the right-hand side, wearing a white robe; and they were dumbfounded. But he said to them, 'Fear nothing; you are looking for Jesus of Nazareth, who was crucified. He has risen; he is not here; look there is the place where they laid him. But go and give this message to his disciples and Peter: "He will go on before you into Galilee and you will see him there, as he told you."' Then they went out and ran away from the tomb, beside themselves with terror. They said nothing to anybody, for they were afraid.

When he had risen from the dead early on Sunday morning he appeared first to Mary of Magdala, from whom he had formerly cast out seven devils. She went and carried the news to his mourning and sorrowful followers, but when they were told that he was alive and that she had seen him they did not believe it.

Later he appeared in a different guise to two of them as they were walking, on their way into the country. These also went and took the news to the others, but again no one believed them.

Afterwards while the Eleven were at table he appeared to them and reproached them for their incredulity and dullness, because they had not believed those who had seen him risen from the dead. Then he said to them: 'Go forth to every part of the world, and proclaim the Good News to the whole creation. Those who believe it and receive baptism will find salvation; those who do not believe will be condemned. Faith will bring with it these miracles: believers will cast out devils in my name and speak in strange tongues; if they handle snakes or drink deadly poison, they will come to no harm; and the sick on whom they lay their hands will recover.'

So after talking with them the Lord Jesus was taken up into heaven, and he took his seat at the right hand of God; but they went out to make their proclamation everywhere, and the Lord worked with them and confirmed their words by the miracles that followed.

3. What Did Christ's Life and Death Mean for His Followers, for the Jews, and for Mankind?

After the death of Jesus on a Roman cross, stories of his resurrection began to circulate. Individuals who believed them had to change their views of his life, ministry, and death. The stories had to be accepted on faith, then as now, and, clearly, most Jews did not believe them. His faithful followers no longer could regard Jesus as the expected king of a new and political Israel. Instead, they held that he was king of a spiritual kingdom of God's children, an Israel of faith.

Soon the followers of Jesus began to preach the message or Gospel of the Son of God risen from the dead. Among these preachers was the man whose life and works influenced the history of Christianity more powerfully than those of any other save Jesus himself: Saul of Tarsus, later called Paul the Apostle. During the last years of Jesus' life on earth, Saul had come to Jerusalem to study in the rabbinic schools there. He was a zealous student and initially very hostile to the Jewish followers of Jesus, even to the point of securing letters of authorization to go from city to city to seek them out and take them back to Jerusalem for trial and punishment.

On one such journey to the city of Damascus, a sudden burst of light blinded Saul, and a vision of the risen Christ directed him on to Damascus, there to await orders. From thence he went alone to the desert, where he communed with the very Christ whose followers he had persecuted. Saul (now known to his Christian friends as Paul) returned to Jerusalem and began the first of his three great missionary journeys. Proceeding from city to city, he would begin his preaching in Jewish synagogues, and carry it from there to the mixed Jewish and Gentile gatherings of his converts. These small communities of new believers were always an object of intense interest and concern to him. He addressed to them the letters of doctrine, interpretation, and advice which form a large part of the Christian New Testament. He dealt with questions that emerged out of the situation and concern of these early Christian communities, these young churches. His activities aroused the enmity of part of the Palestinian Jewish community. Arrested, he claimed the privilege, as a Roman citizen, of trial in Rome. He was sent there and was martyred, probably in the persecution of Christians by the emperor Nero about A.D. 64.

GALATIANS*

St. Paul

But when I saw that [the conduct of some of the Jewish Christians who were refusing to eat with Gentile Christians] did not square with the truth of the Gospel, I said to Cephas,[1] before the whole congregation, 'If you, a Jew born and bred, live like a Gentile, and not like a Jew, how can you insist that Gentiles must live like Jews?'

We ourselves are Jews by birth, not Gentiles and sinners. But we know that no man is ever justified by doing what the law demands, but only through faith in Christ Jesus; so we too have put our faith in Jesus Christ, in order that we might be justified through this faith, and not through deeds dictated by law; for by such deeds, Scripture says, no mortal man shall be justified.

If now, in seeking to be justified in Christ, we ourselves no less than the Gentiles turn out to be sinners against the law, does that mean that Christ is an abettor of sin? No, never! No, if I start building up again a system which I have pulled down, then it is that I show myself up as a transgressor of the law. For through the law I died to law—to live for God. I have been crucified with Christ: the life I now live is not my life, but the life which Christ lives in me; and my present bodily life is lived by faith in the Son of

---

*Galatians 2:14–4:31.

[1] Peter, with whom particularly Paul was having an argument at this time. See above, p. 39, note 3.

God, who loved me and sacrificed himself for me. I will not nullify the grace of God; if righteousness comes by law, then Christ died for nothing.[2]

You stupid Galatians! You must have been bewitched—you before whose eyes Jesus Christ was openly displayed upon his cross! Answer me one question: did you receive the Spirit by keeping the law or by believing the gospel message? Can it be that you are so stupid? You started with the spiritual; do you now look to the material to make you perfect? Have all your great experiences been in vain—if vain indeed they should be? I ask then: when God gives you the Spirit and works miracles among you, why is this? Is it because you keep the law, or is it because you have faith in the gospel message? Look at Abraham: he put his faith in God, and that faith was counted to him as righteousness.

You may take it, then, that it is the men of faith who are Abraham's sons. And Scripture, foreseeing that God would justify the Gentiles through faith, declared the Gospel to Abraham beforehand: 'In you all nations shall find blessing.' Thus it is the men of faith who share the blessing with faithful Abraham.[3]

On the other hand those who rely on obedience to the law are under a curse; for Scripture says, 'Cursed are all who do not persevere in doing everything that is written in the Book of the Law.' It is evident that no one is ever justified before God in terms of law; because we read, 'he shall gain life who is justified through faith.' Now law is not all a matter of having faith: we read, 'he who does this shall gain life by what he does.'

Christ bought us freedom from the curse of the law by becoming for our sake an accursed thing; for Scripture says, 'Cursed is everyone who is hanged on a tree.' And the purpose of it all was that the blessing of Abraham should in Jesus Christ be extended to the Gentiles, so that we might receive the promised Spirit through faith.

My brothers, let me give you an illustration. Even in ordinary life, when a man's will and testament has been duly executed, no one else can set it aside or add a codicil. Now the promises were pronounced to Abraham and to his 'issue.' It does not say 'issues' in the plural, but in the singular, 'and to your issue'; and the 'issue' intended is Christ. What I am saying is this: a testament, or covenant, had already been validated by God; it cannot be invalidated, and its promises rendered ineffective, by a law made four hundred and thirty years later. If the inheritance is by legal right, then it is not by promise; but it was by promise that God bestowed it as a free gift on Abraham.

Then what of the law? It was added to make wrongdoing a legal offence. It was a temporary measure pending the arrival of the 'issue' to whom the promise was made. It was promulgated through angels, and there was an intermediary; but an intermediary is not needed for one party acting alone, and God is one.

Does the law, then, contradict the promises? No, never! If a law had been given which had power to bestow life, then indeed righteousness would have come from keeping the law. But Scripture has declared the whole world to be prisoners in subjection to sin, so that faith in Jesus Christ may be the

---

[2] See Deuteronomy, above, pp. 26–27.
[3] See above, pp. 22–23, for the story of Abraham.

ground on which the promised blessing is given, and given to those who have such faith.

Before this faith came, we were close prisoners in the custody of law, pending the revelation of faith. Thus the law was a kind of tutor in charge of us until Christ should come, when we should be justified through faith; and now that faith has come, the tutor's charge is at an end.

For through faith you are all sons of God in union with Christ Jesus. Baptized into union with him, you have all put on Christ as a garment. There is no such thing as Jew and Greek, slave and freeman, male and female; for you are all one person in Christ Jesus. But if you thus belong to Christ, you are the 'issue' of Abraham, and so heirs by promise.

This is what I mean: so long as the heir is a minor, he is no better off than a slave, even though the whole estate is his; he is under guardians and trustees until the date fixed by his father. . . .

You keep special days and months and seasons and years. You make me fear that all the pains I spent on you may prove to be labour lost. . . .

Tell me now, you who are so anxious to be under law, will you not listen to what the Law says? It is written there that Abraham had two sons, one by his slave and the other by his free-born wife. The slave-woman's son was born in the course of nature, the free woman's through God's promise. This is an allegory. The two women stand for two covenants. The one bearing children into slavery is the covenant that comes from Mount Sinai: that is Hagar. Sinai is a mountain in Arabia and it represents the Jerusalem of today, for she and her children are in slavery. But the heavenly Jerusalem is the free woman; she is our mother. For Scripture says, 'Rejoice O barren woman who never bore child; break into a shout of joy, you who never knew a mother's pangs; for the deserted wife shall have more children than she who lives with the husband.'

And you, my brothers, like Isaac, are children of God's promise. But just as in those days the natural-born son persecuted the spiritual son, so it is today. But what does Scripture say? 'Drive out the slave-woman and her son, for the son of the slave shall not share the inheritance with the free woman's sons.[4] You see, then, my brothers, we are no slave-woman's children; our mother is the free woman.

ROMANS*

St. Paul

Therefore, now that we have been justified through faith, let us continue at peace with God through our Lord Jesus Christ, through whom we have been allowed to enter the sphere of God's grace, where we now stand. Let us exult in the hope of the divine splendour that is to be ours. More than this:

---

[4] This is a reference to the episode in the life of Abraham. Before the birth of Isaac, he had a child by the slave woman Hagar. After the birth of Isaac, Hagar and her son, Ishmael, were driven from Abraham's household.

*Romans 5:1–6:14.

let us even exult in our present sufferings, because we know that suffering trains us to endure, and endurance brings proof that we have stood the test, and this proof is the ground of hope. Such a hope is no mockery, because God's love has flooded our inmost heart through the Holy Spirit he has given us.

For at the very time when we were still powerless, then Christ died for the wicked. Even for a just man one of us would hardly die, though perhaps for a good man one might actually brave death; but Christ died for us while we were yet sinners, and that is God's own proof of his love towards us. And so, since we have now been justified by Christ's sacrificial death, we shall all the more certainly be saved through him from final retribution. For if, when we were God's enemies, we were reconciled to him through the death of his Son, much more, now that we are reconciled, shall we be saved by his life. But that is not all: we also exult in God through our Lord Jesus, through whom we have now been granted reconciliation.

Mark what follows. It was through one man that sin entered the world, and through sin death, and thus death pervaded the whole human race, inasmuch as all men have sinned. For sin was already in the world before there was law, though in the absence of law no reckoning is kept of sin. But death held sway from Adam to Moses, even over those who had not sinned as Adam did, by disobeying a direct command—and Adam foreshadows the Man who was to come.

But God's act of grace is out of all proportion to Adam's wrongdoing. For if the wrongdoing of that one man brought death upon so many, its effect is vastly exceeded by the grace of God and the gift that came to so many by the grace of the one man, Jesus Christ. And again, the gift of God is not to be compared in its effect with that one man's sin; for the judicial action, following upon the one offence, issued in a verdict of condemnation, but the act of grace, following upon so many misdeeds, issued in a verdict of acquittal. For if by the wrongdoing of that one man death established its reign, through a single sinner, much more shall those who receive in far greater measure God's grace, and his gift of righteousness, live and reign through the one man, Jesus Christ.

It follows, then, that as the issue of one misdeed was condemnation for all men, so the issue of just one act is acquittal and life for all men. For as through the disobedience of the one man the many were made sinners, so through the obedience of the one man the many will be made righteous.

Law intruded into this process to multiply law-breaking. But where sin was thus multiplied, grace immeasurably exceeded it, in order that, as sin established its reign by way of death, so God's grace might establish its reign in righteousness, and issue in eternal life through Jesus Christ our Lord.

What are we to say, then? Shall we persist in sin, so that there may be all the more grace? No, no! We died to sin: how can we live in it any longer? Have you forgotten that when we were baptized into union with Christ Jesus we were baptized into his death? By baptism we were buried with him, and lay dead, in order that, as Christ was raised from the dead in the splendour of the Father, so also we might set our feet upon the new path of life.

For if we have become incorporate with him in a death like his, we shall also be one with him in a resurrection like his. We know that the man we once were has been crucified with Christ, for the destruction of the sinful self, so that we may no longer be the slaves of sin, since a dead man is no longer answerable for his sin. But if we thus died with Christ, we believe that we shall also come to life with him. We know that Christ, once raised from the dead, is never to die again: he is no longer under the dominion of death. For in dying as he died, he died to sin, once for all, and in living as he lives, he lives to God. In the same way you must regard yourselves as dead to sin and alive to God, in union with Christ Jesus.

So sin must no longer reign in your mortal body, exacting obedience to the body's desires. You must no longer put its several parts at sin's disposal, as implements for doing wrong. No: put yourselves at the disposal of God, as dead men raised to life; yield your bodies to him as implements for doing right; for sin shall no longer be your master, because you are no longer under law, but under the grace of God.

4. What Is Sin and How Is It Cured?

The apostle John was an early follower of Jesus and was close to him to the very end of his earthly ministry. John lived a long life, perhaps longer than any other who had witnessed the founding of Christianity. He appears to have written the fourth Gospel of the New Testament, as well as its last book, Revelation. But quite late in life, probably just before being exiled to the island of Patmos where he composed Revelation, he, like Paul, wrote a series of epistles. These letters he filled with the advice of a now very old Christian to those whose conversion and progress in the faith he had long watched with hope and fear. Like Paul, John was concerned with man's wickedness and God's care for men in relation to that wickedness.

*FIRST EPISTLE**

St. John

How great is the love that the Father has shown to us! We were called God's children, and such we are; and the reason why the godless world does not recognize us is that it has not known him. Here and now, dear friends, we are God's children; what we shall be has not yet been disclosed, but we know that when it is disclosed we shall be like him, because we shall see him as he is. Everyone who has this hope before him purifies himself, as Christ is pure.

To commit sin is to break God's law: sin, in fact, is lawlessness. Christ appeared, as you know, to do away with sins, and there is no sin in him. No man therefore who dwells in him is a sinner; the sinner has not seen him and does not know him.

---

*I Epistle 3:1–5:21.

My children, do not be misled: it is the man who does right who is righteous, as God is righteous; the man who sins is a child of the devil, for the devil has been a sinner from the first; and the Son of God appeared for the very purpose of undoing the devil's work.

A child of God does not commit sin, because the divine seed remains in him; he cannot be a sinner, because he is God's child. That is the distinction between the children of God and the children of the devil: no one who does not do right is God's child, nor is anyone who does not love his brother. For the message you have heard from the beginning is this: that we should love one another.

Dear friends, let us love one another, because love is from God. Everyone who loves is a child of God and knows God, but the unloving know nothing of God. For God is love; and his love was disclosed to us in this, that he sent his only Son into the world to bring us life. The love I speak of is not our love for God, but the love he showed to us in sending his Son as the remedy for the defilement of our sins. If God thus loved us, dear friends, we in turn are bound to love one another. Though God has never been seen by any man, God himself dwells in us if we love one another; his love is brought to perfection within us.

Here is the proof that we dwell in him and he dwells in us: he has imparted his Spirit to us. Moreover, we have seen for ourselves, and we attest, that the Father sent the Son to be the Saviour of the world, and if a man acknowledges that Jesus is the Son of God, God dwells in him and he dwells in God. Thus we have come to know and believe the love which God has for us.

God is love; he who dwells in love is dwelling in God, and God in him. This is for us the perfection of love, to have confidence on the day of judgement, and this we can have, because even in this world we are as he is. There is no room for fear in love; perfect loves banishes fear. For fear brings with it the pains of judgement, and anyone who is afraid has not attained to love in its perfection. We love because he loved us first. But if a man says, 'I love God,' while hating his brother, he is a liar. If he does not love the brother whom he has seen, it cannot be that he loves God whom he has not seen. And indeed this command comes to us from Christ himself: that he who loves God must also love his brother.

Everyone who believes that Jesus is the Christ is a child of God, and to love the parent means to love his child; it follows that when we love God and obey his commands we love his children too. For to love God is to keep his commands; and they are not burdensome, because every child of God is victor over the godless world. The victory that defeats the world is our faith, for who is victor over the world but he who believes that Jesus is the Son of God?

This is he who came with water and blood: Jesus Christ. He came, not by water alone, but by water and blood; and there is the Spirit to bear witness, because the Spirit is truth. For there are three witnesses, the Spirit, the water, and the blood, and these three are in agreement. We accept human testimony, but surely divine testimony is stronger, and this threefold testimony is indeed that of God himself, the witness he has borne to his Son. He who believes in the Son of God has this testimony in his own heart, but he who disbelieves God, makes him out to be a liar, by refusing to accept God's own witness to his Son. The witness is this: that God has given us eternal life, and that this life is found in his Son. He who possesses the Son has life indeed; he who does not possess the Son of God has not that life.

This letter is to assure you that you have eternal life. It is addressed to those who give their allegiance to the Son of God.

We can approach God with confidence for this reason: if we make requests which accord with his will he listens to us; and if we know that our requests are heard, we also know that the things we ask for are ours.

If a man sees his brother committing a sin which is not a deadly sin, he should pray to God for him, and he will grant him life—that is, when men are not guilty of deadly sin. There is such a thing as deadly sin, and I do not suggest that he should pray about that; but although all wrongdoing is sin, not all sin is deadly sin.

We know that no child of God is a sinner; it is the Son of God who keeps him safe, and the evil one cannot touch him.

We know that we are of God's family, while the whole godless world lies in the power of the evil one.

We know that the Son of God has come and given us understanding to know him who is real; indeed we are in him who is real, since we are in his Son Jesus Christ. This is the true God, this is eternal life. My children, be on the watch against false gods.

5. What Must One Believe in Order To Be a Christian?

During the first centuries after the Crucifixion, loose local groupings of the followers of Christ became increasingly well organized. Moreover, they frequently fell into disagreement with each other about just what true Christians ought to believe about the Lord's work and His nature and their own destiny. Thus, they felt the need for a definitive statement of the basic essentials of their faith. One such statement comes to us as the Apostles' Creed. Although in substance it seems to have come early in Christian history, probably none of the original twelve apostles composed it. It may have received its final form only in the fifth century after Christ, but it purports to set forth what those original followers of Christ must surely have believed. Christians were required to recite some such creed as an affirmation of faith, and some present-day Christian churches still use the Apostles' Creed.

THE APOSTLES' CREED*

I believe in God the Father Almighty, Maker of heaven and earth; and in Jesus Christ his only Son, our Lord, who was conceived by the Holy

---

*Available, among many other places, in Philip Schaff, *The Creeds of Christendom* (New York: Harper and Brothers, 1884), I, 21f., where both the Old Roman and the Received forms are offered.

Ghost, born of the Virgin Mary, suffered under Pontius Pilate, was crucified, died, and buried; he descended into hell; the third day he rose from the dead; he ascended into Heaven, and sitteth at the right hand of God, the Father Almighty; from thence he shall come to judge the quick and the dead. I believe in the Holy Ghost; the holy Catholic Church; the communion of saints; the forgiveness of sins; the resurrection of the body; and the life everlasting. Amen.

II

THE CLASSICAL SOURCE
OF WESTERN TRADITIONS

*All earlier civilized societies and Greek society up to about the sixth century
B.C. had dealt with the problem of explaining the material world of the senses
by means of myths—tales of gods and dragons, of semidivine kings and heroes.
Grounded in the capricious actions of divine beings, those myths were not subjected to scrutiny or judgment by human reason or experience. Myth accounted
for the nature of the material world, its changes and problems, and the fortunes of man, by attributing them to the actions of the gods. Understanding,
and the means of affecting change for the benefit of men, therefore lay with
learning the desires of the gods and persuading them to act in favor of man
through sacrifice, propitiation, and the recitation of incantations, hymns, and
prayers. The knowledge of how to do this rested with the priestly class, who
jealously guarded its secrets as the means to its own power and admitted to
practice only those who were equally persuaded of the value and purpose of
such mythologically explained religion.*

*Beginning in the sixth century B.C., and on through the fourth, Greek-
speaking thinkers became interested in the substance of Near Eastern myth.
Some continued the earlier practice of explaining the world on the basis
of divine cosmology, but some who were free of the intellectual barriers of the
priestly aristocracy began to inquire beneath the surface into the possibility of
a mechanical, "natural," explanation. In doing so they began to bring the whole
range of human concern—the origin, nature, and purpose of the world, of men,
and of communities of men—under rational scrutiny and judgment. By the
late fourth century, Greek speculative thought on these matters had achieved
a level of sophistication so high that down to the present day in at least two
areas, philosophy and politics, men still feel it necessary or desirable to study
carefully the problems raised and the answers given to them by Greek thinkers
almost two and a half millenniums ago. The two greatest formulators and
codifiers of the problems of philosophy and politics as the Greeks saw them
were the Athenian Plato and Aristotle, who was for a time his pupil. Plato,*

however, had been influenced in a major way both in his style of thinking and in the substance of his ideas by his teacher, Socrates.

A. Philosophy

Among the most striking traits of Greek speculation on matters subsequently called philosophical is the speed with which it developed. Such speed, although rare, is not without precedent and not without later analogues. It seems to be connected with the discovery of radically new ways of dealing with perplexities or concerns or activities that previously engaged human effort and action. Such a discovery leads the men involved to set aside traditional ways and to focus all their endeavors on the exploitation of the new ones. This happened, for example, with the rediscovery of Aristotle and Roman law in the Middle Ages, with the discovery of perspective painting in the Renaissance, and with scientific discoveries of the sixteenth and early seventeenth centuries. Such marked acceleration of cultural change need not always entail a conscious and explicit repudiation of old ways by those who embark on the new course, but it is a genuine change. As a result of this turning about—a revolution in the full meaning of the word—Greek philosophers, in two centuries, hit upon a wide range of questions about the nature of the world and man and, employing reason rather than myth, explored many possible answers to such questions. The result was a remarkably intense intellectual activity. The activity, however, did not end in agreement but in a confrontation among several irreconcilable answers and, by the second half of the fifth century, in the emergence of skepticism about the capacity of rational thought to arrive at sure answers to most of the questions it raised.

1. What Is the Justification and What Are the Limits of Human Inquiry?

The Athenian Socrates (469–399 B.C.) sought to cope with the dilemma that the confrontation of irreconcilable opposites posed for the speculative philosopher. By his time, philosophical activity, which earlier had been diffused through the Greek-speaking world from the coast of Asia Minor to Sicily, had come to focus in Athens, which, in the words of one of its leaders, Pericles, had become "the school of Hellas." The son of an Athenian stone mason or perhaps sculptor, Socrates had served with courage if not distinction in the bitter war with Sparta that ended in disaster for Athens. He had also studied philosophy. In his effort to rescue speculative thought from the trap that its practitioners had gotten into, he adopted a method of inquiry that involved the subjection of views, haphazardly though commonly held, to intense rational inquisition. He believed that by this sort of investigation, truth could be distinguished from mere opinion. Eventually, his fellow citizens came to regard Socrates' continual prying into their tradition-bound views not merely as a nuisance but as a menace, a sort of anti-Athenian activity, in view of the dis-oriented political condition of the city during and after its defeat by Sparta. In the end, Socrates' reputation was not improved by his association with a number of rather shady rich young men, including the notorious blasphemer Alcibiades. Socrates was tried for introducing new views and corrupting the youth of Athens and sentenced to death. In the Apology, *his disciple Plato records a version of the trial. In view of the public character of the trial, it seems likely that the views ascribed to Socrates in the* Apology *were those he actually expressed in his own defense.*

THE APOLOGY OF SOCRATES*

Plato

As a matter of fact, gentlemen, I do not feel that it requires much defense to clear myself of Meletus' accusation. What I have said already is enough. But you know very well the truth of what I said in an earlier part of my speech, that I have incurred a great deal of bitter hostility, and this is what will bring about my destruction, if anything does—not Meletus nor Anytus,[1] but the slander and jealousy of a very large section of the people. They have been fatal to a great many other innocent men, and I suppose will continue to do so; there is no likelihood that they will stop at me. But perhaps someone will say, Do you feel no compunction, Socrates, at having followed a line of action which puts you in danger of the death penalty?

I might fairly reply to him, You are mistaken, my friend, if you think that a man who is worth anything ought to spend his time weighing up the prospects of life and death. He has only one thing to consider in performing any action—that is, whether he is acting rightly or wrongly, like a good man or a bad one. On your view the heroes who died at Troy would be poor creatures, especially the son of Thetis.[2] He, if you remember, made light of danger in comparison with incurring dishonor when his goddess mother warned him, eager as he was to kill Hector, in some such words as these, I fancy: My son, if you avenge your comrade Patroclus' death and kill Hector, you will die yourself—'Next after Hector is thy fate prepared.' When he heard this warning, he made light of his death and danger, being much more afraid of an ignoble life and of failing to avenge his friends. 'Let me die forthwith,' said he, 'when I have requited the villain, rather than remain here by the beaked ships to be mocked, a burden on the ground.'[3] Do you suppose he gave a thought to death and danger?

The truth of the matter is this, gentlemen. Where a man has once taken up his stand, either because it seems best to him or in obedience to his orders, there I believe he is bound to remain and face the danger, taking no account of death or anything else before dishonor.

---

*Apology 28a–30b, from *The Last Days of Socrates* trans. and with an introduction by Hugh Tredennick (Harmondsworth, Middlesex: Penguin Books, 1954). By permission.
[1] Socrates' accusers at his trial.
[2] Achilles, whose opponent Hector was the greatest of Troy's warriors.
[3] *Iliad,* xviii.96ff.

This being so, it would be shocking inconsistency on my part, gentlemen, if, when the officers whom you chose to command me assigned me my position at Potidaea and Amphipolis and Delium,[4] I remained at my post like anyone else and faced death, and yet afterward, when God[5] appointed me, as I supposed and believed, to the duty of leading the philosophical life, examining myself and others, I were then through fear of death or of any other danger to desert my post. That would indeed be shocking, and then I might really with justice be summoned into court for not believing in the gods, and disobeying the oracle, and being afraid of death, and thinking that I am wise when I am not. For let me tell you, gentlemen, that to be afraid of death is only another form of thinking that one is wise when one is not; it is to think that one knows what one does not know. No one knows with regard to death whether it is not really the greatest blessing that can happen to a man, but people dread it as though they were certain that it is the greatest evil, and this ignorance, which thinks that it knows what it does not, must surely be ignorance most culpable. This, I take it, gentlemen, is the degree, and this the nature of my advantage over the rest of mankind, and if I were to claim to be wiser than my neighbor in any respect, it would be in this—that not possessing any real knowledge of what comes after death, I am also conscious that I do not possess it. But I do know that to do wrong and to disobey my superior, whether it be God or man, is wicked and dishonorable, and so I shall never feel more fear or aversion for something which, for all I know, may really be a blessing, than for those evils which I know to be evils.

Suppose, then, that you acquit me, and pay no attention to Anytus, who has said that either I should not have appeared before this court at all, or, since I have appeared here, I must be put to death, because if I once escaped your sons would all immediately become utterly demoralized by putting the teaching of Socrates into practice. Suppose that, in view of this, you said to me, Socrates, on this occasion we shall disregard Anytus and acquit you, but only on one condition, that you give up spending your time on this quest and stop philosophizing. If we catch you going on in the same way, you shall be put to death.

Well, supposing, as I said, that you should offer to acquit me on these terms, I should reply, Gentlemen, I am your very grateful and devoted servant, but I owe a greater obedience to God than to you, and so long as I draw breath and have my faculties, I shall never stop practicing philosophy and exhorting you and elucidating the truth for everyone that I meet. I shall go on saying, in my usual way, My very good friend, you are an Athenian and belong to a city which is the greatest and most famous in the world for its wisdom

---

[4] Potidaea was a city in northern Greece which fell to Athens in 430 B.C., after a long and costly siege during the early part of the war between Athens and Sparta. Delium and Amphipolis were two later battles, both of which Athens lost.

[5] There is much confusion for the modern reader in the Greek use of the word "god" in the singular. It often refers to a particular god, as in this instance to Apollo. Elsewhere in these selections, it is used to refer to the divine influence which Plato credits with having designed the world. This does not necessarily mean that Plato was a monotheist, and certainly it does not mean that he was thinking of a single, personal God in the sense found in the Judeo-Christian tradition. In view of the problems entailed in determining Plato's precise meaning, the selections used here follow the translators' lead where they have capitalized the word.

and strength. Are you not ashamed that you give your attention to acquiring as much money as possible, and similarly with reputation and honor, and give no attention or thought to truth and understanding and the perfection of your soul?

And if any of you disputes this and professes to care about these things, I shall not at once let him go or leave him. No, I shall question him and examine him and test him; and if it appears that in spite of his profession he has made no real progress toward goodness, I shall reprove him for neglecting what is of supreme importance, and giving his attention to trivialities. I shall do this to everyone that I meet, young or old, foreigner or fellow citizen, but especially to you, my fellow citizens, inasmuch as you are closer to me in kinship. This, I do assure you, is what my God commands, and it is my belief that no greater good has ever befallen you in this city than my service to my God. For I spend all my time going about trying to persuade you, young and old, to make your first and chief concern not for your bodies nor for your possessions, but for the highest welfare of your souls, proclaiming as I go, Wealth does not bring goodness, but goodness brings wealth and every other blessing, both to the individual and to the state.[6]

2. What Is the Nature of Knowledge and the Obligation of Those Who Attain It?

Born about 429 B.C., Socrates' pupil Plato had intended to become a statesman, but under the influence of Socrates, he soon grew disgusted with contemporary Athenian politics in the period of decline after the city had lost both its empire and its great war with Sparta. He apparently announced to his friends that he would never consider a political career until philosophers became rulers or rulers philosophers. After the execution of Socrates in 399, Plato left Athens to travel. He returned in 387 to found the Academy, a school of philosophers who met outside the city in the grove of Academus. Plato spent the next forty years until his death in 348 lecturing and writing.

The surviving works of Plato, including The Republic, *are dialogues, interchanges of argument among several persons, rather than treatises. The* Republic *starts with a discussion about the nature of justice in individual men. In seeking to run this question to the ground, the participants in the dialogue find they have come up against the problem of the nature of true knowledge, since rightly to rule one's self in a political society, one must know what the right and the true are.*

The scene of the dialogue is in the Piraeus, the harbor town of Athens. A party of friends has gathered at the house of a wealthy merchant after a festival, and has begun to debate the true meaning of justice. "Socrates" (Plato's hero of the dialogue), recounting a previous discussion with Glaucon, one of those present, has just stated his intention of seeking a definition of justice in terms of its operation within the state, rather than within the individual. Glaucon has accepted Socrates' idea that there must be differences in rank

---

[6] Compare this passage with the account of Jesus' arrest and trial above, pp. 39–40.

among participants in the ideal republic and that men must undergo rigorous selection and training for the task of governing. But since this requires everyone in society to accept the principle that not all are fitted for the same privileges, he asks how we may persuade citizens of the republic to accept these differences in status. Socrates' reply begins with the assertion that there are in fact differences in levels of perception. When Glaucon accepts this point, Socrates continues:

THE REPUBLIC*

Plato

Next, said I, compare our nature in respect of education and its lack to such an experience as this. Picture men dwelling in a sort of subterranean cavern with a long entrance open to the light on its entire width. Conceive them as having their legs and necks fettered from childhood, so that they remain in the same spot, able to look forward only, and prevented by the fetters from turning their heads. Picture further the light from a fire burning higher up and at a distance behind them, and between the fire and the prisoners and above them a road along which a low wall has been built, as the exhibitors of puppet shows have partitions before the men themselves, above which they show the puppets.

All that I see, he said.

See also, then, men carrying past the wall implements of all kinds that rise above the wall, and human images and shapes of animals as well, wrought in stone and wood and every material, some of these bearers presumably speaking and others silent.

A strange image you speak of, he said, and strange prisoners.

Like to us, I said. For, to begin with, tell me do you think that these men would have seen anything of themselves or of one another except the shadows cast from the fire on the wall of the cave that fronted them?

How could they, he said, if they were compelled to hold their heads unmoved through life?

And again, would not the same be true of the objects carried past them?

Surely.

If then they were able to talk to one another, do you not think that they would suppose that in naming the things that they saw they were naming the passing objects?

Necessarily.

And if their prison had an echo from the wall opposite them, when one of the passers-by uttered a sound, do you think that they would suppose anything else than the passing shadow to be the speaker?

By Zeus, I do not, said he.

Then in every way such prisoners would deem reality to be nothing else than the shadows of the artificial objects.

* Reprinted by permission of the publishers from The Loeb Classical Library, *Plato's Republic*, vii.514a–520d, trans. Paul Shorey (Cambridge, Mass.: Harvard University Press, 1942), II, 119–143.

Quite inevitably, he said.

Consider, then, what would be the manner of the release and healing from these bonds and this folly if in the course of nature something of this sort should happen to them. When one was freed from his fetters and compelled to stand up suddenly and turn his head around and walk and to lift up his eyes to the light, and in doing all this felt pain and, because of the dazzle and glitter of the light, was unable to discern the objects whose shadows he formerly saw, what do you suppose would be his answer if someone told him that what he had seen before was all a cheat and an illusion, but that now, being nearer to reality and turned toward more real things, he saw more truly? And if also one should point out to him each of the passing objects and constrain him by questions to say what it is, do you not think that he would be at a loss and that he would regard what he formerly saw as more real than the things now pointed out to him?

Far more real, he said.

And if he were compelled to look at the light itself, would not that pain his eyes, and would he not turn away and flee to those things which he is able to discern and regard them as in very deed more clear and exact than the objects pointed out?

It is so, he said.

And if, said I, someone should drag him thence by force up the ascent which is rough and steep, and not let him go before he had drawn him out into the light of the sun, do you not think that he would find it painful to be so haled along, and would chafe at it, and when he came out into the light, that his eyes would be filled with its beams so that he would not be able to see even one of the things that we call real?

Why, no, not immediately, he said.

Then there would be need of habituation, I take it, to enable him to see the things higher up. And at first he would most easily discern the shadows and, after that, the likenesses or reflections in water of men and other things, and later, the things themselves, and from these he would go on to contemplate the appearances in the heavens and heaven itself, more easily by night, looking at the light of the stars and the moon, than by day the sun and the sun's light.

Of course.

And so, finally, I suppose, he would be able to look upon the sun itself and see its true nature, not by reflections in water or phantasms of it in an alien setting, but in and by itself in its own place.

Necessarily, he said.

And at this point he would infer and conclude that this it is that provides the seasons and the courses of the year and presides over all things in the visible region, and is in some sort the cause of all these things that they had seen.

Obviously, he said, that would be the next step.

Well then, if he recalled to mind his first habitation and what passed for wisdom there, and his fellow bondsmen, do you not think that he would count himself happy in the change and pity them?

He would indeed.

And if there had been honors and commendations among them which they bestowed on one another and prizes for the man who is quickest to make out the shadows as they pass and best able to remember their customary precedences, sequences, and coexistences, and so most successful in guessing at what was to come, do you think he would be very keen about such rewards, and that he would envy and emulate those who were honored by these prisoners and lorded it among them, or that he would feel with Homer and greatly prefer while living on earth to be serf of another, a landless man, and endure anything rather than opine with them and live that life?[1]

Yes, he said, I think that he would choose to endure anything rather than such a life.

And consider this also, said I. If such a one should go down again and take his old place would he not get his eyes full of darkness, thus suddenly coming out of the sunlight?

He would indeed.

Now if he should be required to contend with these perpetual prisoners in 'evaluating' these shadows while his vision was still dim and before his eyes were accustomed to the dark—and this time required for habituation would not be very short—would he not provoke laughter, and would it not be said of him that he had returned from his journey aloft with his eyes ruined and that it was not worth while even to attempt the ascent? And if it were possible to lay hands on and to kill the man who tried to release them and lead them up, would they not kill him?

They certainly would, he said.

This image then, dear Glaucon, we must apply as a whole to all that has been said, likening the region revealed through sight to the habitation of the prison, and the light of the fire in it to the power of the sun. And if you assume that the ascent and the contemplation of the things above is the soul's ascension to the intelligible region, you will not miss my surmise, since that is what you desire to hear. But God knows whether it is true. But at any rate, my dream as it appears to me is that in the region of the known the last thing to be seen and hardly seen is the idea of good, and that when seen it must needs point us to the conclusion that this is indeed the cause for all things of all that is right and beautiful, giving birth in the visible world to light, and the author of light and itself in the intelligible world being the authentic source of truth and reason, and that anyone who is to act wisely in private or public must have caught sight of this.

I concur, he said, so far as I am able.

Come then, I said, and join me in this further thought, and do not be surprised that those who have attained to this height are not willing to occupy themselves with the affairs of men, but their souls ever feel the upward urge and the yearning for that sojourn above. For this, I take it, is likely if in this point too the likeness of our image holds.

Yes, it is likely.

And again, do you think it at all strange, said I, if a man returning from divine contemplations to the petty miseries of men cuts a sorry figure

[1] *Odyssey* xi.489.

and appears most ridiculous, if, while still blinking through the gloom, and before he has become sufficiently accustomed to the environing darkness, he is compelled in courtrooms or elsewhere to contend about the shadows of justice or the images that cast the shadows and to wrangle in debate about the notions of these things in the minds of those who have never seen justice itself?

It would be by no means strange, he said.

But a sensible man, I said, would remember that there are two distinct disturbances of the eyes arising from two causes, according as the shift is from light to darkness or from darkness to light, and, believing that the same thing happens to the soul too, whenever he saw a soul perturbed and unable to discern something, he would not laugh unthinkingly, but would observe whether coming from a brighter life its vision was obscured by the unfamiliar darkness, or whether the passage from the deeper dark of ignorance into a more luminous world and the greater brightness had dazzled its vision. And so he would deem the one happy in its experience and way of life and pity the other, and if it pleased him to laugh at it, his laughter would be less laughable than that at the expense of the soul that had come down from the light above.

That is a very fair statement, he said.

Then, if this is true, our view of these matters must be this, that education is not in reality what some people proclaim it to be in their professions. What they aver is that they can put true knowledge into a soul that does not possess it, as if they were inserting vision into blind eyes.

They do indeed, he said.

But our present argument indicates, said I, that the true analogy for this indwelling power in the soul and the instrument whereby each of us apprehends is that of an eye that could not be converted to the light from the darkness except by turning the whole body. Even so this organ of knowledge must be turned around from the world of becoming together with the entire soul, like the scene-shifting machinery in the theater, until the soul is able to endure the contemplation of essence and the brightest region of being.[2] And this, we say, is the good, do we not?

Yes.

Of this very thing, then, I said, there might be an art, an art of the speediest and most effective shifting or conversion of the soul, not an art of producing vision in it, but on the assumption that it possesses vision but does not rightly direct it and does not look where it should, an art of bringing this about.

Yes, that seems likely, he said.

Then the other so-called virtues of the soul do seem akin to those of the body. For it is true that where they do not pre-exist, they are afterward created by habit and practice. But the excellence of thought, it seems, is certainly of a more divine quality, a thing that never loses its potency, but, according to the direction of its conversion, becomes useful and beneficent, or, again, useless and harmful. Have you never observed in those who are popularly spoken of as bad, but smart men how keen is the vision of the little soul,

---

[2] Compare this "essential" knowing with the "revealed" knowing of the selections from the Bible in Section I, above.

how quick it is to discern the things that interest it, a proof that it is not a poor vision which it has, but one forcibly enlisted in the service of evil, so that the sharper its sight the more mischief it accomplishes?

I certainly have, he said.

Observe then, said I, that this part of such a soul, if it had been hammered from childhood, and had thus been struck free of the leaden weights, so to speak, of our birth and becoming, which attaching themselves to it by food and similar pleasures and gluttonies turn downward the vision of the soul—if, I say, freed from these, it had suffered a conversion toward the things that are real and true, that same faculty of the same men would have been most keen in its vision of the higher things, just as it is for the things toward which it is now turned.

It is likely, he said.

Well, then, said I, is not this also likely and a necessary consequence of what has been said, that neither could men who are uneducated and inexperienced in truth ever adequately preside over a state, nor could those who had been permitted to linger on to the end in the pursuit of culture—the one because they have no single aim and purpose in life to which all their actions, public and private, must be directed, and the others, because they will not voluntarily engage in action, believing that while still living they have been transported to the Islands of the Blessed?[3]

True, he said.

It is the duty of us, the founders, then, said I, to compel the best natures to attain the knowledge which we pronounced the greatest, and to win to the vision of the good, to scale that ascent, and when they have reached the heights and taken an adequate view, we must not allow what is now permitted.

What is that?

That they should linger there, I said, and refuse to go down again among those bondsmen and share their labors and honors, whether they are of less or of greater worth.

Do you mean to say that we must do them this wrong, and compel them to live an inferior life when the better is in their power?

You have again forgotten, my friend, said I, that the law is not concerned with the special happiness of any class in the state, but is trying to produce this condition in the city as a whole, harmonizing and adapting the citizens to one another by persuasion and compulsion, and requiring them to impart to one another any benefit which they are severally able to bestow upon the community, and that it itself creates such men in the state, not that it may allow each to take what course pleases him, but with a view to using them for the binding together of the commonwealth.

True, he said, I did forget it.

Observe, then, Glaucon, said I, that we shall not be wronging, either, the philosophers who arise among us, but that we can justify our action when we constrain them to take charge of the other citizens and be their guardians. For we will say to them that it is natural that men of similar quality who spring up in other cities should not share in the labors there. For they grow

---

[3] The Islands of the Blessed were the Greek equivalent of heaven.

up spontaneously from no volition of the government in the several states, and it is justice that the self-grown, indebted to none for its breeding, should not be zealous either to pay to anyone the price of its nurture. But you we have engendered for yourselves and the rest of the city to be, as it were, king bees and leaders in the hive. You have received a better and more complete education than the others, and you are more capable of sharing both ways of life. Down you must go then, each in his turn, to the habitation of the others and accustom yourselves to the observation of the obscure things there. For once habituated you will discern them infinitely better than the dwellers there, and you will know what each of the 'idols' is and whereof it is a semblance, because you have seen the reality of the beautiful, the just and the good. So our city will be governed by us and you with waking minds, and not, as most cities now which are inhabited and ruled darkly as in a dream by men who fight one another for shadows and wrangle for office as if that were a great good, when the truth is that the city in which those who are to rule are least eager to hold office must needs be best administered and most free from dissension, and the state that gets the contrary type of ruler will be the opposite of this.

3. What Are the Gradations of Reality and What Are the Ultimate Realities, the Objects of True Knowledge?

In the course of discussion in The Republic, *Socrates found it necessary to determine what were the essential permanent realities which men could truly know as against the imitations and representations of those realities, about which, since they were always in transit from being to not being, men could only have opinions.*

THE REPUBLIC*

Plato

I. "Truly," I said, "many other considerations assure me that we were entirely right in our organization of the state, and especially, I think, in the matter of poetry." "What about it?" he said. "In refusing to admit at all so much of it as imitative; for that it is certainly not to be received is, I think, still more plainly apparent now that we have distinguished the several parts of the soul." "What do you mean?" "Why, between ourselves—for you will not betray me to the tragic poets and all other imitators—that kind of art seems to be a corruption of the mind of all listeners who do not possess as an antidote a knowledge of its real nature." "What is your idea in saying this?" he said. "I must speak out," I said, "though a certain love and reverence for Homer that has possessed me from a boy would stay me from speaking. For he appears to have been the first teacher and beginner of all these beauties of tragedy. Yet all the same we must not honour a man above truth, but, as I say, speak

* Reprinted by permission of the publishers from The Loeb Classical Library, *Plato's Republic* x.595–599, trans. Paul Shorey (Cambridge, Mass.: Harvard University Press, 1930), II, 419–433.

our minds." "By all means," he said. "Listen, then, or rather, answer my question." "Ask it," he said. "Could you tell me in general what imitation is? For neither do I myself quite apprehend what it would be at." "It is likely, then," he said, "that *I* should apprehend!" "It would be nothing strange," said I, "since it often happens that the dimmer vision sees things in advance of the keener." "That is so," he said; "but in your presence I could not even be eager to try to state anything that appears to me, but do you yourself consider it." "Shall we, then, start the inquiry at this point by our customary procedure? We are in the habit, I take it, of positing a single idea or form[1] in the case of the various multiplicities to which we give the same name. Do you not understand?" "I do." "In the present case, then, let us take any multiplicity you please; for example, there are many couches and tables." "Of course." "But these utensils imply, I suppose, only two ideas or forms, one of a couch and one of a table." "Yes." "And are we not also in the habit of saying that the craftsman who produces either of them fixes his eyes on the idea or form, and so makes in the one case the couches and in the other the tables that we use, and similarly of other things? For surely no craftsman makes the idea itself. How could he?" "By no means." "But now consider what name you would give to this craftsman." "What one?" "Him who makes all the things that all handicraftsmen severally produce." "A truly clever and wondrous man you tell of." "Ah, but wait, and you will say so indeed, for this same handicraftsman is not only able to make all implements, but he produces all plants and animals, including himself, and thereto earth and heaven and the gods and all things in heaven and in Hades under the earth." "A most marvellous sophist," he said. "Are you incredulous?" said I. "Tell me, do you deny altogether the possibility of such a craftsman, or do you admit that in a sense there could be such a creator of all these things, and in another sense not? Or do you not perceive that you yourself would be able to make all these things in a way?" "And in what way, I ask you," he said. "There is no difficulty," said I, "but it is something that the craftsman can make everywhere and quickly. You could do it most quickly if you should choose to take a mirror and carry it about everywhere. You will speedily produce the sun and all the things in the sky, and speedily the earth and yourself and the other animals and implements and plants and all the objects of which we just now spoke." "Yes," he said, "the appearance of them, but not the reality and the truth." "Excellent," said I, "and you come to the aid of the argument opportunely. For I take it that the painter too belongs to this class of producers, does he not?" "Of course." "But you will say, I suppose, that his creations are not real and true. And yet, after a fashion, the painter too makes a couch, does he not?" "Yes," he said, "the appearance of one, he too."

"What of the cabinet-maker? Were you not just now saying that he does not make the idea or form which we say is the real couch, the couch in itself, but only some particular couch?" "Yes, I was." "Then if he does not make that which really is, he could not be said to make real being but something that resembles real being but is not that. But if anyone should say that being in the complete sense belongs to the work of the cabinet-maker

---

[1] 'Form' does not mean 'shape,' but the essential properties which constitute what the thing, by definition, is. [Translator's note.]

or to that of any other handicraftsman, it seems that he would say what is not true." "That would be the view," he said, "of those who are versed in this kind of reasoning." "We must not be surprised, then, if this too is only a dim adumbration in comparison with reality." "No, we must not." "Shall we, then, use these very examples in our quest for the true nature of this imitator?" "If you please," he said. "We get, then, these three couches, one, that in nature, which, I take it, we would say that God produces, or who else?" "No one, I think." "And then there was one which the carpenter made." "Yes," he said. "And one which the painter. Is not that so?" "So be it." "The painter, then, the cabinet-maker, and God, there are these three presiding over three kinds of couches." "Yes, three." "Now God, whether because he so willed or because some compulsion was laid upon him not to make more than one couch in nature, so wrought and created one only, the couch which really and in itself is. But two or more such were never created by God and never will come into being." "How so?" he said. "Because," said I, "if he should make only two, there would again appear one of which they both would possess the form or idea, and that would be the couch that really is in and of itself, and not the other two." "Right," he said. "God, then, I take it, knowing this and wishing to be the real author of the couch that has real being and not of some particular couch, nor yet a particular cabinet-maker, produced it in nature unique." "So it seems." "Shall we, then, call him its true and natural begetter, or something of the kind?" "That would certainly be right," he said, "since it is by and in nature that he has made this and all other things." "And what of the carpenter? Shall we not call him the creator of a couch?" "Yes." "Shall we also say that the painter is the creator and maker of that sort of thing?" "By no means." "What will you say he is in relation to the couch?" "This," said he, "seems to me the most reasonable designation for him, that he is the imitator of the thing which those others produce." "Very good," said I; "the producer of the product three removes from nature you call the imitator?" "By all means," he said. "This, then, will apply to the maker of tragedies also, if he is an imitator and is in his nature three removes from the king and the truth, as are all other imitators." "It would seem so." "We are in agreement, then, about the imitator. But tell me now this about the painter. Do you think that what he tries to imitate is in each case that thing itself in nature or the works of the craftsmen?" "The works of the craftsmen," he said. "Is it the reality of them or the appearance? Define that further point." "What do you mean?" he said. "This: Does a couch differ from itself according as you view it from the side or the front or in any other way? Or does it differ not at all in fact though it appears different, and so of other things?" "That is the way of it," he said; "it appears other but differs not at all." "Consider, then, this very point. To which is painting directed in every case, to the imitation of reality as it is or of appearance as it appears? Is it an imitation of a phantasm or of the truth?" "Of a phantasm," he said. "Then the mimetic art is far removed from truth, and this, it seems, is the reason why it can produce everything, because it touches or lays hold of only a small part of the object and that a phantom; as, for example, a painter, we say, will paint us a cobbler, a carpenter, and other craftsmen, though he himself has no expertness in any of these arts, but nevertheless if he were a good painter, by exhibiting at a distance his picture of a carpenter he would deceive children and foolish men, and make them believe it to be a real carpenter." "Why not?" "But for all that, my friend, this, I take it, is what we ought to bear in mind in all such cases: When anyone reports to us of someone, that he has met a man who knows all the crafts and everything else that men severally know, and that there is nothing that he does not know more exactly than anybody else, our tacit rejoinder must be that he is a simple fellow, who apparently has met some magician or sleight-of-hand man and imitator and has been deceived by him into the belief that he is all-wise, because of his own inability to put to the proof and distinguish knowledge, ignorance and imitation." "Most true," he said.

"Then," said I, "have we not next to scrutinize tragedy and its leader Homer, since some people tell us that these poets know all the arts and all human pertaining to virtue and vice, and all things divine? For the good poet, if he is to poetize things rightly, must, they argue, create with knowledge or else be unable to create. So we must consider whether these critics have not fallen in with such imitators and been deceived by them, so that looking upon their works they cannot perceive that these are three removes from reality, and easy to produce without knowledge of the truth. For it is phantoms, not realities, that they produce.

4. What Course Must Men Follow If They Would Arrive at the Highest Good?

Given that most men lived most of their lives in the darkness of ignorance, accepting mere shadows for reality, still, all men in some sense wanted what was good for themselves, and some, like the guardians of whom Plato spoke at the end of the first passage from the Republic, *above, came close to attaining it. In the* Symposium, *Plato wrote of man's desire for the good and of the way to attain it.*

In this dialogue, several of Socrates' friends in turn have tried to define love. One describes it as the highest possible human motive, another as a sort of mechanical or physiological means of finding harmony between otherwise discordant and uncomfortably incomplete beings. A third, Agathon, chooses to treat it as the god whose name is Love. He describes this divine being as the young and fair source of all that is good among men. Then Socrates begins his approach to a definition of Love, using his young friend Agathon as a foil for his questions:

THE SYMPOSIUM*

Plato

'I was very much struck by your introductory passage, my dear Agathon, where you said that the right thing was first to describe the actual nature

* Reprinted from *Plato: The Symposium* 199c–212c, trans. W. Hamilton (Harmondsworth, Middlesex: Penguin Books, 1951), pp. 75–95. By permission.

of the god, and afterwards to demonstrate the effects which he produces. I like that way of beginning very much. But I should be grateful if you would supplement your otherwise splendid and magnificent account of Love's nature by answering this question. Is the nature of Love such that he must be love of something, or can he exist absolutely without an object? I don't mean "Is Love love of a particular mother or father?"—to ask whether Love is love of a mother or father would be absurd—but I can make my point clear by analogy. If I were to take the single notion *Father* and ask "Does *Father* mean the father of someone or not?" you, if you wanted to give the right answer, would presumably reply that *Father* means the father of a son or a daughter, wouldn't you?'

'Certainly,' said Agathon.

'And similarly with *Mother?*'

'Agreed.'

'Let us go a little further, to make my meaning quite clear. The notion *Brother,* does that intrinsically imply brother of someone, or not?'

'Of course it does.'

'In fact, of a brother or sister?'

'Yes.'

'Very well. Now try to tell me whether Love means love of something, or whether there can be Love which is love of nothing.'

'Quite clearly, it means love of something.'

'Take a firm grasp of this point, then,' said Socrates, 'remembering also, though you may keep it to yourself for the moment, what it is that Love is love of. And now just tell me this: Does Love desire the thing that he is love of, or not?'

'Of course he does.'

'And does he desire and love the same thing that he desires and loves when he is in possession of it or when he is not?'

'Probably when he is not.'

'If you reflect for a moment, you will see that it isn't merely probable but absolutely certain that one desires what one lacks, or rather that one does not desire what one does not lack. To me at any rate, Agathon, it seems as certain as anything con be. What do you think?'

'Yes, I think it is.'

'Good. Now would anybody wish to be big who was big, or strong who was strong?'

'It follows from my previous admission that this is impossible.'

'Because a man who possesses a quality cannot be in need of it?'

'Yes.'

'Suppose a man wanted to be strong who was strong, or swift-footed who was swift-footed. I labour the point in order to avoid any possibility of mistake, for one might perhaps suppose in these and all similar cases that people who are of a certain character or who possess certain qualities also desire the qualities which they possess. But if you consider the matter, Agathon, you will see that these people must inevitably possess these qualities at the present moment, whether they like it or not, and no one presumably would desire what is inevitable. No, if a man says: "I, who am healthy, or who am rich, nonetheless desire to be healthy or rich, as the case may be, and I desire the very qualities which I possess," we should reply: "My friend, what you, who are in possession of health and wealth and strength, really wish, is to have the possession of the qualities continued to you in the future, since at the present moment you possess them whether you wish it or not." Consider, then, whether when you say "I desire what I possess" you do not really mean "I wish that I may continue to possess in the future the things which I possess now." If it were put to him like this, he would agree, I think.'

'Yes,' said Agathon.

'But this is to be in love with a thing which is not yet in one's power or possession, namely the continuance and preservation of one's present blessings in the future.'

'Certainly.'

'Such a man, then, and everyone else who feels desire, desires what is not in his present power or possession, and desire and love have for their object things or qualities which a man does not at present possess but which he lacks.'

'Yes.'

'Come then,' said Socrates, 'let us sum up the points on which we have reached agreement. Are they not first that Love exists only in relation to some object, and second that the object must be something of which he is at present in want?'

'Yes.'

'Now recall also what it was that you declared in your speech to be the object of Love. I'll do it for you, if you like. You said, I think, that the troubles among the gods were composed by love of beauty, for there could not be such a thing as love of ugliness. Wasn't that it?'

'Yes.'

'Quite right, my dear friend, and if that is so, Love will be love of beauty, will he not, and not love of ugliness?'

Agathon agreed.

'Now we have agreed that Love is in love with what he lacks and does not possess.'

'Yes.'

'So after all love lacks and does not possess beauty?'

'Inevitably.'

'Well then, would you call what lacks and in no way possesses beauty beautiful?'

'Certainly not.'

'Do you still think then the Love is beautiful, if this is so?'

'It looks, Socrates, as if I didn't know what I was talking about when I said that.'

'Still, it was a beautiful speech, Agathon. But there is just one more small point. Do you think that what is good is the same as what is beautiful?'

'I do.'

'Then, if Love lacks beauty, and what is good coincides with what is beautiful, he also lacks goodness.'

'I can't find any way of withstanding you, Socrates. Let it be as you say.'

'Not at all, my dear Agathon. It is truth that you find it impossible to withstand; there is never the slightest difficulty in withstanding Socrates.

'But now I will leave you in peace, and try to give the account of Love which I once heard from a woman of Mantinea,[1] called Diotima. She had other accomplishments as well—once, before the plague, when the Athenians had been sacrificing to avert it, she succeeded in postponing it for ten years—but what concerns us at present is that she was my instructress in the art of love. I will try, taking the conclusions on which Agathon and I reached agreement as my starting-point, to give the best consecutive account I can of what she told me. As you were so careful to point out to us, Agathon, one must elucidate the essential nature and characteristics of Love before describing his effects. The easiest thing will be to go through the same questions and answers as she did with me. I had used very much the same language to her as Agathon used to me, and had said that Love is a great god and must be reckoned beautiful, but she employed against me the arguments by which I demonstrated to Agathon that to my way of thinking Love is neither beautiful nor good. "What do you mean, Diotima?" I said. "Is Love ugly and bad?" "Don't say such things," she answered; "do you think that anything that is not beautiful is necessarily ugly?" "Of course I do." "And that anything that is not wisdom is ignorance? Don't you know that there is a state of mind half-way between wisdom and ignorance?" "What do you mean?" "Having true convictions without being able to give reasons for them," she replied. "Surely you see that such a state of mind cannot be called understanding, because nothing irrational deserves the name; but it would be equally wrong to call it ignorance; how can one call a state of mind ignorance which hits upon the truth? The fact is that having true convictions is what I called it just now, a condition half-way between knowledge and ignorance." "I grant you that," said I. "Then do not maintain that what is not beautiful is ugly, and what is not good is bad. Do not suppose that because, on your own admission, Love is not good or beautiful, he must on that account be ugly and bad, but rather that he is something between the two." "And yet," I said, "everybody admits that he is a great god." "When you say everybody, do you mean those who don't know him, or do you include those who do?" "I mean absolutely everybody." She burst out laughing, and said: "Well, Socrates, I don't see how he can be admitted to be a great god by those who say that he isn't even a god at all." "Who are they?" I asked. "You are one of them and I'm another." "What can you mean?" "It's perfectly easy; you'd say, wouldn't you, that all gods are happy and beautiful? You wouldn't dare to suggest that any of the gods is not?" "Good heavens, no." "And by happy you mean in secure enjoyment of what is good and beautiful?" "Certainly." "But you have agreed that it is because he lacks what is good and beautiful that Love desires these very things." "Yes, I have." "But a being who has no share of the good and beautiful cannot be a god?" "Obviously not." "Very well then, you see that you are one of the people who believe that Love is not a god."

' "What can Love be then?" I said. "A mortal?" "Far from it." "Well, what?" "As in my previous examples, he is half-way between mortal and

---

[1]Mantinea was a city in southern Greece.

immortal." "What sort of being is he then, Diotima?" "He is a great spirit, Socrates; everything that is of the nature of a spirit is half-god and half-man." "And what is the function of such a being?" "To interpret and convey messages to the gods from men and to men from the gods, prayers and sacrifices from the one, and commands and rewards from the other. Being of an intermediate nature, a spirit bridges the gap between them, and prevents the universe from falling into two separate halves. Through this class of being come all divination and the supernatural skill of priests in sacrifices and rites and spells and every kind of magic and wizardry. God does not deal directly with man; it is by means of spirits that all the intercourse and communication of gods with men, both in waking life and in sleep, is carried on. A man who possesses skill in such matters is a spiritual man, whereas a man whose skill is confined to some trade or handicraft is an earthly creature. Spirits are many in number and of many kinds, and one of them is Love.'

'"Who are his parents?" I asked. "That is rather a long story," she answered, "but I will tell you. On the day that Aphrodite[2] was born the gods were feasting, among them Contrivance the son of Invention; and after dinner, seeing that a party was in progress, Poverty came to beg and stood at the door. Now Contrivance was drunk with nectar—wine, I may say, had not yet been discovered—and went out into the garden of Zeus,[3] and was overcome by sleep. So Poverty, thinking to alleviate her wretched condition by bearing a child to Contrivance, lay with him and conceived Love. Since Love was begotten on Aphrodite's birthday, and since he has also an innate passion for the beautiful, and so for the beauty of Aphrodite herself, he became her follower and servant. Again, having Contrivance for his father and Poverty for his mother, he bears the following character. He is always poor, and, far from being sensitive and beautiful, as most people imagine, he is hard and weather-beaten, shoeless and homeless, always sleeping out for want of a bed, on the ground, on doorsteps, and in the street. So far he takes after his mother and lives in want. But, being also his father's son, he schemes to get for himself whatever is beautiful and good; he is bold and forward and strenuous, always devising tricks like a cunning huntsman; he yearns after knowledge and is full of resource and is a lover of wisdom all his life, a skilful magician, an alchemist, a true sophist.[4] He is neither mortal nor immortal; but on one and the same day he will live and flourish (when things go well with him), and also meet his death; and then come to life again through the vigour that he inherits from his father. What he wins he always loses, and is neither rich nor poor, neither wise nor ignorant.

'"The truth of the matter is this. No god is a lover of wisdom or desires to be wise, for he is wise already, and the same is true of other wise persons, if there be any such. Nor on the other hand do the ignorant love wisdom and desire to be wise, for the tiresome thing about ignorance is precisely this,

---

[2] Aphrodite was the goddess of love.

[3] Zeus was the chief of the gods.

[4] The Sophists were the people who had learned to use the techniques of logical argument to twist what most of their audiences regarded intuitively as right or true into something wrong and false in order to gain personal advantage. The phrase often used to describe them was that they "made a better argument worse." Their chicanery had brought philosophy along with some of its more honest practitioners into ill repute.

that a man who possesses neither beauty nor goodness nor intelligence is perfectly well satisfied with himself, and no one who does not believe that he lacks a thing desires what he does not believe that he lacks."

' "Who then," I said, "are the lovers of wisdom, if they are neither the wise nor the ignorant?" "A child could answer that question. Obviously they are the intermediate class, of which Love among others is a member. Wisdom is one of the most beautiful of things, and Love is love of beauty, so it follows that Love must be a lover of wisdom, and consequently in a state half-way between wisdom and ignorance. This too springs from the circumstances of his birth; his father was wise and fertile in expedients, his mother devoid of wisdom and helpless. So much for the nature of the spirit, my dear Socrates. As for your thinking as you did about Love, there is nothing remarkable in that; to judge by what you said, you identified Love with the beloved object instead of with what feels love; that is why you thought that Love is supremely beautiful. The object of love is in all truth beautiful and delicate and perfect and worthy to be thought happy, but what feels love has a totally different character such as I have just described."

' "Tell me then, my friend," I said, "for your words carry conviction, what function Love performs among men, if this is his nature." "That is precisely what I am going to try to teach you, Socrates. The nature and parentage of Love are as I have described, and he is also, according to you, love of beauty. But suppose we were to be asked: 'In what does love of beauty consist, Socrates and Diotima?' or, to put it more plainly, 'What is the aim of the love which is felt by the lover of beauty?'" "His aim is to attain possession of beautiful things," I answered. "But that merely raises a further question. What will have been gained by the man who is in possession of beauty?" I said that I could supply no ready answer to this question. "Well," she said, "let us change our terms and substitute good for beautiful. Suppose someone asked you: 'Now, Socrates, what is the aim of the love felt by the lover of the good?'" "Possession of the good," I replied. "And what will have been gained by the man who is in possession of the good?" "I find that an easier question to answer; he will be happy." "Presumably because happiness consists in the possession of the good, and once one has given that answer, the inquiry is at an end; there is no need to ask the further question 'Why does a man desire to be happy?'" "Quite so."

' "Now do you suppose that this desire and this love are characteristics common to all men, and that all perpetually desire to be in possession of the good, or what?" "That is exactly what I mean; they are common to all men." "Why is it then, Socrates, if all men are always in love with the same thing, that we do not speak of all men as being in love, but say that some men are in love and others not?" "I wonder what the reason can be." "There's no need to wonder; the truth is that we isolate a particular kind of love and appropriate for it the name of love, which really belongs to a wider whole, while we employ different names for the other kinds of love." "Can you give me another example of such a usage?" "Yes, here is one. By its original meaning poetry means simply creation, and creation, as you know, can take very various forms. Any action which is the cause of a thing emerging from nonexistence into existence might be called poetry, and all the processes in all the crafts are kinds of poetry, and all those who are engaged in them poets." "Yes." "But yet they are not called poets, but have other names, and out of the whole field of poetry or creation one part, which deals with music and metre, is isolated and called by the name of the whole. This part alone is called poetry, and those whose province is this part of poetry are called poets." "Quite true." "It is just the same with love. The generic concept embraces every desire for good and for happiness; that is precisely what almighty and all-ensnaring love is. But this desire expresses itself in many ways, and those with whom it takes the form of love of money or of physical prowess or of wisdom are not said to be in love or called lovers, whereas those whose passion runs in one particular channel usurp the name of lover, which belongs to them all, and are said to be lovers and in love." "There seems to be truth in what you say," I remarked. "There is indeed a theory," she continued, "that lovers are people who are in search of the other half of themselves, but according to my view of the matter, my friend, love is not desire of the half or the whole, unless that half or whole happens to be good. Men are quite willing to have their feet or their hands amputated if they believe those parts of themselves to be diseased. The truth is, I think, that people are not attached to what particularly belongs to them, except in so far as they can identify what is good with what is their own, and what is bad with what is not their own. The only object of men's love is what is good. Don't you agree?" "Certainly I do." "May we then say without qualification that men are in love with what is good?" "Yes." "But we must add, mustn't we, that the aim of their love is the possession of the good for themselves?" "Yes." "And not only its possession but its perpetual possession?" "Certainly." "To sum up, then, love is desire for the perpetual possession of the good." "Very true."

' "Now that we have established what love invariably is, we must ask in what way and by what type of action men must show their intense desire if it is to deserve the name of love. What will this function be? Can you tell me?" "If I could, Diotima, I should not be feeling such admiration for your wisdom, or putting myself to school with you to learn precisely this." "Well," she said, "I will tell you. The function is that of procreation in what is beautiful, and such procreation can be either physical or spiritual." "What you say needs an interpreter. I don't understand." "I will put it more plainly. All men, Socrates, are in a state of pregnancy, both spiritual and physical, and when they come to maturity they feel a natural desire to bring forth, but they can do so only in beauty and never in ugliness.[5] There is something divine about the whole matter; in pregnancy and bringing to birth the mortal creature is endowed with a touch of immortality. But the process cannot take place in disharmony, and ugliness is out of harmony with everything divine, whereas beauty is in harmony with it. That is why Beauty is the goddess who presides over travail, and why, when a person in a state of pregnancy comes into contact with beauty, he has a feeling of serenity and happy relaxation which makes it possible to bring forth and give birth. But, when ugliness is near, the effect is just the opposite; he frowns and withdraws gloomily into himself

---

[5] Throughout the whole of the discussion which follows, it must be borne in mind that such terms as "conception," "pregnancy," "bringing forth" are used here in a quite general sense and without reference to the specialized functions of male and female.

and recoils and contracts and cannot bring forth, but has painfully to retain the burden of pregnancy. So a person who is pregnant and already great with child is violently attracted towards beauty, because beauty can deliver its possessor from the pains of travail. The object of love, Socrates, is not, as you think, beauty." "What is it then?" "Its object is to procreate and bring forth in beauty." "Really?" "It is so, I assure you. Now, why is procreation the object of love? Because procreation is the nearest thing to perpetuity and immortality that a mortal being can attain. If, as we agreed, the aim of love is the perpetual possession of the good, it necessarily follows that it must desire immortality together with the good, and the argument leads us to the inevitable conclusion that love is love of immortality as well as of the good."[6]

'All this, then, I learnt on the various occasions on which Diotima spoke to me on the subject of love. One day she asked me: "What do you suppose, Socrates, to be the cause of this love and this desire? Look at the behaviour of all animals, both beasts and birds. Whenever the desire to procreate seizes them, they fall a prey to a violent love-sickness. Their first object is to achieve union with one another, their second to provide for their young; for these they are ready to fight however great the odds, and to die if need be, suffering starvation themselves and making any other sacrifice in order to secure the survival of their progeny. With men you might suppose such behaviour to be the result of rational calculation, but what cause is to be ascribed for the occurrence of such love among the beasts? Can you tell me?" I again confessed that I didn't know. "How can you expect ever to become an expert on the subject of love, if you haven't any ideas about this?" "I told you before, Diotima, that this is precisely why I have come to you. I know that I need a teacher. So tell me the cause of this and of all the other phenomena connected with love."

' "Well, if you believe that the natural object of love is what we have more than once agreed that it is, the answer won't surprise you. The same argument holds good in the animal world as in the human, and mortal nature seeks, as far as may be, to perpetuate itself and become immortal. The only way in which it can achieve this is by procreation, which secures the perpetual replacement of an old member of the race by a new. Even during the period for which any living being is said to live and to retain his identity—as a man, for example, is called the same man from boyhood to old age—he does not in fact retain the same attributes, although he is called the same person; he is always becoming a new being and undergoing a process of loss and reparation, which affects his hair, his flesh, his bones, his blood, and his whole body. And not only his body, but his soul as well. No man's character, habits, opinions, desires, pleasures, pains, and fears remain always the same; new ones come into existence and old ones disappear. What happens with pieces of knowledge is even more remarkable; it is not merely that some appear and others disappear, so that we no more retain our identity with regard to knowledge than with regard to the other things I have mentioned, but that each individual piece of knowledge is subject to the same process as we are ourselves. When we use the word recollection we imply by using it that

[6] Compare Plato's conception of love with the Christian conception as explained by John. See above, p. 48.

knowledge departs from us; forgetting is the departure of knowledge, and recollection, by implanting a new impression in the place of that which is lost, preserves it, and gives it a spurious appearance of uninterrupted identity. It is in this way that everything mortal is preserved; not by remaining for ever the same, which is the prerogative of divinity, but by undergoing a process in which the losses caused by age are repaired by new acquisitions of a similar kind. This device, Socrates, enables the mortal to partake of immortality, physically as well as in other ways; but the immortal enjoys immortality after another manner. So do not feel surprise that every creature naturally cherishes its own progeny; it is in order to secure immortality that each individual is haunted by this eager desire and love."

'I was surprised at this account and said: "You may be very wise, Diotima, but am I really to believe this?" "Certainly you are," she replied in true professional style; "if you will only reflect you will see that the ambition of men provides an example of the same truth. You will be astonished at its irrationality unless you bear in mind what I have said, and remember that the love of fame and the desire to win a glory that shall never die have the strongest effects upon people. For this even more than for their children they are ready to run risks, spend their substance, endure every kind of hardship, and even sacrifice their lives. Do you suppose that Alcestis would have died to save Admetus, or Achilles to avenge Patroclus, or your Codrus[7] to preserve his kingdom for his sons, if they had not believed that their courage would live for ever in men's memory, as it does in ours? On the contrary; it is desire for immortal renown and a glorious reputation such as theirs that is the incentive of all actions, and the better a man is, the stronger the incentive; he is in love with immortality. Those whose creative instinct is physical have recourse to women, and show their love in this way, believing that by begetting children they can secure for themselves an immortal and blessed memory hereafter for ever; but there are some whose creative desire is of the soul, and who conceive spiritually, not physically, the progeny which it is the nature of the soul to conceive and bring forth. If you ask what that progeny is, it is wisdom and virtue in general; of this all poets and such craftsmen as have found out some new thing may be said to be begetters; but far the greatest and fairest branch of wisdom is that which is concerned with the due ordering of states and families, whose name is moderation and justice. When by divine inspiration a man finds himself from his youth up spiritually pregnant with these qualities, as soon as he comes of due age he desires to bring forth and to be delivered, and goes in search of a beautiful environment for his children; for he can never bring forth in ugliness. In his pregnant condition physical beauty is more pleasing to him than ugliness, and if in a beautiful body he finds also a beautiful and noble and gracious soul, he welcomes the combination warmly,

---

[7] In Greek mythology, Admetus, the king of Pherae in northern Greece, was doomed by the Fates to die. The god Apollo intervened, however, to secure their acceptance of someone else in Admetus' place if such a person could be found to die for him. Prolonged inquiry revealed that only his wife, Alcestis, was willing to do so.

According to Homer in the *Iliad*, Achilles' revenge against the Trojans for the death of his friend Patroclus turned the tide of war in favor of the Greeks, but it also cost Achilles his own life.

Codrus was a legendary king of early Athens who gave his life to avert an invasion of the city.

and finds much to say to such a one about virtue and the qualities and actions which mark a good man, and takes his education in hand. By intimate association with beauty embodied in his friend, and by keeping him always before his mind, he succeeds in bringing to birth the children of which he has been long in labour, and once they are born he shares their upbringing with his friend; the partnership between them will be far closer and the bond of affection far stronger than between ordinary parents, because the children that they share surpass human children by being immortal as well as more beautiful. Everyone would prefer children such as these to children after the flesh. Take Homer, for example, and Hesiod,[8] and the other good poets; who would not envy them the children that they left behind them, children whose qualities have won immortal fame and glory for their parents? Or take Lycurgus the lawgiver, and consider the children that he left at Sparta to be the salvation not only of Sparta but one may almost say of Greece.[9] Among you Athenians Solon is honoured for the laws which he produced,[10] and so it is in many other places with other men, both Greek and barbarian, who by their many fine actions have brought forth good fruit of all kinds; not a few of them have even won men's worship on account of their spiritual children, a thing which has never yet happened to anyone by reason of his human progeny.

' "So far, Socrates, I have dealt with love-mysteries into which even you could probably be initiated, but whether you could grasp the perfect revelation to which they lead the pilgrim if he does not stray from the right path, I do not know. However, you shall not fail for any lack of willingness on my part: I will tell you of it, and do you try to follow if you can.

' "The man who would pursue the right way to this goal must begin, when he is young, by applying himself to the contemplation of physical beauty, and, if he is properly directed by his guide, he will first fall in love with one particular beautiful person and beget noble sentiments in partnership with him. Later he will observe that physical beauty in any person is closely akin to physical beauty in any other, and that, if he is to make beauty of outward form the object of his quest, it is great folly not to acknowledge that the beauty exhibited in all bodies is one and the same; when he has reached this conclusion he will become a lover of all physical beauty, and will relax the intensity of his passion for one particular person, because he will realize that such a passion is beneath him and of small account. The next stage is for him to reckon beauty of soul more valuable than beauty of body; the result will be that, when he encounters a virtuous soul in a body which has little of the bloom of beauty, he will be content to love and cherish it and to bring forth such notions as may serve to make young people better; in this way he will

---

[8] Hesiod ranks next to Homer as one of early Greece's greatest poets. There is little agreement as to the precise date of either poet, but Hesiod is usually dated later than Homer, and both probably lived and wrote sometime between 800 and 600 B.C.

[9] Lycurgus was an early and perhaps legendary king of Sparta, who was credited with having founded the Spartan military system and government. The view that his reforms enabled Sparta to play the major part it did in turning back the attacks of Persia on the Greeks is the basis of assigning him a great role in the "salvation of Greece."

[10] Solon was chosen sole magistrate in Athens in the early sixth century B.C. His constitutional and social reforms were important in the later development of Athenian democracy.

be compelled to contemplate beauty as it exists in activities and institutions, and to recognize that here too all beauty is akin, so that he will be led to consider physical beauty taken as a whole a poor thing in comparison. From morals he must be directed to the sciences and contemplate their beauty also, so that, having his eyes fixed upon beauty in the widest sense, he may no longer be the slave of a base and mean-spirited devotion to an individual example of beauty, whether the object of his love be a boy or a man or an activity, but, by gazing upon the vast ocean of beauty to which his attention is now turned, may bring forth in the abundance of his love of wisdom many beautiful and magnificent sentiments and ideas, until at last, strengthened and increased in stature by this experience, he catches sight of one unique science whose object is the beauty of which I am about to speak. And here I must ask you to pay the closest possible attention.

' "The man who has been guided thus far in the mysteries of love, and who has directed his thoughts towards examples of beauty in due and orderly succession, will suddenly have revealed to him as he approaches the end of his initiation a beauty whose nature is marvellous indeed, the final goal, Socrates, of all his previous efforts. This beauty is first of all eternal; it neither comes into being nor passes away, neither waxes nor wanes; next, it is not beautiful in part and ugly in part, nor beautiful at one time and ugly at another, nor beautiful in this relation and ugly in that, nor beautiful here and ugly there, as varying according to its beholders; nor again will this beauty appear to him like the beauty of a face or hands or anything else corporeal, or like the beauty of a thought or a science, or like beauty which has its seat in something other than itself, be it a living thing or the earth or the sky or anything else whatever; he will see it as absolute, existing alone with itself, unique, eternal, and all other beautiful things as partaking of it, yet in such a manner that, while they come into being and pass away, it neither undergoes any increase or diminution nor suffers any change.

' "When a man, starting from this sensible world and making his way upward by a right use of his feeling of love for boys, begins to catch sight of that beauty, he is very near his goal. This is the right way of approaching or being initiated into the mysteries of love, to begin with examples of beauty in this world, and using them as steps to ascend continually with that absolute beauty as one's aim, from one instance of physical beauty to two and from two to all, then from physical beauty to moral beauty, and from moral beauty to the beauty of knowledge, until from knowledge of various kinds one arrives at the supreme knowledge whose sole object is that absolute beauty, and knows at last what absolute beauty is.

' "This above all other, my dear Socrates," the woman from Mantinea continued, "is the region where a man's life should be spent, in the contemplation of absolute beauty. Once you have seen that, you will not value it in terms of gold or rich clothing or of the beauty of boys and young men, the sight of whom at present throws you and many people like you into such an ecstasy that, provided that you could always enjoy the sight and company of your darlings, you would be content to go without food and drink, if that were possible, and to pass your whole time with them in the contemplation of their beauty. What may we suppose to be the felicity of the man who sees absolute beauty in its essence, pure and unalloyed, who instead of a beauty tainted by human flesh and colour and a mass of perishable rubbish, is able to apprehend divine beauty where it exists apart and alone? Do you think that it will be a poor life that a man leads who has his gaze fixed in that direction, who contemplates absolute beauty with the appropriate faculty and is in constant union with it? Do you not see that in that region alone where he sees beauty with the faculty capable of seeing it, will he be able to bring forth not mere reflected images of goodness but true goodness, because he will be in contact not with a reflection but with the truth? And having brought forth and nurtured true goodness he will have the privilege of being beloved of God, and becoming, if ever a man can, immortal himself."

5. What Is the Relation Between Knowing in Theory and in Practice?

After the death of Plato in 348 B.C., leadership of the Academy fell to a former pupil whose interest in mathematics seems to have irritated some of the other students. Among those who left the Academy in protest against "the turning of philosophy into mathematics" was Aristotle, a man of thirty-six at the time. He spent the next several years in Asia Minor and on the island of Lesbos, where he engaged in zoological work. Then, around 343, Philip II, king of Macedon, invited him to be the tutor of Philip's son Alexander. This was a brief stay, for little more than two years later, Philip left Macedon on an extended military campaign and made Alexander his regent in his absence. With the prince too busy with official duties to continue his studies, Aristotle returned to Athens. There he rented a grove of trees and some buildings outside the city to found a school of his own, the Lyceum.

The school quickly became a center for the collection of manuscripts and information of all kinds, which Aristotle's students used in their researches. Alexander, who succeeded Philip in 336, is supposed to have sent funds to the philosopher for his work, and while campaigning in the Near East, he had countless specimens of natural life sent back to Athens. Although biology was Aristotle's major scientific interest and talent, his students and associates carried on research and scholarship in many fields. For example, they collected accounts of some one hundred and fifty-eight constitutions of Greek states.

Aristotle's own voluminous writings are a succinct statement of a large and comprehensive system of philosophy. They reveal an intensely practical turn of mind. For him, the meaning of anything is its most obvious, everyday meaning. His early association with Plato had a permanent influence upon him, and the tension between his own matter-of-fact interests and Plato's mathematical and almost mystical ones impelled Aristotle to re-examine many of the problems Plato raised. From the writings of Aristotle, it is difficult to excerpt statements of these central problems, but the following selections let us follow a part of his reasoning as he addressed himself to fundamental questions.

METAPHYSICS*

Aristotle

All men by nature have a desire for knowledge. An indication of this is the joy we take in our perceptions; which we cherish for their own sakes, quite apart from any benefits they may yield us. This is especially true of sight, which we tend to prefer to all the other senses even when it points to no action, and even indeed when no action is in prospect; a preference explained by the greater degree to which sight promotes knowledge by revealing so many differences among things.

It is by nature, again, that animals are born with a faculty of perception, and from this there arises memory in some of them, though not in others. The former class are more intelligent and more capable of learning than those without memory.[1]

But while the other animals live by means of impressions and memories, with only a small amount of what can properly be called experience, the human race lives also by art and reasoning.[2] Memory is what gives rise to experience in men, for it is by having repeated memories of the same thing that our ability to have a single whole experience arises. At first sight experience seems much like knowledge and art, but it is truer to say that experience is the means through which science and art can be acquired; thus Polus rightly declares that "experience has produced art, inexperience chance."[3]

Art arises when out of many reflections upon experience there is produced a single universal judgment about some class of similar objects. To make the judgement that when Callicles was ill of a certain disease a certain remedy was beneficial, and to make a similar judgment about Socrates, and so on, is a matter of experience. Art would consist rather in judging that the remedy is beneficial for all persons of a given type who are suffering from a given disease—e.g., for phlegmatic or bilious people suffering from fever.

From a practical standpoint experience may well be quite as good as art; indeed we often see men of experience succeeding better than those who have theory without experience. The reason for this is that experience is knowledge of particulars, art of universals, and that actions and their effects are always particular. That is to say, the physician does not cure man, except in an incidental sense; he cures Callicles or Socrates or some other namable individual, who has the incidental characteristic of being 'man' as well. Hence, if someone has the theory without the experience, and knows the universal but is ignorant of the particular instance which is before him, he will often

---

Metaphysics ii.i, reprinted from *Aristotle,* trans. Philip Wheelwright (New York: The Odyssey Press, 1951), pp. 67–69. Used by permission.

[1] "Animals that cannot hear sounds, like the bee and similar species, cannot learn, although they have intelligence. Where, on the other hand, an animal has the sense of hearing in addition to memory, it is able to learn."—Aristotle's gloss.

[2] By "art" Aristotle does not mean fine or literary art, but rather the deliberate, purposeful activity by which man constructs things judged to be worth while.

[3] Polus was a Sophist from Agrigentum in Sicily and a younger contemporary of Socrates. He taught rhetoric and discussed the subject in a technical treatise which now is lost, but which very likely is the work from which Aristotle has taken this quotation.

fail to cure, for what has to be cured is always the particular. Nevertheless we think of knowledge and understanding as belonging rather to art than to experience, and we judge artists to be wiser than mere empirics on the ground that wisdom must always involve some knowledge. Empirics know *that* something is, but not *why* it is; artists, on the other hand, know the why and the reason. Similarly, in any craft we regard master-craftsmen as more estimable and as having a wiser understanding of their craft than manual workers because they know the reasons why things are done, whereas we look on manual workers as analogous to those inanimate things which act without knowing what they do, as fire burns for instance, the only difference being that inanimate things behave as they do by nature, manual workers by habit. In short, we regard master-craftsmen as superior not merely because they can do things but because they have a grasp of theory and know the reasons for acting as they do. Broadly speaking, what distinguishes the man who knows from the ignorant man is an ability to teach, and this is why we hold that art and not experience has the character of genuine knowledge—namely, that artists can teach and others [i.e., those who have not acquired an art by study but have merely picked up some skill empirically] cannot.

Sense perceptions, too, we should avoid confusing with wisdom; for although it is true that they are our chief source of knowledge about particulars, still they do not tell us the 'why' of anything—e.g., they do not tell us why fire is hot, but only that it is hot.

6. What Do We Mean by "Change"?

As had other Greek thinkers from the beginning of philosophical inquiry, Aristotle found the problem of being and becoming, of permanence and change, a challenge. Change is always in process, but despite change, things endure. The relation between change and the unchanging, between becoming and being, raised all sorts of problems and perplexities for Greek speculative thought and was indeed the cause of the stalemate in Greek philosophy before Socrates. In a sense, Aristotle centered his whole philosophical enterprise in a systematic attempt to deal with the problem of change in its every aspect. In his Physics, *the following remarks come after an account of the long Greek argument over the number of ultimate realities required to explain what men know about the cosmos, or world.*

PHYSICS*

Aristotle

We pass now to a positive account of our own theory, starting with a general analysis of becoming, or change;[1] for it is the most natural mode of

---

* *Physics* ii.7, reprinted from Aristotle, trans. Philip Wheelwright (New York: The Odyssey Press, 1951), pp. 11–13. Used by permission.

[1] Compare Aristotle's concern with change with Plato's discussion of the ascension of the soul. See above, p. 58.

procedure to speak first of the general characteristics of things and afterwards to investigate the peculiarities of each detail.

When one thing is spoken of as 'coming to be' out of another thing, or out of another kind of thing, the process may be interpreted in both a simple and a compound sense. Here is what I mean. There is a sense in which (1) a man becomes cultured, another in which (2) his previous state of un-culture passes into[2] a state of being cultured, and still another in which (3) an uncultured man become a cultured man. The terms that are regarded as undergoing change in the first two cases (i.e., man and the state of being cultured)[3] as well as what each of them 'becomes' (i.e., cultured) I call simple; but when an uncultured man is regarded as becoming a cultured man both terms of the process are compound. In some cases of becoming, moreover, we can speak of something as coming into existence 'out of' some previously exist-ing state—e.g., being cultured comes into existence 'out of' the state of uncul-ture; while there are other cases where this mode of expression is inappli-cable—e.g., we do not say that the state of being cultured comes into existence 'out of' a man, but simply that a man becomes cultured. Again, as regards the two ways in which a simple thing can be said to 'become something,' in the one case the thing persists through the process of becoming, in the other it does not: a man is still a man on becoming cultured; but his state of unculture, i.e., his not being cultured, does not persist either singly or in combination with the subject.

These distinctions and the several types of becoming that they reveal enable us to conclude that there must be in all cases a subject which, as we say, 'becomes something'—a subject which, though one numerically, is more than one in form. By its form I here mean the specific ways in which the subject is expressed; its two aspects, man and the state of unculture, being of course distinct. The one aspect, man, which has not the character of an oppo-site, survives the process of becoming; while the other aspect—the lacking culture, or the state of being uncultured, or the compound form 'uncultured man'—does not.

'Coming to be' has several senses. In one sense of the word we do not speak of coming into existence but of becoming *something*. It is only sub-stances, or concrete things as such that can be said without qualification to come into existence. Where the becoming is of something other than a concrete substance—a quantity, for example, or a quality, or a relation, or a moment of time, or a being located—a subject is evidently presupposed, and this will be a substance. For it is substance alone that is never predicated of anything, being always the subject to which predications refer. Yet concrete substances too—i.e., anything that can be said without qualification to exist—when they come into existence presuppose some kind of underlying substratum, as will be clear from the sequel. For in every case there is something already present, out of which the resultant thing is born; as animals and plants come from seed.

---

[2] The same word, *gignesthai* or *ginesthai,* is translated "become," "to come to be," "come into existence," or "pass into," according to the requirements of English idiom.

[3] Aristotle obviously did not intend to say that unculture and culture are the same thing, rather he referred to the extent to which a man is cultured as the thing that undergoes change.

7. What Is the Relation of the World Men Actually Perceive to Ultimate Reality?

Plato had tended to devaluate and submerge the individual items of common experience in his quest for an ultimate source of being and reality not subject to the erratic and uncertain changes which affect the items of our experience. Aristotle had to come to grips with the Platonic view.

CATEGORIES*

Aristotle

Expressions which are in no way composite signify substance, quantity, quality, relation, place, time, position, state, action, or affection. To sketch my meaning roughly, examples of substance are 'man' or 'the horse,' of quantity, such terms as 'two cubits long' or 'three cubits long,' of quality, such attributes as 'white,' 'grammatical.' 'Double,' 'half,' 'greater,' fall under the category of relation; 'in the market place,' 'in the Lyceum,' under that of place; 'yesterday,' 'last year,' under that of time. 'Lying,' 'sitting,' are terms indicating 'position'; 'shod,' 'armed,' state; 'to lance,' 'to cauterize,' action; 'to be lanced,' 'to be cauterized,' affection. . . .

Substance, in the truest and primary and most definite sense of the word, is that which is neither predicable of a subject nor present in a subject; for instance, the individual man or horse. But in a secondary sense those things are called substances within which, as species, the primary substances are included; also those which, as genera, include the species. For instance, the individual man is included in the species 'man,' and the genus to which the species belongs is 'animal'; these, therefore—that is to say, the species 'man' and the genus 'animal'—are termed secondary substances. . . .

Everything except primary substances is either predicable of a primary substance or present in a primary substance. This becomes evident by reference to particular instances which occur. 'Animal' is predicated of the species 'man,' therefore of the individual man, for if there were no individual man of whom it could be predicated, it could not be predicated of the species 'man' at all. Again, colour is present in body, therefore in individual bodies, for if there were no indivdual body in which it was present, it could not be present in body at all. Thus everything except primary substances is either predicated of primary substances, or is present in them, and if these last did not exist, it would be impossible for anything else to exist. . . .

All substance appears to signify that which is individual. In the case of primary substance this is indisputably true, for the thing is a unit. In the case of secondary substances, when we speak, for instance, of 'man' or 'animal,' our form of speech gives the impression that we are here also indicating that

* Reprinted by permission of the publishers from *The Works of Aristotle—Categoriae* 4:16, 25–2a, 4 and 5: 2a, 11–18; 2a, 33–26, 6; 36, 10–19; 4a, 10–21, ed. W. D. Ross, trans. E. M. Edghill (Oxford: The Clarendon Press, 1928).

which is individual, but the impression is not strictly true; for a secondary substance is not an individual, but a class with a certain qualification; for it is not one and single as a primary substance is; the words 'man,' 'animal,' are predicable of more than one subject. . . .

The most distinctive mark of substance appears to be that, while remaining numerically one and the same, it is capable of admitting contrary qualities. From among things other than substance, we should find ourselves unable to bring forward any which possessed this mark. Thus, one and the same colour cannot be white and black. Nor can the same one action be good and bad: this law holds good with everything that is not substance. But one and the selfsame substance, while retaining its identity, is yet capable of admitting contrary qualities. The same individual person is at one time white, at another black, at one time warm, at another cold, at one time good, at another bad.

8. What Are the Underlying Principles That Induce Change?

Aristotle's commitment to the reality (and therefore the importance) of the items of our individual experience which are always in the process of changing required him to give close attention to change itself.

PHYSICS*

Aristotle

We have next to consider the question of the factors that make a thing what it is: what they are and how they are to be classified. For knowledge is the object of our studies, and we can hardly be said really to know a thing until we have grasped the 'why' of it—i.e., until we have grasped the factors that are most directly responsible for it. Clearly, then, this must be our aim also with regard to the phenomena of becoming and perishing and all forms of physical change, so that having grasped the underlying principles we may employ them in the explanation of particular phenomena.

[1. *Material Cause.*] In one sense, then, the reason for anything means the material out of which an object is generated and which is immanent in the generated object: e.g., the bronze of a statue, the silver of a bowl, and also the genera to which such materials belong.

[2. *Formal Cause.*] Next, it may mean the form or pattern, i.e., what the thing is defined as being essentially; and also the genus to which this essence belongs. Thus the ratio 2:1 is a formal condition of the musical octave. Generally speaking, number and the factors that make up the definition of a thing are what constitute its formal condition.

[3. *Efficient Cause.*] A third meaning is the immediate source of change or of cessation from change. In this sense a man who gives advice acts as determining agency [on him who receives it], a father on his offspring, and

* *Physics* ii.3, 7, reprinted from *Aristotle,* trans. Philip Wheelwright (New York: The Odyssey Press, 1951), pp. 25–27, 35–37. Used by permission.

generally speaking whatever produces or changes anything on the product or on the thing changed.

[4. *Final Cause*.] Finally the reason for anything may mean the end or purpose for the sake of which a thing is done: e.g., health may be a determining factor in going for a walk. "Why is he taking a walk?" we ask. "In order to be healthy": having said this we think we have given a sufficient explanation. Under this category must also be put all the intermediate steps which the agent must take as means to the end—e.g., taking off weight, loosening the bowels, also drugs and surgical instruments, as means to health. All these are for the sake of an end, although they differ in that some are actions to be performed while others are instruments to be used.

Thus we have enumerated the various ways in which one thing can determine another. Frequently it happens that more than one type of determining factor bears an essential (not merely an incidental) relation to a single thing. It is as a statue and not by virtue of an incidental aspect that a statue owes its existence both to the sculptor who makes it and to the bronze from which it is made; although these are of course related to it in different ways—the one as the force that produces it, the other as its material. Again, some things may be regarded as determining each other reciprocally—e.g., exercise and physical fitness—but not in the same sense, for while exercise is the actual source from which physical fitness proceeds, physical fitness is rather the end toward which exercise is directed. Again, a given factor will often account for quite opposite results: if a certain result can be attributed to its presence we may blame the opposite result on its absence. Thus we attribute a shipwreck to the absence of the pilot whose presence would have brought the ship to safety.

But all of the determining factors just mentioned come under our fourfold classification. In the sense of 'that out of which,' letters are the determinants of syllables, raw materials of manufactured goods, fire and the like of physical bodies, the parts of the whole, and the premises of the conclusion. In each of these cases the first of the related terms is a substratum [or material cause], as parts are to a whole; while the second is the essential character which the substratum receives—its whole or synthesis or form [formal cause]. Again, the seed or sperm, the doctor, the man who gives advice—in short, any agent—is the source in which the starting or stopping of a motion or change originates [efficient cause]. And finally, there are those things which determine in the sense of being a goal, i.e., a good toward which other things tend [final cause]; for the phrase 'for the sake of' connotes both a goal and highest good—whether the good be real or apparent. . . .

It is clear, then, that there are such things as 'determining factors' and that they are of four kinds, as we have stated. These correspond to the four meanings of the question 'why.' The 'why' of anything may be referred: (1) to the 'essential nature of the thing in question,' when it is a question of things that do not involve change[1] (e.g., in mathematics, where our reasoning ultimately falls back upon the definition of a straight line or commensurability or the like); or (2) to the thing that started a movement going (e.g., "Why did they make war? Because they had been raided"); or (3) to the end in view

---

[1] Also when it is a question of changeless aspects of changeable things.

(e.g., [they make war] in order to gain sovereign power); or (4) in the case of things that come into existence, to the material out of which they come. These, then, being the four kinds of determining factor that there are, it is the business of the natural philosopher to understand them all; and his explanations, to be scientifically adequate, must take account of each of them—the matter, the form, the moving force, and the goal.

It sometimes happens that the last three of these determinants coincide. The essential nature of a thing may often be regarded as identical with the fundamental purpose which it serves; and both of these aspects must be identical in kind with the source of the thing's movement—man, for example, being begotten only by man. This latter identity holds true in all cases where the propelling determinant[2] is itself something that changes. As for the opposite sort of case (i.e., where the propelling determinant possesses within itself neither movement nor the power of movement, but is motionless),[3] this falls outside the province of natural science; whence we may distinguish three branches of inquiry—one of things to which movement is foreign, a second of moving but imperishable things, and a third of things that perish.

In short, then, when we explain anything we must take into account at once its material, its essential character, and the source of its movement; this being principally how explanations of occurrences are sought. "What comes into existence, and what has preceded it?" "What was the force or agent that started the process, and on what did it act?"—questions such as these, properly ordered, are essential to every [scientific investigation].

The principles that give rise to and govern physical movement or change are of two kinds. One of them does not itself partake of change, and is therefore not physical: I refer to whatever produces movement or change in other things without itself being affected—the absolutely unalterable and primary [aspect of things], their essential character, or form; hence also their end and goal. And as nature is inherently 'goalful,' the natural scientist must not neglect this aspect. He must, in short, explain the 'why' of things in all four of its aspects, showing how one thing necessarily, or at any rate normally, arises from another [efficient cause]; how one thing is a precondition of another's existence, as premises provide the material for a conclusion [material cause]; how this or that [entity or aspect] manifests a thing's essential nature [formal cause]; and why it is better that this or that should be as it is—not, of course, without qualification but relatively to the whole character of the thing in question [final cause].

9. By What Rule Will a Wise Man Live in a Foolish World?

Two other great schools of philosophy came into being in fourth-century Athens—that of the Epicureans, named after its founder, Epicurus, and that of the Stoics, named after the stoa, or porch, where its founder, Zeno, held forth. In moral philosophy, the former taught a doctrine of temperate quest

---

[2] That is, the efficient cause.

[3] That is, it *has* no principle of change or movement within itself, but it *is* such a principle for other things.

of pleasure, the latter of a self-control through reason that would raise men above both pleasure and pain. After the decline of old standards that resulted from the great expansion of Roman rule and then from the new riches which that expansion brought them, the Roman elite sought a foundation for a viable way of life. About the beginning of the Christian era they found Stoicism more congenial than Epicureanism. It was the moral teaching of the Stoics rather than their cosmology or metaphysics that appealed to the generations on which had fallen the burden of ruling an enormous empire, generations which, moreover, took their duty seriously. Lucius Anneus Seneca (4 B.C.–A.D. 65)—playwright, author, and statesman—was much influenced by the ethical side of Stoic teaching. He had meager speculative gifts, but through him and others of like mind, the Stoic moral outlook became almost the official philosophy of the administrators of the Roman Empire. Seneca himself, after serving as a tutor to the emperor Nero, was ultimately required to commit suicide by that increasingly lunatic ruler for conspiring against him.

ON THE HAPPY LIFE*

Seneca

To live happily, my brother Gallio,[1] is the desire of all men, but their minds are blinded to a clear vision of just what it is that makes life happy; and so far from its being easy to attain the happy life, the more eagerly a man strives to reach it, the farther he recedes from it if he has made a mistake in the road; for when it leads in the opposite direction, his very speed will increase the distance that separates him.

First, therefore, we must seek what it is that we are aiming at; then we must look about for the road by which we can reach it most quickly, and on the journey itself, if only we are on the right path, we shall discover how much of the distance we overcome each day, and how much nearer we are to the goal toward which we are urged by a natural desire. But so long as we wander aimlessly, having no guide, and following only the noise and discordant cries of those who call us in different directions, life will be consumed in making mistakes—life that is brief even if we should strive day and night for sound wisdom. Let us, therefore, decide both upon the goal and upon the way, and not fail to find some experienced guide who has explored the region towards which we are advancing; for the conditions of this journey are different from those of most travel. On most journeys some well-recognized road and inquiries made of the inhabitants of the region prevent you from going astray; but on this one all the best beaten and the most frequented paths are the most deceptive. Nothing, therefore, needs to be more emphasized than the

---

*Reprinted by permission of the publishers from The Loeb Classical Library, Seneca, Moral Essays vi.i, 1–6, 2, "On the Happy Life," trans. John W. Basore (Cambridge, Mass.: Harvard University Press, 1935), II, 99–115.
[1] Gallio was Seneca's elder brother and governor of the province of Achaia (southern Greece) in A.D. 52. It was in this connection that his chief claim to fame arose: he was the Roman official before whom the Jews accused the apostle Paul (Acts 18: 12–17), an event, incidentally, that had already happened when these words were written.

warning that we should not, like sheep, follow the lead of the throng in front of us, travelling, thus, the way that all go and not the way that we ought to go. Yet nothing involves us in greater trouble than the fact that we adapt ourselves to common report in the belief that the best things are those that have met with great approval,—the fact that, having so many to follow, we live after the rule, not of reason, but of imitation. The result of this is that people are piled high, one above another, as they rush to destruction. And just as it happens that in a great crush of humanity, when the people push against each other, no one can fall down without drawing along another, and those that are in front cause destruction to those behind—this same thing you may see happening everywhere in life. No man can go wrong to his own hurt only, but he will be both the cause and the sponsor of another's wrongdoing. For it is dangerous to attach one's self to the crowd in front, and so long as each one of us is more willing to trust another than to judge for himself, we never show any judgment in the matter of living, but always a blind trust, and a mistake that has been passed on from hand to hand finally involves us and works our destruction. It is the example of other people that is our undoing; let us merely separate ourselves from the crowd, and we shall be made whole. But as it is, the populace, defending its own iniquity, pits itself against reason. And so we see the same thing happening that happens at the elections, where, when the fickle breeze of popular favour has shifted, the very same persons who chose the praetors wonder that those praetors were chosen. The same thing has one moment our favour, the next our disfavour; this is the outcome of every decision that follows the choice of the majority.

When the happy life is under debate, there will be no use for you to reply to me, as if it were a matter of votes: "This side seems to be in a majority." For that is just the reason it is the worse side. Human affairs are not so happily ordered that the majority prefer the better things; a proof of the worst choice is the crowd. Therefore let us find out what is best to do, not what is most commonly done—what will establish our claim to lasting happiness, not what finds favour with the rabble, who are the worst possible exponents of the truth. But by the rabble I mean no less the servants of the court than the servants of the kitchen; for I do not regard the colour of the garments that clothe the body. In rating a man I do not rely upon eyesight; I have a better and surer light, by which I may distinguish good of the soul. If the soul ever has leisure to draw breath and to retire within itself—ah! to what self-torture will it come, and how, if it confesses the truth to itself, it will say: "All that I have done hitherto, I would were undone; when I think of all that I have said, I envy the dumb; of all that I have prayed for, I rate my prayers as the curses of my enemies; of all that I have feared—ye gods! how much lighter it would have been than the load of what I have coveted! With many I have been at enmity, and, laying aside hatred, have been restored to friendship with them—if only there can be any friendship between the wicked; with myself I have not yet entered into friendship. I have made every effort to remove myself from the multitude and to make myself noteworthy by reason of some endowment. What have I accomplished save to expose myself to the darts of malice and show it where it can sting me? See you those who praise your eloquence, who trail upon your wealth, who court your favour, who exalt your power?

All these are either now your enemies, or—it amounts to the same thing—can become such. To know how many are jealous of you, count your admirers. Why do I not rather seek some real good—one which I could feel, not one which I could display? These things that draw the eyes of men, before which they halt, which they show to one another in wonder, outwardly glitter, but are worthless within."

Let us seek something that is a good in more than appearance—something that is solid, constant, and more beautiful in its more hidden part; for this let us delve. And it is placed not far off; you will find it—you need only to know where to stretch out your hand. As it is, just as if we groped in darkness, we pass by things near at hand, stumbling over the very objects we desire.

Not to bore you, however, with tortuous detail, I shall pass over in silence the opinions of other philosophers, for it would be tedious to enumerate and refute them all. Do you listen to ours. But when I say "ours," I do not bind myself to some particular one of the Stoic masters; I, too, have the right to form an opinion. Accordingly, I shall follow so-and-so, I shall request so-and-so to divide the question; perhaps, too, when called upon after all the rest, I shall impugn none of my predecessors' opinions, and shall say: "I simply have this much to add." Meantime, I follow the guidance of Nature—a doctrine upon which all Stoics are agreed. Not to stray from and to mould ourselves according to her law and pattern—this is true wisdom.

The happy life, therefore, is a life that is in harmony with its own nature, and it can be attained in only one way. First of all, we must have a sound mind and one that is in constant possession of its sanity; second, it must be courageous and energetic, and, too, capable of the noblest fortitude, ready for every emergency, careful of the body and of all that concerns it, but without anxiety; lastly, it must be attentive to all the advantages that adorn life, but with over-much love for none—the user, but not the slave, of the gifts of Fortune. You understand, even if I do not say more, that, when once we have driven away all that excites or affrights us, there ensues unbroken tranquility and enduring freedom; for when pleasures and fears have been banished, then, in place of all that is trivial and fragile and harmful just because of the evil it works, there comes upon us first a boundless joy that is firm and unalterable, then peace and harmony of the soul and true greatness coupled with kindliness; for all ferocity is born from weakness.

It is possible also to define this good of ours in other terms—that is, the same idea may be expressed in different language. Just as an army remains the same, though at one time it deploys with a longer line, now is massed into a narrow space and either stands with hollowed centre and wings curved forward, or extends a straightened front, and, no matter what its formation may be, will keep the selfsame spirit and the same resolve to stand in defence of the selfsame cause,—so the definition of the highest good may at one time be given in prolix and lengthy form, and at another be restrained and concise. So it will come to the same thing if I say: "The highest good is a mind that scorns the happenings of chance, and rejoices only in virtue," or say: "It is the power of the mind to be unconquerable, wise from experience, calm in action, showing the while much courtesy and consideration in intercourse with others." It may also be defined in the statement that the happy man is he who recognizes no good and evil other than a good and an evil mind—one who cherishes honour, is content with virtue, who is neither puffed up, nor crushed, by the happenings of chance, who knows of no greater good than that which he alone is able to bestow upon himself, for whom true pleasure will be the scorn of pleasures. It is possible, too, if one chooses to be discursive, to transfer the same idea to various other forms of expression without injuring or weakening its meaning. For what prevents us from saying that the happy life is to have a mind that is free, lofty, fearless and steadfast—a mind that is placed beyond the reach of fear, beyond the reach of desire, that counts virtue the only good, baseness the only evil, and all else but a worthless mass of things, which come and go without increasing or diminishing the highest good, and neither subtract any part from the happy life nor add any part to it?

A man thus grounded must, whether he wills or not, necessarily be attended by constant cheerfulness and a joy that is deep and issues from deep within, since he finds delight in his own resources, and desires no joys greater than his inner joys. Should not such joys as these be rightly matched against the paltry and trivial and fleeting sensations of the wretched body? The day a man becomes superior to pleasure, he will also be superior to pain; but you see in that wretched and baneful bondage he must linger whom pleasures and pains, those most capricious and tyrannical of masters, shall in turn enslave. Therefore we must make our escape to freedom. But the only means of procuring this is through indifference to Fortune. Then will be born the one inestimable blessing, the peace and exaltation of a mind now safely anchored, and, when all error is banished, the great and stable joy that comes from the discovery of truth, along with kindliness and cheerfulness of mind; and the source of a man's pleasure in all of these will not be that they are good, but that they spring from a good that is his own.

Seeing that I am employing some freedom in treating my subject, I may say that the happy man is one who is freed from both fear and desire because of the gift of reason; since even rocks are free from fear and sorrow, and no less are the beasts of the field, yet for all that no one could say that these things are "blissful," when they have no comprehension of bliss. Put in the same class those people whose dullness of nature and ignorance of themselves have reduced them to the level of beasts of the field and of inanimate things. There is no difference between the one and the other, since in one case they are things without reason, and in the other their reason is warped, and works their own hurt, being active in the wrong direction; for no man can be said to be happy if he has been thrust outside the pale of truth. Therefore the life that is happy has been founded on correct and trustworthy judgement, and is unalterable. Then, truly, is the mind unclouded and freed from every ill, since it knows how to escape not only deep wounds, but even scratches, and, resolved to hold to the end whatever stand it has taken, it will defend its position even against the assaults of an angry Fortune. For so far as sensual pleasure is concerned, though it flows about us on every side, steals in through every opening, softens the mind with its blandishments, and employs one resource after another in order to seduce us in whole or in part, yet who of mortals, if he has left in him one trace of a human being, would choose to have his senses tickled night and day, and, forsaking the mind, devote his attention wholly to the body?

"But the mind also," it will be said, "has its own pleasures." Let it have them, in sooth, and let it pose as a judge of luxury and pleasures; let it gorge itself with all the things that are wont to delight the senses, then let it look back upon the past, and, recalling faded pleasures, let it intoxicate itself with former experiences and be eager now for those to come, and let it lay its plans, and, while the body lies helpless from present cramming, let it direct its thoughts to that to come—yet from all this, it seems to me, the mind will be more wretched than ever, since it is madness to choose evils instead of goods. But no man can be happy unless he is sane, and no man can be sane who searches for what will injure him in place of what is best. The happy man, therefore, is one who has right judgement; the happy man is content with his present lot, no matter what it is, and is reconciled to his circumstances; the happy man is he who allows reason to fix the value of every condition of existence.

10. How Is Alienated Man To Be Restored to the True Being from Which He Is Alienated?

Roman Stoicism became the world view of Roman men of action in the great days of the Empire. By the end of the second century after Christ, those days were numbered. In a decaying Empire, many men could no longer find in the Stoic ethic that rational satisfaction in duty done according to reason that was the Stoic version of the older Roman sense of civic responsibility. For such men, philosophies of withdrawal from obligations in this world came to hold more powerful charms than philosophies of the active life. The most effective philosophy of withdrawal was Neoplatonism.

Aside from the Christian Scriptures, few writings from Antiquity have influenced medieval life—particularly medieval mysticism—as much as those on Neoplatonism. Among the Neoplatonists, Plotinus was pre-eminent. He was born in Egypt in A.D. 205 and studied at Alexandria before going to Rome to become the center of a group of intellectuals. He wrote nothing until he was nearing fifty years of age. The present selection comes from the collection of Plotinus' writings known as the Enneads. *In the course of his work, he provided what scholars often have called the last completing link between pagan philosophy and Christian theology. His concerns reflect the deep and dark sense of alienation which afflicted so many men in the last centuries of antiquity. Directly or indirectly, he dealt with the problem that such alienation raised.*

THE ENNEADS*

Plotinus

What can it be that has brought the souls to forget the father, God, and, though members of the Divine and entirely of that world, to ignore at once themselves and It?

Fifth En"ead 1–4, reprinted by permission from *Plotinus: The Divine Mind*, trans. Stephen MacKenna (New York: Pantheon, 1926), IV, 1–5.

The evil that has overtaken them has its source in self-will, in the entry into the sphere of process, and in the primal differentiation with the desire for self ownership. They conceived a pleasure in this freedom and largely indulged their own motion; thus they were hurried down the wrong path, and in the end, drifting further and further, they came to lose even the thought of their origin in the Divine. A child wrenched young from home and brought up during many years at a distance will fail in knowledge of its father and of itself: the souls, in the same way, no longer discern either the divinity or their own nature; ignorance of their rank brings self-depreciation; they misplace their respect, honouring everything more than themselves; all their awe and admiration is for the alien, and, clinging to this, they have broken apart, as far as a soul may, and they make light of what they have deserted; their regard for the mundane and their disregard of themselves bring about their utter ignoring of the divine.

Admiring pursuit of the external is a confession of inferiority; and nothing thus holding itself inferior to things that rise and perish, nothing counting itself less honourable and less enduring than all else it admires could ever form any notion of either the nature or the power of God.

A double discipline must be applied if human beings in this pass are to be reclaimed, and brought back to their origins, lifted once more towards the Supreme and One and First.

There is the method . . . [of] declaring the dishonour of the objects which the soul holds here in honour; the second teaches or recalls to the soul its race and worth; this latter is the leading truth, and, clearly brought out, is the evidence of the other.

It must occupy us now for it bears closely upon our enquiry (as to the Divine Hypostases) to which it is the natural preliminary: the seeker is [the] soul and it must start from a true notion of the nature and quality by which [the] soul may undertake the search; it must study itself in order to learn whether it has the faculty for the enquiry, the eye for the object proposed, whether in fact we ought to seek; for if the object is alien the search must be futile, while if there is relationship the solution of our problem is at once desirable and possible.

Let every soul recall, then, at the outset the truth that Soul [itself][1] is the author of all living things, that it has breathed the life into them all, whatever is nourished by earth and sea, all the creatures of the air, the divine stars in the sky; it is the maker of the sun; it formed and ordered this vast heaven and conducts all that rhythmic motion: and it is a principle distinct from all these to which it gives law and movement and life, and it must of necessity be more honourable than they, for they gather or dissolve as Soul brings them life or abandons them, but Soul, since it never can abandon itself, is of eternal being.

How life was purveyed to the universe of things and to the separate beings in it may be thus conceived:—

That great Soul must stand pictured before another soul, one not mean,

---

[1] By "Soul," Plotinus meant the divine all-pervading Soul of which each individual human soul is a part. For purposes of clarity, every reference to the divine soul is capitalized in the material to follow.

a soul that has become worthy to look, emancipated . . . from all that binds its fellows in bewitchment, holding itself in quietude. Let not merely the enveloping body be at peace, body's turmoil stilled, but all that lies around, earth at peace, and sea at peace, and air and the very heavens. Into that heaven, all at rest, let the great Soul be conceived to roll inward at every point, penetrating, permeating, from all sides pouring in its light. As the rays of the sun throwing their brilliance upon a lowering cloud make it gleam all gold, so Soul entering the material expanse of the heavens has given life, has given immortality: What was abject it has lifted up; and the heavenly system, moved now in endless motion by Soul that leads it in wisdom, has become a living and a blessed thing; the Soul domiciled within, it takes worth where, before Soul, it was stark body—clay and water—or, rather, the blankness of Matter, the absence of Being, and, as an author says, "the execration of the Gods."

Soul's nature and power will be brought out more clearly, more brilliantly, if we consider next how it envelops the heavenly system and guides all to its purposes: for it has bestowed itself upon all that huge expanse so that every interval, small and great alike, all has been ensouled.

The material body[2] is made up of parts, each holding its own place, some in mutual opposition and others variously interdependent; Soul is in no such condition; it is not whittled down so that life tells of a part of Soul and springs where some such separate portion impinges;[3] each separate life lives by the [one] Soul entire, [which is] omnipresent in the likeness of the engendering father, entire in unity and entire in diffused variety. By the power of Soul the manifold and diverse heavenly system is a unit: through Soul this universe is a God: and the sun is a God because it is ensouled; so too the stars: and whatsoever we ourselves may be, it is all in virtue of Soul; for "dead is viler than dung."

This, by which the gods are divine, must be the oldest God of them all: and our own soul is of that same Ideal nature, so that to consider it, purified, freed from all accruement, is to recognize in ourselves that same value which we have found Soul to be, honourable above all that is bodily. For what is body but earth, and, taking fire itself (the noblest of material things), what (but Soul) is its burning power? So it is with all the compounds of earth and fire, even with water and air added to them?

If, then, it is the presence of Soul that brings worth, how can a man slight himself and run after other things? You honour Soul elsewhere; honour then yourself.[4]

The soul once seen to be thus precious, thus divine, you may hold the faith that by its possession you are already nearing . . . [the Divine]: in the strength of this power make upwards towards It: at no great distance you must attain: there is not much between.[5]

---

[2] That is, the material body of objects which make up the world of sense experience.

[3] Plotinus apparently meant to stress the point here that the all-pervading Soul is not divided into sections which are separate in and spring from those individual objects of the universe that seem to indicate the presence of Soul because they have life.

[4] Because your own soul is a manifestation of the great Soul.

[5] That is, the seeker need not go far to attain realization of the Divine once he has seen that his own soul is a part of it.

But over this Divine, there is a still diviner: grasp the upward neighbor of Soul, its prior and source.

Soul, for all the worth we have shown to belong to it, is yet a secondary, an image of [Thought]:[6] reason uttered is an image of the reason stored within the soul, and in the same way Soul is an utterance of [Thought]: it is even the total of its activity, the entire stream of life sent forth by that [Thought] to the production of further being; it is the forthgoing heat of a fire which has also heat essentially inherent. But within the Supreme we must see energy not as an overflow but in the double aspect of integral inherence with the establishment of a new being. Sprung, in other words, from [Thought], Soul is intellective, but with an intellection operating by the method of reasonings: for its perfecting it must look to that Divine Mind, which may be thought of as a father watching over the development of his child born imperfect in comparison with himself.

Thus its [Soul's] substantial existence comes from [Thought]; and the Reason within it becomes Act in virtue of its contemplation of that prior [the antecedent Thought]; for its thought and act are its own intimate possession when it looks to the Supreme Intelligence; those only are soul-acts which are of this intellective nature and are determined by its own character; all that is less noble is foreign (traceable to Matter) and is accidental to the soul in the course of its peculiar task.

In two ways, then, [Thought] enhances the divine quality of Soul, as father and as immanent presence; nothing separates them but the fact that they are not one and the same, that there is succession, that over against a recipient there stands the ideal-form received; but this recipient, Matter to the Supreme Intelligence, is also noble as being at once informed by divine intellect and uncompounded.

What [this] Thought [or Supreme Intelligence] must be is carried in the single word that Soul, itself so great, is still inferior.

But there is yet another way to this knowledge:—

Admiring the world of sense as we look out upon its vastness and beauty and the order of its eternal march, thinking of the gods within it, seen and hidden, and the celestial spirits and all the life of animal and plant, let us mount to its archetype, to the yet more authentic sphere: there we are to contemplate all things as members of the Intellectual—eternal in their own right, vested with a self-springing consciousness and life—and, presiding over all these, the unsoiled Intelligence and the unapproachable wisdom.

That archetypal world is the true Golden Age, age of Kronos,[7] who is the [Supreme] Intelligence as being the offspring or exuberance of God. For here is contained all that is immortal: nothing here but is Divine Mind; all is God; this is the place of every soul. Here is rest unbroken: for how can that

---

[6] The translator here has used "Intellectual-Principle" for Plotinus' Greek word *nous*, which means "mind," or "intelligence." It is clear that he means the thought behind Soul, not the individual intellect of the human soul.

[7] In Greek mythology, the Age of Kronos was a time of unique peace and blessedness in the beginning of the world, before warfare among the gods despoiled creation. Apparently because Kronos gave birth to many of the gods of Olympus, including Zeus, Plotinus took him to be the genuine representation of God, even though Kronos was later superseded by Zeus. Therefore, Plotinus called the archetypal world the "offspring of God (Kronos)."

seek change, in which all is well; what need that reach to, which holds all within itself; what increase can that desire, which stands utterly achieved? All its content, thus, is perfect, that itself may be perfect throughout, as holding nothing that is less than the divine, nothing that is less than intellective. Its knowing is not by search but by possession, its blessedness inherent, not acquired; for all belongs to it eternally and it holds the authentic Eternity imitated by Time which, circling round Soul, makes towards the new thing and passes by the old. Soul deals with thing after thing—now Socrates; now a horse: always some one entity from among beings—but [Thought] is all and therefore its entire content is sumultaneously present in that identity: this is pure being in eternal actuality; nowhere is there any future, for every then is a now; nor is there any past, for nothing there has ever ceased to be; everything has taken its stand for ever, an identity well pleased, we might say, to be as it is; and everything, in that entire content, is [Thought] and True Being; and the total of all is [Thought] entire and Being entire. [Thought] by its intellective act establishes Being, which in turn, as the object of intellection, becomes the cause of intellection and of existence to the [Thought]—though, of course, there is another cause of intellection which is also a cause to Being, both rising in a source distinct from either.

Now while these two are coalescents, having their existence in common and are never apart, still the unity they form is two-sided; there is [Thought] as against Being, the intellectual agent as against the object of intellection; we consider the intellective act and we have the [Thought]; we think of the object of that act and we have Being.

Such difference there must be if there is to be any intellection; but similarly there must also be identity (since, in perfect knowing, subject and object are identical).

B. Politics

The preceding section displayed the Greeks as the first people in history to turn the full resources of the human intellect, all its rational and speculative capacities, uninhibited by commitment to myth, into the work of exploring the nature of the world and of man. Man being, as Aristotle said, "a political animal," any exploration of his nature must involve an inquiry into human political organizations.

The Greeks, originally organized in city-states, found themselves under attack by the Persian Empire at the beginning of the fifth century B.C. Their success against this onslaught served to confirm the Greek assumption that the city-state, or polis, *offered the best possible device for human political organization. It had withstood its test against Oriental despotism; consequently, when in the course of the expansion of their philosophic concern in the fifth century, Greeks began to make politics a subject of intellectual speculation and inquiry, the triumphant* polis *was naturally the political structure on which they focused their attentions.*

A further stimulus to political speculation was provided by the long and bitter war of almost three decades between the two most powerful Greek city-

states, Sparta and Athens, which began in 431 B.C. Sparta was a poor garrison state maintained by the exploitation of an enserfed peasantry for the support of a highly trained, rigorously disciplined infantry in a constant state of military readiness. The achievement of this military strength had brought Sparta's cultural contributions to a standstill. Athens, on the other hand, was a rich commercial society with a large body of free citizens, all of whom took an active part in the political life of the city. It was the center of Greek activity in the arts, poetry, and philosophy; it seemed to some of its citizens a nearly perfect embodiment of the idea of the polis.

1. Why Should Civilized Men Sacrifice Themselves for a Free Political Society?

Born about 455 B.C., Thucydides was a young man when the war between Athens and Sparta, the Peloponnesian War, began. He fashioned his career in the years of conflict, during which he rose to the rank of general. His military service ended when the Spartan general Brasidas defeated him at the battle of Amphipolis in 424. Thereupon he retired, and, relying upon the closeness of his past association with the Athenian high command and upon diligent inquiry, he wrote a history of the war.

The first selection from Thucydides dates from the end of the first year of the war. The chief citizen of Athens and its leader during the first years was Pericles, a man from a great ancient Athenian family, whom Thucydides much admired. The Athenians had chosen Pericles to deliver a funeral oration for those who had fallen in the early campaigns. He sought to raise the morale of his fellow citizens in the face of battle losses and threatening enemies by answering questions that he realized the bereaved families must be asking.

HISTORY OF THE PELOPONNESIAN WAR*

Thucydides

'I shall begin by speaking about our ancestors, since it is only right and proper on such an occasion to pay them the honour of recalling what they did. In this land of ours there have always been the same people living from generation to generation up till now, and they, by their courage and their virtues, have handed it on to us, a free country. They certainly deserve our praise. Even more so do our fathers deserve it. For to the inheritance they had received they added all the empire we have now, and it was not without blood and toil that thy handed it down to us of the present generation. And then we ourselves, assembled here to-day, who are mostly in the prime of life, have, in most directions, added to the power of our empire and have organized our State in such a way that it is perfectly well able to look after itself both in peace and in war.

---

* Reprinted by permission of the publishers from *Thucydides: The Peloponnesian War* ii.4, trans. Rex Warner (London: The Bodley Head, 1954), pp. 116–120.

'I have no wish to make a long speech on subjects familiar to you all: so I shall say nothing about the warlike deeds by which we acquired our power or the battles in which we or our fathers gallantly resisted our enemies, Greek or foreign. What I want to do is, in the first place, to discuss the spirit in which we faced our trials and also our constitution and the way of life which has made us great. After that I shall speak in praise of the dead, believing that this kind of speech is not inappropriate to the present occasion, and that this whole assembly, of citizens and foreigners, may listen to it with advantage.

'Let me say that our system of government does not copy the institutions of our neighbours. It is more the case of our being a model to others, than of our imitating anyone else. Our constitution is called a democracy because power is in the hands not of a minority but of the whole people. When it is a question of settling private disputes, everyone is equal before the law; when it is a question of putting one person before another in positions of public responsibility, what counts is not membership of a particular class, but the actual ability which the man possesses. No one, so long as he has it in him to be of service to the state, is kept in political obscurity because of poverty. And, just as our political life is free and open, so is our day-to-day life in our relations with each other. We do not get into an argument with our next-door neighbor if he enjoys himself in his own way, nor do we give him the kind of black looks which, though they do no real harm, still do hurt people's feelings. We are free and tolerant in our private lives; but in public affairs we keep to the law. This is because it commands our deep respect.

'We give our obedience to those whom we put in positions of authority, and we obey the laws themselves, especially those which are for the protection of the oppressed, and those unwritten laws which it is an acknowledged shame to break.

'And here is another point. When our work is over, we are in a position to enjoy all kinds of recreation for our spirits. There are various kinds of contests and sacrifices regularly throughout the year; in our own homes we find a beauty and a good taste which delight us every day and which drive away our cares. Then the greatness of our city brings it about that all the good things from all over the world flow in to us, so that to us it seems just as natural to enjoy foreign goods as our own local products.

'Then there is a great difference between us and our opponents, in our attitude towards military security. Here are some examples: Our city is open to the world, and we have no periodical deportations in order to prevent people observing or finding out secrets which might be of military advantage to the enemy. This is because we rely, not on secret weapons, but on our own real courage and loyalty. There is a difference, too, in our educational systems. The Spartans, from their earliest boyhood, are submitted to the most laborious training in courage; we pass our lives without all these restrictions, and yet are just as ready to face the same dangers as they are. Here is proof of this: When the Spartans invade our land, they do not come by themselves, but bring all their allies with them; whereas we, when we launch an attack abroad, do the job by ourselves, and, though fighting on foreign soil, do not often fail to defeat opponents who are fighting for their own hearths and homes. As a matter of fact none of our enemies has ever yet been confronted with our total strength, because we have to divide our attention between our navy and the many missions on which our troops are sent on land. Yet, if our enemies engage a detachment of our forces and defeat it, they give themselves credit for having thrown back our entire army; or, if they lose, they claim that they were beaten by us in full strength. There are certain advantages, I think, in our way of meeting danger voluntarily, with an easy mind, instead of with a laborious training, with natural rather than with state-induced courage. We do not have to spend our time practising to meet sufferings which are still in the future; and when they are actually upon us we show ourselves just as brave as these others who are always in strict training. This is one point in which, I think, our city deserves to be admired. There are also others:

'Our love of what is beautiful does not lead to extravagance; our love of the things of the mind does not make us soft. We regard wealth as something to be properly used, rather than as something to boast about. As for poverty, no one need be ashamed to admit it: the real shame is in not taking practical measures to escape from it. Here each individual is interested not only in his own affairs but in the affairs of the state as well: even those who are mostly occupied with their own business are extremely well-informed on general politics—this is a peculiarity of ours: we do not say that a man who takes no interest in politics is a man who minds his own business; we say that he has no business here at all. We Athenians, in our own persons, take our decisions on policy or submit them to proper discussions: for we do not think that there is an incompatibility between words and deeds; the worst thing is to rush into action before the consequences have been properly debated: And this is another point where we differ from other people. We are capable at the same time of taking risks and of estimating them beforehand. Others are brave out of ignorance; and, when they stop to think, they begin to fear. But the man who can most truly be accounted brave is he who best knows the meaning of what is sweet in life and of what is terrible, and then goes out undeterred to meet what is to come.

'Again, in questions of general good feeling there is a great contrast between us and most other people. We make friends by doing good to others, not by receiving good from them. This makes our friendship all the more reliable, since we want to keep alive the gratitude of those who are in our debt by showing continued goodwill to them: whereas the feelings of one who owes us something lack the same enthusiasm, since he knows that, when he repays our kindness, it will be more like paying back a debt than giving something spontaneously. We are unique in this. When we do kindnesses to others, we do not do them out of any calculations of profit or loss: we do them without afterthought, relying on our free liberality. Taking everything together then, I declare that our city is an education to Greece,[1] and I declare that in my opinion each single one of our citizens, in all the manifold aspects of life, is able to show himself the rightful lord and owner of his own person, and do this, moreover, with exceptional grace and exceptional versatility. And to show that this is no empty boasting for the present occasion, but real tangible fact, you have only to consider the power which our city possesses

---

[1] This is Pericles' famous phrase, calling Athens the "School of Hellas," here translated differently, however.

and which has been won by those very qualities which I have mentioned. Athens, alone of the states we know, comes to her testing time in a greatness that surpasses what was imagined of her. In her case, and in her case alone, no invading enemy is ashamed at being defeated, and no subject can complain of being governed by people unfit for their responsibilities. Mighty indeed are the marks and monuments of our empire which we have left. Future ages will wonder at us, as the present age wonders at us now. We do not need the praises of a Homer, or of anyone else whose words may delight us for the moment, but whose estimation of facts will fall short of what is really true. For our adventurous spirit has forced an entry into every sea and into every land; and everywhere we have left behind us everlasting memorials of good done to our friends or suffering inflicted on our enemies.

'This, then, is the kind of city for which these men, who could not bear the thought of losing her, nobly fought and nobly died. It is only natural that every one of us who survive them should be willing to undergo hardships in her service. And it was for this reason that I have spoken at such length about our city, because I wanted to make it clear that for us there is more at stake than there is for others who lack our advantages; also I wanted my words of praise for the dead to be set in the bright light of evidence. And now the most important of these words has been spoken. I have sung the praises of our city; but it was the courage and gallantry of these men, and of people like them, which made her splendid. Nor would you find it true in the case of many of the Greeks, as it is true of them, that no words can do more than justice to their deeds.'

2. What Rule Determines the Relationship Between States?

As the war progressed, other Greek city-states were drawn into the vortex as allies of Athens or of Sparta. Most of the cities on the islands of the Aegean were subject-allies of Athens, whose sea power was vastly superior to that of Sparta and her allies. Almost alone among the Aegean cities, Melos remained neutral. Athens summoned Melos to submit, and when the Melian rulers refused, the following parley ensued, according to Thucydides.

HISTORY OF THE PELOPONNESIAN WAR*

Thucydides

. . . The Athenian envoys spoke as follows:—

Athenians.—'Since the negotiations are not to go on before the people, in order that we may not be able to speak straight on without interruption, and deceive the ears of the multitude by seductive arguments which would pass without refutation (for we know that this is the meaning of our being brought before the few), what if you who sit there were to pursue a method more

* Reprinted by permission of the publishers from *Thucydides: The Peloponnesian War* v.7, trans. Rex Warner (London: The Bodley Head, 1954), pp. 393–399.

cautious still! Make no set speech yourselves, but take us up at whatever you do not like, and settle that before going any farther. And first tell us if this proposition of ours suits you.'

The Melian commissioners answered:—

Melians.—'To the fairness of quietly instructing each other as you propose there is nothing to object; but your military preparations are too far advanced to agree with what you say, as we see you are come to be judges in your own cause, and that all we can reasonably expect from this negotiation is war, if we prove to have right on our side and refuse to submit, and in the contrary case, slavery.'

Athenians.—'If you have met to reason about presentiments of the future, or for anything else than to consult for the safety of your state upon the facts that you see before you, we will give over; otherwise we will go on.'

Melians.—'It is natural and excusable for men in our position to turn more ways than one both in thought and utterance. However, the question in this conference is, as you say, the safety of our country; and the discussion, if you please, can proceed in the way which you propose.'

Athenians.—'For ourselves, we shall not trouble you with specious pretences—either of how we have a right to our empire because we overthrew the Mede, or are now attacking you because of wrong that you have done us—and make a long speech which would not be believed; and in return we hope that you, instead of thinking to influence us by saying that you did not join the Lacedæmonians,[1] although their colonists, or that you have done us no wrong, will aim at what is feasible, holding in view the real sentiments of us both; since you know as well as we do that right, as the world goes, is only in question between equals in power, while the strong do what they can and the weak suffer what they must.'

Melians.—'As we think, at any rate, it is expedient—we speak as we are obliged, since you enjoin us to let right alone and talk only of interest—that you should not destroy what is our common protection, the privilege of being allowed in danger to invoke what is fair and right, and even to profit by arguments not strictly valid if they can be got to pass current. And you are as much interested in this as any, as your fall would be a signal for the heaviest vengeance and an example for the world to meditate upon.'

Athenians.—'The end of our empire, if end it should, does not frighten us: a rival empire like Lacedæmon, even if Lacedæmon was our real antagonist, is not so terrible to the vanquished as subjects who by themselves attack and overpower their rulers. This, however, is a risk that we are content to take. We will now proceed to show you that we are come here in the interest of our empire, and that we shall say what we are now going to say, for the preservation of your country; as we would fain exercise that empire over you without trouble, and see you preserved for the good of us both.'

Melians.—'And how, pray, could it turn out as good for us to serve as for you to rule?'

Athenians.—'Because you would have the advantage of submitting before suffering the worst, and we should gain by not destroying you.'

---

[1] That is, the Spartans—the "Mede" earlier in the sentence refers to the Persians.

Melians.—'So that you would not consent to our being neutral, friends instead of enemies, but allies of neither side.'

Athenians.—'No; for your hostility cannot so much hurt us as your friendship will be an argument to our subjects of our weakness, and your enmity of our power.'

Melians.—'Is that your subjects' idea of equity, to put those who have nothing to do with you in the same category with peoples that are most of them your own colonists, and some conquered rebels?'

Athenians.—'As far as right goes they think one has as much of it as the other, and that if any maintain their independence it is because they are strong, and that if we do not molest them it is because we are afraid; so that besides extending our empire we should gain in security by your subjection; the fact that you are islanders and weaker than others rendering it all the more important that you should not succeed in baffling the masters of the sea.'

Melians.—'But do you consider that there is no security in the policy which we indicate? For here again if you debar us from talking about justice and invite us to obey your interest, we also must explain ours, and try to persuade you, if the two happen to coincide. How can you avoid making enemies of all existing neutrals who shall look at our case and conclude from it that one day or another you will attack them? And what is this but to make greater the enemies that you have already, and to force others to become so who would otherwise have never thought of it?'

Athenians.—'Why, the fact is that continentals generally give us but little alarm; the liberty which they enjoy will long prevent their taking precautions against us; it is rather islanders like yourselves, outside our empire, and subjects smarting under the yoke, who would be the most likely to take a rash step and lead themselves and us into obvious danger.'

Melians.—'Well then, if you risk so much to retain your empire, and your subjects to get rid of it, it were surely great baseness and cowardice in us who are still free not to try everything that can be tried, before submitting to your yoke.'

Athenians.—'Not if you are well advised, the contest not being an equal one, with honour as the prize and shame as the penalty, but a question of self-preservation and of not resisting those who are far stronger than you are.'

Melians.—'But we know that the fortune of war is sometimes more impartial than the disproportion of numbers might lead one to suppose; to submit is to give ourselves over to despair, while action still preserves for us a hope that we may stand erect.'

Athenians.—'Hope, danger's comforter, may be indulged in by those who have abundant resources, if not without loss at all events without ruin; but its nature is to be extravagant, and those who go so far as to put their all upon the venture see it in its true colours only when they are ruined; but so long as the discovery would enable them to guard against it, it is never found wanting. Let not this be the case with you, who are weak and hang on a single turn of the scale; nor be like the vulgar, who, abandoning such security as human means may still afford, when visible hopes fail them in extremity, turn to invisible, to prophecies and oracles, and other such inventions that delude men with hopes to their destruction.'

Melians.—'You may be sure that we are as well aware as you of the difficulty of contending against your power and fortune, unless the terms be equal. But we trust that the gods may grant us fortune as good as yours, since we are just men fighting against unjust, and that what we want in power will be made up by the alliance of the Lacedæmonians, who are bound, if only for very shame, to come to the aid of their kindred. Our confidence, therefore, after all is not so utterly irrational.'

Athenians.—'When you speak of the favour of the gods, we may as fairly hope for that as yourselves; neither our pretensions nor our conduct being in any way contrary to what men believe of the gods, or practise among themselves. Of the gods we believe, and of men we know, that by a necessary law of their nature they rule wherever they can. And it is not as if we were the first to make this law, or to act upon it when made: we found it existing before us, and shall leave it to exist for ever after us; all we do is to make use of it, knowing that you and everybody else, having the same power as we have, would do the same as we do. Thus, as far as the gods are concerned, we have no fear and no reason to fear that we shall be at a disadvantage. But when we come to your notion about the Lacedæmonians, which leads you to believe that shame will make them help you, here we bless your simplicity but do not envy your folly. The Lacedæmonians, when their own interests or their country's laws are in question, are the worthiest men alive; of their conduct towards others much might be said, but no clearer idea of it could be given than by shortly saying that of all the men we know they are most conspicuous in considering what is agreeable honourable, and what is expedient just. Such a way of thinking does not promise much for the safety which you now unreasonably count upon.'

Melians.—'But it is for this very reason that we now trust to their respect for expediency to prevent them from betraying the Melians, their colonists, and thereby losing the confidence of their friends in Hellas and helping their enemies.'

Athenians.—'Then you do not adopt the view that expediency goes with security, while justice and honour cannot be followed without danger; and danger the Lacedæmonians generally court as little as possible.'

Melians.—'But we believe that they would be more likely to face even danger for our sake, and with more confidence than for others, as our nearness to Peloponnese makes it easier for them to act, and our common blood insures our fidelity.'

Athenians.—'Yes, but what an intending ally trusts to, is not the good-will of those who ask his aid, but a decided superiority of power for action; and the Lacedæmonians look to this even more than others. At least, such is their distrust of their home resources that it is only with numerous allies that they attack a neighbour; now is it likely that while we are masters of the sea they will cross over to an island?'

Melians.—'But they would have others to send. The Cretan sea is a wide one, and it is more difficult for those who command it to intercept others, than for those who wish to elude them to do so safely. And should the Lacedæmonians miscarry in this, they would fall upon your land, and upon those left of your allies whom Brasidas did not reach; and instead of places which are not yours, you will have to fight for your own country and your own confederacy.'

Athenians.—'Some diversion of the kind you speak of you may one day experience, only to learn, as others have done, that the Athenians never once yet withdrew from a siege for fear of any. But we are struck by the fact, that after saying you would consult for the safety of your country, in all this discussion you have mentioned nothing which men might trust in and think to be saved by. Your strongest arguments depend upon hope and the future, and your actual resources are too scanty, as compared with those arrayed against you, for you to come out victorious. You will therefore show great blindness of judgment, unless, after allowing us to retire, you can find some counsel more prudent than this. You will surely not be caught by that idea of disgrace, which in dangers that are disgraceful, and at the same time too plain to be mistaken, proves so fatal to mankind; since in too many cases the very men that have their eyes perfectly open to what they are rushing into, let the thing called disgrace, by the mere influence of a seductive name, lead them on to a point at which they become so enslaved by the phrase as in fact to fall wilfully into hopeless disaster, and incur disgrace more disgraceful as the companion of error, than when it comes as the result of misfortune. This, if you are well advised, you will guard against; and you will not think it dishonourable to submit to the greatest city in Hellas,[2] when it makes you the moderate offer of becoming its tributary ally, without ceasing to enjoy the country that belongs to you; nor when you have the choice given you between war and security, will you be so blinded as to choose the worse. And it is certain that those who do not yield to their equals, who keep terms with their superiors, and are moderate towards their inferiors, on the whole succeed best. Think over the matter, therefore, after our withdrawal, and reflect once again that it is for your country that you are consulting, that you have not more than one, and that upon this one deliberation depends its prosperity or ruin.'

3. What Arrangements for Living Together Best Serve the Ends for Which Men Join into Political Communities?

The defeat of Athens in the Peloponnesian War disillusioned many Athenians. In some, it raised grave doubts about the assumptions of their fellow citizens with respect to the sound forms of political association. Among the doubters was Plato. His doubts were accentuated when the citizens of Athens democratically condemned his teacher Socrates to death. His meditations on the problem of politics led him to question the very nature and basis of political life. His investigations appear in The Republic. *The dialogue pictures the debate led by Socrates. With him as participants in this section are Adimantus and Glaucon. Socrates speaks first in his interchange with Adimantus.*

---

[2] That is, Greece.

THE REPUBLIC*

Plato

The origin of the city . . . is to be found in the fact that we do not severally suffice for our own needs, but each of us lacks many things. Do you think any other principle establishes the state, [Adimantus]?

No other, said he.

As a result of this, then, one man calling in another for one service and another for another, we, being in need of many things, gather many into one place of abode as associates and helpers, and to this dwelling together we give the name city or state, do we not?

By all means.

And between one man and another there is an interchange of giving, if it so happens, and taking, because each supposes this to be better for himself.

Certainly.

Come, then, let us create a city from the beginning, in our theory. Its real creator, as it appears, will be our needs.

Obviously.

Now the first and chief of our needs is the provision of food for existence and life.

Assuredly.

The second is housing and the third is raiment and that sort of thing.

That is so.

Tell me, then, said I, how our city will suffice for the provision of all these things. Will there not be a farmer for one, and a builder, and then again a weaver? And shall we add thereto a cobbler and some other purveyor for the needs of the body?

Certainly.

The indispensable minimum of a city, then, would consist of four or five men.

Apparently.

What of this, then? Shall each of these contribute his work for the common use of all? I mean, shall the farmer, who is one, provide food for four and spend fourfold time and toil on the production of food and share it with the others, or shall he take no thought for them and provide a fourth portion of the food for himself alone in a quarter of the time and employ the other three-quarters, the one in the provision of a house, the other of a garment, the other of shoes, and not have the bother of associating with other people, but, himself for himself, mind his own affairs?

And Adimantus said, But, perhaps Socrates, the former way is easier.

It would not, by Zeus, be at all strange, said I, for now that you have

---

*Reprinted by permission of the publishers from The Loeb Classical Library, Plato's Republic ii.369b–375b, iii.415–417b, v.473b–e, trans. Paul Shorey (Cambridge, Mass.: Harvard University Press, 1930), I, 149–169, 305–313, 507–509.

mentioned it, it occurs to me myself that, to begin with, our several natures are not all alike but different. One man is naturally fitted for one task, and another for another. Don't you think so?

I do.

Again, would one man do better working at many tasks or one at one?

One at one, he said.

And, furthermore, this, I fancy, is obvious—that if one lets slip the right season, the favorable moment in any task, the work is spoiled.

Obvious.

That, I take it, is because the business will not wait upon the leisure of the workman, but the workman must attend to it as his main affair, and not as a bywork.

He must indeed.

The result, then, is that more things are produced, and better and more easily when one man performs one task according to his nature, at the right moment, and at leisure from other occupations.

By all means.

Then, Adimantus, we need more than four citizens for the provision of the things we have mentioned. For the farmer, it appears, will not make his own plow if it is to be a good one, nor his hoe, nor his other agricultural implements, nor will the builder, who also needs many, and similarly the weaver and cobbler.

True.

Carpenters, then, and smiths and many similar craftsmen, associating themselves with our hamlet, will enlarge it considerably.

Yet it still wouldn't be very large even if we should add to them neat-herds and shepherds and other herders, so that the farmers might have cattle for plowing, and the builders oxen to use with the farmers for transportation, and the weavers and the cobblers hides and fleeces for their use.

It wouldn't be a small city, either, if it had all these.

But further, said I, it is practically impossible to establish the city in a region where it will not need imports.

It is.

There will be further need, then, of those who will bring in from some other city what it requires.

There will.

And again, if our servitor goes forth empty-handed, not taking with him any of the things needed by those from whom they procure what they themselves require, he will come back with empty hands, will he not?

I think so.

Then their home production must not merely suffice for themselves but in quality and quantity meet the needs of those of whom they have need.

It must.

So our city will require more farmers and other craftsmen.

Yes, more.

And also of other ministrants who are to export and import the merchandise. These are traders, are they not?

Yes.

We shall also need traders, then.

Assuredly.

And if the trading is carried on by sea, we shall need quite a number of others who are expert in maritime business.

Quite a number.

But again, within the city itself how will they share with one another the products of their labor? This was the very purpose of our association and establishment of a state.

Obviously, he said, by buying and selling.

A market place, then, and money as a token for the purpose of exchange will be the result of this.

By all means.

If, then, the farmer or any other craftsman taking his products to the market place does not arrive at the same time with those who desire to exchange with them, is he to sit idle in the market place and lose time from his own work?

By no means, he said, but there are men who see this need and appoint themselves for this service—in well-conducted cities they are generally those who are weakest in body and those who are useless for any other task. They must wait there in the agora[1] and exchange money for goods with those who wish to sell, and goods for money with as many as desire to buy.

This need, then, said, I, creates the class of shopkeepers in our city. Or is not 'shopkeepers' the name we give to those who, planted in the agora, serve us in buying and selling, while we call those who roam from city to city merchants?

Certainly.

And there are, furthermore, I believe, other servitors who in the things of the mind are not altogether worthy of our fellowship, but whose strength of body is sufficient for toil; so they, selling the use of this strength and calling the price wages, are designated, I believe, 'wage earners,' are they not?

Certainly.

Wage earners, then, it seems, are the complement that helps to fill up the state.

I think so.

Has our city, then, Adimantus, reached its full growth, and is it complete?

Perhaps.

Where then, can justice or injustice be found in it? And along with which of the constituents that we have considered do they come into the state?

I cannot conceive, Socrates, he said, unless it be in some need that those very constituents have of one another.

Perhaps that is a good suggestion, said I. We must examine it and not hold back.

First of all, then, let us consider what will be the manner of life of men thus provided. Will they not make bread and wine and garments and shoes? And they will build themselves houses and carry on their work in summer

---

[1] The marketplace.

for the most part unclad and unshod and in winter clothed and shod sufficiently. And for their nourishment they will provide meal from their barley
and flour from their wheat, and kneading and cooking these they will serve
noble cakes and loaves on some arrangement of reeds or clean leaves. And,
reclined on rustic beds strewed with bryony and myrtle, they will feast with
their children, drinking of their wine thereto, garlanded and singing hymns
to the gods in pleasant fellowship, not begetting offspring beyond their means
lest they fall into poverty or war.

Here Glaucon broke in. No relishes apparently, he said, for the men you
describe as feasting.

True, said I, I forgot that they will also have relishes—salt, of course,
and olives and cheese, and onions and greens, the sort of things they boil in
the country, they will boil up together. But for dessert we will serve them figs
and chick-peas and beans, and they will toast myrtle berries and acorns before
the fire, washing them down with moderate potations. And so, living in peace
and health, they will probably die in old age and hand on like life to their
offspring.

And he said, If you were founding a city of pigs, Socrates, what other
fodder than this would you provide?

Why, what would you have, Glaucon? said I.

What is customary, he replied. They must recline on couches, I presume,
if they are not to be uncomfortable, and dine from tables and have dishes and
sweetmeats such as are now in use.

Good, said I. I understand. It is not merely the origin of a city, it seems,
that we are considering but the origin of a luxurious city. Perhaps that isn't
such a bad suggestion, either. For by observation of such a city it may be we
could discern the origin of justice and injustice in states. The true state I
believe to be the one we have described—the healthy state, as it were. But if it
is your pleasure that we contemplate also a fevered state, there is nothing to
hinder. For there are some, it appears, who will not be contented with this
sort of fare or with this way of life, but couches will have to be added thereto
and tables and other furniture, yes, and relishes and myrrh and incense and
girls and cakes—all sorts of all of them. And the requirements we first mentioned, houses and garments and shoes, will no longer be confined to necessities,
but we must set painting to work and embroidery, and procure gold and ivory
and similar adornments, must we not?

Yes, he said.

Then shall we not have to enlarge the city again? For that healthy state
is no longer sufficient, but we must proceed to swell out its bulk and fill it up
with a multitude of things that exceed the requirements of necessity in states,
as, for example, the entire class of huntsmen, and the imitators, many of them
occupied with figures and colors and many with music—the poets and their
assistants, rhapsodists, actors, chorus dancers, contractors—and the manufac-
turers of all kinds of articles, especially those that have to do with women's
adornment. And so we shall also want more servitors. Don't you think that
we shall need tutors, nurses wet and dry, beauty-shop ladies, barbers, and yet
again cooks and chefs? And we shall have need, further, of swineherds; there
were none of these creatures in our former city, for we had no need of them,

but in this city there will be this further need. And we shall also require other cattle in great numbers if they are to be eaten, shall we not?

Yes.

Doctors, too, are something whose services we shall be much more likely to require if we live thus than as before?

Much.

And the territory, I presume, that was then sufficient to feed the then population, from being adequate will become too small. Is that so or not?

It is.

Then we shall have to cut out a parcel of our neighbor's land if we are to have enough for pasture and plowing, and they in turn of ours if they too abandon themselves to the unlimited acquisition of wealth, disregarding the limits set by our necessary wants.

Inevitably, Socrates.

We shall go to war as the next step, Glaucon—or what will happen?

What you say, he said.

And we are not yet to speak, said I, of any evil or good effect of war, but only to affirm that we have further discovered the origin of war, namely, from those things from which the greatest disasters, public and private, come to states when they come.

Certainly.

Then, my friend, we must still further enlarge our city by no small increment, but by a whole army, that will march forth and fight it out with assailants in defense of all our wealth and the luxuries we have just described.

How so? he said. Are the citizens themselves not sufficient for that?

Not if you, said I, and we all were right in the admission we made when we were molding our city. We surely agreed, if you remember, that it is impossible for one man to do the work of many arts well.

True, he said.

Well, then, said I, don't you think that the business of fighting is an art and a profession?

It is indeed, he said.

Should our concern be greater, then, for the cobbler's art than for the art of war?

By no means.

Can we suppose, then, that while we were at pains to prevent the cobbler from attempting to be at the same time a farmer, a weaver, or a builder instead of just a cobbler, to the end that we might have the cobbler's business well done, and similarly assigned to each and every one man one occupation, for which he was fit and naturally adapted and at which he was to work all his days, at leisure from other pursuits and not letting slip the right moments for doing the work well, and that yet we are in doubt whether the right accomplishment of the business of war is not of supreme moment? It is so easy that a man who is cultivating the soil will be at the same time a soldier and one who is practicing cobbling or any other trade, though no man in the world could make himself a competent expert at checkers or dice who did not practice that and nothing else from childhood but treated it as an occasional business? And are we to believe that a man who takes in hand a shield or any other instrument of war springs up on that very day a competent combatant in heavy armor or in any other form of warfare—though no other tool will make a man be an artist or an athlete by his taking it in hand, nor will it be of any service to those who have neither acquired the science of it nor sufficiently practiced themselves in its use?

Great indeed, he said, would be the value of tools in that case!

Then, said I, in the same degree that the task of our guardians is the greatest of all, it would require more leisure than any other business and the greatest science and training.

I think so, said he.

Does it not also require a nature adapted to that very pursuit?

Of course.

It becomes our task, then, it seems, if we are able, to select which and what kind of natures are suited for the guardianship of a state.

Yes, ours.

Upon my word, said I, it is no light task that we have taken upon ourselves. But we must not faint so far as our strength allows.

No, we mustn't.

Do you think, said I, that there is any difference between the nature of a well-bred hound for this watchdog's work and that of a wellborn lad?

What point do you have in mind?

I mean that each of them be keen of perception, quick in pursuit of what it has apprehended, and strong too if it has to fight it out with its captive.

Of course.

And will a creature be ready to be brave that is not high-spirited, whether horse or dog or anything else? Have you never observed what an irresistible and invincible thing is spirit, the presence of which makes every soul in the face of everything fearless and unconquerable?

I have.

The physical qualities of the guardian, then, are obvious.

Yes.

And also those of his soul, namely that he must be of high spirit.

Socrates later proceeds to raise the question of how the ordinary citizens can be persuaded to submit to the rule of the wise guardians. He suggests that they be told a tale.

While all of you in the city are brothers, we will say in our tale, yet God in fashioning those of you who are fitted to hold rule mingled gold in their generation, for which reason they are the most precious—but in the helpers silver, and iron and brass in the farmers and other craftsmen. And as you are all akin, though for the most part you will breed your kinds, it may sometimes happen that a golden father would beget a silver son and that a golden offspring would come from a silver sire and that the rest would in like manner be born of one another. So that the first and chief injunction that the god lays upon the rulers is that of nothing else are they to be such careful guardians and so intently observant of the intermixing of these metals in the souls of their offspring, and if sons are born to them with an infusion of brass or iron they shall by no means give way to pity in their treatment of them, but shall assign to each the status due to his nature and thrust them out among the artisans or the farmers. And again, if from these there are born sons with unexpected gold or silver in their composition they shall honor such and bid them go up higher, some to the office of guardian, some to the assistantship, alleging that there is an oracle that the state shall then be overthrown when the man of iron or brass is its guardian. Do you see any way of getting them to believe this tale?

No, not these themselves, he said, but I do their sons and successors and the rest of mankind who come after.

Well, said I, even that would have a good effect in making them more inclined to care for the state and one another. For I think I apprehend your meaning. And this shall fall out as tradition guides. But let us arm these sons of earth and conduct them under the leadership of their rulers. And when they have arrived they must look out for the fairest site in the city for their encampment, a position from which they could best hold down rebellion against the laws from within and repel aggression from without as of a wolf against the fold. And after they have encamped and sacrificed to the proper gods they must make their lairs, must they not?

Yes, he said.

And these must be of a character to keep out the cold in winter and be sufficient in summer?

Of course. For I presume you are speaking of their houses.

Yes, said I, the houses of soldiers, not of money-makers.

What distinction do you intend by that? he said.

I will try to tell you, I said. It is surely the most monstrous and shameful thing in the world for shepherds to breed the dogs who are to help them with their flocks in such wise and of such a nature that from indiscipline or hunger or some other evil condition the dogs themselves shall attack the sheep and injure them and be likened to wolves instead of dogs.

A terrible thing, indeed, he said.

Must we not then guard by every means in our power against our helpers' treating the citizens in any such way and, because they are the stronger, converting themselves from benign assistants into savage masters?

We must, he said.

And would they not have been provided with the chief safeguard if their education has really been a good one?

But surely it has, he said.

That, said I, dear Glaucon, we may not properly affirm, but what we were just now saying we may, that they must have the right education, whatever it is, if they are to have what will do most to make them gentle to one another and to their charges.

That is right, he said.

In addition, moreover, to such an education a thoughtful man would affirm that their houses and the possessions provided for them ought to be such as not to interfere with the best performance of their own work as guardians and not to incite them to wrong the other citizens.

He will rightly affirm that.

Consider then, said I, whether, if that is to be their character, their habitations and ways of life must not be something after this fashion. In the first place, none must possess any private property save the indispensable. Secondly, none must have any habitation or treasure house which is not open for all to enter at will. Their food, in such quantities as are needful for athletes of war sober and brave, they must receive as an agreed stipend from the other citizens as the wages of their guardianship, so measured that there shall be neither superfluity at the end of the year nor any lack. And resorting to a common mess like soldiers on campaign they will live together. Gold and silver, we will tell them, they have of the divine quality from the gods always in their souls, and they have no need of the metal of men nor does holiness suffer them to mingle and contaminate that heavenly possession with the acquisition of mortal gold, since many impious deeds have been done about the coin of the multitude, while that which dwells within them is unsullied. But for these only of all the dwellers in the city it is not lawful to handle gold and silver and to touch them nor yet to come under the same roof with them, nor to hang them as ornaments on their limbs nor to drink from silver and gold. So living they would save themselves and save their city. But whenever they shall acquire for themselves land of their own and houses and coin, they will be householders and farmers instead of guardians, and will be transformed from the helpers of their fellow citizens to their enemies and masters, and so in hating and being hated, plotting and being plotted against, they will pass their days without—and then even then laying the course of near shipwreck for themselves and the state. For all these reasons, said I, let us declare that such must be the provision for our guardians in lodging and other respects and so legislate. Shall we not?

By all means, said Glaucon.

Having earlier in The Republic *sought to establish the nature of knowledge and its importance for the just governing of states,*[2] *Socrates then raises the question of the readiest means to bring about their right governing.*

. . . We must try to discover and point out what it is that is now badly managed in our cities, and that prevents them from being so governed, and what is the smallest change that would bring a state to this manner of government, preferably a change in one thing, if not, then in two, and, failing that, the fewest possible in number and the slightest in potency.

By all means, he said.

There is one change, then, said I, which I think that we can show would bring about the desired transformation. It is not a slight or an easy thing but it is possible.

What it that? said he.

I am on the very verge, said I, of what we likened to the greatest wave of paradox. But say it I will, even if, to keep the figure, it is likely to wash us away on billows of laughter and scorn. Listen.

I am all attention, he said.

---

[2] See above, pp. 56–61.

Unless, said I, either philosophers become kings in our states or those whom we now call our kings and rulers take to the pursuit of philosophy seriously and adequately, and there is a conjunction of these two things, political power and philosophical intelligence, while the motley horde of the natures who at present pursue either apart from the other are compulsorily excluded, there can be no cessation of troubles, dear Glaucon, for our states, nor, I fancy, for the human race either. Nor, until this happens, will this constitution which we have been expounding in theory ever be put into practice within the limits of possibility and see the light of the sun. But this is the thing that has made me so long shrink from speaking out, because I saw that it would be a very paradoxical saying. For it is not easy to see that there is no other way of happiness either for private or public life. . . .

4. What Is the Nature of Goodness in Men?

Aristotle's work on politics again presents him as the "master of those who know." But in politics as in other matters, for Aristotle knowing was not the same thing that it was for Plato. He believed that the route to the knowledge of politics and of other realities lay through the analysis of every-day experience. While Plato wrote of an ideal republic, Aristotle examined real men and real states and considered what made them good or bad. For it is evident that good states need good men.

NICHOMACHEAN ETHICS*

Aristotle

. . . The virtue of a man . . . will be the state of character which makes a man good and which makes him do his own work well.

How this is to happen . . . will be made plain . . . by the following consideration of the specific nature of virtue. In everything that is continuous and divisible it is possible to take more, less, or an equal amount, and that either in terms of the thing itself or relatively to us; and the equal is an intermediate between excess and defect. By the intermediate in the object I mean that which is equidistant from each of the extremes, which is one and the same for all men; by the intermediate relatively to us that which is neither too much nor too little—and this is not one, nor the same for all. For instance, if ten is many and two is few, six is the intermediate, taken in terms of the object; for it exceeds and is exceeded by an equal amount; this is intermediate according to arithmetical proportion. But the intermediate relatively to us is not to be taken so; if ten pounds are too much for a particular person to eat and two too little, it does not follow that the trainer will order six pounds for this also is perhaps too much for the person who is to take it, or too little

---

* Reprinted by permission of the publishers from *The Works of Aristotle*, Vol. IX, *Ethica Nichomachea* 1106a, 22–1109a, 29, ed. and trans. W. D. Ross (Oxford: The Clarendon Press, 1915, reprinted 1954).

... The same is true of running and wrestling. Thus a master of any art avoids excess and defect, but seeks the intermediate and chooses this—the intermediate not in the object but relatively to us.

If it is thus, then, that every art does its work well—by looking to the intermediate and judging its works by this standard (so that we often say of good works of art that it is not possible either to take away or to add anything, implying that excess and defect destroy the goodness of works of art, while the mean perserves it; and good artists, as we say, look to this in their work), and if, further, virtue is more exact and better than any art, as nature also is, then virtue must have the quality of aiming at the intermediate. I mean moral virtue; for it is this that is concerned with passions and actions, and in these there is excess, defect, and the intermediate. For instance, both fear and confidence and appetite and anger and pity and in general pleasure and pain may be felt both too much and too little, and in both cases not well; but to feel them at the right times, with reference to the right objects, towards the right people, with the right motive, and in the right way, is what is both intermediate and best, and this is characteristic of virtue. Similarly with regard to actions also there is excess, defect, and intermediate. Now virtue is concerned with passions and actions, in which excess is a form of failure, and so is defect, while the intermediate is praised and is a form of success; and being praised and being successful are both characteristic of virtue. Therefore virtue is a kind of mean, since, as we have seen, it aims at what is intermediate.[1]

Again, it is possible to fail in many ways (for evil belongs to the class of the unlimited, . . . and good to that of the limited), while to succeed is possible only in one way (for which reason also one is easy and the other difficult—to miss the mark easy, to hit it difficult); for these reasons also, then, excess and defect are characteristic of vice, and the mean of virtue;

For men are good in but one way, but bad in many.

Virtue, then, is a state of character concerned with choice, lying in a mean, i.e. the mean relative to us, this being determined by a rational principle, and by that principle by which the man of practical wisdom would determine it. Now it is a mean between two vices, that which depends on excess and that which depends on defect; and again it is a mean because the vices respectively fall short of or exceed what is right in both passions and actions, while virtue both finds and chooses that which is intermediate. Hence in respect of its substance and the definition which states its essence virtue is a mean, with regard to what is best and right an extreme.

But not every action nor every passion admits of a mean; for some have names that already imply badness, e.g. spite, shamelessness, envy, and in the case of actions adultery, theft, murder; for all of these and suchlike things imply by their names that they are themselves bad, and not the excesses or deficiencies of them. It is not possible, then, ever to be right with regard to them; one must always be wrong. Nor does goodness or badness with regard to such things depend on committing adultery with the right woman, at the right time, and in the right way, but simply to do any of them is to do wrong. It would be equally absurd, then, to expect that in unjust, cowardly, and

---

[1] Compare Aristotle's conception of virtue with Jesus' conception of blessedness, above, pp. 35–36.

voluptuous action there should be a mean, an excess, and a deficiency; for at that rate there would be a mean of excess and of deficiency, an excess of excess, and a deficiency of deficiency. But as there is no excess and deficiency of temperance and courage because what is intermediate is in a sense an extreme, so too of the actions we have mentioned there is no mean nor any excess and deficiency, but however they are done they are wrong; for in general there is neither a mean of excess and deficiency, nor excess and deficiency of a mean.

We must, however, not only make this general statement, but also apply it to the individual facts. For among statements about conduct those which are general apply more widely, but those which are particular are more genuine, since conduct has to do with individual cases, and our statements must harmonize with the facts in these cases. We may take these cases from our table. With regard to feelings of fear and confidence courage is the mean; of the people who exceed, he who exceeds in fearlessness has no name (many of the states have no name), while the man who exceeds in confidence is rash, and he who exceeds in fear and falls short in confidence is a coward. With regard to pleasures and pains—not all of them, and not so much with regard to the pains—the mean is temperance, the excess is self-indulgence. Persons deficient with regard to the pleasures are not often found; hence such persons have received no name. But let us call them 'insensible.'

With regard to giving and taking of money the mean is liberality, the excess and defect prodigality and meanness. In these actions people exceed and fall short in contrary ways; the prodigal exceeds in spending and falls short in taking, while the mean man exceeds in taking and falls short in spending. (At present we are giving a mere outline or summary, and are satisfied with this; later these states will be more exactly determined.) With regard to money there are also other dispositions—a mean, magnificence (for the magnificent man differs from the liberal man; the former deals with large sums, the latter with small ones), an excess, tastelessness and vulgarity, and a deficiency, niggardliness; these differ from the states opposed to liberality, and the mode of their difference will be stated later.

With regard to honor and dishonor the mean is proper pride, the excess is known as a sort of 'empty vanity,' and the deficiency is undue humility; and as we said liberality was related to magnificence, differing from it by dealing with small sums, so there is a state similarly related to proper pride, being concerned with small honors while that is concerned with great. For it is possible to desire honor as one ought, and more than one ought, and less, and the man who falls short unambitious, while the intermediate person has no name. The dispositions are also nameless, except that that of the ambitious man is called ambition. Hence the people who are at the extremes lay claim to the middle place; and we ourselves sometimes call the intermediate person ambitious and sometimes unambitious, and sometimes praise the ambitious man and sometimes the unambitious . . .

With regard to anger also there is an excess, a deficiency, and a mean. Although they can scarcely be said to have names, yet since we call the intermediate person good-tempered let us call the mean good temper; of the persons at the extremes let the one who exceeds be called irascible, and his vice irascibility, and the man who falls short an inirascible sort of person, and the deficiency inirascibility.

There are also three other means, which have a certain likeness to one another, but differ from one another: for they are all concerned with intercourse in words and actions, but differ in that one is concerned with truth in this sphere, the other two with pleasantness; and of this one kind is exhibited in giving amusement, the other in all the circumstances of life. We must therefore speak of these too, that we may the better see that in all things the mean is praiseworthy, and the extremes neither praiseworthy nor right, but worthy of blame. Now most of these states also have no names, but we must try, as in the other cases, to invent names ourselves so that we may be clear and easy to follow. With regard to truth, then, the intermediate is a truthful sort of person and the mean may be called truthfulness, while the pretence which exaggerates is boastfulness and the person characterized by it a boaster, and that which understates is mock modesty and the person characterized by it mock-modest. With regard to pleasantness in the giving of amusement the intermediate person is ready-witted and the disposition ready wit, the excess is buffoonery and the person characterized by it a buffoon, while the man who falls short is a sort of boor and his state is boorishness. With regard to the remaining kind of pleasantness, that which is exhibited in life in general, the man who is pleasant in the right way is friendly and the mean is friendliness, while the man who exceeds is an obsequious person if he has no end in view, a flatterer if he is aiming at his own advantage, and the man who falls short and is unpleasant in all circumstances is a quarrelsome and surly sort of person.

There are also means in the passions and concerned with the passions; since shame is not a virtue, and yet praise is extended to the modest man. For even in these matters one man is said to be intermediate, and another to exceed, as for instance the bashful man who is ashamed of everything; while he who falls short or is not ashamed of anything at all is shameless, and the intermediate person is modest. Righteous indignation is a mean between envy and spite, and these states are concerned with the pain and pleasure that are felt at the fortunes of our neighbors; the man who is characterized by righteous indignation is pained at undeserved good fortune, the envious man, going beyond him, is pained at all good fortune, and the spiteful man falls so far short of being pained that he even rejoices. . . .

There are three kinds of disposition, then, two of them vices, involving excess and deficiency respectively, and one a virtue, viz. the mean, and all are in a sense opposed to all; for the extreme states are contrary both to the intermediate state and to each other, and the intermediate to the extremes; as the equal is greater relatively to the less, less relatively to the greater, so the middle states are excessive relatively to the deficiencies, deficient relatively to the excesses, both in passions and in actions. For the brave man appears rash relatively to the coward, and cowardly relatively to the rash man; and similarly the temperate man appears self-indulgent relatively to the insensible man, insensible relatively to the self-indulgent, and the liberal man prodigal relatively to the mean man, mean relatively to the prodigal. Hence also the people at the extremes push the intermediate man each over to the other, and the brave man is called rash by the coward, cowardly by the rash man, and correspondingly in the other cases.

These states being thus opposed to one another, the greatest contrariety is that of the extremes to each other, rather than to the intermediate; for these are further from each other than from the intermediate, as the great is further from the small and the small from the great than both are from the equal. Again, to the intermediate some extremes show a certain likeness, as that of rashness to courage and that of prodigality to liberality; but the extremes show the greatest unlikeness to each other; no contraries are defined as the things that are furthest from each other, so that things that are further apart are more contrary.

To the mean in some cases the deficiency, in some the excess is more opposed; e.g., it is not rashness, which is an excess, but cowardice, which is a deficiency, that is more opposed to courage, and not insensibility, which is a deficiency, but self-indulgence, which is an excess, that is more opposed to temperence. This happens from two reasons, one being drawn from the thing itself; for because one extreme is nearer and liker to the intermediate, we oppose not this but rather its contrary to the intermediate. E.g., since rashness is thought liker and nearer to courage, and cowardice more unlike, we oppose rather the latter to courage; for things that are further from the intermediate are thought more contrary to it. This, then, is one cause, drawn from the thing itself; another is drawn from ourselves; for the things to which we ourselves more naturally tend to seem more contrary to the intermediate. For instance, we ourselves tend more naturally to pleasures, and hence are more easily carried away towards self-indulgence than towards propriety. We describe as contrary to the mean, then, rather the directions in which we more often go to great length; and therefore self-indulgence, which is an excess, is the more contrary to temperance.

That moral virtue is a mean, then, and in what sense it is so, and that it is a mean between two vices, the one involving excess, the other deficiency, and that it is such because its character is to aim at what is intermediate in passions and in actions, has been sufficiently stated. Hence also it is no easy task to be good. For in everything it is no easy task to find the middle, e.g., to find the middle of a circle is not for every one but for him who knows; so, too, any one can get angry—that is easy—or give or spend money; but to do this to the right person, to the right extent, at the right time, with the right motive, and in the right way, *that* is not for everyone, nor is it easy; wherefore goodness is both rare and laudable and noble.

5. What Are the Natural Forms of Human Association?

Having established his view of the nature of goodness in men in the Nicomachean Ethics, *Aristotle went on to deal with questions about a special characteristic of men: man, the "political animal," always lives in association with other men. There are, however, a variety of human associations. Some, like the family, are universal; others, like slavery and the* polis, *are not uni-*

versal. Inquiry into the forms of human association, their origin, and their justification was therefore the necessary basis of the study of politics.

POLITICS*

Aristotle

Every state is a community of some kind, and every community is established with a view to some good; for mankind always act in order to obtain that which they think good. But, if all communities aim at some good, the state or political community, which is the highest of all, and which embraces all the rest, aims at good in a greater degree than any other, and at the highest good.

Some people think that the qualifications of a statesman, king, householder, and master are the same, and that they differ, not in kind, but only in the number of their subjects. For example, the ruler over a few is called a master; over more, the manager of a household; over a still larger number, a statesman or king, as if there were no difference between a great household and a small state. The distinction which is made between the king and the statesman is as follows: When the government is personal, the ruler is a king; when, according to the rules of the political science, the citizens rule and are ruled in turn, then he is called a statesman.

But all this is a mistake; for governments differ in kind, as will be evident to any one who considers the matter according to the method which has hitherto guided us. As in other departments of science, so in politics, the compound should always be resolved into the simple elements or least parts of the whole. We must therefore look at the elements of which the state is composed, in order that we may see in what the different kinds of rule differ from one another, and whether any scientific result can be attained about each one of them.

He who thus considers things in their first growth and origin, whether a state or anything else, will obtain the clearest view of them. In the first place there must be a union of those who cannot exist without each other; namely, of male and female, that the race may continue (and this is a union which is formed, not of deliberate purpose, but because, in common with other animals and with plants, mankind have a natural desire to leave behind them an image of themselves), and of natural ruler and subject, that both may be preserved. For that which can foresee by the exercise of mind is by nature intended to be lord and master, and that which can with its body give effect to such foresight is a subject, and by nature a slave; hence master and slave have the same interest. Now nature has distinguished between the female and the slave. For she is not niggardly, like the smith who fashions the Delphian knife for many uses; she makes each thing for a single use, and every instrument is best made when intended for one and not for many uses. But among barbarians no

* Reprinted by permission of the publishers from *The Works of Aristotle—Politics* 1252a–1253a; 1253b, 15–1255a, 3; 1274b, 31–1275b, 21, ed. W. D. Ross, trans. Benjamin Jowett (Oxford: The Clarendon Press, 1921, revised).

distinction is made between women and slaves, because there is no natural ruler among them: they are a community of slaves, male and female. Wherefore the poets say,—

It is meet that Hellenes should rule over barbarians';[1]

as if they thought that the barbarian and the slave were by nature one.

Out of these two relationships between man and woman, master and slave, the first thing to arise is the family, and Hesiod is right when he says,—

'First house and wife and an ox for the plough,'[2]

for the ox is the poor man's slave. The family is the association established by nature for the supply of men's everyday wants . . . but when several families are united, and the association aims at something more than the supply of daily needs, the first society to be formed is the village. And the most natural form of the village appears to be that of a colony from the family, composed of the children and grandchildren, who are said to be 'suckled with the same milk.' And this is the reason why Hellenic states were originally governed by kings; because the Hellenes were under royal rule before they came together, as the barbarians still are. Every family is ruled by the eldest, and therefore in the colonies of the family the kingly form of government prevailed because they were of the same blood. As Homer says:

'Each one gives law to his children and to his wives.'[3]

For they lived dispersedly, as was the manner in ancient times. Wherefore men say that the Gods have a king, because they themselves either are or were in ancient times under the rule of a king. For they imagine, not only the forms of the Gods, but their ways of life to be like their own.

When several villages are united in a single complete community, large enough to be nearly or quite self-sufficing, the state comes into existence, originating in the bare needs of life, and continuing in existence for the sake of a good life. And therefore, if the earlier forms of society are natural, so is the state, for it is the end of them, and the nature of a thing is its end. For what each thing is when fully developed, we call its nature, whether we are speaking of a man, a horse, or a family. Besides, the final cause and end of a thing is the best, and to be self-sufficing is the end and the best.

Hence it is evident that the state is a creation of nature, and that man is by nature a political animal.[4] And he who by nature and not by mere accident is without a state, is either a bad man or above humanity; he is like the

'Tribeless, lawless, heartless one,'[5]

whom Homer denounces—the natural outcast is forthwith a lover of war; he may be compared to an isolated piece at [checkers].[6]

Now, that man is more of a political animal than bees or any other gregarious animals is evident. Nature, as we often say, makes nothing in vain,

---

[1] Euripides *Iphigenaea in Aulis* 1400.
[2] *Works and Days* 405.
[3] *Odyssey* ix.114.
[4] The word "politics" comes to us from the Greek word *polis*, "city." For Aristotle, therefore, "politics" and "state" usually referred to the city. In his discussion of the interactions which comprise the state in the sections to be considered later, however, he occasionally employed these terms in reference to units larger than the city.
[5] *Iliad* ix.63.
[6] The translator's word "draughts" has here been changed to "checkers."

and man is the only animal whom she has endowed with the gift of speech. And whereas mere voice is but an indication of pleasure or pain, and is therefore found in other animals (for their nature attains to the perception of pleasure and pain and the intimation of them to one another, and no further), the power of speech is intended to set forth the expedient and inexpedient, and therefore likewise the just and the unjust. And it is a characteristic of man that he alone has any sense of good and evil, of just and unjust, and the like, and the association of living beings who have this sense makes a family and a state.

Further, the state is by nature clearly prior to the family and to the individual, since the whole is of necessity prior to the part; for example, if the whole body be destroyed, there will be no foot or hand, except in an equivocal sense, as we might speak of a stone hand; for when destroyed the hand will be no better than that. But things are defined by their working and power; and we ought not to say that they are the same when they no longer have their proper quality, but only that they have the same name. The proof that the state is a creation of nature and prior to the individual is that the individual, when isolated, is not self-sufficing; and therefore he is like a part in relation to the whole. But he who is unable to live in society, or who has no need because he is sufficient for himself, must be either a beast or a god: he is no part of a state. A social instinct is implanted in all men by nature, and yet he who first founded the state was the greatest of benefactors. For man, when perfected, is the best of animals, but, when separated from law and justice, he is the worst of all; since armed injustice is the more dangerous, and he is equipped at birth with arms, meant to be used by intelligence and virtue, which he may use for the worst ends. Wherefore, if he have not virtue, he is the most unholy and the most savage of animals, and the most full of lust and gluttony. But justice is the bond of men in states, for the administration of justice, which is the determination of what is just, is the principle of order in political society.

Aristotle then proceeded to deal with a form of association very common in his day among Greeks.

Let us . . . speak of master and slave, looking to the needs of practical life and also seeking to attain some better theory of their relation than exists at present. For some are of opinion that the rule of a master is a science, and that the management of a household, and the mastership of slaves, and the political and royal rule, . . . are all the same. Others affirm that the rule of a master over slaves is contrary to nature, and that the distinction between slave and freeman exists by law only, and not by nature; and being an interference with nature is therefore unjust.

Property is a part of the household, and the art of acquiring property is a part of the art of managing the household; for no man can live well, or indeed live at all, unless he be provided with necessaries. And as in the arts which have a definite sphere the workers must have their own proper instruments for the accomplishment of their work, so it is in the management of a household. Now instruments are of various sorts; some are living, others lifeless; in the rudder, the pilot of a ship has a lifeless, in the lookout man, a living instrument; for in the arts the servant is a kind of instrument. Thus, too, a possession is an instrument for maintaining life. And so, in the arrangement of the family, a slave is a living possession, and the property a number of such instruments; and the servant is himself an instrument which takes precedence of all other instruments. For if every instrument could accomplish its own work, obeying or anticipating the will of others . . . —if the shuttle would weave and the plectrum touch the lyre without a hand to guide them, chief workmen would not want servants, nor masters slaves. Here, however, another distinction must be drawn: the instruments commonly so called are instruments of production, whilst a possession is an instrument of action. The shuttle, for example, is not only of use; but something else is made by it, whereas of a garment or of a bed there is only the use. Further, as production and action are different in kind, and both require instruments, the instruments which they employ must likewise differ in kind. But life is action and not production, and therefore the slave is a minister of action. Again, a possession is spoken of as a part is spoken of; for the part is not only a part of something else, but wholly belongs to it; and this is also true of a possession. The master is only the master of the slave; he does not belong to him, whereas the slave is not only the slave of his master, but wholly belongs to him. Hence we see what is the nature and office of a slave; he who is by nature not his own but another's man, is by nature a slave; and he may be said to be another's man who, being a human being, is also a possession. And a possession may be defined as an instrument of action, separable from the possessor.

But is there any one thus intended by nature to be a slave, and for whom such a condition is expedient and right, or rather is not all slavery a violation of nature?

There is no difficulty in answering this question, on the grounds both of reason and of fact. For that some should rule and others be ruled is a thing not only necessary, but expedient; from the hour of their birth, some are marked out for subjection, other for rule.

And there are many kinds both of rulers and subjects (and that rule is better which is exercised over better subjects—for example, to rule over men is better than to rule over wild beasts; for the work is better which is executed by better workmen, and where one man rules and another is ruled, they may be said to have a work); for in all things which form a composite whole and which are made up of parts, whether continuous or discrete, a distinction between the ruling and the subject element comes to light. Such a duality exists in living creatures, but not in them only; it originates in the constitution of the universe; even in things which have no life there is a ruling principle, as in a musical mode. But we are wandering from the subject. We will therefore restrict ourselves to the living creature, which, in the first place, consists of soul and body: and of these two, the one is by nature the ruler, and the other the subject. But then we must look for the intentions of nature in things which retain their nature, and not in things which are corrupted. And therefore we must study the man who is in the most perfect state both of body and soul, for in him we shall see the true relation of the two; although in bad or corrupted natures the body will often appear to rule over the soul, because they are in an evil and unnatural condition. At all events we may firstly observe in living creatures both a despotical and a constitutional rule, whereas the intellect rules the appetites with a constitutional and royal rule. And it is clear that the rule of the soul over the body, and of the mind and the rational element over the passionate, is natural and expedient; whereas the equality of the two or the rule of the inferior is always hurtful. The same holds good of animals in relation to men; for tame animals have a better nature than wild, and all tame animals are better off when they are ruled by man; for then they are preserved. Again, the male is by nature superior, and the female inferior; and the one rules, and the other is ruled; this principle, of necessity, extends to all mankind. Where then there is such a difference as that between soul and body, or between men and animals (as in the case of those whose business is to use their body, and who can do nothing better), the lower sort are by nature slaves, and it is better for them as for all inferiors that they should be under the rule of a master. For he who can be, and therefore is, another's, and he who participates in rational principle enough to apprehend, but not to have, such a principle, is a slave by nature. Whereas the lower animals cannot even apprehend a principle; they obey their instincts. And indeed the use made of slaves and of tame animals is not very different; for both with their bodies minister to the needs of life. Nature would like to distinguish between the bodies of freemen and slaves, making the one strong for servile labour, the other upright, and although useless for such services, useful for political life in the arts both of war and peace. But the opposite often happens—that some have the souls and others have the bodies of freemen. And doubtless if men differed from one another in the mere forms of their bodies as much as the statues of gods do from men, all would acknowledge that the inferior class should be slaves of the superior. And if this is true of the body, how much more just that a similar distinction should exist in the soul? but the beauty of the body is seen, whereas the beauty of the soul is not seen. It is clear, then, that some men are by nature free, and others slaves, and that for these latter slavery is both expedient and right.

Later, Aristotle turned to the question of the nature and the differing forms of the state. Although in his day the Greek city-state was in the process of being superseded by the great empire of his own former pupil Alexander, he gave no consideration to the latter type of political structure, but only to the former.

He who would inquire into the essence and attributes of various kinds of government must first of all determine 'What is a state?' At present this is a disputed question. Some say that the state has done a certain act; others, no, not the state, but the oligarchy or the tyrant. And the legislator or statesman is concerned entirely with the state; a constitution or government being an arrangement of the inhabitants of a state. But a state is composite, like any other whole made up of many parts;—these are the citizens, who compose it. It is evident, therefore, that we must begin by asking, Who is the citizen, and what is the meaning of the term? For here again there may be a difference of opinion. He who is a citizen in a democracy will often not be a citizen in an oligarchy. Leaving out of consideration those who have been made citizens, or who have obtained the name of citizen in any other accidental manner, we may say, first, that a citizen is not a citizen because he lives in a certain place, for resident aliens and slaves share in the place; nor is he a citizen who has no legal right except that of suing and being sued; for this right may be enjoyed under the provisions of a treaty. Nay, resident aliens in many places do not possess even such rights completely, for they are obliged to have a patron, so that they do but imperfectly participate in citizenship, and we call them citizens only in a qualified sense, as we might apply the term to children who are too young to be on the register, or to old men who have been relieved from state duties. Of these we do not say quite simply that they are citizens, but add in the one case that they are not of age, and in the other, that they are past the age, or something of that sort; the precise expression is immaterial, for our meaning is clear. Similar difficulties to those which I have mentioned may be raised and answered about deprived citizens and about exiles. But the citizen whom we are seeking to define is a citizen in the strictest sense, against whom no such exception can be taken, and his special characteristic is that he shares in the administration of justice, and in offices. Now of offices some are discontinuous, and the same persons are not allowed to hold them twice, or can only hold them after a fixed interval; others have no limit of time,—for example, the office of dicast or ecclesiast.[7] It may, indeed, be argued that these are not magistrates at all, and that their functions give them no share in the government. But surely it is ridiculous to say that those who have the supreme power do not govern. Let us not dwell further upon this, which is a purely verbal question; what we want is a common term including both dicast and ecclesiast. Let us, for the sake of distinction, call it 'indefinite office,' and we will assume that those who share in such office are citizens. This is the most comprehensive definition of a citizen, and best suits all those who are generally so called.

But we must not forget that things of which the underlying principles differ in kind, one of them being first, another second, another third, have, when regarded in this relation, nothing or hardly anything, worth mentioning in common. Now we see that governments differ in kind, and that some of them are prior and that others are posterior; those which are faulty or perverted are necessarily posterior to those which are perfect. (What we mean by perversion will be hereafter explained.) The citizen then of necessity differs under each form of government; and our definition is best adapted to the citizen of a democracy; but not necessarily to other states. For in some states the people are not acknowledged, nor have they any regular assembly, but only extraordinary ones; and suits are distributed by sections among the magistrates. At Lacedaemon, for instance, the Ephors[8] determine suits about contracts, which they distribute among themselves, while the elders are judges of homicide, and other causes are decided by other magistrates. A similar principle prevails at Carthage; there certain magistrates decide all causes. We may, indeed, modify our definition of the citizen so as to include these states. In them it is the holder of a definite, not of an indefinite office, who legislates and

---

[7] "Dicasts" were members of the Athenian law courts, where they combined the modern functions of judge and jury. The "ecclesiast" was a member of the assembly of all the citizens.
[8] Members of the board of five officials who took charge of much of Sparta's public business.

judges, and to some or all such holders of definite offices is reserved the right of deliberating or judging about some things or about all things. The conception of the citizen now begins to clear up.

He who has the power to take part in the deliberative or judicial administration of any state is said by us to be a citizen of that state; and, speaking generally, a state is a body of citizens sufficing for the purposes of life.

*　　*　　*

Having determined these questions [the proper definition of a citizen], we have next to consider whether there is only one form of government or many, and if many, what they are, and how many, and what are the differences between them.

A constitution is the arrangement of magistracies in a state, especially of the highest of all. The government is everywhere sovereign in the state, and the constitution is in fact the government. For example, in democracies the people are supreme, but in oligarchies, the few; and, therefore, we say that these two forms of government also are different: and so in other cases.

First, let us consider what is the purpose of a state, and how many forms of government there are by which human society is regulated. We have already said, in the first part of this treatise, when discussing household management and the rule of a master, that man is by nature a political animal. And therefore, men, even when they do not require one another's help, desire to live together; not but that they are also brought together by their common interests in proportion as they severally attain to any measure of well-being. This is certainly the chief end, both of individuals and of states. And also for the sake of mere life (in which there is possibly some noble element so long as the evils of existence do not greatly overbalance the good) mankind meet together and maintain the political community. And we all see that men cling to life even at the cost of enduring great misfortune, seeming to find in life a natural sweetness and happiness.

There is no difficulty in distinguishing the various kinds of authority; they have been often defined already . . . The rule of a master, although the slave by nature and the master by nature have in reality the same interests, is nevertheless exercised primarily with a view to the interest of the master, but accidentally considers the slave, since, if the slave perish, the rule of the master perishes with him. On the other hand, the government of a wife and children and of a household, which we have called household management, is exercised in the first instance for the good of the governed or for the common good of both parties, but essentially for the good of the governed, as we see to be the case in medicine, gymnastic, and the arts in general, which are only accidentally concerned with the good of the artists themselves. For there is no reason why the trainer may not sometimes practise gymnastics, and the helmsman is always one of the crew. The trainer or the helmsman considers the good of those committed to his care. But, when he is one of the persons taken care of, he accidentally participates in the advantage, for the helmsman is also a sailor, and the trainer becomes one of those in training. And so in politics: when the state is framed upon the principle of equality and likeness, the citizens think that they ought to hold office by turns. Formerly, as is natural, every one would take his turn of service; and then again, somebody else would look after his interest, just as he, while in office, had looked after theirs. But nowadays, for the sake of the advantage which is to be gained from the public revenues and from office, men want to be always in office. One might imagine that the rulers, being sickly, were only kept in health while they continued in office; in that case we may be sure that they would be hunting after places. The conclusion is evident: that governments which have a regard to the common interest are constituted in accordance with strict principles of justice, and are therefore true forms; but those which regard only the interest of the rulers are all defective and perverted forms, for they are despotic, whereas a state is a community of freemen.

Having determined these points, we have next to consider how many forms of government there are, and what they are; and in the first place what are the true forms, for when they are determined the perversions of them will at once be apparent. The words constitution and government have the same meaning, and the government, which is the supreme authority in states, must be in the hands of one, or of a few, or of the many. The true forms of government, therefore, are those in which the one, or the few, or the many, govern with a view to the common interest; but governments which rule with a view to the private interest, whether of the one, or of the few, or of the many, are perversions. For the members of a state, if they are truly citizens, ought to participate in its advantages. Of forms of government in which one rules, we call that which regards the common interests, kingship or royalty; that in which more than one, but not many, rule, aristocracy; and it is so called, either because the rulers are the best men, or because they have at heart the best interests of the state and of the citizens. But when the citizens at large administer the state for the common interest, the government is called by the generic name—a constitution. And there is a reason for this use of language. One man or a few may excel in virtue; but as the number increases it becomes more difficult for them to attain perfection in every kind of virtue, though they may in military virtue, for this is found in the masses. Hence in a constitutional government the fighting-men have the supreme power, and those who possess arms are the citizens.

Of the above-mentioned forms, the perversions are as follows:— of royalty, tyranny; of aristocracy, oligarchy; of constitutional government, democracy. For tyranny is a kind of monarchy which has in view the interest of the monarch only; oligarchy has in view the interest of the wealthy; democracy, of the needy: none of them the common good of all.

6. What Traits of the Roman Republic Gave It Resilience and Durability?

With the rise of Rome to world power at the end of the third century B.C., *the Greeks developed a serious interest in Roman affairs, particularly in the unusual strength of Roman political organization. Two things about the Romans sharply struck the Greeks: first, their extraordinary and rapid military triumphs; second, their success in avoiding the political extremes of tyranny and mob rule so frequent among the cities of Greece. The best Greek account of Rome's achievement is by Polybius.*

Polybius (c. 203–120 B.C.) was a Greek hostage seized by the Romans, along with one thousand of his countrymen, because of doubts of their loyalty to their alliance with Rome during the Third Macedonian War (171–168 B.C.). At Rome, he became friendly with a few highly placed Roman officials and was allowed to go with them on military campaigns. His complete personal freedom in Italy and his opportunity to examine Roman official records put him in a unique position to write a history of Rome. In the selection used here, he gave an analysis of Rome's constitution at the time of her worst defeat by the Carthaginian general Hannibal during the Second Punic War, the disastrous battle of Cannae in 216 B.C., a defeat despite which, surprisingly, she was able later to rally and finally to triumph.

HISTORIES*

Polybius

As for the Roman constitution, it had three elements, each of them possessing sovereign powers: and their respective share of power in the whole state had been regulated with such a scrupulous regard to equality and equilibrium, that no one could say for certain, not even a native, whether the constitution as a whole were an aristocracy or democracy or despotism. And no wonder: for if we confine our observation to the power of the Consuls[1] we should be inclined to regard it as despotic; if to that of the Senate, as aristocratic; and if finally one looks at the power possessed by the people it would seem a clear case of a democracy. What the exact powers of these several parts were, and still, with slight modifications, are, I will now state.

The consuls, before leading out the legions, remain in Rome and are supreme masters of the administration. All other magistrates, except the tribunes, are under them and take their orders. They introduce foreign ambassadors to the senate; bring matters requiring deliberation before it; and see to the execution of its decrees. If, again, there are any matters of state which require the authorisation of the people, it is their business to see to them, to summon the popular meetings, to bring the proposals before them, and to carry out the decrees of the majority. In the preparations for war also, and in a word in the entire administration of a campaign, they have all but absolute power. It is competent to them to impose on the allies such levies as they think good, to appoint the military tribunes, to make up the roll for soldiers and

---

* *The Histories of Polybius* vi.11–18, trans. Evelyn S. Shuckburgh (London: Macmillan & Co. 1889), pp. 468–474.

[1] Two consuls were elected annually at Rome as the chief administrative officials. During time of war, they were also the supreme military leaders and so commanded the legions, the large units into which the army was divided.

select those that are suitable.[2] Besides they have absolute power of inflicting punishment on all who are under their command while on active service: and they have authority to expend as much of the public money as they choose, being accompanied by a quaestor who is entirely at their orders. A survey of these powers would in fact justify our describing the constitution as despotic,—a clear case of royal government. . . .

The senate has first of all the control of the treasury, and regulates the receipts and disbursements alike.[3] For the quaestors cannot issue any public money for the various departments of the state without a decree of the senate, except for the service of the consuls.[4] The Senate controls also what is by far the largest and most important expenditure, that, namely which is made by the censors every *lustrum* for the repair or construction of public buildings; this money cannot be obtained by the censors except by the grant of the senate.[5] Similarly all crimes committed in Italy requiring a public investigation, such as treason, conspiracy, poisoning, or wilful murder, are in the hands of the senate. Besides, if any individual or state among the Italian allies requires a controversy to be settled, a penalty to be assessed, help or protection to be afforded,—all this is the province of the senate. Or again, outside Italy, if it is necessary to send an embassy to reconcile warring communities, or to remind them of their duty, or sometimes to impose requisitions upon them or to receive their submission, or finally to proclaim war against them—this too is the business of the senate. In like manner the reception to be given to foreign ambassadors in Rome, and the answers to be returned to them, are decided by the senate. With such business the people have nothing to do. Consequently, if one were staying at Rome when the consuls were not in town, one would imagine the constitution to be a complete aristocracy: and this has been the idea entertained by many Greeks, and by many kings as well, from the fact that nearly all the business they had with Rome was settled by the senate.

After this one would naturally be inclined to ask what part is left for the people in the constitution, when the senate has these various functions, especially the control of the receipts and expenditure of the exchequer; and when the consuls, again, have absolute power over the details of military preparation, and an absolute authority in the field? There is, however, a part left the people, and it is a most important one. For the people is the sole fountain of honour and of punishment; and it is by these two things and these alone that dynasties and constitutions and, in a word, human society are held together: for where the distinction between them is not sharply drawn both in theory and practice, there no undertaking can be properly administered,—as

---

[2] Roman full military force consisted of a substantial number of troops from allies in addition to the legions. The treaties of alliance usually permitted the consuls to specify the amount of help required for any given campaign. Military tribunes were subordinate military officials under the consuls.

[3] The Roman Senate consisted in this period of the three hundred leaders of the state's most important tribes. It represented the views of the aristocracy.

[4] Quaestors were the quartermaster officials of the state. They also served as assistants to the consuls.

[5] The censors were elected for eighteen months once every five years to supervise the *lustrum*, a purification ceremony for the whole state. At this time, they took the census, supervised the registration of new citizens, and considered the qualifications of those who wished to enter the Senate, in addition to letting the public contracts to which Polybius referred.

indeed we might expect when good and bad are held in exactly the same honour. The people then are the only court to decide matters of life and death; and even in cases where the penalty is money, if the sum to be assessed sufficiently serious, and especially when the accused have held the higher magistracies. And in regard to this arrangement there is one point deserving especial commendation and record. Men who are on trial for their lives at Rome, while sentence is in process of being voted,—if even only one of the tribes whose votes are needed to ratify the sentence has not voted,—have the privilege at Rome of openly departing and condemning themselves to a voluntary exile.[6] Such men are safe at Naples or Praeneste or at Tibur, and at other towns with which this arrangement has been duly ratified on oath.

Again, it is the people who bestow offices on the deserving, which are the most honourable rewards of virtue. It has also the absolute power of passing or repealing laws; and, most important of all, it is the people who deliberate on the question of peace or war. And when provisional terms are made for alliance, suspension of hostilities, or treaties, it is the people who ratify them or the reverse.

These considerations again would lead one to say that the chief power in the state was the people's, and that the constitution was a democracy.

Such, then, is the distribution of power between the several parts of the state. I must now show how each of these several parts can, when they choose, oppose or support each other.

The consul, then, when he has started on an expedition with the powers I have described, is to all appearance absolute in the administration of the business in hand; still he has need of the support both of people and senate, and, without them, is quite unable to bring the matter to a successful conclusion. For it is plain that he must have supplies sent to his legions from time to time; but without a decree of the senate they can be supplied neither with corn, nor clothes, nor pay, so that all the plans of a commander must be futile, if the senate is resolved either to shrink from danger or hamper his plans. And again, whether a consul shall bring any undertaking to a conclusion or no depends entirely upon the senate: for it has absolute authority at the end of a year to send another consul to supersede him, or to continue the existing one in his command. Again, even to the successes of the generals the senate has the power to add distinction and glory, and on the other hand to obscure their merits and lower their credit. For these high achievements are brought in tangible form before the eyes of the citizens by what are called "triumphs." But these triumphs the commanders cannot celebrate with proper pomp, or in some cases celebrate at all, unless the senate concurs and grants the necessary money. As for the people, the consuls are pre-eminently obliged to court their favour, however distant from home may be the field of their operations; for it is the people, as I have said before, that ratifies, or refuses to ratify, terms of peace and treaties; but most of all because when laying down their office they have to give an account of their administration before it. Therefore in no case is it safe for the consuls to neglect either the Senate or the goodwill of the people.

---

[6] In the assemblies of the people, which occasionally sat as a court of appeal in cases involving severe penalties, the vote was taken by tribe.

As for the senate, which possesses the immense power I have described, in the first place it is obliged in public affairs to take the multitude into account, and respect the wishes of the people; and it cannot put into execution the penalty for offences against the republic, which are punishable with death, unless the people first ratify its decrees. Similarly even in matters which directly affect the senators,—for instance, in the case of a law diminishing the senate's traditional authority, or depriving senators of certain dignities and offices, or even actually cutting down their property,—even in such cases the people have the sole power of passing or rejecting the law. But most important of all is the fact that, if the tribunes interpose their veto, the senate not only are unable to pass a decree, but cannot even hold a meeting at all, whether formal or informal.[7] Now, the tribunes are always bound to carry out the decree of the people, and above all things to have regard to their wishes: therefore, for all these reasons the senate stands in awe of the multitude, and cannot neglect the feelings of the people.

In like manner the people on its part is far from being independent of the senate, and is bound to take its wishes into account both collectively and individually. For contracts, too numerous to count, are given out by the censors in all parts of Italy for the repairs or construction of public buildings; there is also the collection of revenue from many rivers, harbours, gardens, mines, and land—everything, in a word, that comes under the control of the Roman government: and in all these the people at large are engaged; so that there is scarcely a man, so to speak, who is not interested either as a contractor or as being employed in the works. For some purchase the contracts from the censors for themselves; and others go partners with them; while others again go security for these contractors, or actually pledge their property to the treasury for them. Now over all these transactions the senate has absolute control. It can grant an extension of time; and in case of unforeseen accident can relieve the contractors from a portion of their obligation, or release them from it altogether, if they are absolutely unable to fulfil it. And there are many details in which the Senate can inflict great hardships, or, on the other hand, grant great indulgences to the contractors: for in every case the appeal is to it. But the most important point of all is that the judges are taken from its members in the majority of trials, whether public or private, in which the charges are heavy. Consequently, all citizens are much at its mercy; and being alarmed at the uncertainty as to when they may need its aid, are cautious about resisting or actively opposing its will. And for a similar reason men do not rashly resist the wishes of the consuls, because one and all may become subject to their absolute authority on a campaign.

The result of this power . . . of the several interest groups [in the state] for mutual help . . . or harm is a union sufficiently firm for all emergencies, and a constitution than which it is impossible to find a better. For whenever any danger from without compels them to unite and work together, the strength which is developed by the State is so extraordinary, that every-

---

[7] The tribunes were the people's representatives in the government, dating from earlier days when the commoners, the plebeians, had few personal rights. Initially, the tribunes were empowered to block action by any magistrate against the person of a plebeian. Later, when this social division was no longer important, they still were elected by the people in the tribal assembly, and still could veto public action.

thing required is unfailingly carried out by the eager rivalry shown by all classes to devote their whole minds to the need of the hour, and to secure that any determination come to should not fail for want of promptitude; while each individual works, privately and publicly alike, for the accomplishment of the business in hand. Accordingly, the peculiar constitution of the State makes it irresistible, and certain of obtaining whatever it determines to attempt. Nay, even when these external alarms are past, and the people are enjoying their good fortune and the fruits of their victories, and, as usually happens, growing corrupted by flattery and idleness, show a tendency to violence and arrogance,—it is in these circumstances, more than ever, that the constitution is seen to possess within itself the power of correcting abuses. For when any one of the three classes becomes puffed up, and manifests an inclination to be contentious and unduly encroaching, the mutual interdependency of all the three, and the possibility of the pretensions of any one being checked and thwarted by the others, must plainly check this tendency: and so the proper equilibrium is maintained by the impulsiveness of the one part being checked by its fear of the other.

7. What Is the Relation of Law to Justice, to Nature, and to God?

Marcus Tullius Cicero (106–43 B.C.) came from a moderately wealthy but politically obscure family outside of Rome. His education was the best possible for his time, including a period of study in Athens. He chose a career in the law courts, where his oratorical abilities enabled him to rise to important public office in the last years of the Roman Republic. He finally became consul in 63 B.C. Cicero was one of the casualities of the revolution in which the Republic gave way to one-man rule. He was killed by the agents of Mark Antony, the man with whom Octavian had to contend for leadership of the popular party before becoming the first emperor.

The following selection is from Cicero's Concerning the Laws, *begun in 52, some ten years after his consulship. It explores a number of fundamental issues concerning the law.*

Cicero was not only a copious speaker, he was a prolific author. His writings helped popularize Greek philosophy and political speculation in the Latin-speaking western part of the Roman state. His preoccupation with law gave a character to his writings on politics different from that of the great political theorists of Greece.

CONCERNING THE LAWS*

Cicero

. . . Out of all the material of the philosophers' discussions, surely there comes nothing more valuable than the full realization that we are born for

*Reprinted by permission of the publishers from The Loeb Classical Library, *Cicero, De Re Publica, De Legibus,* trans. Clinton Walker Keyes, *De Legibus* I.x.28–xii.34; xiv.40–xvi.45; xxiv.62 (Cambridge, Mass.: Harvard University Press, 1928), pp. 329–335, 341–347, 367.

Justice, and that right is based, not upon men's opinions, but upon Nature. This fact will immediately be plain if you once get a clear conception of man's fellowship and union with his fellow-men. For no single thing is so like another, so exactly its counterpart, as all of us are to one another. Nay, if bad habits and false beliefs did not twist the weaker minds and turn them in whatever direction they are inclined, no one would be so like his own self as all men would be like all others. And so, however we may define man, a single definition will apply to all. This is a sufficient proof that there is no difference in kind between man and man; for if there were, one definition could not be applicable to all men; and indeed reason, which alone raises us above the level of the beasts and enables us to draw inferences, to prove and disprove, to discuss and solve problems, and to come to conclusions, is certainly common to us all, and, though varying in what it learns, at least in the capacity to learn it is invariable. For the same things are invariably perceived by the senses, and those things which stimulate the senses, stimulate them in the same way in all men; and those rudimentary beginnings of intelligence to which I have referred, which are imprinted on our minds, are imprinted on all minds alike; and speech, the mind's interpreter, though differing in the choice of words, agrees in the sentiments expressed. In fact, there is no human being of any race who, if he finds a guide, cannot attain to virtue.

The similarity of the human race is clearly marked in its evil tendencies as well as in its goodness. For pleasure also attracts all men; and even though it is an enticement to vice, yet it has some likeness to what is naturally good. For it delights us by its lightness and agreeableness; and for this reason, by an error of thought, it is embraced as something wholesome. It is through a similar misconception that we shun death as though it were a dissolution of nature, and cling to life because it keeps us in the sphere in which we were born; and that we look upon pain as one of the greatest of evils, not only because of its cruelty, but also because it seems to lead to the destruction of nature. In the same way, on account of the similarity between moral worth and renown, those who are publicly honoured are considered happy, while those who do not attain fame are thought miserable. Troubles, joys, desires, and fears haunt the minds of all men without distinction, and even if different men have different beliefs, that does not prove, for example, that it is not the same quality of superstition that besets those races which worship dogs and cats as gods, as that which torments other races. But what nation does not love courtesy, kindliness, gratitude, and remembrance of favours bestowed? What people does not hate and despise the haughty, the wicked, the cruel, and the ungrateful? Inasmuch as these considerations prove to us that the whole human race is bound together in unity, it follows, finally that knowledge of the principles of right living is what makes men better. . . .

The next point, then, is that we are so constituted by Nature as to share the sense of Justice with one another and to pass it on to all men. And in this whole discussion I want it understood that what I shall call Nature is [that which is implanted in us by Nature]; that, however, the corruption caused by bad habits is so great that the sparks of fire, so to speak, which Nature has kindled in us are extinguished by this corruption, and the vices which are their opposites spring up and are established. But if the judgments of men were in agreement with Nature, so that, as the poet says, they considered "nothing alien to them which concerns mankind,"[1] then Justice would be equally observed by all. For those creatures who have received the gift of reason from Nature have also received the gift of Law, which is right reason applied to command and prohibition. And if they have received Law, they have received Justice also. Now all men have received reason; therefore all men have received Justice. Consequently Socrates was right when he cursed, as he often did, the man who first separated utility from Justice; for this separation, he complained, is the source of all mischief.[2] . . . From this it is clear that, when a wise man shows toward another endowed with equal virtue the kind of benevolence which is so widely diffused among men, that will then have come to pass which, unbelievable as it seems to some, is after all the inevitable result—namely, that he loves himself no whit more than he loves another. For what difference can there be among things which are all equal? But if the least distinction should be made in friendship, then the very name of friendship would perish forthwith; for its essence is such that, as soon as either friend prefers anything for himself, friendship ceases to exist.

* * *

. . . And so men pay the penalty, not so much through decisions of the courts (for once there were no courts anywhere, and to-day there are none in many lands; and where they do exist, they often act unjustly after all); but guilty men are tormented and pursued by the Furies, not with blazing torches, as in the tragedies,[3] but with the anguish of remorse and the torture of a guilty conscience.

But if it were a penalty and not Nature that ought to keep men from injustice, what anxiety would there be to trouble the wicked when the danger of punishment was removed? But in fact there has never been a villain so brazen as not to deny that he had committed a crime, or else invent some story of just anger to excuse its commission, and seek justification for his crime in some natural principle of right. Now if even the wicked dare to appeal to such principles, how jealously should they be guarded by the good! But if it is a penalty, the fear of punishment, and not the wickedness itself, that is to keep men from a life of wrongdoing and crime, then no one can be regarded as imprudent; furthermore, those of us who are not influenced by virtue itself to be good men, but by some consideration of utility and profit, are merely shrewd, not good. For to what lengths will that man go in the dark who fears nothing but a witness and a judge? What will he do if, in some desolate spot, he meets a helpless man, unattended, whom he can rob of a fortune? Our virtuous man, who is just and good by nature, will talk with such a person, help him, and guide him on his way; but the other, who does nothing for another's sake, and measures every act by the standard of his

---

[1] Terence *Heautontimorumenos* 77.

[2] This statement was apparently attributed to Socrates by Cleanthes, the second head of the Stoic school, about 250 B.C.

[3] As for instance in Aeschylus' *Eumenides,* where the Furies pursue Orestes for the murder of his mother, Clytaemnestra.

own advantage—it is clear enough, I think, what he will do! If, however, the latter does deny that he would kill the man and rob him of his money, he will not deny it because he regards it as a naturally wicked thing to do, but because he is afraid that his crime may become known—that is, that he may get into trouble. Oh, what a motive, that might well bring a blush of shame to the cheek, not merely of the philosopher, but even of the simple rustic!

But the most foolish notion of all is the belief that everything is just which is found in the customs or laws of nations. Would that be true, even if these laws had been enacted by tyrants? . . . For Justice is one; it binds all human society, and is based on one Law, which is right reason applied to command and prohibition. Whoever knows not this Law, whether it has been recorded in writing anywhere or not, is without Justice.

But if Justice is conformity to written laws and national customs, and if, as the same persons claim, everything is to be tested by the standard of utility, then anyone who thinks it will be profitable to him will, if he is able, disregard and violate the laws. It follows that Justice does not exist at all, if it does not exist in Nature, and if that form of it which is based on utility can be overthrown by that very utility itself. And if Nature is not to be considered the foundation of Justice, that will mean the destruction [of the virtues on which human society depends]. For where then will there be a place for generosity, or love of country, or loyalty, or the inclination to be of service to others or to show gratitude for favours received? For these virtues originate in our natural inclination to love our fellow-men, and this is the foundation of Justice. Otherwise not merely consideration for men but also rites and pious observances in honour of the gods are done away with; for I think that these ought to be maintained, not through fear, but on account of the close relationship which exists between man and God. But if the principles of Justice were founded on the decrees of peoples, the edicts of princes, or the decisions of judges, then Justice would sanction robbery and adultery and forgery of wills, in case these acts were approved by the votes or decrees of the populace. But if so great a power belongs to the decisions and decrees of fools that the laws of Nature can be changed by their votes, then why do they not ordain that what is bad and baneful shall be considered good and salutary? Or, if a law can make Justice out of Injustice, can it not also make good out of bad? But in fact we can perceive the difference between good laws and bad by referring them to no other standard than Nature; indeed, it is not merely Justice and Injustice which are distinguished by Nature, but also and without exception things which are honourable and dishonourable. For since an intelligence common to us all makes things known to us and formulates them in our minds, honourable actions are ascribed by us to virtue, and dishonourable actions to vice; and only a madman would conclude that these judgments are matters of opinion, and not fixed by Nature. For even what we, by a misuse of the term, call the virtue of a tree or of a horse, is not a matter of opinion, but is based on Nature. And if that is true, honourable and dishonourable actions must also be distinguished by Nature. For if virtue in general is to be tested by opinion, then its several parts must also be so tested; who, therefore, would judge a man of prudence and, if I may say so, hard common sense, not by his own character but by some external circumstance?

For virtue is reason completely developed; and this certainly is natural; therefore everything honourable is likewise natural.[4]

* * *

And when it [the mind] realizes that it is born to take part in the life of a State, it will think that it must employ not merely the customary subtle method of debate, but also the more copious continuous style, considering, for example, how to rule nations, establish laws, punish the wicked, protect the good, honour those who excel, publish to fellow-citizens precepts conducive to their well-being and credit, so designed as to win their acceptance; how to arouse them to honourable actions, recall them from wrongdoing, console the afflicted, and hand down to everlasting memory the deeds and counsels of brave and wise men, and the infamy of the wicked.

8. What Can Citizens of a Highly Civilized State Learn from the Study of a Primitive People?

The expansion of the Roman state from the time of the Punic Wars on was accompanied by a deterioration of the institutions of the Republic, suited for the rule of a confederation of Italian towns, but not for the rule of a world empire. After a century of crisis, institutions were remodelled, adapted, and supplemented by Octavian, who became Rome's first emperor, taking the name Augustus (63 B.C.–A.D. 14), to meet the needs of that vast empire. These imperial institutions enabled Rome to keep peace in the Mediterranean world which had for centuries been torn by strife.

Very little is known of Cornelius Tacitus (c. A.D. 55–c. 120), considering the quality of his writings and the force of his opinions. He was the admiring son-in-law of the general Agricola (whose military successes in Britain ended when the emperor Domitian recalled him). Tacitus enjoyed a reputation as an accomplished orator in Rome before serving as governor of Asia in 112–113. His writings reveal the fondness of the Roman aristocrat for the Republic, and a distaste for the increasingly autocratic government of the emperors. The historian did much of his work during the calm of the pax Romana *(Roman peace) in the late first and early second centuries. He used the stability and enlightenment of Trajan's reign (98–117) to write scathingly of the erratic behavior of many of Trajan's predecessors. The present selection comes from his* De origine et situ Germanorum *(The Origins, Land, and Peoples of the Germans) a usually favorable description of the life of this primitive society.*

GERMANIA*

Tacitus

For myself I accept the view that the people of Germany have never been tainted by intermarriage with other peoples, and stand out as a nation

---

[4] Compare this view of law with the views set forth in the selections from the Bible in Section I, above.

* Reprinted by permission of the publishers from *Tacitus on Britain and Germany*, trans. H. Mattingly (Harmondsworth, Middlesex: Penguin Books, 1948), pp. 103–117.

peculiar, pure and unique of its kind. Hence the physical type, if one may generalize at all about so vast a population, is everywhere the same—wild, blue eyes, reddish hair and huge frames that excel only in violent effort. They have no corresponding power to endure hard work and exertion, and have little capacity to bear thirst and heat; but their climate and soil have taught them to bear cold and hunger.

The country in general, while varying somewhat in character, either bristles with woods or festers with swamps. It is wetter where it faces Gaul, windier where it faces . . . [north and east]. Though fertile in grain crops, it is unkind to fruit trees. It is rich in flocks, but they are for the most part undersized. Even the cattle lack the splendid brows that are their natural glory. It is numbers that please, numbers that constitute their only, their darling, form of wealth. Heaven has denied them gold and silver—shall I say in mercy or in wrath? But I would not go so far as to assert that Germany has no lodes of silver and gold. Who has ever prospected for them? The Germans take less than the normal pleasure in owning and using them. One may see among them silver vessels, which have been given as presents to their envoys and chiefs, as lightly esteemed as earthenware. The Germans nearest us do, however, value gold and silver for their use in trade, and recognize and prefer certain types of Roman money. The peoples of the interior, truer to the plain old ways, employ barter. They like money that is old and familiar, denarii[1] with the notched edge and the type of the two-horse chariot. Another point is that they try to get silver in preference to gold. They have no predilection for the metal, but find plenty of silver change more serviceable in buying cheap and common goods.

There is not even any great abundance of iron, as may be inferred from the character of their weapons. Only a very few use swords or lances. The spears that they carry . . . have short and narrow heads, but are so sharp and easy to handle, that the same weapon serves at need for close or distant fighting. The horseman asks no more than his shield and spear, but the infantry have also javelins to shower, several per man, and can hurl them to a great distance; for they are either naked or only lightly clad in their cloaks. There is nothing ostentatious in their equipment. Only the shields are picked out with carefully selected colors. Few have breastplates; only here and there will you see a helmet of metal or hide. Their horses are not distinguished either for beauty or for speed, nor are they trained in Roman fashion to execute various turns. They ride them straight ahead or with a single swing to the right, keeping the wheeling line so perfect that no one drops behind the rest. On a general survey, their strength is seen to lie rather in their infantry, and that is why they combine the two arms in battle. The men whom they select from the whole force and station in the van are fleet of foot and fit admirably into cavalry action.[2] The number of these select men is exactly fixed. A hundred are drawn from each district, and 'the hundred' is the name they bear at home. What began as a mere number ends as a title of distinction. The line is made up of wedge formations. To retreat, provided that you return to the attack, is considered crafty rather than cowardly. They bring in the bodies of the fallen even

---

[1] The *denarius* was one of the basic coins of the Roman monetary system.

[2] The van was the party of warriors used in advance of the main body of troops.

when the battle hangs in the balance. To throw away one's shield is the supreme disgrace; the guilty wretch is debarred from sacrifice or council. Men have often survived battle only to end their shame by hanging themselves.

They choose their kings for their noble birth, their leaders for their valor. The power even of the kings is not absolute or arbitrary. As for the leaders, it is their example rather than their authority that wins them special admiration—for their energy, their distinction, or their presence in the front of the fight. Capital punishment, imprisonment and even flogging are allowed to none but the priests, and are not inflicted merely as punishments or on the leaders' orders, but in obedience to the god whom they believe to preside over battle. They also carry into the fray figures and emblems taken from their sacred groves. Not chance or the accident of mustering makes the troop or wedge, but family and friendship, and this is a very powerful incitement to valor. A man's dearest possessions are at hand; he can hear close to him the laments of his women and the wailing of his children. These are the witnesses that a man reverences most, to them he looks for his highest praise. The men take their wounds to their mothers and wives, and the latter are not afraid of counting and examining their blows, and bring food and encouragement to the fighting men.

It stands on record that armies wavering on the point of collapse have been restored by the women. They have pleaded heroically with their men, thrusting their bosoms before them and forcing them to realize the imminent prospect of their enslavement—a fate which they fear more desperately for their women than for themselves. It is even found that you can secure a surer hold on a state if you demand among the hostages girls of noble family. More than this, they believe that there resides in women an element of holiness and prophecy, and so they do not scorn to ask their advice or lightly disregard their replies. . . .

* * *

On matters of minor importance only the chiefs debate, on major affairs the whole community; but, even where the commons have the decision, the case is carefully considered in advance by the chiefs. Except in case of accident or emergency they assemble on fixed days, when the moon is either crescent or nearing her full orb . . . It is a defect of their freedom that they do not assemble at once or in obedience to orders, but waste two or three days in their dilatory gathering. When the mass so decide, they take their seats fully armed. Silence is then demanded by the priests, who on that occasion have also power to enforce obedience. Then such hearing is given to the king or chief as age, rank, military distinction or eloquence can secure; but it is rather their prestige as counsellors than their authority that tells. If a proposal displeases them, the people roar out their dissent; if they approve, they clash their spears. No form of approval can carry more honor than praise expressed by arms. . . .

On the field of battle it is a disgrace to the chief to be surpassed in valor by his companions, to the companions not to come up to the valor of their chief. As for leaving a battle alive after your chief has fallen, *that* means lifelong infamy and shame. To defend and protect him, to put down one's own acts of heroism to his credit—that is what they really mean by 'allegiance!'

The chiefs fight for victory, the companions for their chief. Many noble youths, if the land of their birth is stagnating in a protracted peace, deliberately seek out other tribes, where some war is afoot. The Germans have no taste for peace; renown is easier won among perils, and you cannot maintain a large body of companions except by violence and war. The companions are prodigal in their demands on the generosity of their chiefs. It is always 'give me that warhorse' or 'give me that bloody and victorious spear.' As for meals with their plentiful, if homely, fare, they count simply as pay. Such open-handedness must have war and plunder to feed it. You will find it harder to persuade a German to plough the land and to await its annual produce with patience than to challenge a foe and earn the prize of wounds. He thinks it spiritless and slack to gain by sweat what he can buy with blood.

When not engaged in warfare, they spend some little time in hunting, but more in idling, abandoned to sleep and gluttony. All the heroes and grim warriors dawdle their time away, while the care of house, hearth and fields is left to the women, old men and weaklings of the family. The warriors themselves lose their edge. They are so strangely inconsistent. They love indolence, but they hate peace. It is usual for states to make voluntary and individual contributions of cattle or agricultural produce to the chiefs. These are accepted as a token of honor, but serve also to relieve essential needs. The chiefs take peculiar pleasure in gifts from neighboring states, such as are sent not only by individuals, but by the community as well—choice horses, splendid arms, metal discs and collars; the practice of accepting money payments they have now learnt—from us.

* * *

. . . German women live in a chastity that is impregnable, uncorrupted by the temptations of public shows or the excitements of banquets. Clandestine love-letters are unknown to men and women alike. Adultery in that populous nation is rare in the extreme, and punishment is summary and left to the husband. He shaves off his wife's hair, strips her in the presence of kinsmen, thrusts her from his house and flogs her through the whole village. They have, in fact, no mercy on a woman who prostitutes her chastity. Neither beauty, youth nor wealth can find the sinner a husband. No one in Germany finds vice amusing, or calls it 'up-to-date' to debauch and be debauched. It is still better with those states in which only virgins marry, and the hopes and prayers of a wife are settled once and for all. They take one husband, like the one body or life that they possess. No thought or desire must stray beyond him. They must not love the husband so much as the married state. To restrict the number of children or to put to death any born after the heir is considered criminal. Good morality is more effective in Germany than good laws in some places we know.[3]

9. What Were the Merits of Roman Rule?

Aelius Aristides, an itinerant orator of the second century A.D., *travelled about the eastern end of the Empire giving speeches in an artfully developed*

---

[3] Compare Tacitus' whole attitude to the Germans with Aristotle's to barbarians. See above, pp. 113–14.

style. He lectured on many subjects, but is best known for his eulogies of Athens, Smyrna, and Rome and his heavy compliments to the emperor. The selection here comes from the oration he delivered in Rome in 156 during the benevolent and relatively quiet reign of Antoninus Pius (138–161). Even if Aristides' oration contains flattery, it helps us understand something about the Romans during the great age of the Roman Empire. It shows what he thought would please the great men of Rome. The many enthusiastic inscriptions found in the imperial provinces from the second century indicate that other men of the day had the same attitude.

TO ROME*

Aelius Aristides

Vast and comprehensive as is the size of it, your empire is much greater for its perfection than for the area which its boundaries encircle. There are no pockets of the empire held by . . . others, land which some have occupied by force, others have detached by revolt, who cannot be captured. Nor is it merely called the land of the *King,* while really the land of all who are able to hold it.[1] Nor do satraps fight one another as if they had no king; nor are cities at variance, some fighting against these and some against those, with garrisons being dispatched to some cities and being expelled from others.[2] But for the eternal duration of this empire the whole civilized world prays all together, emitting, like a flute after a thorough cleaning, one note with more perfect precision than a chorus; so beautifully is it harmonized by the leader in command. . . . All directions are carried out by the chorus of the civilized world at a word or gesture of guidance more easily than at some plucking of a chord; and if anything need be done, it suffices to decide and there it is already done.

The governors sent out to the city-states and ethnic groups are each of them rulers of those under them, but in what concerns themselves and their relations to each other they are all equally among the ruled, and in particular they differ from those under their rule in that it is they . . . who first show how to be the right kind of subject.[3] So much respect has been instilled in all men for him who is the great governor, who obtains for them their all, [that] they think . . . he knows what they are doing better than they do themselves. Accordingly they fear his displeasure and stand in greater awe of him than one would of a despot, a master who was present and watching and uttering commands. No one is so proud that he can fail to be moved upon hearing

---

* Adapted by permission from Aelius Aristides *To Rome* 29,31–38, trans. James H. Oliver in "The Ruling Power," *Transactions of the American Philosophical Society,* N. S. XLIII, 4 (1953), 898f.

[1] That is, the land does not just nominally belong to the ruler while actually under the control of others.

[2] Satraps were governors of the provinces of the Persian Empire and were infamous in the classical world for their constant strife with each other.

[3] Some Roman governors were sent to cities, but some went to provinces which were not far enough advanced to have cities. These Aristides calls "ethnic groups."

even the mere mention of the Ruler's name, but, rising, he praises and worships him and breathes two prayers in a single breath, one to the gods on the Ruler's behalf, one for his own affairs to the Ruler himself. And if the governors should have even some slight doubt whether certain claims are valid in connection with either public or private lawsuits and petitions from the governed, they straightway send to him with a request for instructions what to do, and they wait until he renders a reply, like a chorus waiting for its trainer. Therefore he has no need to wear himself out traveling around the whole empire nor, by appearing personally, now among some, then among others, to make sure of each point when he has the time to tread their soil. It is very easy for him to stay where he is and manage the entire civilized world by letters, which arrive almost as soon as they are written, as if they were carried by winged messengers.[4]

But that which deserves as much wonder and admiration as all the rest together, and constant expression of gratitude both in word and action, shall now be mentioned. You who hold so vast an empire and rule it with such a firm hand and with so much unlimited power have very decidedly won a great success, which is completely your own. For of all who have ever gained empire you alone rule over men who are free. . . . [Sections of the empire have not been given to this or that ruler]; nor is the country said to be enslaved, as household of so-and-so, to whomsoever it has been turned over, a man himself not free.[5] But just as those in states [that are composed of only] one city appoint the magistrates to protect and care for the governed, so you, who conduct public business in the whole civilized world exactly as if it were one city state, appoint the governors, as is natural after elections, to protect and care for the governed, not to be slave masters over them. Therefore governor makes way for governor unobtrusively, when his time is up, and far from staying too long and disputing the land with his successor, he might easily not stay long enough even to meet him.

Appeals to a higher court are made with . . . ease . . . [and] with no greater menace for those who make them than for those who have accepted the local verdict. Therefore one might say that the men of today are ruled by the governors who are sent out, only in so far as they are content to be ruled. Are not these advantages beyond the old "Free Republic" of every people?[6] For under Government by the People it is not possible to go outside after the verdict has been given in the city's court nor even to other jurors, but . . . one must ever be content with the local verdict. But now . . . there is another judge, a mighty one, whose comprehension no just claim ever escapes.

---

[4] Here Aristides was alluding to the highly developed bureaucratic organization of the Empire in the second century. Provinces were carefully graded as to importance and were policed by adequate forces. Communications were swift and sure, and instructions were carried out to the letter by a corps of officials who had much to gain in the closely watched civil service.

[5] In the Near East, the land of a kingdom often belonged exclusively to the king, to be managed as his personal estate. Here, Aristides pointed out that even where local territories were managed by the delegation of this kind of authority, the subordinate chieftain was himself not free.

[6] This may be an oblique reference to any republican sentiment that still remained in Rome. In any case, it stresses the point that where the people are sovereign, there is no appeal from their decision—a direct comparison between ordered government and the unruly freedoms of earlier Greece.

10. What Are the Bases and Sources of Roman Law?

His voluminous works make Gaius (second century after Christ) one of Rome's greatest legal writers despite the fact that he apparently held no imperial post as a jurist. His long commentary on provincial law has led some scholars to believe he was a provincial jurist, but his contemporaries made no mention of him. Whatever popularity he may have lacked in his own time, however, is more than made up by his influence upon the codification of Roman law under the Byzantine emperor Justinian (527–565). The following selection from his Institutes *summarizes the common view of the jurists on sources or constitutive elements of the law of Rome.*

INSTITUTES*

Gaius

Every people that is governed by statutes and customs observes partly its own peculiar law and partly the common law of all mankind. That law which a people establishes for itself is peculiar to it, and is called *ius ciuile* (civil law) as being the special law of that *ciuitas* (State), while the law that natural reason establishes among all mankind is followed by all peoples alike, and is called *ius gentium* (law of nations, or law of the world) as being the law observed by all mankind. Thus the Roman people observes partly its own peculiar law and partly the common law of mankind. . . .

The laws of the Roman people consist of *leges* (comitial enactments), plebiscites, senatusconsults, imperial constitutions, edicts of those possessing the right to issue them, and answers of the learned. A *lex* is a command and ordinance of the *populus*. A plebiscite is a command and ordinance of the *plebs*. The *plebs* differs from the *populus* in that the term *populus* designates all citizens including patricians, while the term *plebs* designates all citizens excepting patricians.[1] Hence in former times the patricians used to maintain that they were not bound by plebiscites, these having been made without their authorization. But a *L. Hortensia* was passed, which provided the plebiscites should bind the entire *populus*.[2] Thereby plebiscites were equated to *leges*. A senatusconsult is a command and ordinance of the senate; it has the force of *lex*, though this has been questioned. An imperial constitution is what the emperor by decree, edict, or letter ordains; it has never been doubted that this has the force of *lex*, seeing that the emperor himself receives his *imperium* (sovereign power) through a *lex*. The right of issuing edicts is possessed by

---

* Reprinted by permission of the publishers from Francis de Zulueta, *The Institutes of Gaius* I.i.2–7 (Oxford: The Clarendon Press, 1951), pp. 3–5.

[1] In the Republican period, much was made of the difference between the upper-class patricians and the lower-class plebeians. Gaius here was commenting on part of the legal battle by which the plebeians won equality with the patricians.

[2] This particular *Lex Hortensius*, so called because it was passed after being presented by an official named Hortensius, became law in 287 B.C. Its passage was the key event in the victory of the plebeians.

magistrates of the Roman people. Very extensive law is contained in the edicts of the two praetors, the urban and the peregrine,[3] whose jurisdiction is possessed in the provinces by the provincial governors; also in the edicts of the curule aediles,[4] whose jurisdiction is possessed in the provinces of the Roman people by quaestors; no quaestors are sent to the provinces of Caesar,[5] and consequently the aedilician edict is not published there. The answers of the learned are the decisions and opinions of those who are authorized to lay down the law. If the decisions of all of them agree, what they so hold has the force of *lex*, but if they disagree, the judge is at liberty to follow whichever decision he pleases. This is declared by a rescript of the late emperor Hadrian.

---

[3] These praetors were judicial officials, one for Roman citizens within the city, the other for foreigners.

[4] The aediles were officials within the city whose chief function it was to supervise the care and maintenance of public buildings and the staging of public games. Since this was an extensive responsibility involving much valuable property, the annual statement issued by each aedile upon taking office had considerable importance. Like the praetor's edicts, these statements tended to accumulate as definitions of legal and judicial policy.

[5] Those provinces which demanded large standing armies, which were particularly restive, or which offered the greatest opportunities for exploitation were regularly held under the personal control of the emperor and kept apart from the public administration of the senatorial provinces.

III

THE CONFRONTATION OF
THE JUDEO-CHRISTIAN AND
THE GRECO-ROMAN TRADITIONS

During the three centuries which followed Jesus' death, Christianity changed from a persecuted sect into the official religion of the Roman Empire. But this did not mean the Church's problems were solved. For the early persecutors of the Christians had been reared in classical culture; Christian converts were mainly Greek- and Latin-speaking people steeped in the traditions of the classical world; certainly the Empire, for which Christianity now was assuming spiritual responsibility, had been founded in classical culture.

The Christian tradition therefore confronted the classical tradition in its persecutors, in its converts, and, finally, in the society over which it assumed religious dominion. As a result, these same three centuries found men exploring the terms on which such widely divergent traditions might adjust to one another to achieve at least a truce if not full concord.

The selections which follow differ from those presented so far. They do not, so to speak, stand on their own, but rather relate to each other. Through them we can glimpse early Christianity as it coped with its external antagonist, classical civilization, while at the same time it tried to straighten out its own institutional and organizational problems. This is thus the first of several "source clusters" which appear in this book.

1. How Shall the Roman State Deal With Those Who Refuse To Perform the Rites Lawfully Due to the Emperor?

The cult of "emperor worship" began concurrently with the origins of Christianity and came to be legally required of subjects of the Roman state. Christians refused to perform the rites of this cult. Since in common opinion, the security of the Empire and therefore the public welfare depended on these rites, this refusal posed a problem for the Roman administrators. One of them, the writer Pliny (A.D. 62–113), laid his difficulties before the emperor Trajan, who ruled from A.D. 98 to 117. The emperor's answer is included.

LETTERS*

Pliny the Younger

PLINY TO TRAJAN

It is my custom, Sire, to refer to you in all cases where I do not feel sure, for who can better direct my doubts or inform my ignorance? I have never been present at any legal examination of the Christians, and I do not know, therefore, what are the usual penalties passed upon them, or the limits of those penalties, or how searching an inquiry should be made. I have hesitated a great deal in considering whether any distinctions should be drawn according to the ages of the accused; whether the weak should be punished as severely as the more robust; whether if they renounce their faith they should be pardoned, or whether the man who has once been a Christian should gain nothing by recanting; whether the name itself, even though otherwise innocent of crime, should be punished, or only the crimes that gather round it.

In the meantime, this is the plan which I have adopted in the case of those Christians who have been brought before me. I ask them whether they are Christians; if they say yes, then I repeat the question a second time and a third time, warning them of the penalties it entails, and if they still persist, I order them to be taken away to prison. For I do not doubt, that whatever the character of the crime may be which they confess, their pertinacity and inflexible obstinacy certainly ought to be punished. There were others who showed similar mad folly whom I reserved to be sent to Rome, as they were Roman citizens. Subsequently, as is usually the way, the very fact of my taking up this question led to a great increase of accusations, and a variety of cases were brought before me. A pamphlet was issued anonymously, containing the names of a number of people. Those who denied that they were or had been Christians and called upon the gods in the usual formula, reciting the words after me, those who offered incense and wine before your image, which I had given orders to be brought forward for this purpose, together with the statues of the deities—all such I considered should be discharged, especially as they cursed the name of Christ, which, it is said, those who are really Christians cannot be induced to do. Others, whose names were given me by an informer, first said that they were Christians and afterwards denied it, declaring that they had been but were so no longer, some of them having recanted many years before, and more than one so long as twenty years back. They all worshipped your image and the statues of the deities, and cursed the name of Christ. But they declared that the sum of their guilt or their error only amounted to this, that on a stated day they had been accustomed to meet before daybreak and to

---

* Reprinted from *Documents Illustrative of the History of the Church*, Vol. I, *to A.D. 313*, ed. Beresford James Kidd (London: Society for Promoting Christian Knowledge, 1933), Nos. 14 and 15, pp. 38–40.

recite a hymn among themselves to Christ, as though he were a god, and that so far from binding themselves by oath to commit any crime, their oath was to abstain from theft, robbery, adultery, and from breach of faith, and not to deny trust-money placed in their keeping when called upon to deliver it. When this ceremony was concluded, it had been their custom to depart and meet again to take food; but it was of no special character and quite harmless, and they had ceased this practice after the edict in which, in accordance with your orders, I had forbidden all secret societies. I thought it the more necessary, therefore, to find out what truth there was in these statements by submitting two women, who were called deaconesses, to the torture, but I found nothing but a debased superstition carried to great lengths. So I postponed my examination, and immediately consulted you. The matter seems to me worthy of your consideration, especially as there are so many people involved in the danger. Many persons of all ages and of both sexes alike are being brought into peril of their lives by their accusers, and the process will go on. For the contagion of this superstition has spread not only through the free cities, but into the villages and the rural districts, and yet it seems to me that it can be checked and set right. It is beyond doubt that the temples, which have been almost deserted, are beginning again to be thronged with worshippers, that the sacred rites which have for a long time been allowed to lapse are now being renewed, and that the food for the sacrificial victims is once more finding a sale, whereas, up to recently, a buyer was hardly to be found. From this it is easy to infer what vast numbers of people might be reclaimed if only they were given an opportunity of repentance.

Trajan to Pliny

You have adopted the proper course, my dear Pliny, in examining into the cases of those who have been denounced to you as Christians, for no hard and fast rule can be laid down to meet a question of such wide extent. The Christians are not to be hunted out; if they are brought before you and the offence is proved, they are to be punished, but with this reservation—that if any one denies that he is a Christian and makes it clear that he is not, by offering prayers to our deities, then he is to be pardoned because of his recantation, however suspicious his past conduct may have been. But pamphlets published anonymously must not carry any weight whatever, no matter what the charge may be, for they are not only a precedent of the very worst type, but they are not in consonance with the spirit of our age.

2. Can Rome and the Church, Christianity and Classical Culture, Be Harmonized?

The peculiarities of the Christians, seen from the point of view of both the rulers of the Roman Empire and the populace, alike heirs of the classical Greco-Roman tradition, brought upon them all sorts of charges from atheism to immorality. The great Christian apologist, Tertullian, supplies some of the answers to these accusations. Born about A.D. 155, Tertullian received a legal education and attained some eminence as a lawyer before his conversion to

Christianity about A.D. *180. Zeal for the new faith quickly won for him appointment as elder of the church at Carthage in Africa. Relying upon his training and experience, he turned his talents to writing, both to answer the charges and also to meet what he regarded as a greater danger from men who professed themselves Christians but failed in one way or another to keep the faith. Seeking to meet the philosophy of the classical world on its own ground, some of Tertullian's contemporaries and others of his time sought to reason their way into a syncretism that would provide Christian answers to the intellectual problems that both Christianity and the philosophy of the ancient world had posed. He took a more intransigeant position.*

APOLOGY*

Tertullian

We [Christians], then, alone are without crime. Is there aught wonderful in that, if it be a very necessity with us? For a necessity indeed it is. Taught of God himself what goodness is, we have both a perfect knowledge of it as revealed to us by a perfect Master; and faithfully we do His will, as enjoined on us by a Judge we dare not despise. But your ideas of virtue you have got from mere human opinion; on human authority, too, its obligation rests: hence your system of practical morality is deficient, both in the fulness and authority requisite to produce a life of real virtue. Man's wisdom to point out what is good, is no greater than his authority to exact the keeping of it; the one is as easily deceived as the other is despised. And so, which is the ampler rule, to say, "Thou shalt not kill," or to teach, "Be not even angry?" Which is more perfect, to forbid adultery, or to restrain from even a single lustful look? Which indicates the higher intelligence, interdicting evil-doing, or evil-speaking? Which is more thorough, not allowing an injury, or not even suffering an injury done to you to be repaid? . . . what is the real authority of human laws, when it is in man's power both to evade them, by generally managing to hide himself out of sight in his crimes, and to despise them sometimes, if inclination or necessity leads him to offend? Think of these things, too, in the light of the brevity of any punishment you can inflict—never to last longer than till death. On this ground Epicurus makes light of all suffering and pain, maintaining that if it is small, it is contemptible; and if it is great, it is not long-continued. No doubt about it, we, who receive our awards under the judgment of an all-seeing God, and who look forward to eternal punishment from Him for sin,—we alone make real effort to attain a blameless life, under the influence of our ampler knowledge, the impossibility of concealment, and the greatness of the threatened torment, not merely long-enduring but everlasting. . . .

We have sufficiently met, as I think, the accusation of the various crimes on the ground of which these fierce demands are made for Christian blood. We have made a full exhibition of our case; and we have shown you how we

---

* Reprinted from *The Antenicene Fathers*, ed. A. Roberts and J. Donaldson (Buffalo: The Christian Literature Publishing Co., 1885), III, 50–51.

are able to prove that our statement is correct, from the trustworthiness, I mean, and antiquity of our sacred writings, and from the confession likewise of the powers of spiritual wickedness themselves. Who will venture to undertake our refutation; not with skill of words, but, as we have managed our demonstration, on the basis of reality? But while the truth we hold is made clear to all, unbelief meanwhile, at the very time it is convinced of the worth of Christianity, which has now become well known for its benefits as well as from the intercourse of life, takes up the notion that it is not really a thing divine, but rather a kind of philosophy. These are the very things, it says, the philosophers counsel and profess—innocence, justice, patience, sobriety, chastity. Why, then, are we not permitted an equal liberty and impunity for our doctrines as they have, with whom, in respect of what we teach, we are compared? or why are not they, as so like us, not pressed to the same offices, for declining which our lives are imperilled? For who compels a philosopher to sacrifice or take an oath, or put out useless lamps at midday? Nay, they openly overthrow your gods, and in their writings they attack your superstitions; and you applaud them for it. Many of them even, with your countenance, bark out against your rulers, and are rewarded with statues and salaries, instead of being given to the wild beasts. . . .

He proceeded to compare the conduct of famous philosophers with that of simple Christians to the detriment of the former. Then he continued.

The truth which philosophers, these mockers and corrupters of it, with hostile ends merely affect to hold, and in doing so deprave, caring for nought but glory, Christians both intensely and intimately long for and maintain in its integrity, as those who have a real concern about their salvation. So that we are like each other neither in our knowledge nor our ways, as you imagine . . . But it will be said that some of us, too, depart from the rules of our discipline. In that case, however, we count them no longer Christians; but the philosophers who do such things retain still the name and the honour of wisdom. So, then, where is there any likeness between the Christian and the philosopher? between the disciple of Greece and of heaven? between the man whose object is fame, and whose object is life? between the talker and the doer? between the man who builds up and the man who pulls down? between the friend and the foe of error? between one who corrupts the truth, and one who restores and teaches it?

ON PRESCRIPTION AGAINST HERETICS*

Tertullian

In his On Prescription against Heretics, *Tertullian emphasized more vigorously still what he deemed the real relation between true Christianity, heresy, and philosophy.*

---

* Reprinted from *The Antenicene Fathers,* ed. A. Roberts and J. Donaldson (Buffalo: The Christian Literature Publishing Co., 1885), III, 246.

These are "the doctrines" of men and "of demons" produced for itching ears of the spirit of this world's wisdom: this the Lord called "foolishness," and "chose the foolish things of the world" to confound even philosophy itself. For (philosophy) it is which is the material of the world's wisdom, the rash interpreter of the nature and the dispensation of God. Indeed heresies are themselves instigated by philosophy. . . . The same subject-matter is discussed over and over again by the heretics and the philosophers; the same arguments are involved. Whence comes evil? Why is it permitted? What is the origin of man? and in what way does he come? Besides the question . . . very lately proposed—Whence comes God? . . . Unhappy Aristotle! who invented for these men dialectics, the art of building up and pulling down; an art so evasive in its propositions, so far-fetched in its conjectures, so harsh, in its arguments, so productive of contentions—embarrassing even to itself, retracting everything, and really treating of nothing! Whence spring those "fables and endless genealogies," and "unprofitable questions," and "words which spread like a cancer?" From all these, when the apostle[1] would restrain us, he expressly names *philosophy* as that which he would have us be on our guard against. Writing to the Colossians, he says, "See that no one beguile you through philosophy and vain deceit, after the tradition of men, and contrary to the wisdom of the Holy Ghost." He had been at Athens, and had in his interviews (with its philosophers) become acquainted with that human wisdom which pretends to know the truth, whilst it only corrupts it, and is itself divided into its own manifold heresies, by the variety of its mutually repugnant sects. What indeed has Athens to do with Jerusalem? What concord is there between the Academy and the Church? what between heretics and Christians? Our instruction comes from "the porch of Solomon," who had himself taught that "the Lord should be sought in simplicity of heart." Away with all attempts to produce a mottled Christianity of Stoic, Platonic, and dilectic composition! We want no curious disputation after possessing Christ Jesus, no inquisition after enjoying the gospel! With our faith, we desire no further belief. For this is our palmary faith, that there is nothing which we ought to believe besides.

3. How Did God Provide for the Unity of Christianity?

From early in its history, Christianity underwent a very considerable persecution by individual pagans and by the Roman government. Simultaneously, the Church found itself wracked by internal conflict, in grave danger of losing all sense of unity. Questions that might split this militant community of believers thus became a matter of life and death for the Church. The Christians had to stand together, a united front against the world. Hence, such questions as whether those individuals who had defected under pressure were still members of the Church had more than a purely theological significance.

Like Tertullian, Cyprian was born in Africa, probably at Carthage around A.D. *200. Similarly, he received a legal education and was also successful*

---

[1] Tertullian was referring to Paul.

as a teacher of rhetoric. After conversion to Christianity, he won the position of Bishop of Carthage. This honor came so quickly, however, as to cause discontent among other candidates for the office. Their efforts to displace Cyprian by claiming their own competence to serve as bishops embroiled him in controversy over who properly could administer the sacraments of the Church, especially baptism. He lived during the period when the persecution of the emperor Decius (ruled A.D. 249-251) largely dispersed the North African church. During the persecution, Cyprian fled Carthage, while the imperial government set up a special board before which those suspected of being Christian had to declare that they were not members of the faith. Under such pressure, from within and without the Christian community, Cyprian devised his views on the unity of the Church.

THE UNITY OF THE CATHOLIC CHURCH*

Cyprian

We must guard against wily trickery and subtle deceit no less than open and obvious perils. And could anything more subtle and wily have been devised than this? The enemy had been exposed and laid low by the coming of Christ, light came to the nations, the sun of salvation shined to save mankind, so that the deaf received the hearing of spiritual grace, the blind opened their eyes to the Lord, the weak recovered strength in eternal health, the lame ran to church, the dumb prayed aloud. Yet, when he saw the idols abandoned and his seats and temples deserted through the host of believers, our enemy thought of a new trick, to deceive the unwary under cover of the name Christian. He invented heresies and schisms to undermine faith, pervert truth, and break unity. Unable to keep us in the dark ways of former error, he draws us into a new maze of deceit. He snatches men away from the Church itself and, just when they think they have drawn near to the light and escaped the night of the world, he plunges them unawares into a new darkness. Though they do not stand by the gospel and discipline and law of Christ, they call themselves Christians. Though they are walking in darkness, they think they are in the light, through the deceitful flattery of the adversary who, as the Apostle said, transforms himself into an angel of light and adorns his ministers as ministers of righteousness[1] who call night day, death salvation, despair hope, perfidy faith, antichrist Christ, cunningly to frustrate truth by their lying show of truth. That is what happens, my brothers, when we do not return to the fount of truth, when we are not looking to the head and keeping the doctrine taught from heaven.

Due consideration of these points renders lengthy discussion and argument unnecessary. Faith finds ready proof when the truth is stated succinctly.

---

* Cyprian, "The Unity of the Catholic Church" 3-5. Reprinted by permission of the publishers from *Early Latin Theology*, Vol. V. LCC, ed. S. L. Greenslade (London: Student Christian Movement Press, and Philadelphia: Westminster Press, 1956), pp. 125-127.

[1] II Corinthians 11:14-15.

The Lord says to Peter: "I say unto thee that thou art Peter, and upon this rock I will build my Church; and the gates of hell shall not prevail against it. I will give unto thee the keys of the kingdom of heaven: and whatsoever thou shalt bind on earth shall be bound in heaven; and whatsoever thou shalt loose on earth shall be loosed also in heaven.[2] He builds the Church upon one man. True, after the resurrection he assigned the like power to all the apostles, saying: "As the Father hath sent me, even so send I you. Receive ye the Holy Ghost: whose soever sins ye remit, they shall be remitted unto him; whose soever ye retain, they shall be retained."[3] Despite that, in order to make unity manifest, he arranged by his own authority that this unity should, from the start, take its beginning from one man. Certainly the rest of the apostles were exactly what Peter was; they were endowed with an equal share of office and power. But there was unity at the beginning before any development, to demonstrate that the Church of Christ is one. This one Church is also intended in the *Song of Songs,* when the Holy Spirit says, in the person of the Lord: "My dove, my perfect one, is but one; she is the only one of her mother, the choice one of her that bare her."[4] Can one who does not keep this unity of the Church believe that he keeps the faith? Can one who resists and struggles against the Church be sure that he is in the Church? For the blessed apostle Paul gives the same teaching and declares the same mystery of unity when he says: "There is one body and one spirit, one hope of your calling, one Lord, one faith, one baptism, one God."[5]

It is particularly incumbent upon those of us who preside over the Church as bishops to uphold this unity firmly and to be its champions, so that we may prove the episcopate also to be itself one and undivided. Let no one deceive the brotherhood with lies or corrupt the true faith with faithless treachery. The episcopate is a single whole, in which each bishop's share gives him a right to, and a responsibility for, the whole. So is the Church a single whole, though she spreads far and wide into a multitude of churches as her fertility increases. We may compare the sun, many rays, but one light, or a tree, many branches but one firmly rooted trunk. When many streams flow from one spring, although the bountiful supply of water welling out has the appearance of plurality, unity is preserved in the source. Pluck a ray from the body of the sun, and its unity allows no division of the light. Break a branch from the tree, and when it is broken off it will not bud. Cut a stream off from its spring, and when it is cut off it dries up. In the same way the Church, bathed in the light of the Lord, spreads her rays throughout the world, yet the light everywhere diffused is one light and the unity of the body is not broken. In the abundance of her plenty she stretches her branches over the whole earth, far and wide she pours her generously flowing streams. Yet there is one head, one source, one mother boundlessly fruitful. Of her womb we are born, by her milk we are nourished, by her breath we are quickened.

---

[2] Matthew 16:18–19.

[3] John 20:21–23.

[4] Song of Solomon 6:9.

[5] Ephesians 4:4–6.

4. How Shall the Enemies of Christianity Be Dealt With in the Christian Empire?

After the conversion of the emperor Constantine about A.D. *312, the Christian Church had to cope with the problem of its relationship with rulers who fostered Christianity but who were nevertheless responsible for the security of an empire, many of whose inhabitants were not Christian, rulers, moreover, not readily receptive to limitations on their authority in any sphere. A decree of the Christian emperor Theodosius (*A.D. *379–395) sought to deal with the surviving non-Christian cults in the Empire.*

CODEX THEODOSIANUS*

Hereafter no one of whatever race or dignity, whether placed in office or discharged therefrom with honour, powerful by birth or humble in condition and fortune, shall in any place in any city sacrifice an innocent victim to a senseless image, venerate with fire the household deity by a more private offering, as it were the genius of the house, or the Penates,[1] and burn lights, place incense, or hang up garlands.

If any one undertakes by way of sacrifice to slay a victim, or to consult the smoking entrails,[2] let him, as guilty of lese-majesty, receive the appropriate sentence, having been accused by a lawful indictment, even though he shall not have sought anything against the safety of the princes or concerning their welfare. It constitutes a crime of this nature to wish to repeal the laws, to spy into lawful things, to reveal secrets, or to attempt things forbidden, to seek the end of another's welfare, or to promise the hope of another's ruin.

If any one, by placing incense, venerates either images made by mortal labour, or those which are enduring, or if any one in ridiculous fashion forthwith venerates what he has represented, either by a tree encircled with garlands or an altar of cut turfs (though the advantage of such service is small, the injury to religion is complete), let him, as guilty of sacrilege, be punished by the loss of that house or possession in which he worshipped according to the heathen superstition. For all places which shall smoke with incense, if they shall be proved to belong to those who burn incense, shall be confiscated.

But if, in temples or public sanctuaries or buildings and fields belonging to another, any one should venture this sort of sacrifice, if it shall appear that the acts were performed without the knowledge of the owner, let him be compelled to pay a fine of twenty-five pounds of gold, and let the same penalty apply to those who connive at this crime as well as those who sacrifice.

---

* Reprinted by permission of the publishers from *Codex Theodosianus* XVI.x.12, "The Suppression of Pagan Worship," in *A Source-Book for Ancient Church History*, ed. J. C. Ayers (New York: Charles Scribner's Sons, 1913), pp. 346–348.

[1] The Penates were the spirits which, especially in early Roman times, were believed to guard the family larder. Their worship was part of private, family cult practice.

[2] A very important part of animal sacrifice in the pagan world was the examination of the entrails as a means of foretelling the future.

We will also that this command be observed by judges, defensors, and curials of each and every city,[3] to the effect that those things noted by them be reported to the court, and by the acts charged be punished. But if they believe anything to be overlooked by favour or allowed to pass through negligence, they will lie under a judicial warning. And when they have been warned, if by any negligence they fail to punish, they will be fined thirty pounds of gold, and the members of their court are to be subjected to a like punishment.

5. Where in the Church Does Religious Authority Lie?

By the middle of the fourth century A.D., *the organization of the Church began to undergo an important change. Removal of the imperial capital from Rome to Constantinople (modern Istanbul) had left the West with weakened government control, and a heresy called Arianism won a following among many bishops.[1] The situation evoked from the Council of Sardica (*A.D. *344) and from Julius, Bishop of Rome (ruled* A.D. *337–352), claims more precise than Cyprian's as to the location of supreme authority in the Church.*

THE COUNCIL OF SARDICA*

. . . But if in any province a bishop have a matter in dispute against his brother bishop, one of the two shall not call in as judge a bishop from another province.

But if judgment have gone against a bishop in any cause, and he think that he has a good case, in order that the question may be reopened, let us, if it be your pleasure, honour the memory of St. Peter the Apostle, and let those who tried the case write to Julius, the bishop of Rome, and if he shall judge that the case should be retried, let that be done, and let him appoint judges; but if he shall find that the case is of such a sort that the former decision need not be disturbed, what he has decreed shall be confirmed.

Is this the pleasure of all? The synod answered, It is our pleasure.

POPE JULIUS†

. . . Let us grant the "removal," as you write, of Athanasius and Marcellus[1] from their own places; yet what must one say of the case of the other

---

[3] These were the local judicial and legislative officers in the cities of the Empire.

[1] Arianism was the position taken by one of the parties to a particularly difficult controversy of the fourth century. It involved the question of the relationship of Christ to God the Father within the Trinity, but since the controversy died out in Antiquity, it has not been presented in detail here.

* Reprinted by permission of the publishers from *The Select Library of Nicene and Post-Nicene Fathers of the Christian Church*, Second Series, Vol. XIV, *The Seven Ecumenical Councils*, ed. Philip Schaff and Henry Wace (Grand Rapids, Mich.: Eerdmans, 1956), p. 417.

† Reprinted from *Documents Illustrative of the History of the Church*, Vol. II, *313–461 A.D.*, ed. Beresford James Kidd (London: Society for Promoting Christian Knowledge, 1938), No. 17, p. 30.

[1] These were two prelates deposed during the course of the Arian controversy. The issue, as the text of the letter makes clear, is the question of whether the Council of Antioch, to which the letter was written, or any church council for that matter, should bow to the will of the emperor and submit to secular condemnation of *any* party in a religious controversy.

bishops and presbyters who, as I said before, came hither from various parts, and who complained that they also had been forced away, and had suffered the like injuries? O dearly beloved, the decisions of the Church are no longer according to the Gospel, but tend only to banishment and death. Supposing, as you assert, that some offence rested upon these persons, the case ought to have been conducted against them, not after this manner, but according to the Canon of the Church. Word should have been written of it to us all, that so a just sentence might proceed from all. For the sufferers were bishops, and churches of no ordinary note, but those which the Apostles themselves had governed in their own persons.

And why was nothing said to us concerning the church of the Alexandrians in particular? Are you ignorant that the custom has been for word to be written first to us, and then for a just sentence to be passed from this place? If, then, any such suspicion rested upon the bishop there, notice thereof ought to have been sent to the church of this place; whereas, after neglecting to inform us, and proceeding on their own authority, as they pleased, now they desire to obtain our concurrence in their decisions, though we never condemned him. Not so have the constitutions of the Paul, not so have the traditions of the Fathers directed. What we have received from the blessed Apostle Peter, that I signify to you.

6. Can Man's Freedom Be Reconciled with God's Foreknowledge, Man's Punishment for Sin with God's Love and Mercy?

The conversion of Constantine and the favor he showed the Church in consequence of it ended the long period of persecution and allowed Christianity to cross over into smoother, though not always safer, waters. Still, to say that the Christians were now at peace with the Empire is not quite the same thing as saying they were at peace with the world. Despite Theodosius' decree, the Empire itself was still largely pagan, and those who had not accepted Christianity were quick to blame it for most of the troubles that faced a state and society approaching collapse. Particularly they blamed it for the sack of Rome in A.D. 410 by Alaric and the Visigoths, whom the crumbling imperial defenses could no longer keep out. The opponents of the Church argued that this shocking disaster was the result of the rejection of the ancient gods of Rome under whom the city had acquired its greatness. Since the pagans made the sack a practical test of the relative validity of the two religious systems, their allegations called for complete answer by the Christians. That answer came in the City of God, *the greatest work of one of the later ancient Church fathers, Augustine, Bishop of Hippo in North Africa.*

Aurelius Augustinus was born in A.D. 345 in Numidia in North Africa, the son of a pagan father and a Christian mother. Like so many earlier Christian leaders of North Africa, he was trained in rhetoric. Before he reached the age of thirty, he was lucratively employed as a teacher of rhetoric in Rome and Milan. As a youth, Augustine sowed his wild oats abundantly. The prayers of his mother, however, bore fruit when the young man came under the influence of Ambrose, Bishop of Milan. For suddenly he gave up his mistress, accepted

*Christianity, received baptism by Ambrose in 387, sold his goods, and distrib-
uted the proceeds among the poor. He remained in Italy for a short time,
devoting himself to the affairs of the Church, and then began a return trip to
Africa with his mother, only to have her die on the way. Back in Africa, he
was soon chosen elder of the church at Hippo, and in 391 became the city's
bishop. He spent the rest of his life administering affairs of the Church, practicing mild asceticism, and writing his many works of theology, apologetics,
meditation, and confession. He is often called the ancient world's greatest mind
since Plato, and his works show a thorough acquaintance with all the philosophical and literary learning of his age.*

*Augustine's experience and insights allowed him to plumb the depths
of human nature. His memory of a seemingly trivial youthful prank permitted
him to present in his* Confessions *a graphic picture of what he found in those
depths.*

CONFESSIONS*
St. Augustine

Theft is punished by Thy law, O Lord, and by the law written in men's
hearts, which iniquity itself cannot blot out. For what thief will suffer a thief?
Even a rich thief will not suffer him who is driven to it by want. Yet had I
a desire to commit robbery, and did so, compelled neither by hunger, nor
poverty, but through a distaste for well-doing, and lustiness of iniquity. For I
pilfered that of which I had already sufficient, and much better. Nor did I
desire to enjoy what I pilfered, but the theft and sin itself. There was a pear-
tree close to our vineyard, heavily laden with fruit, which was tempting neither
for its colour nor its flavour. To shake and rob this some of us wanton young
fellows went, late one night (having, according to our disgraceful habit, prolonged our games in the streets until then), and carried away great loads, not
to eat ourselves, but to fling to the very swine, having only eaten some of them;
and to do this pleased us all the more because it was not permitted. Behold
my heart, O my God; behold my heart, which Thou hadst pity upon when in
the bottomless pit. Behold, now, let my heart tell Thee what it was seeking
there, that I should be gratuitously wanton, having no inducement to evil but
the evil itself. It was foul, and I loved it. I loved to perish. I loved my own
error—not that for which I erred, but the error itself. Base soul, falling from
Thy firmament to utter destruction—not seeking aught through the shame
but the shame itself!

In the City of God, *Augustine not only answered pagan criticism of
Christianity, but showed that God has always dealt with mankind, even though
His true nature remained hidden from unbelievers. The author echoes a theme
raised earlier by St. Paul in a speech before the assembly of elders of the city
of Athens in Acts 17: that to pagan eyes there is an* Unknown God *who inter-
venes even in the affairs of those who do not know Him. Therefore, a double*

* Reprinted by permission of the publishers from Augustine, *Confessions* iv.9, *The Select
Library of the Nicene and Post-Nicene Fathers of the Christian Church*, Vol I, *The Confessions
and Letters of St. Augustine*, ed. Philip Schaff (Grand Rapids, Mich.: Eerdmans, 1956), p. 57.

community always has existed in the world, made up of believers on the one hand, and everyone else on the other.

In Books ii to x, Augustine refuted "the arguments of those enemies of the City of God who prefer their own gods to its Founder, Christ, and who hate His followers savagely, to the havoc of their own souls."[1] When, in the course of this discussion, he came to the question of God's part in all this and the implications of divine control over those who do not know Him, he had the following to say:

THE CITY OF GOD*

St. Augustine

There are some who define fate, not as the arrangement of stars at conception, birth, or other beginning-to-be, but as the total series of causes which brings about all that happens. With these there is no need to enter into a lengthy debate on the use of words, since they attribute to the will and power of God the order and dependence of causes. They are perfectly right in believing that God allows nothing to remain unordered and that He knows all things before they come to pass. He is the Cause of all causes, although not of all choices.

It is easy to prove that by Fate they mean, primarily, the will of the supreme God whose power cannot be prevented from reaching everywhere. It was Annaeus Seneca,[1] I think, who wrote in verse:

> Lead where Thou wilt, Father and Lord of the world.
> Mine to obey, boldly, without delay.
> Should e'er my will resist the right and good,
> I'll take in tears whatever ill may come.
> Fate leads or drags men—willy-nilly—on.[2]

Obviously, in the last line he means by fate the will of the 'Father and Lord' mentioned in the first line. This will he is ready to obey—to be led willingly or, if need be, dragged reluctantly. The fact is that 'Fate leads or drags men—willy-nilly[3]—on.'

There is the same idea in some lines of Homer which Cicero, when he put them into Latin, took to mean:

> Men's minds are led by whatsoever rays
> High Jove has cast upon their earthly ways.[4]

---

[1] Augustine, *City of God,* xviii.1. All selections from this work are reprinted by permission of the publishers from *Fathers of the Church,* Vols. VIII, XIV, XXIV: *The Writings of St. Augustine,* Vols. VI, VII, VIII, trans. Demetrius B. Zema, S. J., Gerald G. Walsh, S. J., Grace Monahan, O. S. U., and Daniel J. Honan (Washington, D.C.: The Catholic University of America Press, 1950, 1952, 1954).

* *City of God,* v.8–10; viii.4–5; xiv.26–28; xix.16–17.

[1] For some of Seneca's own writing, and for reference to the Stoic doctrine which Augustine cited here, see above, pp. 83–87.

[2] Seneca *Letters* cvii.

[3] Seneca: "When willing they are led, when unwilling, dragged."

[4] *Odyssey* xvii.136–137.

Not, of course, that Cicero thought the poet's opinion has any authority in such matters, but he notes that the Stoic philosophers used to cite these lines of Homer when they were defending the power of fate. Thus, there is question here, not of the opinion of the poet, but of the thought of the philosopher. It is clear from these verses, which they used in their discussions, that they meant by fate the supreme divinity, whom they called Jupiter, and from whom all destinies depend.

Cicero attempts to refute these Stoics,[5] but he can find no way of doing so without getting rid of divination; this he does by denying all knowledge of what is future. He makes every effort to prove that there can be no foreknowledge, whether in God or in man, and, therefore, no possibility of prediction. Thus, he denies the foreknowledge of God and seeks to get rid even of the clearest cases of prophecy by baseless arguments and by limiting himself to such oracles as are easy to refute. The fact is that he does not confute even these. However, he makes a masterly refutation of the conjectures of the astrologers—for the simple reason that their mutual contradictions are their best refutation.

Nevertheless, for all their sidereal fates, the astrologers are nearer the truth than Cicero with his denial of all knowledge of the future, for it is plain nonsense for a man to admit that God exists and then to deny that He can know the future. Cicero realized this, but was rash enough to fulfill the words of the Scripture: 'The fool has said in his heart: There is no God.'[6] It is true, he does not do this in his own name. This, he knew, was too risky. Instead, in his work *On the Nature of the Gods* he lets Cotta[7] play the role, in arguing against the Stoics, of denying the existence of any divine nature. Cicero chose to give his vote to Lucilius Balbus, who defended the Stoic position, but, in his work *On Divination,* Cicero openly and in his own name attacks all foreknowledge of the future.

It is true, he seems to do this only to save free will and to reject the necessity of fate. His point is that, once any knowledge of the future is admitted, it is logically impossible to deny fate.

But, be these tortuous strifes and disputations of the philosophers what they will, we who profess belief in the supreme and true God confess, likewise, His will, His supreme power, His foreknowledge. Nor are we dismayed by the difficulty that what we choose to do freely is done of necessity, because He whose foreknowledge cannot be deceived foreknew that we would choose to do it. This was the fear that made Cicero oppose foreknowledge. It was this fear, too, that led the Stoics to admit that not everything happened of necessity, even though they held that everything happens by fate.

Let us examine, then, this fear of foreknowledge which led Cicero to attempt to deny it in his detestable disputation. He argues thus. If all that is future is foreknown, each event will occur in the order in which it is foreknown that it will occur. But if things happen in this order, the order of things is known for certain in the mind of God who foreknows them. But,

---

[5] *De Divinatione (On Divination)* ii and following.
[6] *Psalms* 13:1.
[7] Gaius Aurelius Cotta was consul in 75 B.C. and was noted for the sharp and incisive character of his oratory. In Cicero's *De Natura Deorum (On the Nature of the Gods)* (iii.145), he championed the philosophy of the Academy in Athens.

if the order of events is known for certain, then the order of causes is known for certain—since nothing can happen without a preceding efficient cause. If, however, the order of causes, by which all that happens is known for certain, then, he says, all that happens happens by fate. But, if this is so, nothing is left to our own power and, therefore, there is no choice in our will. But, he goes on, once we admit this, all human life becomes topsy-turvy; laws are made in vain; there is no point in reproaches or in praise, in scolding or in exhortation; there is no ground in justice for rewarding the good or punishing the wicked.

Thus, his motive for rejecting foreknowledge of the future was to avoid unworthy, absurd and dangerous implications for human society. He narrows down the choices of a devout mind to one or other of these alternatives: *either* the power of choice *or* foreknowledge. It seemed to him impossible that both could exist. If one stands, the other falls. If we choose foreknowledge, we lose free choice; if we choose free choice, we must lose knowledge of the future.

Magnanimous and learned as he was, and with no thought but to save human nature as best he could, Cicero made his choice. He chose free choice. To make it certain, he denied foreknowledge. Thus, to make men free, he made them give up God.

A man of faith wants both. He professes both and with a devout faith he holds both firmly. But how, one asks? For, if there is foreknowledge of the future, logical step follows logical step until we reach a point where nothing is left in the will. On the other hand, if we start from power in the will, the steps lead in the opposite direction until we come to the conclusion that fore-knowledge is non-existent. This is how the reverse argument runs. If there is free choice, not all is fixed by fate. If not all is fixed by fate, there is no certain order of all causes. If there is no certain order of causes, there is no certain order of events known in the mind of God, since events cannot happen without preceding and efficient causes. If the order of events is not certain in the foreknowledge of God, not all things happen as He foresaw they would happen. But, if all does not happen as He foresaw it would happen, then, Cicero argues, in God there is no foreknowledge of all that is to happen.

Our stand against such bold and impious attacks on God is to say that God knows all things before they happen; yet, we act by choice in all those things where we feel and know that we cannot act otherwise than willingly. And yet, so far from saying that everything happens by fate, we say that nothing happens by fate—for the simple reason that the word 'fate' means nothing. The word means nothing, since the only reality in the mind of those who use the word—namely, the arrangement of the stars at the moment of conception or birth—is, as we show, pure illusion.

We do not deny, of course, an order of causes in which the will of God is all-powerful. On the other hand, we do not give this order the name fate, except in a sense in which the word 'fate' is derived from *fari,* to speak. For, of course, we cannot reject what is written in Holy Scripture: 'God hath spoken once, these two things have I heard, that power belongeth to God and mercy to Thee, O Lord, for Thou wilt render to everyone according to his works.'[8] The 'once' here means 'once and for all.' God spoke once and for all

---

[8] Psalms 62:11f.

because He knows unalterably all that is to be, all that He is to do. In this way, we might use the word 'fate' to mean what God has 'spoken' [*fatum*], except that the meaning of the word has already taken a direction in which we do not want men's minds to move.

However, our main point is that, from the fact that to God the order of all causes is certain, there is no logical deduction that there is no power in the choice of our will. The fact is that our choices fall within the order of the causes which is known for certain to God and is contained in His foreknowledge—for, human choices are the causes of human acts. It follows that He who foreknew the causes of all things could not be unaware that our choices were among those causes which were foreknown as the causes of our acts.

In this matter it is easy enough to refute Cicero by his own admission, namely, that nothing happens without a preceding efficient cause. It does not help him to admit that nothing happens without a cause and then to argue that not every cause is fated, since some causes are either fortuitous or natural or voluntary. He admits that nothing happens without a preceding cause; that is enough to refute him.

As for the causes which are called fortuitous—hence, the name of fortune—we do not say they are unreal. We say they are latent, in the sense that they are hidden in the will either of the true God or one of His spirits. And, of course, still less do we dissociate from the will of Him who is the Author and Builder of all nature, the causes which Cicero calls 'natural.' There remain the voluntary causes. They are the choices of God or of angels or of men or of certain animals—if, indeed we may call 'choices' the instinctive movements of irrational animals by which they seek or avoid what is good or bad for their nature. By the choices of angels I mean those of the good ones we call the angels of God or of the wicked ones we call demons or the angels of the Devil. So of men, there are the choices of good men and of bad men.

From this we conclude that the only efficient causes of all things are voluntary causes, that is to say, causes of the same nature as the spirit or breath of life. Of course, the air or wind can be said to breathe; but, being a body, it is not the breath or spirit of life. The Spirit of Life, which gives life to all and is the Creator of all matter and of every created spirit is God, a Spirit, indeed, but uncreated. In His will is the supreme power which helps the good choices of created spirits, judges the evil ones, and orders all of them, giving powers to some and not to others.

As He is the Creator of all natures, so is He the giver of all powers—though He is not the maker of all choices. Evil choices are not from Him, for they are contrary to the nature which is from Him. Thus, bodies are subject to wills. Some bodies are subject to our wills—to the wills of all mortal animals, but especially those of men rather than of beasts. Some bodies are subject to the wills of angels. And absolutely all bodies are subject to the will of God; as, indeed, are all wills, too, since they have no power save what He gave them.

Thus, God is the Cause of all things—a cause that makes but is not made. Other causes make, but they are themselves made—for example, all created spirits and, especially, rational spirits. Material causes which are rather passive than active are not to be included among efficient causes, for their power is limited to what the wills of spirits work through them.

It does not follow, therefore, that the order of causes, known for certain though it is in the foreknowing mind of God, brings it about that there is no power in our will, since our choices themselves have an important place in the order of causes.

And so, let Cicero argue with those who hold that this order of causes is fixed by fate, or, rather, is the reality they call fate. Our main objection is to the word fate, which is usually given a false sense. As for Cicero, we object to him even more than the Stoics do when he denies that the order of all causes is fixed and clearly known in the foreknowledge of God. Cicero must either deny that God exists—and this, in fact, is what he attempts to do in the name of Cotta in his work *On the Nature of the Gods*—or else, if he admits God's existence while denying His foreknowledge, what he says amounts to nothing more than what 'the fool hath said in his heart: There is no God.' The fact is that one who does not foreknow the whole of the future is most certainly not God.

Our conclusion is that our wills have power to do all that God wanted them to do and foresaw they could do. Their power, such as it is, is a real power. What they are to do they themselves will most certainly do, because God foresaw both that they could do it and that they would do it and His knowledge cannot be mistaken. Thus, if I wanted to use the word 'fate' for anything at all, I should prefer to say that 'fate' is the action of a weak person, while 'choice' is the act of the stronger man who holds the weak man in his power, rather than to admit that the choice of our will is taken away by that order of causes which the Stoics arbitrarily call fate.

It follows that we need not be afraid of that necessity which frightened the Stoics into distinguishing various kinds of causes. They sought to free certain causes from necessity while others were subject to it. Among the causes which they wanted free from necessity they reckoned our wills. Obviously, wills could not be free if subject to necessity.

Now, if by necessity we mean one that is in no way in our power, but which has its way even when our will is opposed to it, as is the case with the necessity to die, then, our choices of living well or ill obviously are not subject to this kind of necessity. The fact is that we do many things which we would most certainly not do if we did not choose to do them. The most obvious case is our willing itself. For, if we will, there is an act of willing; there is none if we do not want one. We would certainly not make a choice if we did not choose to make it. On the other hand, if we take necessity to mean that in virtue of which something must be so and so or must happen in such and such a way, I do not see that we should be afraid of such necessity taking away our freedom of will. We do not put the life of God and the foreknowledge of God under any necessity when we say that God *must* live an eternal life and *must* know all things. Neither do we lessen His power when we say He cannot die or be deceived. This is the kind of inability which, if removed, would make God less powerful than He is. God is rightly called omnipotent, even though He is unable to die and be deceived. We call Him omnipotent because He does whatever He wills to do and suffers nothing that He does not will to suffer. He would not, of course, be omnipotent, if He had to suffer anything against His will. It is precisely because He is omnipotent that for Him some things are impossible.

So with us, when we say we *must* choose freely when we choose at all, what we say is true; yet, we do not subject free choice to any necessity which destroys our liberty. Our choices, therefore, are our own, and they effect, whenever we choose to act, something that would not happen if we had not chosen. Even when a person suffers against his will from the will of others, there is a voluntary act—not, indeed, of the person who suffers. However, a human will prevails—although the power which permits this is God's. (For, wherever there is a mere will without power to carry out what it chooses, it would be impeded by a stronger will. Even so, there would be no will in such a condition unless there were a will, and not merely the will of another but the will of the one choosing, even though he is unable to carry out his choice.) Therefore, whatever a man has to suffer against his will is not to be attributed to the choices of man or of angels or of any created spirit, but to His choice who gives to wills whatever power they have.

It does not follow, therefore, that there is no power in our will because God foreknew what was to be the choice in our will. For, He who had this foreknowledge had some foreknowledge. Further, if He who foresaw what was to be in our will foresaw, not nothing, but something, it follows that there is a power in our will, even though He foresaw it.

The conclusion is that we are by no means under compulsion to abandon free choice in favor of divine foreknowledge, nor need we deny—God forbid!—that God knows the future, as a condition for holding free choice. We accept both. As Christians and philosophers, we profess both—foreknowledge, as a part of our faith; free choice, as a condition of responsible living. It is hard to live right if one's faith in God is wrong.

Far be it from us, then, to deny, in the interest of our freedom, the foreknowledge of God by whose power we are—or are to be—free. It follows, too, that laws are not in vain, nor scoldings and encouragements, nor praise and blame. He foresaw that such things should be. Such things have as much value as He foresaw they would have. So, too, prayers are useful in obtaining these favors which He foresaw He would bestow on those who should pray for them. There was justice in instituting rewards and punishments for good and wicked deeds. For, no one sins because God foreknew that he would sin. In fact, the very reason why a man is undoubtedly responsible for his own sin, when he sins, is because He whose foreknowledge cannot be deceived foresaw, not the man's fate or fortune or what not, but that the man himself would be responsible for his own sin. No man sins unless it is his choice to sin; and his choice not to sin, that, too, God foresaw.

Augustine, who felt the need to confront and master the problems that classical philosophers posed for Christians, could not be wholly satisfied with Tertullian's forthright dilemma—Athens or Jerusalem.[9] He had said that he would repudiate "all who do not carry philosophy into religious observance or philosophize in a religious spirit."[10] And in the eighth book of the City of God, *he discussed the meaning of this repudiation for a Christian who was thoroughly familiar with the philosophical writings of his pagan predecessors.*

[9] See the selection from Tertullian above, p. 142.
[10] *De Vera Religione* (*On the True Religion*) vii[12].

Of the pupils of Socrates, Plato was so remarkable for his brilliance that he has deservedly outshone all the rest. He was born in Athens of a good family and by his marvelous ability easily surpassed all his fellow disciples. Realizing, however, that neither his own genius nor Socratic training was adequate to evolve a perfect system of philosophy, he traveled far and wide to wherever there was any hope of gaining some valuable addition to knowledge. Thus, in Egypt he mastered the lore which was there esteemed. From there he went to lower Italy, famous for the Pythagorean School, and there successfully imbibed from eminent teachers all that was then in vogue in Italian philosophy.

However, Plato's special affection was for his old master—so much so that in practically all the Dialogues he makes Socrates, with all his charm, the mouthpiece not only of his own moral arguments but of all that Plato learned from others or managed to discover himself.

Now, the pursuit of wisdom follows two avenues—action and contemplation. Thus, one division of philosophy may be called active; the other part, contemplative. The former deals with the conduct of life; that is to say, with the cultivation of morals. Contemplative philosophy considers natural causality and truth as such. Socrates excelled in practical wisdom; Pythagoras favored contemplation, and to this he applied his whole intelligence.

It is to Plato's praise that he combined both in a more perfect philosophy, and then divided the whole into three parts: first, moral philosophy which pertains to action; second, natural philosophy whose purpose is contemplation; third, rational philosophy which discriminates between truth and error. Although this last is necessary for both action and contemplation, it is contemplation especially which claims to reach a vision of the truth. Hence, this three fold division in no way invalidates the distinction whereby action and contemplation are considered the constituent elements of the whole of philosophy. Just what Plato's position was in each of these three divisions—that is to say, just what he knew or believed to be the end of all action, the cause of all nature, the light of all reason—I think it would be rash to affirm and would take too long to discuss at length.

Plato was so fond of following the well-known habit of his master of dissimulating his knowledge or opinions that in Plato's own works (where Socrates appears as a speaker) it is difficult to determine just what views he held even on important questions. However, of the views which are set forth in his writings, whether his own or those of others which seemed to have pleased him, a few must be recalled and included here. In some places, Plato is on the side of the true religion which our faiths accepts and defends. At other times he seems opposed; for example, on the respective merits of monotheism and polytheism in relation to genuine beatitude after death.

Perhaps this may be said of the best disciples of Plato—of those who followed most closely and understood most clearly the teachings of a master rightly esteemed above all other pagan philosophers—that they have perceived, at least, these truths about God: that in Him is to be found the cause of all being, the reason of all thinking, the rule of all living. The first of these truths belongs to natural, the second to rational, the third to moral philosophy. . . .

In Books xi–xiv, the author dealt with the origins of the "two cities": the Earthly City, the world of men apart from God; and the Heavenly City, the community of believers in the true God of whatever age in human history. He closed this discussion as follows:

. . . God Almighty the ultimate and supremely good Creator and Ruler of all living creatures, the Giver of grace and glory to all good wills, and the God who abandons bad wills to the doom they deserve, was not without His own definite plan of populating the City of God with that fixed number of saints which His divine wisdom had ordained, even though the City had to be filled with citizens chosen from the ranks of a fallen human race. Of course, once the whole mass of mankind was, as it were, cankered in its roots, there was no question of men meriting a place in His City. They could only be marked out by His grace; and how great that grace was they could see not only in their own deliverance but in the doom meted out to those who were not delivered from damnation. For, no one can help but acknowledge how gratuitous and undeserved is the grace which delivers him when he sees so clearly the contrast between his privileged, personal immunity and the fate of the penalized community whose punishment he was justly condemned to share.

Here we have an answer to the problem why God should have created men whom He foresaw would sin. It was because both in them and by means of them He could reveal how much was deserved by their guilt and condoned by His grace, and, also, because the harmony of the whole of reality which God has created and controls cannot be marred by the perverse discordancy of those who sin.

What I have just said applies to both angelic and human sinners. They can do nothing to interfere with 'the great works of God which are accomplished according to His will.'[11] God who both foresees all things and can do all things, when He distributes to each of His creatures their appropriate endowments, knows how to turn to good account both good and evil. Hence, there was no reason why God should not make a good use even of the bad angel who was so doomed to obduracy, in punishment of the sin that issued from the primal bad will, that a return to good will became for him impossible. This God did by permitting the bad angel to tempt the first man who had been created good, in the sense of having a will that was good by nature.

The point here is that the first man had been so constituted that if, as a good man, he had relied on the help of God, he could have overcome the bad angel, whereas he was bound to be overcome if he proudly relied on his own will in preference to this wisdom of his maker and helper, God; and he was destined to a merited reward if his will remained firm with the help of God, and to an equally deserved doom if his will wavered because of his desertion from God. Notice here that, whereas the reliance on the help of God was a positive act that was only possible by the help of God, the reliance on his own will was a negative falling away from favors of divine grace, and this was a possibility of his own choice.

There is an analogy to this in living. The act of living in a body is a

---

[11] Psalms 111:2.

positive act which is not a matter of choice but is only possible by the help of nourishment; whereas the choice not to live in the body is a negative act which is in our human power, as we see in the case of suicide. Thus, to remain living as one ought to live was not a matter of choice, even in Eden, but depended on the help of God, whereas to live ill, as one ought not to live, was in man's power; therefore, man was justly responsible for the cutting short of his happiness and the incurring of the penalty that followed.

Since, then, God was not without knowledge of man's future fall, He could well allow man to be tempted by the angel who hated and envied man. God was in no uncertainty regarding the defect which man would suffer; but, what matters more, God foresaw the defeat which the Devil would suffer at the hands of a descendant of Adam, and with the help of divine grace, and that this would be to the greater glory of the saints. Now, all this was so accomplished that nothing in the future escaped the foreknowledge of God, yet nothing in the foreknowledge compelled anyone to sin. God's further purpose was to reveal to all rational creatures, angelic and human, in the light of their own experience, the difference between the fruits of presumption, angelic or human, and the protection of God. For of course, no one would dare to believe or declare that it was beyond God's power to prevent the fall of either angel or man. But, in fact, God preferred not to use His own power, but to leave success or failure to the creature's choice. In this way, God could show both the immense evil that flows from the creature's pride and also the even greater good that comes from His grace.

What we see, then, is that two societies have issued from two kinds of love. Worldly society has flowered from a selfish love which dared to despise even God, whereas the communion of saints is rooted in a love of God that is ready to trample on self. In a word, this latter relies on the Lord, whereas the other boasts that it can get along by itself. The city of man seeks the praise of men, whereas the height of glory for the other is to hear God in the witness of conscience. The one lifts up its head in its own boasting; the other says to God: 'Thou art my glory, thou liftest up my head.'[12]

In the city of the world both the rulers themselves and the people they dominate are dominated by the lust for domination; whereas in the City of God all citizens serve one another in charity, whether they serve by the responsibilities of office or by the duties of obedience. The one city loves its leaders as symbols of its own strength; the other says to its God: 'I love thee, O Lord, my strength.'[13] Hence, even the wise men in the city of man live according to man, and their only goal has been the goods of their bodies or of the mind or of both; though some of them have reached a knowledge of God, 'they did not glorify him as God or give thanks but became vain in their reasonings, and their senseless minds have been darkened. For while professing to be wise' (that is to say, while glorying in their own wisdom, under the domination of pride), 'they have become fools, and they have changed the glory of the incorruptible God for an image made like to corruptible man and to birds and four-footed beasts and creeping things' (meaning that they either led their people, or imitated them, in adoring idols shaped like these things), 'and they wor-

---

[12] Psalms 3:3.
[13] Psalms 18:1.

shipped and served the creature rather than the Creator who is blessed for-ever.'[14] In the City of God, on the contrary, there is no merely human wisdom, but there is a piety which worships the true God as He should be worshiped and has as its goal that reward of all holiness whether in the society of saints on earth or in that of angels of heaven, which is 'that God may be all in all.'[15]

Augustine's discussion in Books xv through the first part of xix develops the simultaneous history of the two cities, drawing heavily upon the account of the events in the lives of the early Hebrews as given in the Old Testament. He closed this discussion with a specific statement about the community of believers, and then continued:

Our holy Fathers in the faith, to be sure, had slaves, but in the regula-tion of domestic peace it was only in matters of temporal importance that they distinguished the position of their children from the status of their servants. So far as concerns the worship of God—from whom all must hope for eternal blessings—they had like loving care for all the household without exception. This was what nature demanded, and it was from this kind of behavior that there grew the designation 'father of the family,' which is so widely accepted that even wicked and domineering men love to be so called.

Those who are true fathers are as solicitous for every one in their house-holds as for their own children to worship and to be worthy of God. They hope and yearn for all to arrive in that heavenly home where there will be no further need of giving orders to other human beings, because there will be no longer any duty to help those who are happy in immortal life. In the meantime, fathers ought to look upon their duty to command as harder than the duty of slaves to obey.

Meanwhile, in case anyone in the home behaves contrary to its peace, he is disciplined by words or whipping or other kind of punishment lawful and licit in human society, and for his own good, to readjust him to the peace he has abandoned. For, there is no more benevolence and helpfulness in bring-ing about the loss of a greater good than there is innocence and compassion in allowing a culprit to go from bad to worse. It is the duty of a blameless person not just to do no wrong, but to keep others from wrong-doing and to punish it when done, so that the one punished may be improved by the experience and others be warned by the example.

Now, since every home should be a beginning or fragmentary constitu-ent of a civil community, and every beginning related to some specific end, and every part to the whole of which it is a part, it ought to follow that domestic peace has a relation to political peace. In other words, the ordered harmony of authority and obedience between those who live together has a relation to the ordered harmony of authority and obedience between those who live in a city. This explains why a father must apply certain regulations of civil law to the governance of his home so as to make it accord with the peace of the whole community.

While the homes of unbelieving men are intent upon acquiring tem-

---

[14] Romans 1:21–25.
[15] I Corinthians 15:28.

poral peace out of the possessions and comforts of this temporal life, the families which live according to faith look ahead to the good things of heaven promised as imperishable, and use material and temporal goods in the spirit of pilgrims, not as snares or obstructions to block their way to God, but simply as helps to ease and never to increase the burdens of this corruptible body which weighs down the soul. Both types of homes and their masters have this in common, that they must use things essential to this mortal life. But the respective purposes to which they put them are characteristic and very different.

So, too, the earthly city which does not live by faith seeks only an earthly peace, and limits the goal of its peace, of its harmony of authority and obedience among its citizens, to the voluntary and collective attainment of objectives necessary to mortal existence. The heavenly City, meanwhile—or, rather, that part that is on pilgrimage in mortal life and lives by faith—must use this earthly peace until such time as our mortality which needs such peace has passed away. As a consequence, so long as her life in the earthly city is that of a captive and an alien (although she has the promise of ultimate delivery and the gift of the Spirit as a pledge), she has no hesitation about keeping in step with the civil law which governs matters pertaining to our existence here below. For, as mortal life is the same for all, there ought to be common cause[16] between the two cities in what concerns our purely human living.

Now comes the difficulty. The city of this world, to begin with, has had certain 'wise men' of its own mold, whom true religion must reject, because either out of their own daydreaming or out of demonic deception these wise men came to believe that a multiplicity of divinities was allied with human life, with different duties, in some strange arrangement, and different assignments: this one over the body, that one over the mind; in the body itself, one over the head, another over the neck, still others, one for each bodily part; in the mind, one over the intelligence, another over learning, another over temper, another over desires; in the realities, related to life, that lie about us, one over flocks and one over wheat, one over wine, one over oil, and another over forests, one over currency, another over navigation, and still another over warfare and victory, one over marriage, a different one over fecundity and childbirth, so on and so on.

The heavenly City, on the contrary, knows and, by religious faith, believes that it must adore one God alone and serve Him with that complete dedication which the Greeks call *latreía* and which belongs to Him alone. As a result, she has been unable to share with the earthly city a common religious legislation, and has had no choice but to dissent on this score and so to become a nuisance to those who think otherwise. Hence, she has had to feel the weight of their anger, hatred, and violence, save in those instances when, by sheer numbers and God's help, which never fails, she has been able to scare off her opponents.

So long, then, as the heavenly City is wayfaring on earth, she invites citizens from all nations and all tongues, and unites them into a single pilgrim band. She takes no issue with that diversity of customs, laws, and traditions whereby human peace is sought and maintained. Instead of nullifying or

---

[16] Augustine's word here is *concordia*, "agreement, harmony."

tearing down, she preserves and appropriates whatever in the diversities of divers races is aimed at one and the same objective of human peace, provided only that they do not stand in the way of the faith and worship of the one supreme and true God.

Thus, the heavenly City, so long as it is wayfaring on earth, not only makes use of earthly peace but fosters and actively pursues along with other human beings a common platform in regard to all that concerns our purely human life and does not interfere with faith and worship. Of course, though, the City of God subordinates this earthly peace to that of heaven.[17] For the latter is not merely true peace, but, strictly speaking, for any rational creature, the only real peace, since it is, as I said, 'the perfectly ordered and harmonious communion of those who find their joy in God and in one another in God.'

When this peace is reached, man will be no longer haunted by death, but plainly and perpetually endowed with life, nor will his body, which now wastes away and weighs down the soul, be any longer animal, but spiritual, in need of nothing and completely under the control of his[18] will.

This peace the pilgrim City already possesses by faith and it lives holily and according to this faith so long as, to attain its heavenly completion, it refers every good act done for God or for his fellow man.[19] I say 'fellow man' because, of course, any community life must emphasize social relationships.

---

[17] The Latin of this part of Augustine's very complicated sentence is, *eamque terrenam pacem refert ad caelestem pacem,* "and this earthly peace is related to the peace of heaven." The rest of his sentence clarifies the meaning of *refert:* true peace is found only among those with a joyful relationship to God and to each other; therefore genuine peace in the world depends upon the prior establishment of heavenly peace.

[18] The translators here have used "our will," but "his will" seems to fit the context.

[19] Here again, Augustine used the word *refert* in the special sense of "subordination" as noted in note 17 above. Every good act done to secure the heavenly peace must be subordinated to God's purposes and society's needs.

THE MIDDLE AGES,

Edited by Peter Riesenberg

I

THE EARLY MIDDLE AGES

What went on in western Europe from, roughly, 400 to 1100 is much too complex to be described in a single negative term, the "Dark Ages." To be sure, there were many changes toward simplicity of life. Some Roman cities were deserted; the population in others gathered for safety near the stone walls built in a more vigorous past; the once active commercial routes of the Empire fell into disuse; the vast majority of Europeans lived out their lives in the countryside, many of them bound by law or custom to the soil. And in the centuries when these things happened, two equally significant changes in politics took place: rudimentary local government replaced the highly organized and centralized Roman bureaucracy; and, in countless localities, an official of the Church, the bishop, took over the responsibilities of ruling. Thus, the Church in this period provided not only the ultimate goals of organized society, but day-to-day leadership in government as well.

The Church was the generative power of the era, and from it came institutions that have influenced the Western world ever since. The bishop of Rome offered himself as spiritual leader to all Christians, and by the late eleventh century, his primacy was respected throughout western and central Europe. In many areas local bishops had served their people as both governor and pastor for hundreds of years by then, and were therefore a focus for local affection and respect. Everywhere, too, monasteries had been founded, and during the centuries of violence, the monks had given refuge to the needy and weak, built magnificent churches, and preserved learning. At the same time, more active ascetics had gone into the wilds of central Germany, England, Ireland, and Scandinavia to convert the heathen and to bring more souls into Christendom through their message of peace. Starting from the civilization of the Roman Mediterranean basin, such Christians, many of them of Germanic origin, were accomplishing an early "expansion of Europe." All this activity achieved a remarkable penetration of civilization among barbarian peoples, and is hardly given its due by the usual "Dark Ages."

Along with government and colonization, churchmen constantly dealt with a problem of education. They were attempting to influence the conduct of the warrior Germans who, by the end of the fifth century, had largely replaced the descendants of Romans as political rulers throughout the West. The value system of the Germans can be discerned in such epic poetry as the Nibelungenlied *or the* Song of Roland. *Although these poems were written down hundreds of years after the events they purport to narrate, their normative values are still overwhelmingly martial, and many centuries were yet to pass before the Christian ethic of peace was clearly understood—if even now it is understood.*

Yet Roland's leader, Charlemagne (742–814), did attempt to realize a Christian kingdom on earth. Guided as he was by ecclesiastics, his statements of policy and his actions evidence an appreciation of the unity of Christian life. Charlemagne ordered universal elementary education in an effort to improve the minds of his subjects; he built roads and bridges to provide the material prerequisites for a healthy economy in which no Christian would benefit from injury inflicted on a fellow Christian in need. But, if for Charlemagne the purpose of government was salvation for his people, such was not the object of the land-hungry horsemen who served him and his less able successors. Nevertheless, the imperial dream survived.

Two hundred and fifty years after Charlemagne's death, Europe entered a remarkable era of progress. By the last third of the eleventh century, after several hundred years of feudal warfare, peace had emerged over large areas of France and Germany, and there were men in power competent to maintain it. During those same centuries, the Church had continued to preach and to exert its influence, with the result that, in the second half of the eleventh century, Europe experienced a great religious revival. Those who took part in this revival placed their goods and their lives in the hands of the Church, founded churches and monasteries, went on crusades, and listened when the pope spoke from Rome.

Out of this Europe, more peaceful than at any time since the Roman Empire, however, there were to develop powerful tensions between the doctrines of introspection, resignation, and contemplation preached by the Church as its highest ideals, and the virtues of strength and activity approved by the incipient leaders of secular society, the warrior-noble, the merchant, and the prince.

1. How Should Man Serve God?

Of the great Western fathers of the early Church, Gregory I, the Great (540–604), probably ranks immediately below Augustine in influence. He was born into a distinguished Roman family and trained for the civil service. After a public career, he became a monk, withdrew into one of the seven monasteries he had founded, and led the cloistered life. Later, against his will, he was drawn back into the world to serve as papal envoy in Constantinople and, eventually, as Pope.

Gregory's works include many letters, sermons, saints' lives, and biblical studies, of which the most widely read in the Middle Ages was the Moralia in Job (Morals on the Book of Job), *from which the first of the following selections is taken. Not only his ideas, but also his approach to the interpretation of*

Scripture were accepted by many in the Church for a millennium. As the following document shows, the tension between the active and the contemplative life did not originate with Christianity, nor were Christians the first to try to cope with it. It was from Gregory, however, that the problems it raised received intellectual formulation in Christian terms which greatly influenced the way men actually acted throughout the medieval period.

MORALIA IN JOB*

St. Gregory

Ver. 26. Thou shalt come to thy grave in fulness, like as a shock of corn cometh in in his season.

For what is denoted by the name of the grave, saving a life of contemplation? which as it were buries us, dead to this world, in that it hides us in the interior world away from all earthly desires. For they being dead to the exterior life, were also buried by contemplation, to whom Paul said, *For ye are dead, and your life is hid with Christ in God.* An active life also is a grave, in that it covers us, as dead, from evil works; but the contemplative life more perfectly buries us, in that it wholly severs us from all worldly courses. Whoever then has already subdued the insolencies of the flesh in himself, has this task left him, to discipline his mind by the exercises of holy practice. And whosoever opens his mind in holy works, has over and above to extend it to the secret pursuits of inward contemplation. For he is no perfect preacher, who either, from devotion to contemplation, neglects works that ought to be done, or, from urgency in business, puts aside the duties of contemplation. For it is hence that Abraham buries his wife after death in a double sepulchre, in that every perfect preacher buries his soul, dead to the desires of the present life, under the covering of good practice and of contemplation, that the soul which aforetime, sensible of the desires of the world, was living in death, may as it were, without being obnoxious to sense, lie buried from carnal concupiscence under an active and contemplative life. It is hence that the Redeemer of mankind in the day time exhibits His miracles in cities, and spends the night in devotion to prayer upon the mountain, namely, that He may teach all perfect preachers, that they should neither entirely leave the active life, from love of the speculative, nor wholly slight the joys of contemplation from excess in working, but in quiet imbibe by contemplation, what in employment they may pour back to their neighbours by word of mouth. For by contemplation they rise into the love of God, but by preaching they return back to the service of their neighbour. Hence with Moses, whilst a heifer is slaughtered in sacrifice, scarlet wool twice dyed is enjoined to be offered together with hyssop and cedar wood. For we slay a heifer, when we kill our flesh to its lust of gratification; and this we offer with hyssop and cedar and scarlet wool, in that together with the mortifying of the flesh, we burn the incense of faith, hope, and charity. The hyssop is of use to purify our inward parts; and Peter says,

---

*Gregory I, the Great, *Morals on the Book of Job,* trans. J. H. Parker (Oxford, 1844–1850), pp. 355–361.

purifying their hearts by faith. Cedar wood never decays by rotting, in that no end finishes the hope of heavenly things. Whence too Peter saith, *He hath begotten us again by a lively hope by the resurrection of Jesus Christ from the dead; to an inheritance incorruptible, undefiled, and that fadeth not away.* Scarlet wool flames with the redness of its hue, in that charity sets on fire the heart she fills. Whence also 'Truth' saith in the Gospel, *I am come to send fire on the earth.* But scarlet wool twice dyed is ordered to be offered, that in the sight of the internal Judge our charity may be coloured with the love both of God and of our neighbour, that the converted soul may neither so delight in repose for the sake of the love of God, as to put aside the care and service of our neighbour, nor busying itself for the love of our neighbour, be so wedded thereto, that entirely forsaking quiet, it extinguish in itself the fire of love of the Most High. Whosoever then has already offered himself as a sacrifice to God, if he desires perfection, must needs take care that he not only stretch himself out to breadth of practice, but likewise up to the heights of contemplation.[1]

But herein it is above all things necessary to know, that [souls have divers compositions], for there are some of such inactivity of mind, that, if the labours of business fall upon them, they give way at the very beginning of their work, and there be some so restless, that if they have cessation from labour, they have only the worse labour, in that they are subject to worse tumults of mind, in proportion as they have more time and liberty for their thoughts. Whence it behoves that neither the tranquil mind should open itself wide in the immoderate exercising of works, nor the restless mind stint itself in devotion to contemplation. For often they, who might have contemplated God in quiet, have fallen, being overcharged with business; and often they, who might live advantageously occupied with the service of their fellow-creatures, are killed by the sword of the quiescence. It is hence that some restless spirits, whilst by contemplation they hunt out more than their wits compass, launch out even to the length of wrong doctrines, and, whilst they have no mind to be the disciples of Truth in a spirit of humility, they become the masters of falsities. It is hence that 'Truth'[2] saith by His own lips, *And if thy right eye offend thee, pluck it out, and cast it from thee; for it is profitable for thee to enter into life with one eye, rather than having two eyes be cast into hell fire.* For the two lives, the active and the contemplative, when they be preserved in the soul, are accounted as two eyes in the face. Thus the right eye is the contemplative life, and the left the active life. But, as we have said, there be some, who are quite unable to behold the world above, and spiritual things, with the eye of discernment, yet enter upon the heights of contemplation, and therefore, by the mistake of a perverted understanding, they fall away into the pit of misbelief. These then the contemplative life, adopted to an extent beyond their powers, obliges to fall from the truth, which same persons the active life by itself might have kept safe in lowliness of mind in the firm seat of their uprightness. To these 'Truth' rightly addresses the warning which we said before, *And if thy right eye offend thee, pluck it out, and cast it from thee; for it is good for thee to enter into life with one eye, rather than having two*

---

[1] Compare this with the portion of Plato's *Republic* above, pp. 60–61.
[2] That is, Christ.

eyes to be cast into hell fire. As if He said in plain words; 'When thou art not qualified for the contemplative life by a fitting degree of discretion, keep more safely the active life alone, and when thou failest in that which thou choosest as great, be content with that which thou heedest as very little, that if by the contemplative life thou art forced to fall from the knowledge of the truth, thou mayest by the active life alone be able to enter into the kingdom of heaven at least with one eye.' . . .

But herein it is necessary to know, that often at one and the same time love stimulates inactive souls to work, and fear keeps back restless souls in the exercise of contemplation. . . . Whence it is necessary that whoever eagerly prosecutes the exercises of contemplation, first question himself with particularity, how much he loves. For the force of love is an engine of the soul, which, while it draws it out of the world, lifts it on high. Let him then first examine whether in searching after the highest things he loves, whether in loving he fears, whether he knows either how to apprehend unknown truths, while he loves them, or not being apprehended to reverence them in cherishing fear. For in contemplation, if love does not stimulate the mind, the dulness of its tepidity stupefies it. . . . First then the soul must be cleansed from all affection for earthly glory, and from the gratification of carnal concupiscence, and next it is to be lifted up in the ken of contemplation. Hence too, when the Law is given to them, the people are forbidden the Mount,[3] namely, that they who, by the frailty of their minds, still have their affections set upon earthly objects, may not venture to take cognizance of things above. And hence it is rightly said, *And if a beast touch the mountain, it shall be stoned.* For 'a beast touches the mountain,' when the mind, which is bowed down to irrational desires, lifts itself to the heights of contemplation. . . .

Let all then that strive to lay hold of the summit of perfection, when they desire to occupy the citadel of contemplation, first try themselves, by exercising, in the field of practice, that they may heedfully acquaint themselves, if they now no longer bring mischiefs upon their neighbours, if when brought upon them by their neighbours, they bear them with composure of mind, if when temporal advantages are put in their way, the mind is never dissipated by joy, if, when they are withdrawn, it is not stung by overmuch regret, and then let them reflect, if, when they return inwardly to themselves, in this work of theirs of exploring spiritual things, they never draw along with them the shadows of corporeal objects, or when drawn along, as they may be, if they drive them off with the hand of discretion; if, when they long to behold the unencompassed light, they put down all images of their own compass, or in that which they seek to reach unto above themselves, conquer that which they are. Hence it is rightly said here, *Thou shalt come to thy grave in abundance.* For the perfect man does 'come to the grave in abundance,' in that he first gathers together the works of an active life, and then by contemplation wholly hides from this world his fleshly sense, which is now dead. Hence too it is fitly subjoined,

Like as a shock of corn cometh in in his season.

For the season for action comes first, for contemplation last. Whence

---

[3] Gregory was referring to Moses on Mount Sinai. See above, pp. 24–26.

it is needful that every perfect man first discipline his mind in virtuous habits, and afterwards lay it up in the granary of rest. For it is hence that he, who was left of the legion of devils at the bidding of our Lord, seats himself at His Saviour's feet, receives the words of instruction, and eagerly desires to leave his country in company with the Author of his recovery, but That very 'Truth' Himself, Who vouchsafed to him recovery, tells him, *Return first unto thine own house, and shew what great things God hath done unto thee.* For when we have the least particle imparted to us of the knowledge of God, we are no longer inclined to return to our human affairs, and we shrink from burthening ourselves with the wants of our neighbours. We seek the rest of contemplation, and love only that which refreshes without toil. But after we are cured, the Lord sends us home, He bids us relate the things that have been done with us, so as that in fact the soul should first spend itself in labour, and that afterwards it may be refreshed by contemplation.

It is hence that Jacob serves for Rachel, and gets Leah, and that it is said to him, *It is not the custom in our country to give the youngest before the first-born.* For Rachel is rendered 'the beginning seen,' but 'Leah,' 'laborious.' And what is denoted by Rachel but the contemplative life? What by Leah, but the active life? For in contemplation 'the Beginning,' which is God, is the object we seek, but in action we labour under a weighty bundle of wants. Whence on the one hand Rachel is beautiful but barren, Leah weak eyed, but fruitful, truly in that when the mind seeks the ease of contemplation, it sees more, but it is less productive in children to God. But when it betakes itself to the laborious work of preaching, it sees less, but it bears more largely. Accordingly after the embrace of Leah, Jacob attains to Rachel, in that every one that is perfect is first joined to an active life in productiveness, and afterwards united to a contemplative life in rest. For that the life of contemplation is less indeed in time, but greater in value than the active, we are shewn by the words of the Holy Gospel, wherein two women are described to have acted in different ways. For Mary sat at our Redeemer's feet, hearing His words, but Martha eagerly prosecuted bodily services; and when Martha made complaint against Mary's inactivity, she heard the words, *Martha, Martha, thou art careful and troubled about many things; but one thing is needful: and Mary hath chosen that good part, which shall not be taken away from her.* For what is set forth by Mary, who sitting down gave ear to the words of our Lord, saving the life of contemplation? and what by Martha, so busied with outward services, saving the life of action? Now Martha's concern is not reproved, but that of Mary is even commended. For the merits of the active life are great, but of the contemplative, far better. Whence Mary's part is said to be 'never taken away from her,' in that the works of the active life pass away together with the body, while the joys of the contemplative life are made more lively at the end.

2. How Should the Flock of Christ Be Tended?

Gregory, like Augustine two centuries earlier, was bishop as well as theologian, which is to say that he constantly had to struggle with problems related to property, politics, and law. As administrator of the papal see, his concerns necessarily ranged over all of Italy and involved him in relations with Byzantium. As spiritual leader, he bore responsibility for his immediate Roman flock, and in days of growing papal ascendancy throughout western Europe, for the welfare of Christendom as a whole. Out of this varied experience came the Pastoral Rule, *or handbook for bishops. It shaped episcopal conduct for centuries and was thought so important that King Alfred himself translated the book into Old English.*

PASTORAL CARE*

St. Gregory

THE RULER[1] SHOULD BE A NEIGHBOUR IN COMPASSION TO EVERYONE AND EXALTED ABOVE ALL IN THOUGHT

Let the ruler be neighbour in compassion to everyone and exalted above all in thought, so that by the love of his heart he may transfer to himself the infirmities of others, and by the loftiness of his contemplation transcend even himself in his apsirations for the invisible things. Otherwise, while he has lofty aspirations, he will be disregarding the infirmities of his neighbours, or in accommodating himself to the weak, will cease to seek that which is above.

* * *

Thus Moses frequently goes in and out of the Tabernacle; and while within he is caught up in contemplation, outside he devotes himself to the affairs of the weak. Inwardly he considers the hidden things of God, outwardly he bears the burdens of carnal men. In doubtful matters, too, he always returns to the Tabernacle to consult the Lord in front of the Ark of the Covenant. He thus, no doubt, sets an example to rulers, that when they are uncertain what dispositions to make in secular matters, they should always return to reflection, as though to the Tabernacle, and there, as it were, standing before the Ark of the Covenant, should consult the Lord, whether they should seek a solution of their problems in the pages of the Sacred Word.

Thus the Truth Itself, manifested to us by assuming our human nature, engaged in prayer on the mountain and worked miracles in the towns. He thus showed the way to be followed by good rulers, who, though they strive after the highest things by contemplation, should nevertheless by their compassion share in the needs of the weak. Then, indeed, charity rises to sublime heights, when in pity it is drawn by the lowly things of the neighbour, and the more kindly it stoops to infirmity, the mightier is its reach to the highest.

But those who rule others should show themselves such that their subjects are unafraid to reveal their hidden secrets to them. Thus, when these little ones are enduring the waves of temptation, they will have recourse to

---

*Gregory I, the Great, *Pastoral Care,* trans. Henry Davis, S. J. (Westminster: The Newman Press, 1950), pp. 56–73.

[1] The reference here is to the bishop.

the pastor's understanding as to a mother's bosom; and in the solace of his comforting words and in their prayerful tears they will cleanse themselves when they see themselves defiled by the sin that buffets them.

Hence also it is that in front of the doors of the Temple there is a sea of brass for washing the hands of those who enter the Temple, that is to say, a laver, supported by twelve oxen, whose faces are plainly visible, but whose hinder parts are not visible.[2] What else is symbolised by the twelve oxen but the whole order of pastors? Of these the Law says, as Paul reports: *Thou shalt not muzzle the mouth of the ox that treadeth out the corn.* We see the work they do openly, but do not see the rest that later awaits them in the secret requital of the strict Judge. Those, however, who make ready in their patient condescension to cleanse the confessed sins of the neighbour, support the laver, as it were, in front of the door of the Temple. Whosoever, then, is striving to enter the gate of eternity, may reveal his temptations to the mind of the pastor, and cleanse the hands of thought or deed, as it were, in the laver of the oxen.

Now, it happens frequently that, while the ruler's mind in his condescension learns of the trials of others, he also is assailed by the temptations which he gives ear to; for in the case of the laver, too, that was mentioned as serving the cleansing of the multitude, it is certainly defiled. In receiving the filth of those who wash in it, it loses its limpid clearness. But the pastor need not fear these things at all, for when God weighs all things exactly, the pastor is the more easily delivered from temptation, as he is the more compassionately afflicted by the temptations of others.

THE RULER SHOULD IN HUMILITY BE THE COMRADE OF THOSE WHO LIVE THE GOOD LIFE; BUT IN HIS ZEAL FOR RIGHTEOUSNESS HE SHOULD BE STERN WITH THE VICES OF EVIL-DOERS

The ruler should in humility be the comrade of those who lead good lives, but stern with the vices of evil-doers. He must not set himself over the good in any way, and when the sins of the wicked demand it, he must assert the power of his supremacy at once. Thus, waiving aside his rank, he regards himself the equal of his subjects who lead good lives, but does not shrink from exercising the laws of rectitude against the perverse. For, as I remember to have said in the *Books of Morals,* it is clear that nature brought forth all men in equality, while guilt has placed some below others, in accordance with the order of their varying demerits. This diversity, which results from vice, is a dispensation of the divine judgment, much as one man must be ruled by another, since all men cannot be on an equal footing.

Wherefore, all who are superiors should not regard in themselves the power of their rank, but the equality of their nature; and they should find their joy not in ruling over men, but in helping them. For our ancient fathers are recorded to have been not kings of men, but shepherds of flocks. And when the Lord said to Noe[3] and his sons: *Increase and multiply and fill the earth,* He at once added: *And let the fear and dread of you be upon all the beasts of*

---

[2] III Kings 7:23ff.
[3] That is, Noah.

the earth. Fear and dread were prescribed for all the beasts of the earth, but forbidden to be exercised over men. By nature a man is made superior to the beasts, but not to other men; it is, therefore, said to him that he is to be feared by beasts, but not by men. Evidently, to wish to be feared by an equal is to lord it over others, contrary to the natural order.

Yet it is necessary that rulers should be feared by subjects, when they see that the latter do not fear God. Lacking fear of God's judgments, these must at least fear sin out of human respect. It is not at all a case of exhibiting pride when superiors seek to inspire fear, whereby they do not seek personal glory, but the righteousness of their subjects. In fact, in inspiring fear in those who lead evil lives, superiors lord it, as it were, over beasts, not over men, because, in so far as their subjects are beasts, they ought also to be subjugated by fear.

Often, however, a ruler by the very fact of his pre-eminence over others becomes conceited; and because everything is at his service, because his orders are quickly executed to suit his wishes, because all his subjects praise him for what he has done well, but have no authority to criticise what he has done amiss and because they usually praise even what they ought to blame, his mind, led astray by those below him, is lifted above itself. While he is outwardly surrounded by abounding favours, the truth within him is made void. Forgetful of what he is, he is diverted by the commendations of others, and believes himself to be such as he hears himself outwardly proclaimed to be, not such as he should inwardly judge himself. He despises his subjects and does not acknowledge them to be his equals in the order of nature; and those whom he has excelled by the fortuity of power, he believes he has also surpassed by the merits of his life. He esteems himself to be wiser than any of those whom he sees he exceeds in power. For he puts himself on an eminence in his own estimation, and though he has his own limitations by reason of the equality of nature with others, he disdains to regard others as being on his level. He thus brings himself to be the like of him of whom Scripture says: *He beholdeth every high thing, and he is king over all the children of pride.* He who aspired to singular eminence and disdained life in common with the angels, said: *I will place my seat in the North, I will be like the Most High.* By a wonderful decree, therefore, he finds within himself the pit of his downfall, while outwardly exalting himself on the pinnacle of power. Man is made like the apostate angel when he disdains, though a man, to be like other men.

In this way Saul, after having distinguished himself for his humility, was swollen with pride in the eminence of his power; by his humility he was advanced, by his pride, rejected, as the Lord attested, saying: *When thou wast a little one in thy own eyes, did I not make thee the head of the tribes of Israel?* He had previously seen himself a little one in his own eyes, but relying on temporal power, he no longer saw himself to be a little one. Preferring himself to others, he regarded himself great above all others, because he had greater power than they. And in a wonderful way, while a little one in his own esteem, he was great with God, but when he thought himself to be great, he was little with God.

Usually, then, when the mind of a man is inflated with a multitude of subjects under him, he becomes corrupted and moved to pride by the eminence of his power which panders to the mind. But such power is truly well-controlled by one who knows how both to assert and oppose it. He controls it well who knows how through it to obtain the mastery over sin, and knows how with it to associate with others on terms of equality. For the human mind is prone to pride even when not supported by power; how much more, then, does it exalt itself when it has that support! But he disposes his power aright, who knows how, with great care, both to derive from it what is profitable, and to subdue the temptations which it creates, and how, though in possession of it, to realise his equality with others, and at the same time set himself above sinners in his zeal for retribution.

This is a distinction which will be more fully understood when we consider the examples given by the first Pastor. Peter, who held from God the primacy in Holy Church, refused to accept excessive veneration from Cornelius though he acted rightly in humbly prostrating himself; but Peter acknowledged in him his equal, when he said: *Arise, do not act so; I myself also am a man.* But when the guilt of Ananias and Sapphira[4] were discovered by him, he at once showed with what great authority he had been made pre-eminent over others. By his word he smote their life when he laid it bare by his penetrating spirit. He recalled to his mind that in the question of opposition to sin he was supreme in the Church, but such distinction was not present to his mind when among upright brethren honour was eagerly exhibited to him. In the one instance holy conduct was met by the assertion of common equality; in the other, zeal for retributive justice revealed the right of authority. . . .

Supreme rank is, therefore, well-administered, when the superior lords it over vices rather than over brethren. When rulers correct their delinquent subjects, it is incumbent on them to observe carefully that, while they smite faults with due discipline in virtue of their authority, they acknowledge, by observing humility, that they are only the equals of the brethren whom they correct. But we should as a regular practice in thoughtful silence prefer to ourselves those whom we correct, for it is through us that their vices are smitten with rigorous discipline, whereas in the case of our own vices we are not chastised even by verbal censure of anyone. Therefore, we are the more bounden before the Lord, inasmuch as we sin with impunity before men. On the other hand, our discipline renders our subjects the more exempt from the divine judgment, as it does not exempt them here from punishment for their faults.

Consequently, humility must be preserved in the heart, and discipline in action. Between these two, we must diligently beware not to relax the rights of government by immoderate adherence to the virtue of humility, for if the superior depreciates himself unduly, he may be unable to restrain the lives of subjects under the bond of discipline.[5] Let rulers, therefore, uphold externally what they undertake for the service of others, and internally retain their fear in their estimate of themselves. Nevertheless, let the subjects themselves perceive, by signs becomingly manifested, that their rulers are humble in their

---

[4] Cornelius was the first gentile convert to Christianity; he and his family and friends listened to St. Peter and then were baptized. Ananias and his wife, Sapphira, were members of the primitive church at Jerusalem. When Ananias' gift to the community treasury was revealed as less than he had stated, he fell dead.

[5] See Aristotle, *Nichomachean Ethics,* above, pp. 108–109.

own estimation. They should thus apprehend both what they ought to fear from authority, and what to imitate in the sphere of humility.

* * *

. . . One who has been cast away is brought back when, after having fallen into sin, he is recalled to the state of righteousness by the influence of pastoral care; and the ligature binds a fracture when discipline subdues sin, lest the wound's continued flow lead to death if a tight compress does not bind it up. Often, however, the fracture is made worse by an unskilful ligature, so that the lesion causes even greater pain from being bound up too tightly.

Wherefore, it is necessary that when the wound of sin in the subject is repressed by correction, even the restraint must be most carefully moderated, lest the feeling of kindness be extinguished by the manner in which the principles of discipline are exercised against the sinner. For care must be taken that loving-kindness, like that of a mother, be displayed by the ruler towards his subjects, and correction given as by a father. In all such cases treatment must be bestowed with care and circumspection, lest discipline be too rigid, or loving-kindness too lax.

. . . Either discipline or compassion is greatly wanting, if one is exercised independently of the other. But rulers in their relations with subjects should be animated by compassion duly considerate and by discipline affectionately severe. . . . In other words, gentleness is to be mingled with severity; a compound is to be made of both, so that subjects may not be exasperated by too great harshness, nor enervated by excessive tenderness. . . .

There should, then, be love that does not enervate, vigour that does not exasperate, zeal not too immoderate and uncontrolled, loving-kindness that spares, yet not more than is befitting. Thus, while justice and clemency are blended in supreme rule, the ruler will soothe the hearts of his subjects even when he inspires fear, and yet in soothing them, hold them to reverential awe for him.

In His Preoccupation with External Matters the Ruler Should Not Relax His Care for the Inner Life, Nor Should His Solicitude for the Inner Life Cause Neglect of the External

Let the ruler not relax the care of the inner life by preoccupying himself with external matters, nor should his solicitude for the inner life bring neglect of the external, lest, being engrossed with what is external, he be ruined inwardly, or being preoccupied with what concerns only his inner self, he does not bestow on his neighbors the necessary external care. For often some persons, forgetting that they are superiors of their brethren for the sake of their souls, devote themselves with all concentration of heart to secular cares. These they gladly attend to when the occasion offers, but when the occasion is not present, hanker after them day and night with the surge of a disordered mind. When they find a respite from these occupations, because the occasion for them has gone by, they are the more wearied by the respite itself. For they take it as a pleasure to be weighed down by such activities, and regard it laborious not to be labouring in earthly concerns. And so it happens that, while they rejoice in being weighed down with tumultuous worldly business, they disregard those interior matters which they ought to be teaching others. Consequently, the life of their subjects undoubtedly grows languid, because, though these wish to make spiritual progress, they are confronted with the stumbling-block, as it were, of the example of their superior.

For when the head languishes, the members have no vigour. It is in vain that an army, seeking contact with the enemy, hurries behind its leader, if he has lost the way. No exhortation then uplifts the minds of subjects, no reproof castigates their faults, for when one who is a spiritual guardian fulfils the office of a judge of the world, the shepherd's care of the flock is lacking; and subjects cannot see the light of the truth, for when earthly cares occupy the pastor's mind, dust, driven by the winds of temptation, blinds the eyes of the Church. . . .

Subjects, then, are to transact inferior matters, rulers to attend to the highest, so that the eye, which is set above for guiding the steps, may not be dimmed by annoying dust. For all rulers are the heads of their subjects, and surely the head ought to look forward from above, that the feet may be able to go onward on a straight path. Otherwise, if the body's upright posture becomes bent and if the head stoops toward the earth, the feet will drag in the way of progress. But with what conscience can the ruler of souls use his pastoral rank among others, if he himself is engaged in those earthly occupations which he should reprehend in others? This is, indeed, what the Lord in the anger of His just retribution threatened through the Prophet when He said: *And there shall be like people like priest.* Priest is, indeed, like people, when a man performing a spiritual office does what they do who are still adjudged in terms of carnal pursuits. This is contemplated and deplored by the Prophet Jeremias in the great grief of his charity, under the symbol of the destruction of the Temple, when he says: *How is the gold become dim, the finest colour is changed, the stones of the sanctuary are scattered in the top of every street!* And indeed, what is meant by gold which surpasses all other metals, but surpassing holiness? What is meant by the finest colour, but the reverence paid to religion, beloved by all men? What, by the stones of the sanctuary, but persons in Sacred Orders? What is signified by the term streets, but the expanse of this life? Since in the Greek language width is expressed by *platos,* obviously streets (*plateae*) are so termed for their expanse. The Truth Himself says: *Wide and broad is the way that leadeth to destruction.*

*　*　*

Some . . . undertake the charge of the flock, but wish to be so free for spiritual occupations, as not to give any time at all to external matters. Now, when such people wholly neglect to attend to what pertains to the body, they afford no help to their subjects. It is no wonder that their preaching is disregarded for the most part, for while chiding the deeds of sinners, and not giving them the necessities of the present life, their words certainly do not find sympathetic listeners. Doctrine taught does not penetrate the minds of the needy, if a compassionate heart does not commend it to the hearts of hearers;

but the seed of the word does germinate promptly, when the kindness of a preacher waters it in the hearer's heart. Therefore, that the ruler may be able to plant within, he must also, with irreproachable intention, make provision for what is external. Let pastors, then, give their entire devotion to the inner life of their subjects, yet not neglect to provide for the exterior life also.

. . . The mind of the flock is, as it were, justified in being averse to accepting the words of the preacher, if the pastor neglects the duty of affording external help. Wherefore, too, the first Pastor gave this earnest admonition, saying: *The ancients that are among you, I beseech, who am myself also an ancient, and a witness of the sufferings of Christ, as also a partaker of that glory which is to be revealed in time to come, feed the flock of God which is among you.* In this place he makes it clear whether it was the feeding of the heart or of the body that he was urging, when he presently added: *taking care of it, not by constraint, but willingly, according to God, not for filthy lucre's sake, but voluntarily.*

In these words obviously a kindly forewarning is given to pastors lest, while they satisfy the needs of those under them, they slay themselves with the dagger of ambition, and when the neighbours are refreshed with succour given to the body, the pastors themselves remain bereft of the bread of righteousness.

3. Who Is the Appropriate Hero of Christian Men?

For centuries, the Germans had extolled the virtues of war. The missionaries who were attempting to convert them drew on the Latin language and literature as well as on Christian doctrine to influence these tribesmen toward a more peaceful way of life.

Eventually, monks and others wrote thousands of saints' lives to memorialize the pious deeds of exemplary men, to illustrate the power of Christ or one of His chosen, or to teach Christian principles of conduct in a simple way. It has been said that the saint is the Christian equivalent of the warrior hero in the epics of the Germanic peoples, and that the simplicity of their listeners forced Christian teachers to get their message across by the means of naive biography. St. Benedict (c. 480– c. 543), the traditional founder of Western monasticism, lived a life of exemplary goodness and sacrifice. In his own lifetime, his goodness inspired men to follow the hard monastic way. Gregory the Great's decision to write a life of Benedict suggests the respect in which Benedict was already held less than a century after his death and suggests, too, the hopes Gregory had of monasticism as an example and instrument of conversion.

Like Gregory, Benedict came from a good family and received the best education possible in his day. But he never entered the active governmental life that still, in the fifth century, was considered the proper career for one of his class. Rather, in early manhood, he withdrew to a cave in the Appenine Mountains near Subiaco and there gained a reputation for purity and leadership that attracted disciples. Eventually, he founded twelve communities dedicated to the life of prayer and work and wrote for them the Rule which to this day serves as the guide for Benedictine communities everywhere.

LIFE OF ST. BENEDICT*

St. Gregory

There was a man of venerable life, blessed by grace and blessed in name, for he was called *Benedictus* or Bennet, who from his [youth] carried always the mind of an old man; for his age was inferior to his virtue. All vain pleasure he contemned, and though he were in the world and might freely have enjoyed such commodities as it yieldeth, yet did he nothing esteem it nor the vanities thereof. He was born in the province of Nursia of honourable parentage and brought up at Rome in the study of humanities. But for as much as he saw many by reason of such learning to fall to dissolute and lewd life, he drew back his foot, which he had as it were now set forth into the world, lest, entering too far in acquaintance therewith, he likewise might have fallen into that dangerous and godless gulf. Wherefore, giving over his books and forsaking his father's house and wealth, with a resolute mind only to serve God, he sought for some place where he might attain to the desire of his holy purpose; and in this sort he departed, instructed with learned ignorance and furnished with unlearned wisdom.[1] All the notable things and acts of his life I could not learn; but those few, which I mind now to report, I had by the relation of four of his disciples. . . .

How He Made a Broken Sieve Whole and Sound

Bennet having now given over the school with a resolute mind to lead his life in the wilderness, his nurse alone, who did tenderly love him, would not by any means give him over. Coming, therefore, to a place called Enside and remaining there in the church of St. Peter, in the company of other virtuous men which for charity lived in that place, it fell so out that his nurse borrowed of the neighbours a sieve to make clean wheat, which being left negligently upon the table, by chance it was broken in two pieces. Whereupon she fell pitifully a-weeping, because she had borrowed it. The devout and religious youth Bennet, seeing his nurse so lamenting, moved with compassion, took away with him both the pieces of the sieve and with tears fell to his prayers; and after he had done, rising up he found it so whole that the place could not be seen where before it was broken. And coming straight to his nurse and comforting her with good words, he delivered her the sieve safe and sound. Which miracle was known to all the inhabitants thereabout and so much admired that the townsmen for a perpetual memory did hang it up at the church door, to the end that not only men then living but also their posterity might understand how greatly God's grace did work with him upon his first renouncing of the world. The sieve continued there many years after, . . . where it did hang over the church door.

---

* Gregory I, the Great, *The Dialogues,* trans. P. W. Gardner and rev. E. G. Gardner (London: P. L. Warner, 1911) pp. 59–77. Reprinted by permission of the Medici Society, Ltd.

[1] Compare Gregory's conception of a life of exemplary virtue with Aristotle's and Tertullian's, above, pp. 108–112 and 142.

But Bennet, desiring rather the miseries of the world than the praises of men, rather to be wearied with labour for God's sake than to be exalted with transitory commendation, fled privily from his nurse and went into a desert place called Subiacum, distant almost forty miles from Rome. In that place there was a fountain springing forth cool and clear water, the abundance whereof doth first in a broad place make a lake and afterward, running forward, cometh to be a river. As he was travelling to this place, a certain monk called Romanus met him and demanded whither he went; and understanding his purpose, he both kept it close, furthered him what he might, vested him with the habit of holy conversation, and as he could did minister and serve him.

The man of God, Bennet, coming to this foresaid place, lived there in a strait cave, where he continued three years unknown to all men except to Romanus, who lived not far off, under the rule of Abbot Theodacus, and very virtuously did steal certain hours, and likewise sometime a loaf given for his own provision, which he did carry to Bennet. And because from Romanus' cell to that cave there was not any way, by reason of an high rock which did hang over it, Romanus, from the top thereof, upon a long rope, did let down the loaf, upon which also with a band he tied a little bell, that by the ringing thereof the man of God might know when he came with his bread and so be ready to take it. But the old enemy of mankind, envying at the charity of the one and the refection of the other, seeing a loaf upon a certain day let down, threw a stone and brake the bell; but yet, for all that, Romanus gave not over to serve him by all the possible means he could.

How He Overcame a Great Temptation of the Flesh

Upon a certain day when Bennet was alone, the tempter was at hand; for a little black bird, commonly called a merle or an ousel, began to fly about his face and that so near as the holy man, if he would, might have taken it with his hand. But after he had blessed himself with the sign of the Cross, the bird flew away; and forthwith the holy man was assaulted with such a terrible temptation of the flesh as he never felt the like in all his life. A certain woman there was which some time he had seen, the memory of which the wicked spirit put into his mind, and by the representation of her did so mightily inflame with concupiscence the soul of God's servant, which did so increase that, almost overcome with pleasure, he was of mind to have forsaken the wilderness. But suddenly assisted with God's grace, he came to himself and, seeing many thick briers and nettle-bushes to grow hard by, off he cast his apparel, and threw himself into the midst of them and there wallowed so long that, when he rose up, all his flesh was pitifully torn; and so by the wounds of his body he cured the wounds of his soul, in that he turned pleasure into pain and by [suffering] outward burning quenched that fire which, being nourished before with the fuel of carnal [thoughts], did inwardly burn his soul. And by this means he overcame the sin because he made a change of the fire. From which time forward, as himself did afterward report unto his disciples, he found all temptation of pleasure so subdued that he never felt any such thing. Many after this began to abandon the world and to become his scholars; for being now freed from the vice of temptation, worthily and with great reason is he made a master of virtue.

* * *

How Bennet, by the Sign of the Holy Cross, Brake a Drinking-Glass in Pieces

. . . When this great temptation was thus overcome, the man of God, like unto a piece of ground well tilled and weeded, of the seed of virtue brought forth plentiful store of fruit; and by reason of the great report of his wonderful holy life, his name became very famous. Not far from the place where he remained there was a monastery, the Abbot whereof was dead. Whereupon the whole convent came unto the venerable man Bennet, entreating him very earnestly that he would vouchsafe to take upon him the charge and government of their abbey. Long time he denied them, saying that their manners were divers from his and therefore that they should never agree together; yet at length, overcome with their entreaty, he gave his consent. Having now taken upon him the charge of the abbey, he took order that regular life should be observed so that none of them could, as before they used, through unlawful acts decline from the path of holy conversation either on the one side or on the other. Which the monks perceiving, they fell into a great rage, accusing themselves that ever they desired him to be their Abbot, seeing their crooked conditions could not endure his virtuous kind of government. And therefore when they saw that under him they could not live in unlawful sort, and were loath to leave their former conversation, and found it hard to be enforced with old minds to meditate and think upon new things, and because the life of virtuous men is always grievous to those that be of wicked conditions, some of them began to devise how they might rid him out of the way. And therefore, taking counsel together, they agreed to poison his wine. Which being done and the glass wherein that wine was, according to the custom, offered to the Abbot to bless, he, putting forth his hand, made the sign of the cross; and straightway the glass, that was holden far off, brake in pieces, as though the sign of the Cross had been a stone thrown against it. Upon which accident the man of God by and by perceived that the glass had in it the drink of death, which could not endure the sign of life; and therefore rising up, with a mild countenance and quiet mind he called the monks together and spake thus unto them: "Almighty God have mercy upon you, and forgive you; why have you used me in this manner? Did not I tell you beforehand that our manner of living could never agree together? Go your ways and seek ye out some other father suitable to your own conditions, for I intend not now to stay any longer amongst you." When he had thus discharged himself, he returned back to the wilderness which so much he loved and dwelt alone with himself in the sight of his Creator, who beholdeth the hearts of all men.

* * *

How Bennet Reformed a Monk That Would Not Stay at His Prayers

In one of the monasteries which he had built in those parts, a monk there was who could not continue at prayers; for when the other monks knelt down to serve God, his manner was to go forth and there with wandering mind to busy himself about some earthly and transitory things. And when he had been often by his abbot admonished of this fault without any amendment, at length he was sent to the man of God, who did likewise very much rebuke him for his folly. Yet notwithstanding, returning back again, he did scarce two days follow the holy man's admonition; for upon the third day he fell again to his old custom and would not abide within at the time of prayer. Word whereof being once more sent to the man of God by the father of the abbey whom he had there appointed, he returned him answer that he would come himself and reform what was amiss, which he did accordingly. And it fell so out that when the singing of psalms was ended and the hour come in which the monks betook themselves to prayer, the holy man perceived that the monk which used at that time to go forth was by a little black boy drawn out by the skirt of his garment; upon which sight he spake secretly to Pompeianus, father of the abbey, and also to Maurus, saying: "Do you not see who it is that draweth this monk from his prayers?" And they answered him that they did not. "Then let us pray," quoth he, "unto God, that you also may behold whom this monk doth follow." And after two days Maurus did see him, but Pompeianus could not. Upon another day, when the man of God had ended his devotions, he went out of the oratory, where he found the foresaid monk standing idle, whom for the blindness of his heart he strake with a little wand, and from that day forward he was so freed from all allurement of the little black boy that he remained quietly at his prayers as other of the monks did. For the old enemy was so terrified that he durst not any more suggest any such cogitations, as though by that blow not the monk but himself had been strooken.

Of the Destruction of the Altar of Apollo

. . . The holy man, changing his place, did not for all that change his enemy. For afterward he endured so much the more grievous battles, by how much he had now the master of all wickedness fighting openly against him. For the town which is called Cassino standeth upon the side of an high mountain, which containeth as it were in the lap thereof the foresaid town and afterward so riseth in height the space of three miles that the top thereof seemeth to touch the very heavens. In this place there was an ancient chapel in which the foolish and simple country people, according to the custom of the old gentiles, worshipped the god Apollo. Round about it likewise upon all sides there were woods for the service of the devils, in which, even to that very time, the mad multitude of infidels did offer most wicked sacrifice. The man of God, coming thither, beat in pieces the idol, overthrew the altar, set fire on the woods, and in the temple of Apollo he built the oratory of St. Martin, and where the altar of the same Apollo was he made an oratory of St. John. And by his continual preaching he brought the people dwelling in those parts to embrace the faith of Christ. The old enemy of mankind, not taking this in good part, did not now privily or in a dream but in open sight present himself to the eyes of that holy father, and with great outcries complained that he had offered him violence. The noise which he made the monks did hear, but himself they could not see; but, as the venerable father told them, he appeared visibly unto him most fell and cruel and as though, with his fiery mouth and flaming eyes, he would have torn him in pieces. What the devil said unto him, all the monks did hear; for first he would call him by his name, and because the man of God vouchsafed him not any answer, then would he fall a-reviling and railing at him: for when he cried out, calling him "Blessed Bennet," and yet found that he gave him no answer, straightways he would turn his tune and say: "Cursed Bennet and not blessed, what hast thou to do with me? And why dost thou thus persecute me?" Wherefore new battles of the old enemy against the servant of God are to be looked for, against whom willingly did he make war, but, against his will, did he give him occasion of many notable victories.

How Venerable Bennet Revived a Boy, Crushed to Death with the Ruin of a Wall

Again, as the monks were making a certain wall somewhat higher because that was requisite, the man of God in the meantime was in his cell at his prayers. To whom the old enemy appeared in an insulting manner, telling him that he was now going to his monks that were a-working. Whereof the man of God in all haste gave them warning, wishing them to look unto themselves, because the devil was at that time coming amongst them. The message was scarce delivered when as the wicked spirit overthrew the new wall which they were a-building, and with the fall slew a little young child, a monk, who was the son of a certain courtier. At which pitiful chance all were passing sorry and exceedingly grieved, not so much for the loss of the wall as for the death of their brother; and in all haste they sent this heavy news to the venerable man Bennet, who commanded them to bring unto him the young boy, mangled and maimed as he was, which they did, but yet they could not carry him any otherwise than in a sack, for the stones of the wall had not only broken his limbs but also his very bones. Being in that manner brought unto the man of God, he bade them to lay him in his cell and in that place upon which he used to pray; and then, putting them all forth, he shut the door and fell more instantly to his prayers than he used at other times. And O strange miracle! for the very same hour he made him sound and as lively as ever he was before, and sent him again to his former work that he also might help the monks to make an end of that wall, of whose death the old serpent thought he should have insulted over Bennet and greatly triumphed.

* * *

How Holy Bennet Wrote a Rule for His Monks

. . . Desirous I am . . . to tell you many things of this venerable father, but some of purpose I let pass, because I make haste to entreat also of the acts of other holy men. Yet I would not have you to be ignorant but that the man of God amongst so many miracles, for which he was so famous in the world, was also sufficiently learned in divinity; for he wrote a rule for his monks, both excellent for discretion and also eloquent for the style. Of whose life and conversation, if any be curious to know further, he may in the institution of that rule understand all his manner of life and discipline; for the holy man could not otherwise teach than himself lived.

———

Despite the tone of the preceding selections, the early Middle Ages were not filled with peace and light, with universally beloved churchmen establishing Christianity, justice, and learning everywhere in Europe. War and violence were usual, and many missionaries found martyrdom in violent death. In the early Middle Ages, the warrior rulers of western Europe were an illiterate lot, more at home on the hunt and on the battlefield than with a good book. These men were nominally Christian, but it took centuries for them to make any sense of the Christian message of peace. And by the year 1100 or thereabouts, the measure of general tranquillity which Europe enjoyed resulted from the interaction of many forces, only one of which was brotherhood as preached by the Church.

At about the same time, men unknown to us began to write down the epic poems of the feudal era, the chansons de geste. *The deeds of Charlemagne and his great barons constitute the central subject of these poems, of which the* Song of Roland *was probably the earliest to be put in writing and is surely the greatest. As historical record, it is a better guide to the conditions and values of the early twelfth century than to those of the late eighth. Nevertheless, the virtues cherished in feudal Europe stand out clearly.*

THE SONG OF ROLAND*

In the initial verses of the poem, we learn that the Moslems have decided to try to trick Charlemagne, whose army has been destroying their towns and villages in Spain. In return for peace, the Moslem embassy led by Blanchandrin is to promise Charlemagne that King Marsila will follow him to France, there to be baptized. To quiet Charlemagne's suspicions, Blanchandrin promises him twenty noble hostages.

Under a pine tree, where his golden throne
Was placed, he called his bravest knights together.
And first the Archbishop Turpin came, and then
Gerin and Gerier, Tybalt—he of Rheims—
And many more as brave and wise as they;
And likewise Roland came, and at his side
His comrade Oliver. Ay, and with the rest
Ganelon came, the traitor. So began
The fateful council, fraught with woe for France.

And the King spake, and said: "Fair sirs, to us
The Paynim sends his messengers, with store

---

* Reprinted with permission of The Macmillan Company from *The Song of Roland*, trans. Frederick B. Luquiens, pp. 8–9, 11–12, 36–43, 51, 52–53, 58, 60–61, 69–70, 77–81. Copyright 1952 by The Macmillan Company.

Of precious gifts, lions and shaggy bears,
Camels and falcons, mules weighed down with gold
Of Araby—more than we may take away
In fifty of our wains. But he demands
We turn again to our own land, and he
Will follow us straightway, and there subscribe
In all things to our law and glorious faith,
Turn Christian, be my liegeman—ay, and yet
I fathom not his real intent." He spake,
And the Franks cried: "It is a trap—take heed!"

*Up spring the great nobles to offer advice. Charlemagne's nephew Roland
wants the war to continue, but Ganelon, the aged and respected Naimon, and
many others counsel peace. Most agree with Ganelon, and the discussion turns
to the choice of the Frankish ambassador to King Marsila.*

But then the Archbishop rose, Turpin of Rheims,
"Let be your peers, for they have toiled enough
In this accursed land. Give me your staff
And glove, and I shall seek the Paynim King,
Shall cunningly discern, mayhap, his heart
And real intent." But then again did Charles
Make answer, angrily: "Nay, you shall not go."

"My lords," so spake the King, "choose me a man
Fearless enough, and true." And Roland cried:
"Let it be Ganelon. He is valiant—ay,
And true." And straightway all the Franks approved
With a great shout. But Ganelon, leaping up
In sudden anger, throwing aside his cloak,
And standing forth in silken tunic, with hate
In his grey eyes, and yet so passing fair
That all wondered, cried unto Roland: "Fool!
Think not to hide your purpose! All men know
I am your stepsire, and for that alone
You hate me, and would send me into Spain.
If God permit that I return, I swear
To bring upon you great unhappiness,
Which shall endure through all your wretched life."
Then Roland: "You are mad! What all men know
Is this—that I care not for threats! But hold!
The King should send a prudent man. Stand back!
And let him give his glove and staff to me."

And Ganelon answered: "These are empty words,
For you are not my liegeman—nay, nor I
Your lawful lord, to bid you do my hest.
You may not go for me to the dread court
Of Marsila. Charles has spoken. I must go

To Saragossa.—Yea, but there shall I
Liefer some madness do, than not assuage
Mine anger." But Roland, hearing, laughed aloud.

And as he laughed, the heart in Ganelon's breast
Flamed with a sudden rage. He scarce could stand,
So swirled all sense within him. Then he cried:
"I hate you, Roland, hate you. You have brought
This cruel choice upon me, you alone.—
King of the Franks, I stand at your behest.

*On the journey to the Moslem king, Blanchandrin plays upon Ganelon's
hatred of Roland, and together they plot the hero's death. Marsila enters the
plot and agrees to attack Charlemagne's rear guard which Ganelon means to
have Roland command. The traitor's scheme succeeds, and while the Moslem
forces gather for the attack, Roland, his trusted companion Oliver, and Archbishop Turpin assume command of the twenty thousand in the rear guard.*

The Paynims bound their coats of linkèd mail
About their shoulders, laced upon their heads
Their Saragossan helmets, girt their sides
With golden-hilted swords of shimmering steel
Forged in Vienna. Then they took their shields,
And slender lances of Valencian make,
Astream with pennons blue and white and red,
And all with a great shout leapt on their steeds
And rode in serried ranks, a fearful horde.
The day was clear, resplendent shone the sun,
Each several bit of armor flamed again.
And all the trumpets of the host rang loud;
The echoing rumor, borne on the west wind,
Found out the straight defile of Ronceval . . .
And then spake Oliver, saying: "Roland, friend,
We know that sound of old! The Saracens
Are near!" But Roland laughed, and answered him:
"God give your words be true! Then for our King
Here may we stand and fight as brave men should.
For his liege lord a knight ungrudgingly
Must bear distress and aching toil, nor shrink
From scorching sun or blast of winter wind,
Nor reck of life or limb. Soldiers of France,
Deal mighty blows, and so, when songs are sung,
This day's emprise shall not be held in scorn.
We fight for right, the Paynims fight for wrong!
And so, let come what may, we cannot yield!"

But Oliver climbed a lofty hill, and thence
Looked into Spain. Far, far away he saw

The host of Paynims riding. And he called
To Roland, saying: "Lo, from out of Spain
A fearful brightness comes—the blinding gleam
Of hauberks white and helmets all aflame
In the hot sun. Ay, Ganelon has betrayed
Us all, for he it was besought the King
To leave us here." But Roland answered him:
"Your words are madness, friend; it cannot be."

But Oliver climbed a high and jutting crag
Which looked toward Spain. There rode the Paynim host!
He saw the distant gleam of countless helms
Crusted with gold and set with priceless gems.
He saw the shining of bright shields, the hues
Of broidered coats of mail, and rows of spears
With pennons fluttering three-tongued from the tips.
Numberless was the host. He tried to count
The ranks, and could not. So, with hurrying steps
He turned him from the crag, and climbing down
Among the boulders, joined his friends again.

And then he cried: "From yonder pointed rock
I saw the Paynims riding. Never, I think,
Hath living man seen more of them. Alone
The vanguard rides a hundred thousand strong!
Shield upon shining shield they surge, as far
As eye can reach. Their helms and coats of mail
Are laced upon them. Heavenward point their spears,
The burnished tips bright-gleaming. Franks of France,
You shall have battle such as never was
Till now. Be strong in God! Nor yield of ground
The measure of this lance!" And all the Franks
Cried with one voice: "A curse on him who flees!
Not one of us will fail you in this hour!"

And Oliver cried to Roland: "The black host
Is numberless, and we, alas, are few.
Good comrade, wind your horn. The King will hear
The ringing blast, and turning back to Spain,
Will help us." Then did Roland answer him:
"Friend, I were mad to heed you. I should lose
The praise of men forever in sweet France.
Nay, I shall draw my sword, and steep the blade
In Paynim blood up to the hilt. Fore God!
The Paynims shall not thrive in Ronceval!
I pledge you, comrade, they shall die this day!"

"Roland, dear comrade, wind your ivory horn!
And Charles, though far away in France, shall hear,

With all his host shall come to succor us."
But Roland answered, saying: "God forbid
That I bring low my kindred, or become
The instrument of my dear land's dishonor.
Nay, rather shall I draw my sword, my tried
And trusted Durendal, and you shall see
Drenched in red blood the gleaming blade thereof.
The wretched Paynims here in Ronceval
Shall meet their doom—I pledge you, they shall die!"

"Roland, dear comrade, wind for us your horn!
The King will hear, and—this do I pledge you—
Will come to us." But Roland: "God forfend!
No living man shall say I winded horn
For Paynims! Such indignity shall not
Abase my kindred! When the fight is on,
Mine arm shall tire not. Nay, for you shall see
The steel of Durendal adrip with blood.
The Franks are soldiers good and true; their foes
Are doomed—yea, here in Ronceval they die!"

But Oliver said once more: "Let be, dear friend,
For I have seen the Paynims. Over hill
And wide-stretched plain they swarm. The stranger host
Is numberless, and we, all told, are few."
But Roland answered: "All the more I thirst
For battle, praying God that glorious France
Shall never lose through me her proud estate.
Ay, even death were sweeter than long life
Of utter shame, without the King's great love—
And he loves best a giver of stout blows."

Roland is brave. His friend is brave—and wise.
Both are good knights and true in word and deed.
Nor Oliver will yield him, though he die,
After the fight is on. And while they spake,
They heard the onrushing Paynims. Near at hand
Their battle cries rang loud. And Oliver said:
"Behold, proud Roland, where they ride. But Charles
Is far away. You would not wind your horn,
Hearkening not our prayers, and now we die
Unaided. Yonder, in the pass, our men
Prepare them for the strife, but sadly. None
Shall fight again." But Roland answered him:
"Enough! I know the heart within your breast
Is not turned craven. Stand we side by side,
And handle well our swords, let come what may."[1]

---

[1] Here and throughout the selection, compare with Tacitus' account of the ideals of the rman warrior, above, pp. 129–132.

And Roland, fearless as lion or leopard brought
To bay at last, called to the men of France
With words inspiriting. Then once more replied
To Oliver: "Friend, of this no more! for here
In Ronceval are twenty thousand Franks,
But not one coward. It is Frankish law
That every man must suffer for liege lord
Or good or ill, or fire or wintry blast,
Ay, truly, must not reck of life or limb.
Bestir you, comrade! Grasp your lance, and I
My Durendal, bestowed by the King's hand.
Whoever wears it after me shall say:
'This was the sword of one who fought till death.'"

Meanwhile Archbishop Turpin, he of Rheims,
Urging his steed with prick of spur, rode up
The mountain side a space, and from a rock,
As from a pulpit, called upon the Franks:
"Soldiers of France, when King Charles left us here,
He deemed us willing, in extremity,
To suffer death for his dear sake. Nay, more,
He deemed us soldiers of the Christian faith,
Willing to die for God. The hour of proof
Is come. The foes of Charles and God are here
Before you. Now confess your sins, and pray
God's bounteous mercy. Then shall I absolve you,
And if you die, the crown of martyrdom
Is yours, and yours great Paradise." He spake,
And so the Franks, dismounting, knelt them down,
And Turpin signed them with the cross of God,
And for a penance bade them deal stout blows.

The Franks arose with strengthened hearts, absolved
From sin, by Turpin signed with the true cross.
They leapt astride their chargers. Goodly knights
Were they, and armed as knights should be, and all
Athirst for battle. Then did Roland speak
To his dear friend: "O comrade, it is truth—
For gold and silver has my stepsire sold
The rear guard. Ay, the King of Spain hath made
A bargain for our blood. Come! Let us pay
The score with steel! Charles will avenge our deaths!"

And through the strait defile of Ronceval
He galloped, driving the spurs in his good steed.
His armor sat upon him pleasingly;
Within his iron grasp a splendid spear
Was brandished, pointing heavenward, and down

The shaft a pennon of pure white let fall
A fringe of gold across his hand. His face
Was laughing, as the face of one who goes
To dance, not die. And all the Franks acclaimed
Their leader. Roland, hearing, gave them thanks.
A gentle kindliness illumed the eyes
Which flashed a fearful wrath for Paynims. Then
He said: "Ride forward slowly, for the foe
Is coming fast enough to death. Shrink not
Before their spears, which soon shall be your own!"
And even as he spake, the rushing hosts
Were joining in the shock of mortal strife.

And Oliver said: "You winded not your horn,
And now we needs must fight our last good fight
Unaided. But the King is not at fault,
Nor they who, at his side, are going down
To France. Forward, my lords! Fight with the strength
Of desperate men, and stoutly give and take
The blows of battle, shouting the rally cry
Of the great King of France!" And so they cried
"Montjoy!" O, would you all had heard! for so
You never would forget what bravery
Is like! And then they charge—O God!
With what fierce pride! goading their horses' flanks
With frenzied spurs until they bleed again.
So rush to death. What else could brave knights do?
Nor do the Paynim hosts abate their speed.
Paynims and Franks—behold them joined in war.

*The poet then recounts the many valorous deeds of the Frankish
warriors.*

The Franks had held the field with heart and hand
Untiring. An hundred thousand foes had charged,
And scarce two thousand fled. And Roland spake,
Saying: "The men who fight this fight are good
And true. There is no king in the wide world
Has better men, and therefore is it writ
In Frankish story that our King is great."
But even while he spake, and while his Franks
Sought for their dead or dying through the field,
Weeping for friends or kindred, a new horde
Of Paynims came, led by the King himself.

The Paynim King had seen his people slain,
And, sounding horn and clarion, rode apace
To vengeance, leading a new host.—And first
Galloped a Paynim black as molten pitch;

No wickeder than he in all the swarm;
Spotted with many sins, believing not
In God, the Son of Mary; loving more
Treason and murder of his fellow men
Than good Galician gold; so fell that none
Had ever seen him laugh or play; but bold,
And so by Marsila loved, who this day laid
His flag, a painted dragon, in his hand.
And the Archbishop, seeing, loved him not
With Christian love, but yearned to smite him, thus
Communing with his heart: "The wretch, methinks,
Is far the worst of unbelievers—yea—
If now I slay him I shall do no wrong.
Whatever tide, a coward love I not."

And so the Archbishop Turpin led the Franks
Against the Paynim host, riding the steed
Of a great king whom he aforetime slew
In Denmark—swifter than wind, with little feet
And slender legs, but strong, short thighs, wide croup,
And lofty back, with yellow mane and head,
Whereon two tiny ears sat saucily.
On him the good Archbishop rode to meet
The leader of the Paynims, on whose arm
Was fastened a round shield ablaze with gems
From overseas—a demon fashioned it
In some dark cavern, far from haunts of men.
But Turpin smote, and when his blow had split
The splendid buckler, it was little worth.
And the swart Paynim, riven clean in twain
By that one stroke, fell dead upon the field.
Then cried the Franks: "Here is true knightlihood!
In the Archbishop's hand the Cross is safe."

But when the Franks beheld the Paynim hordes
On every side, and hiding the green grass
Utterly, cried they out in sudden dread
To Roland, and to Oliver, and the Peers.
But Turpin bade them think no craven thought,
Nor yield an inch of the red field, lest men
Sing shameful songs thereof. "Much better die
In fight," he said. "And die we must. This day
Shall be our last in life. But of one thing
May I be surety—blessèd Paradise
Is opened wide for you, and with the Saints
Shall you be singing ere the sun hath set."
And when they heard, the Franks forgot straightway
The fear of imminent death, and cried "Montjoy!"

And Roland called to Oliver, saying: "Look,
The Archbishop handles lance and sword as well
As hallowed crosier." And his friend replied:
"In very sooth, the man of God shall teach
The men of battle." So the Franks fought on,
Though sore beset. Would you had seen the fight!
Would you had seen Count Roland and his friend
Smite with their swords! and with his pointed spear
The good Archbishop! Thousands did they slay—
So it is written in the Book of France—
Four battles did they fight, and win—the fifth
Went not so well. Alas, of all the Franks
Sixty alone are left, whom God has spared
Till now—and dearly will they sell their lives.

With almost all the Franks gone, Roland accedes to Oliver's request and blows the great horn, Oliphant, to summon Charlemagne.

And Roland cried: "Why are you wroth with me?"
The other answered: "Comrade, all the fault
Is yours. To temper knightlihood with sense
Is not unknightly; valor must be joined
With measure. Through your foolish arrogance
The Franks are dead, and nevermore will fight
For Charles. If you had given heed, the King
Would now be here. We should have fought and won.
Marsila, long ere this, were put to flight
Or slain. Roland, your reckless hardihood
Was fraught with woe for us. And now the King
Shall lose you, and your like shall never be
Unto the end of all things. You shall die,
And France shall be forlorn. This fearful day
Shall our dear friendship end, and the black night
Shall come upon us parted—and for aye."

But now the good Archbishop, hearing, drave
His spurs of purest gold into his steed,
And came where they contended, and spake thus,
Reproving them: "Sir Roland, ay, and you,
Comrade of Roland, in the name of God
Dispute not thus together. True, the horn
Will save us not. It is too late. And yet
It is the better way. Let the King come;
He will avenge us, and the Paynim hordes
Shall not turn joyous back to Spain. Our Franks,
Dismounting even here, will find us dead
And hewn asunder, but with gentle hands
Us will they lift on sumpters, while they weep

And call us by our names, and take us home
And bury us in some far church of France,
And we shall not be food for wolves or dogs."

Wounded, Roland finally sounds the horn, and, as Oliver lies dying,
Charlemagne turns the army about and comes to the rescue.

The wounded knight feels the approach of death.
He cannot see or hear. So he dismounts
And kneels him down, raising on high his voice
Confesses him, clasping his hands implores
The gift of Paradise, and prays to God
For Charles his glorious King, and for sweet France,
But most of all for Roland, his companion.
His heart falters, his helmèd head sinks down
On his great breast, and slowly to the ground
He droops, and lies in death. His blessèd soul
Tarries no longer. Roland, when he saw,
Did cry aloud. A cry so terrible
Was never wrung from heart of mortal man.

When Roland saw his dear companion dead,
Lying face downward on the earth, his grief
Was uncontrolled. He called to him: "Sir friend,
Your valor merited a better meed
Than this! Day after day, year after year,
Have we been linked together in great love.
Life without you were deeper suffering
Than I could bear." And once again he swooned.
Held by his stirrups of gold, at the wild will
Of his mad steed, he traversed the red field.

Then, as the sound of the rescuing army is heard, and as the Paynim
flee, Roland prepares to die.

Roland, for death was imminent—from his wounds
A crimson flood was flowing—prayed to God
For the great Peers, and prayed for his own soul
To Gabriel the Archangel. Then he took
His horn in his left hand, and in his right
His trusted sword, lest any man reproach
His fair name afterward, and so went forth
Through a green field toward Paynim Spain, as far
As arrow flies from bow, and climbed a hill
Where two great trees flung heavenward their arms,
And covered with their shadows four hewn blocks
Of marble. There, on the soft grass, he fell
Headlong, and swooned, and death was near at hand.

The hills were high, and high upsprang the trees
Over the four white stones, and the green grass.
A Paynim, feigning death, had smeared his face
And all his frame with blood, and thrown him down
On a great heap of dead men. Now he rose
To his full height, a stalwart man and strong,
And ran to Roland, laying craven hand
Upon him. And he cried aloud: "Now yields
The nephew of great Charles; this sword shall I
Take home to Araby!" So he spake, and touched
The golden hilt, and Roland came to sense.

When Roland felt that a strange hand had grasped
His Durendal, he opened his dim eyes,
And cried: "Hold! You are not a friend, methinks."
And seized the horn beside him, and did smite
So fearfully upon the Paynim's helm,
He crushed both helm and head, and threw him down
A lifeless clod. And then he said: "You coward!
How were you ever bold enough, for right
Or wrong, to lay on me your arrogant hands?
Unhappy wretch! for all who hear of this
Shall deem you madman—but mine ivory horn
Is shattered, and the golden rim is broken."

And Roland, though his eyes were dimmed, though death
Was near at hand, gathered his strength once more,
And stood upon his feet. Before him lay
A marble stone. In pain and fearful wrath
He swung bright Durendal, and smote upon
The unyielding rock. The quivering steel rang loud,
But broke not, nor was splintered, and he cried:
"Saint Mary, aid me! Durendal my sword,
In evil hour they forged you. I must you
Forsake, and cherish you no more—with whom
So many battles have I fought, and won
So many lands, which he of the white beard
Now holds. God give that none possess you now
Save that he know not cowardice. Good sword,
A valiant knight and true has wielded you.
A better man is not—mayhap—in France."

And Roland smote the marble stone. The steel
Rang loud, but splintered not. And when he knew
He could not break the tempered blade, he cried:
"O Durendal, how white you are, and how
You gleam, aflame in the bright sun! The King—
They say—was holding court in Morianne,

And lo, an herald came from God, and bade
That you be given to one of his great captains—
Then girt he all your brightness upon me.
With you I conquered Brittany for the King,
Normandy, Aquitania, Lombardy,
And all Roumania. And with you I won
Bavaria and great Flanders, Burgundy,
Poland and far Stamboul, which swore to serve
My master always, and his will is law
Among the fair-haired Saxons. And with you
I conquered for him Scotland and fierce Wales,
And Ireland, and he holds for his domain
All England too. With you I overcame
All the broad lands that Charles of the white beard
Now holds. But I grieve for you, my Durendal,
Thinking that you shall stay henceforth in Spain—
With Saracens! O God, let not this be!"

And Roland smote the stone, and hewed away
A fragment. The good steel rang loud and clear,
Yet shattered not nor splintered, but upsprang
Toward heaven, and Roland knew it would not break
For all his desperate strength. And tenderly then
He spake to it: "O Durendal, how fair
You are, and holy, for your pommel hides
Good store of relics—ay, a tooth of Peter,
A vial of Basil's martyred blood, and hair
Of good Saint Dennis, and the blessèd hem
Of Mary's garment. He who wields you now
Must be a Christian. And may God forfend
That Saracens possess you, or a man
Who ever falters. O sweet Durendal,
How many lands has Roland won with you,
Now held by Charles the Great, whose beard is white
As driven snow, ruler of all the Franks."

And then he knew that death was taking hold
Of his great frame, creeping from head to heart.
Under a lofty pine, on the green grass
He cast him down, laying his horn and sword
Beneath him, turning his face where fled
The affrighted Paynims, that the King might know
He died a conqueror still, and lifted voice
To heaven, confessing him to his liege lord,
Tendering him the glove of his right hand.

Ay—Roland knew that death was near. He lay
On a high hill, looking toward Paynim Spain,

And beat his breast, crying: "Forgive, O God,
The wrongs that I have wrought Thee, since the day
When I was born unto this day when here
I am fordone." He raised his iron glove
To the blue sky, and so the angels came
On wings of gold to take his soul to God.

   Under a lofty pine he lay, and turned
Toward Spain, and called to memory many things—
The lands that he had conquered, and sweet France,
His kindred, and Great Charles, who cherished him
As his own son. And yet, for all his grief,
Remembered how a knight should pray, and said:
"Father whose word is truth, who from the grave
Didst ransom Lazarus, and from ravening lions
Didst rescue Daniel, rescue now my soul
From suffering for the sins which I have sinned
All my life long." And so upon his arm
His head sank slowly down. With joinèd hands,
Praying, he died. And as he died there came
On golden wings a spirit, and beside
Saint Michael of the Peril of the Deep,
And the Archangel Gabriel, and these three
Carried his soul to heaven, and to God.

II

THE HIGH MIDDLE AGES

After the passing of the slowly creative centuries that followed the collapse of Roman government, the pattern of institutions, ideas, and styles that we generally term "medieval" began to appear around the year 1100. First Romanesque and then Gothic churches were built from Palermo in Sicily to Durham in northern England. Higher schools that by the thirteenth century were to serve as international universities began to offer instruction at Bologna and Paris, where the faculties specialized in law and theology, respectively. In Sicily and Rome, as well as in England, rationally directed governments collected taxes and formally assumed an obligation to rule with justice. The twelfth century, roughly conceived as the period 1090–1215, witnessed these great creative acts which established institutions and values that were to shape European civilization for centuries.

Before the last quarter of the eleventh century, Christian Europe had produced little political theory. Then the struggle between the Holy Roman Emperor Henry IV and Pope Gregory VII, the investiture controversy,[1] stimulated nearly one hundred tracts, treatises, and analyses, and, in fact, launched the great tradition of medieval and modern political thought. From its beginning, medieval theory had an overtone that had been lacking in ancient thought about man and society: always implied in the search for right was the danger of final and total damnation if one were wrong. Political arguments were ultimately religious arguments in the Middle Ages, and the same was true of economic thinking.

The issues raised during the investiture controversy were argued throughout the Middle Ages: the proper relation, within Christendom, between Church and State, pope and emperor; the source of political authority; the proper structure of authority within the Church or kingdom. In the twelfth

---

[1] This is the term applied to the whole range of issues that divided the Church and secular authority from about 1070 to 1122. Involved were such matters as appointment of bishops and reform of clergy. Not only the Emperor was involved in controversy with the Pope; the reform Papacy disputed and eventually reached agreement with the kings of France and England and lesser princes.

century, stimulated by the revival of the study of Roman law, men began to think more coherently about law and justice and, in later years, carried on the examination of them with much technicality and finesse. Discussion of such matters was endless, but the impression that one has heard all this before should be qualified by the realization that a statement similar to the one made centuries earlier has a different impact when made in a different institutional environment.

The relationship between theories and institutions is nowhere better evidenced than in the effect of legal thinking upon legal institutions during the Middle Ages. Given their great concern to do right, which was, of course, a religious as well as a political duty, and given, too, the prestige that accompanied the exercise of justice, rulers consciously built elaborate judicial systems. This is as true of pope and bishop as of king, baron, or city fathers. At the same time, a concern for personal and group privileges and rights and rule of law that may be termed "constitutionalism" served as a basis for the development all over Europe, in ecclesiastical as well as secular government, of parliamentary devices. Estates or parliaments were not democratic in the Middle Ages (with the possible exception of the citizen assemblies of the Italian towns) and indeed were usually creatures of the king or prince, but nevertheless they did serve as a means to the solution of conflicts through talk, as the very word "parliament" (from the French parler, "to speak") suggests.

This medieval concern for justice, so often described in Cicero's terms as "giving each man his due," was carried over into financial and commercial matters. From the twelfth century, money began to play a more and more important role in medieval life. The Church developed financial needs and the finance bureaus to satisfy them. In towns of considerable size, the marketplace or fair became the normal mechanism of distribution; and in some towns workers produced goods in quantity for an export market of international proportions. Commerce and industry created great wealth and several other conventional features of a complex business world such as fraud and exploitation of the ignorant and weak. Christian theory had little place for riches or for such abuses. So, in this age in which justice was considered the principal purpose of government, theologians as well as theorists of both the canon (ecclesiastical) and Roman laws worried and wrote about the nature of justice in economic and social relations and the means of assuring it.

During these same years, the active burgesses of the towns built their cloth halls and told the tales that suggest to us the tensions between traditional verities and current performance. Toward the end of the Middle Ages, it became very difficult to hold those tensions in balance, as the criticisms of Chaucer, Langland, and others testify.

Brushing shoulders with the merchants in Paris, Oxford, Bologna, Salamanca, and, eventually, Cologne, Prague, and Cracow, were Europe's scholars. They, like the merchants, were unacceptable to some in the Christian community, and not the least of their achievements, apart from substantive advance in many technical fields, was to make learning itself necessary and respectable. That is to say, a place was found for science in the theoretical framework of Christian society. By the end of the thirteenth century, few thinking men questioned the value of the learned professions: lawyers served governments that *properly ordered their subjects' lives and brought them peace; physicians healed the body; and scientists and mathematicians now boldly attempted to describe the material universe, seen as God's creation and therefore fully worthy of human investigation.*

1. Who Leads the Christian Commonwealth?

For most of the thousand years before the reign of Pope Gregory VII (1073–1085), the Church in western Europe was dependent upon and often controlled by laymen. Some, like Charlemagne, were imbued with the idealism of the Church, protected it, and attempted to organize the territory they ruled according to Christian principles. Others, although baptized, were little influenced by the priests in their service and used religion and ecclesiastics for personal advantage.

By the second half of the eleventh century, a reform movement had emerged, its headquarters in Rome, its goal, in a broad sense, to purify the Church and lead all men to salvation. Study of theology and canon law, intensification of religious and ascetic spirit institutionalized in a monastic revival, interference in religious affairs by deeply concerned members of the laity: these were a few of the sources of the reform.

One layman who interfered was the emperor Henry III. In 1046, Henry marched on Rome, ended a contest for office among three claimants to the papal throne, and then put his own man on it. His choice was a fine one, and thus the Emperor added his weight to the reform movement, fulfilling in his interference what he considered to be a traditional imperial responsibility. Before his death in 1056 and during the minority of his son, a line of reputable and efficient popes began to construct the Roman Church and the papal institutions that in so many ways were to dominate all aspects of European life for the following two centuries.

Gradually, the Papacy freed itself from imperial control, developed bureaucratic institutions that made it efficient, and then, relying upon the religious consciousness that several centuries of preaching and teaching had finally awakened, used this advanced form of government to achieve its ends. It proclaimed its own leadership of Western society and attempted to provide that leadership. This vast movement has been called the "Gregorian Revolution," not because Gregory VII started it, but because he led it during the great crisis, the struggle with the emperor Henry IV, and because he consolidated lines of ideological and institutional development that served the Papacy for several hundred years.

At the same moment that deeply religious popes were attempting to extricate themselves and the German bishops from imperial tutelage, the young emperor Henry IV (1056–1106) was attempting to create the institutions of "modern" centralized monarchy in Germany. In the 1070's, when he faced the determined Gregory VII, Henry still had to depend in war upon the thousands of horsemen that the German bishops traditionally had furnished the secular ruler who had granted them their vast lands. The Papacy was opposed to continued use of the Church in this way, but Henry knew that in past history there was support for his view of the proper relations between Church and State. And if the Pope could advance theories based upon law, Scripture, and history, so, too, could the Emperor. In the following source cluster we can trace the movement of ideas and claims about the sources and nature of political authority from the late eleventh to the early fourteenth century.

LETTERS OF POPE GREGORY VII AND EMPEROR HENRY IV

To Hermann of Metz, in Defense of the Papal Policy Toward Henry IV*

Gregory . . . to his beloved brother in Christ, Hermann, bishop of Metz,[1] greeting . . .

You ask us to fortify you against the madness of those who babble with accursed tongues about the authority of the Holy Apostolic See not being able to excommunicate King Henry as one who despises the law of Christ, a destroyer of churches and of the empire, a promoter and partner of heresies, nor to release anyone from his oath of fidelity to him; but it has not seemed necessary to reply to this request, seeing that so many and such convincing proofs are to be found in Holy Scripture. Nor do we believe that those who abuse and contradict the truth to their utter damnation do this as much from ignorance as from wretched and desperate folly. And no wonder! It is ever the way of the wicked to protect their own iniquities by calling upon others like themselves; for they think it of no account to incur the penalty of falsehood.

To cite but a few out of the multitude of proofs: Who does not remember the words of our Lord and Savior Jesus Christ: "Thou art Peter and on this rock I will build my Church, and the gates of hell shall not prevail against it. And I will give thee the keys of the kingdom of heaven and whatsoever thou shalt bind on earth shall be bound in heaven and whatsoever thou shalt loose on earth shall be loosed in heaven." Are kings excepted here? Or are they not of the sheep which the Son of God committed to St. Peter? Who, I ask, thinks himself excluded from this universal grant of the power of binding and loosing to St. Peter unless, perchance, that unhappy man who, being unwilling to bear the yoke of the Lord, subjects himself to the burden of the Devil and refuses to be numbered in the flock of Christ? His wretched liberty shall profit him nothing; for if he shakes off from his proud neck the power divinely granted to Peter, so much the heavier shall it be for him in the day of judgment.

This institution of the divine will, this foundation of the rule of the Church, this privilege granted and sealed especially by a heavenly decree to

---

* *The Correspondence of Pope Gregory VII*, trans. with an introduction by E. Emerton (New York: Columbia University Press, 1932), pp. 166–175.

[1] One of the more important bishops in Germany whom Gregory was especially anxious to win to his side. The extent to which Gregory developed his ideas in his letters to Hermann suggests that the ideas were somewhat unusual and needed explication.

St. Peter, chief of the Apostles, has been accepted and maintained with great reverence by the holy fathers, and they have given to the Holy Roman Church, as well in general councils as in their other acts and writings, the name of "universal mother." They have not only accepted her expositions of doctrine and her instructions in [our] holy religion, but they have also recognized her judicial decisions. They have agreed as with one spirit and one voice that all major cases, all especially important affairs and the judgments of all churches ought to be referred to her as to their head and mother, that from her there shall be no appeal, that her judgments may not and cannot be reviewed or reversed by anyone.

Thus Pope Gelasius, writing to the emperor Anastasius,[2] gave him these instructions as to the right theory of the principate of the Holy and Apostolic See, based upon divine authority:

> Although it is fitting that all the faithful should submit themselves to all priests who perform their sacred functions properly, how much the more should they accept the judgment of that prelate who has been appointed by the supreme divine ruler to be superior to all priests and whom the loyalty of the whole later Church has recognized as such. Your Wisdom sees plainly that no human capacity [*concilium*] whatsoever can equal that of him whom the word of Christ raised above all others and whom the reverend Church has always confessed and still devotedly holds as its Head.

So also Pope Julius,[3] writing to the eastern bishops in regard to the powers of the same Holy and Apostolic See, says:

> You ought, my brethren, to have spoken carefully and not ironically of the Holy Roman and Apostolic Church, seeing that our Lord Jesus Christ addressed her respectfully [*decenter*], saying, "Thou art Peter and upon this rock I will build my church, and the gates of hell shall not prevail against it; and I will give thee the keys of the kingdom of heaven." For it has the power, granted by a unique privilege, of opening and shutting the gates of the celestial kingdom to whom it will.

To whom, then, the power of opening and closing Heaven is given, shall he not be able to judge the earth? God forbid! Do you remember what the most blessed Apostle Paul says: "Know ye not that we shall judge angels? How much more things that pertain to this life?"

So Pope Gregory[4] declared that kings who dared to disobey the orders

---

[2] Gelasius was a Roman pope (492–496) famous for his theory of the proper relation between Church and State. He wrote that "there are two powers by which this world is chiefly ruled: the sacred authority of the priesthood and the authority of kings." He is held to have meant that both ecclesiastical and civil power are of divine origin, and that each is to rule in its own independent sphere of action. Anastasius I (ruled 491–518) was emperor of the Eastern Roman Empire.

[3] Pope Julius I (ruled 337–352) was active in the doctrinal controversy with the Arians over the nature of the Trinity. In disputing with them, he claimed that the Popes possessed appellate jurisdiction over the entire Church. See Julius' statement, above, pp. 146–147.

[4] Pope Gregory I (590–604) was, in his own episcopacy of Rome, a model of aggressive action. When Rome was threatened by the Lombards, he negotiated with the attackers, thus affronting the dignity of the Roman emperor who should have been protecting the holy city. However, in his theoretical statements, Gregory espoused the doctrine of divided and complementary papal and imperial powers.

of the Apostolic See should forfeit their office. He wrote to a certain senator and abbot in these words:

> If any king, priest, judge or secular person shall disregard this decree of ours and act contrary to it, he shall be deprived of his power and his office and shall learn that he stands condemned at the bar of God for the wrong that he has done. And unless he shall restore what he has wrongfully taken and shall have done fitting penance for his unlawful acts he shall be excluded from the sacred body and blood of our Lord and Savior Jesus Christ and at the last judgment shall receive condign punishment.

Now then, if the blessed Gregory, most gentle of doctors, decreed that kings who should disobey his orders about a hospital for strangers should be not only deposed but excommunicated and condemned in the last judgment, how can anyone blame us for deposing and excommunicating Henry, who not only disregards apostolic judgments, but so far as in him lies tramples upon his mother the Church, basely plunders the whole kingdom and destroys its churches—unless indeed it were one who is a man of his own kind?

As we know also through the teaching of St. Peter in his letter touching the ordination of Clement, where he says: "If any one were friend to those with whom he [Clement] is not on speaking terms, that man is among those who would like to destroy the Church of God and, while he seems to be with us in the body, he is against us in mind and heart, and he is a far worse enemy than those who are without and are openly hostile. For he, under the forms of friendship, acts as an enemy and scatters and lays waste the Church." Consider then, my best beloved, if he passes so severe a judgment upon him who associates himself with those whom the pope opposes on account of their actions, with what severity he condemns the man himself to whom the pope is thus opposed.

But now, to return to our point: Is not a sovereignty invented by men of this world who were ignorant of God subject to that which the providence of Almighty God established for his own glory and graciously bestowed upon the world? The Son of God we believe to be God and man, sitting at the right hand of the Father as High Priest, head of all priests and ever making intercession for us. He despised the kingdom of this world wherein the sons of this world puff themselves up and offered himself as a sacrifice upon the cross.

Who does not know that kings and princes derive their origin from men ignorant of God who raised themselves above their fellows by pride, plunder, treachery, murder—in short, by every kind of crime—at the instigation of the Devil, the prince of this world, men blind with greed and intolerable in their audacity? If, then, they strive to bend the priests of God to their will, to whom may they more properly be compared than to him who is chief over all the sons of pride? For he, tempting our High Priest, head of all priests, son of the Most High, offering him all the kingdoms of this world, said: "All these will I give thee if thou wilt fall down and worship me."

Does anyone doubt that the priests of Christ are to be considered as fathers and masters of kings and princes and of all believers? Would it not be regarded as pitiable madness if a son should try to rule his father or a pupil his master and to bind with unjust obligations the one through whom he expects to be bound or loosed, not only on earth but also in heaven? Evidently recognizing this the emperor Constantine the Great,[5] lord over all kings and princes throughout almost the entire earth, as St. Gregory relates in his letter to the emperor Mauritius,[6] at the holy synod of Nicaea took his place below all the bishops and did not venture to pass any judgment upon them but, even addressing them as gods, felt that they ought not to be subject to his judgment but that he ought to be bound by their decisions.

Pope Gelasius, urging upon the emperor Anastasius not to feel himself wronged by the truth that was called to his attention said: "There are two powers, O august Emperor, by which the word is governed, the sacred authority of the priesthood and the power of kings. Of these the priestly is by so much the greater as they will have to answer for kings themselves in the day of divine judgment;" and a little further: "Know that you are subject to their judgment, not that they are to be subjected to your will."

In reliance upon such declarations and such authorities, many prelates have excommunicated kings or emperors. . . .

Your Fraternity should remember also that greater power is granted to an exorcist[7] when he is made a spiritual emperor for the casting out of devils, than can be conferred upon any layman for the purpose of earthly dominion. All kings and princes of this earth who live not piously and in their deeds show not a becoming fear of God are ruled by demons and are sunk in miserable slavery. Such men desire to rule, not guided by the love of God, as priests are, for the glory of God and the profit of human souls, but to display their intolerable pride and to satisfy the lusts of their mind. Of these St. Augustine says in the first book of his Christian doctrine: "He who tries to rule over men—who are by nature equal to him—acts with intolerable pride." Now if exorcists have power over demons, as we have said, how much more over those who are subject to demons and are limbs of demons! And if exorcists are superior to these, how much more are priests superior to them!

Furthermore, every Christian king when he approaches his end asks the aid of a priest as a miserable suppliant that he may escape the prison of hell, may pass from darkness into light and may appear at the judgment seat of God freed from the bonds of sin. But who, layman or priest, in his last moments has ever asked the help of any earthly king for the safety of his soul? And what king or emperor has power through his office to snatch any Christian from the might of the Devil by the sacred rite of baptism, to confirm him among the sons of God and to fortify him by the holy chrism? Or—and this is the greatest thing in the Christian religion—who among them is able by his own word to create the body and blood of the Lord? or to whom among them is given the power to bind and loose in Heaven and upon earth? From

---

[5] Constantine I (c. 288–337), called "the Great" in Western history because he was the first emperor to embrace Christianity (albeit the Arian form eventually declared heretical) and the first to involve himself with the internal affairs of the Church. It was he who called the Council of Nicaea, 325.

[6] A general, later a Byzantine emperor (c. 539–602), who was active in defense against both Persians and Avars.

[7] Although its exercise is strictly regulated by church law, the Catholic Church claims to possess the power to rid a person of evil spirits. In the early days of the Church, the title of one with such powers was exorcist. Already in the Middle Ages, the exorcist was regarded as one of the lesser clergy.

this it is apparent how greatly superior in power is the priestly dignity.

Or who of them is able to ordain any clergyman in the Holy Church—much less to depose him for any fault? For bishops, while they may ordain other bishops, may in no wise depose them except by authority of the Apostolic See. How, then, can even the most slightly informed person doubt that priests are higher than kings? But if kings are to be judged by priests for their sins, by whom can they more properly be judged than by the Roman pontiff?

In short, all good Christians, whosoever they may be, are more properly to be called kings than are evil princes; for the former, seeking the glory of God, rule themselves rigorously; but the latter, seeking their own rather than the things that are of God, being enemies to themselves, oppress others tyrannically. The former are the body of the true Christ; the latter, the body of the Devil. The former rule themselves that they may reign forever with the supreme ruler. The power of the latter brings it to pass that they perish in eternal damnation with the prince of darkness who is king over all the sons of pride.

It is no great wonder that evil priests take the part of a king whom they love and fear on account of honors received from him. By ordaining any person whomsoever, they are selling their God at a bargain price. For as the elect are inseparably united to their Head, so the wicked are firmly bound to him who is head of all evil—especially against the good. But against these it is of no use to argue, but rather to pray God with tears and groans that he may deliver them from the snares of Satan, in which they are caught, and after trial may lead them at last into knowledge of the truth.

So much for kings and emperors who, swollen with the pride of this world, rule not for God but for themselves. But since it is our duty to exhort everyone according to his station, it is our care with God's help to furnish emperors, kings and other princes with the weapons of humility that thus they may be strong to keep down the floods and waves of pride. We know that earthly glory and the cares of this world are wont especially to cause rulers to be exalted, to forget humility and, seeking their own glory, strive to excel their fellows. It seems therefore especially useful for emperors and kings, while their hearts are lifted up in the strife for glory, to learn how to humble themselves and to know fear rather than joy. Let them therefore consider carefully how dangerous, even awesome is the office of emperor or king, how very few find salvation therein, and how those who are saved through God's mercy have become far less famous in the Church by divine judgment than many humble persons. From the beginning of the world to the present day we do not find in all authentic records [seven] emperors or kings whose lives were as distinguished for virtue and piety as were those of a countless multitude of men who despised the world—although we believe that many of them were saved by the mercy of God. Not to speak of Apostles and Martyrs, who among emperors and kings was famed for his miracles as were St. Martin, St. Antony and St. Benedict?[8] What emperor or king ever raised the dead, cleansed lepers

---

[8] St. Martin of Tours (316–c. 397) is famous for his charity: he is often represented in the act of sharing his cloak with a beggar. Although a bishop, he preferred to live the monastic life; in his monastery near Tours he was active in the training of missionaries. St. Antony (c. 251–350) was one of the "founders" of Christian monasticism. He was active in establishing communities of monks, an innovation, for before his time the characteristic holy life was that of the hermit. St. Benedict was founder of the Benedictine order and of European monasticism. See above, pp. 176–181.

or opened the eyes of the blind? True, Holy Church praises and honors the emperor Constantine of pious memory, Theodosius and Honorius, Charles and Louis,[9] as lovers of justice, champions of the Christian faith and protectors of churches, but she does not claim that they were illustrious for the splendor of their wonderful works. Or to how many names of kings or emperors has Holy Church ordered churches or altars to be dedicated or masses to be celebrated?

Let kings and princes fear lest the higher they are raised above their fellows in this life, the deeper they may be plunged in everlasting fire. Wherefore it is written: "The mighty shall suffer mighty torments." They shall render unto God an account for all men subject to their rule. But if it is no small labor for the pious individual to guard his own soul, what a task is laid upon princes in the care of so many thousands of souls! And if Holy Church imposes a heavy penalty upon him who takes a single human life, what shall be done to those who send many thousands to death for the glory of this world? These, although they say with their lips, *mea culpa,* for the slaughter of many, yet in their hearts they rejoice at the increase of their glory and neither repent of what they have done nor regret that they have sent their brothers into the world below. So that, since they do not repent with all their hearts and will not restore what they have gained by human bloodshed, their penitence before God remains without the fruits of a true repentance. . . .[10]

All Christians, therefore, who desire to reign with Christ are to be warned not to reign through ambition for wordly power. They are to keep in mind the admonition of that most holy pope Gregory in his book on the pastoral office: "Of all these things what is to be followed, what held fast, except that the man strong in virtue shall come to his office under compulsion? Let him who is without virtue not come to it even though he be urged thereto." If, then, men who fear God come under compulsion with fear and trembling to the Apostolic See where those who are properly ordained become stronger through the merits of the blessed Apostle Peter, with what awe and hesitation should men ascend the throne of a king where even good and humble men like Saul and David become worse! What we have said above is thus stated in the decrees of the blessed pope Symmachus[11]— though we have learned it by experience: "He, that is St. Peter, transmitted to his successors an unfailing endowment of merit together with an inheritance of innocence;" and again: "For who can doubt that he is holy who is raised to the height of such an office, in which if he is lacking in virtue acquired by

[9] The Roman emperor Theodosius (c. 346–395), called "Great" by the Church because he condemned the Arian view of the Trinity as heretical, established the Creed of Nicaea, and used the force of the government to crush opposition to the new orthodoxy. Honorius (384–423) was the successor of Theodosius. During his reign, the barbarian generals of the Roman armies rose to significant power. The Visigoths under Alaric sacked Rome, and the split widened between the ways of life in the eastern and western parts of the Empire. In accordance with Christian doctrine, he abolished the gladitorial games in Rome, thus ending a very evident survival of paganism. Charles is of course Charlemagne, who translated the ideas of his ecclesiastical advisors into all manner of legislation and activity. Louis the Pious (778–840), Charlemagne's son and successor, was too much in the hands of his priests, thought the great Frankish nobles who wished a warrior for a leader, not a king who prayed and surrounded himself with idealistic churchmen.

[10] Refer to the *Song of Roland,* above, pp. 181–193, for an example of this kind of person.

[11] Pope (498–514) whose election was confirmed by Theodoric, and one of whose problems was the proper relation between the orthodox majority in Italy and the ruling Ostrogoths, who were Arians.

his own merits, that which is handed down from his predecessor is sufficient. For either he [Peter] raises men of distinction to bear this burden or he glorifies them after they are raised up."

Wherefore let those whom Holy Church, of its own will and with deliberate judgment, not for fleeting glory but for the welfare of multitudes, has called to royal or imperial rule—let them be obedient and ever mindful of the blessed Gregory's declaration in that same pastoral treatise: "When a man disdains to be the equal of his fellow men, he becomes like an apostate angel. Thus Saul, after his period of humility, swollen with pride, ran into excess of power. He was raised in humility, but rejected in his pride, as God bore witness, saying: 'Though thou wast little in thine own sight, wast thou not made the head of the tribes of Israel?'" and again: "I marvel how, when he was little to himself he was great before God, but when he seemed great to himself he was little before God." Let them watch and remember what God says in the Gospel: "I seek not my own glory," and, "He who would be first among you, let him be the servant of all." Let them ever place the honor of God above their own; let them embrace justice and maintain it by preserving to everyone his right; let them not enter into the counsels of the ungodly, but cling to those of religion with all their hearts. Let them not seek to make Holy Church their maid-servant or their subject, but recognizing priests, the eyes of God, as their masters and fathers, strive to do them becoming honor.

If we are commanded to honor our fathers and mothers in the flesh, how much more our spiritual parents! If he that curseth his father or his mother shall be put to death, what does he deserve who curses his spiritual father or mother? Let not princes, led astray by carnal affection, set their own sons over that flock for whom Christ shed his blood if a better and more suitable man can be found. By thus loving their own son more than God they bring the greatest evils upon the Church. For it is evident that he who fails to provide to the best of his ability so great and necessary an advantage for our holy mother, the Church, does not love God and his neighbor as befits a Christian man. If this one virtue of charity be wanting, then whatever of good the man may do will lack all saving grace.

But if they do these things in humility, keeping their love for God and their neighbor as they ought, they may count upon the mercy of him who said: "'Learn of me, for I am meek and lowly of heart." If they humbly imitate him, they shall pass from their servile and transient reign into the kingdom of eternal liberty.[12]

EMPEROR HENRY IV TO POPE GREGORY VII*

Henry, King not by usurpation, but by the pious ordination of God, to Hildebrand, now not Pope, but false monk:

You have deserved such a salutation as this because of the confusion you have wrought; for you left untouched no order of the Church which you could

---

[12] Compare this whole argument with St. Gregory's *Pastoral Care*, above, pp. 169–175, and with the statements of the Council of Sardica and Pope Julius, above, pp. 146–147.

* Reprinted from *Imperial Lives and Letters of the Eleventh Century*, trans. T. E. Mommsen and K. R. Morrison, ed. R. Benson (New York: Columbia University Press, 1962), pp. 150–151.

make a sharer of confusion instead of honor, of malediction instead of benediction.

For to discuss a few outstanding points among many: Not only have you dared to touch the rectors of the holy Church—the archbishops, the bishops, and the priests, anointed of the Lord as they are—but you have trodden them under foot like slaves who know not what their lord may do. In crushing them you have gained for yourself acclaim from the mouth of the rabble. You have judged that all these know nothing, while you alone know everything. In any case, you have sedulously used this knowledge not for edification, but for destruction, so greatly that we may believe Saint Gregory,[1] whose name you have arrogated to yourself, rightly made this prophesy of you when he said: "From the abundance of his subjects, the mind of the prelate is often exalted, and he thinks that he has more knowledge than anyone else, since he sees that he has more power than anyone else."

And we, indeed, bore with all these abuses, since we were eager to preserve the honor of the Apostolic See. But you construed our humility as fear, and so you were emboldened to rise up even against the royal power itself, granted to us by God. You dared to threaten to take the kingship away from us—as though we had received the kingship from you, as though kingship and empire were in your hand and not in the hand of God.

Our Lord, Jesus Christ, has called us to kingship, but has not called you to the priesthood. For you have risen by these steps: namely, by cunning, which the monastic profession abhors, to money; by money to favor; by favor to the sword. By the sword you have come to the throne of peace, and from the throne of peace you have destroyed the peace. You have armed subjects against their prelates; you who have not been called by God have taught that our bishops who have been called by God are to be spurned; you have usurped for laymen the bishops' ministry over priests, with the result that these laymen depose and condemn the very men whom the laymen themselves received as teachers from the hand of God, through the imposition of the hands of bishops.[2]

You have also touched me, one who, though unworthy, has been anointed to kingship among the anointed. This wrong you have done to me, although as the tradition of the holy Fathers has taught, I am to be judged by God alone and am not to be deposed for any crime unless—may it never happen—I should deviate from the Faith. For the prudence of the holy bishops entrusted the judgment and the deposition even of Julian the Apostate[3] not to themselves, but to God alone. The true pope Saint Peter also exclaims, "Fear God, honor the king." You, however, since you do not fear God, dishonor me, ordained of Him.

Wherefore, when Saint Paul gave no quarter to an angel from heaven if the angel should preach heterodoxy, he did not except you who are now

---

[1] Pope Gregory I, whose *Pastoral Care* appears above, pp. 169–175.

[2] Henry's reference here is to a recent letter from the Pope excommunicating several German bishops and one archbishop. In the eyes of the Emperor and of many of the German clergy, the Pope's violent and arbitrary actions were overturning the established order of things.

[3] A Roman emperor (ruled 360–363) who made an attempt during his short reign to stop the growing political power of Christianity. He legislated against the Christians and for the pagans, especially in matters of education.

teaching heterodoxy throughout the earth. For he says, "If anyone, either I or an angel from heaven, preach any other gospel unto you than that which we have preached unto you, let him be accursed." Descend, therefore, condemned by this anathema and by the common judgment of all our bishops and of ourself. Relinquish the Apostolic See which you have arrogated. Let another mount the throne of Saint Peter, another who will not cloak violence with religion but who will teach the pure doctrine of Saint Peter.[4]

I, Henry, King by the grace of God, together with all our bishops, say to you: Descend! Descend!

Emperor Henry IV to the German Bishops*

Henry, King by the grace of God, sends to A.,[1] the grace, greeting, and love which he sends not to all men, but only to a few:

In the greatest affairs there is need for the greatest counsels of the greatest men, who externally should have power and within should not be lacking in good will, so that they may be both willing and able to deliberate well about that matter for which they wish well. For in the advancement of any enterprise, neither power without good will nor good will without power is useful. O most faithful subject, you possess, we think, each of these in equal proportion. To tell the truth, although as one of the great, you possess great power, your good will for our advantage and for that of our kingdom grows even greater than this great power—if we know you well and have properly noted your fidelity. From past actions faithfully done, the hope grows that future actions will be done yet more faithfully. We trust to your love, however, that your fidelity may not fall short of our hope, since from the fidelity of none of the kingdom's princes do we hope for greater things than from yours. Thus until this very time, we have rejoiced not only in what past affairs reveal but also in your promise of things still to be hoped for.

Let your good will stand by us, therefore, together with your power at this opportune time, the good will for which not only our need is earnestly longing, but also that of all your fellow bishops and brethren, nay rather, that of the whole oppressed Church. Certainly, you are not ignorant of this oppression. Only see to it that you do not withdraw assistance from the oppressed Church, but rather that you give your sympathy to the kingship and to the priesthood. Just as hitherto the Church was exalted by each of these offices, so now, alas, it is laid low, bereft of each; since one man has arrogated both for himself, he has injured both, and he who has neither wanted nor was able to be of benefit in either has been useless in each.

To keep you in suspense no longer as to the name of the man under discussion, learn of whom we speak: it is the monk Hildebrand (a monk indeed in habit), so-called pope who, as you yourself know clearly, presides in

---

[4] This letter came to Gregory from the Emperor who was in council with his great nobles, lay and ecclesiastical, at Worms. Henry, fresh from a victory over Saxon rebels and sure of the support of many German bishops, was in no mood to compromise with Pope Gregory.

* Reprinted from *Imperial Lives and Letters of the Eleventh Century,* trans. T. E. Mommsen and K. R. Morrison, ed. R. Benson (New York: Columbia University Press, 1962), pp. 151–154.

[1] This was an encyclical letter sent to all his German bishops. "A" therefore stands for the name of the bishop that the scribe, following a form, was to insert.

the Apostolic See not with the care of a pastor but with the violence of a usurper and from the throne of peace dissolves the bond of the one catholic peace. To cite to a few things among the many: without God's knowledge he has usurped for himself the kingship and the priesthood. In this deed he held in contempt the pious ordinance of God, which especially commanded these two—namely, the kingship and the priesthood—should remain, not as one entity, but as two. In his Passion, the Savior Himself meant the figurative sufficiency of the two swords to be understood in this way: When it was said to him, "Lord, behold there are two swords here," He answered, "It is enough," signifying by this sufficient duality, that the spiritual and the carnal swords are to be used in the Church and that by them every hurtful thing is to be cut off. That is to say, He was teaching that every man is constrained by the priestly sword to obey the king as the representative of God but by the kingly sword both to repel enemies of Christ outside and to obey the priesthood within. So in charity the province of one extends into the other, as long as neither the kingship is deprived of honor by the priesthood nor the priesthood is deprived of honor by the kingship. You yourself have found out, if you have wanted to discover it, how the Hildebrandine madness has confounded this ordinance of God; for in his judgment, no one may be a priest unless he begs that [honor] from his arrogance. He has also striven to deprive me of the kingship—me whom God has called to the kingship (God, however, has not called him to the priesthood)—since he saw that I wished to hold my royal power from God and not from him and since he himself had not constituted me as king. And further, he threatened to deprive me of kingship and life, neither of which he had bestowed.

Although he often contrived these outrages against us, and others like them, as you yourself know, nonetheless he was not satisfied unless from day to day he cast new and coarse sorts of affliction upon us. . . .

Wherefore, be not ashamed, most cherished friend, be not ashamed to satsify the petition we make in common with your fellow bishops: that you come to Worms at Pentecost and hear many things there with the other princes, a few of which this letter mentions, and advise us what is to be done. For you are besought by the love of your fellow bishops, admonished through the advantage of the Church, and bound by the honor of our life and of the whole kingdom.

EMPEROR HENRY IV TO THE ROMAN CARDINALS*

Behold, with the favor of God we shall come to Rome on the set date. If he should wish, let everything be done there. If it is more agreeable to come with our messengers to meet us, we approve that plan also. Come with him yourselves, as many of you as wish; come, hear, judge. If he can and ought to be pope, we shall obey him; but if the opposite is true in your judgment and ours, let another, one whom the Church requires, be provided for the Church.[1]

---

* Reprinted from *Imperial Lives and Letters of the Eleventh Century*, trans. T. E. Mommsen and K. R. Morrison, ed. R. Benson (New York: Columbia University Press, 1962), pp. 164–165.

[1] By 1082, the date of this letter, Henry, although formally deposed, was in command of Rome, and Pope Gregory, the "he" in the letter, was in exile among his Norman supporters. Now it was the Emperor who was proposing an assembly—one to decide whether Gregory was fit to be Pope.

You ought not to reject this proposal. If it is righteous to heed a priest, it is righteous also to obey a king. Why does Hildebrand strive to destroy the dispensation of God? And if he attempts this, why do you not oppose him? God has said not that one, but that two swords are sufficient. But Hildebrand intends that there be only one, since he struggles to ruin us, whom (though unworthy) God ordained king from our very cradle. God has shown daily that He had so ordained us; as anyone can see who considers well how He guarded us from the ambushes of Hildebrand and his partisans. For we still reign, though against his will; it was the Lord who destroyed our knight, the perjurer whom Hildebrand ordained king over us.

In the name of the faith which you kept for the emperors, our grandfather and our father Henry [III], and which you ought to keep for us and indeed did keep well until the time of Hildebrand, we ask that you not deny us our patrimonial honor bestowed by you upon us through the hand of our father. On the other hand, if you wish to deny it to us, we ask that you say why you deny it, since we are prepared to do all justice to you, to reserve all honor to Saint Peter, and to reward all who are deserving, whoever they may be. We have come to assail not you, but those who are assailing you.

Do not oppress the Church any longer through Hildebrand; do not fight with him against justice. Let there be a trial in the sight of the Church. If it is just that you should consider him pope, defend him as pope. Do not defend him as a thief seeking his lair.

What does he gain by sacrificing justice for power? Does he, therefore, wish to be more unjust, because more exalted? These are his very words, "That he ought to be judged by no one." And his meaning is the same as if he had said: "He may do as he pleases." But this is not the rule of Christ, where it is said, "He who is greater among you will be your servant." And so it is unjust for him who names himself servant of the servants of God to oppress the servants of God through his power. It ought not to shame him to be reduced to a low estate in order to remove a scandal common to all the faithful by whose common obedience he ought to be exalted. "For whoso," said the Lord, "shall offend one of these little ones which believe in me, it were better for him that a millstone were hanged about his neck." Lo, little ones and great ones cry out against the scandal he presents and ask that it be removed from their midst.

Let him, therefore, come bravely. If his conscience is pure, assuredly he will rejoice in that all are present, since when these things have been refuted together, the glory will be his. Let him be certain that his life will not be in danger, even if by your judgment and the authority of the canons it be decided that he ought to be deprived of his unjustly held dignity. We are ready to do nothing without you but all things with you, if only we do not find you resisting our good acts.

Finally, we ask nothing except that justice abide in the place where it is most fitting for justice to be. We wish to find justice among you; and with the favor of God, we are resolved to reward it when found. Farewell.

The Church which Innocent III ruled as Pope from 1198 to 1216 was quite different from that of Gregory VII. Between the reigns of those two ecclesiastical statesmen had intervened one of the great events in Western history: the intellectual revival that witnessed the recovery of much of the law, literature, and philosophy of classical antiquity. Gregory VII had had little formal higher education. Innocent III studied theology at the new University of Paris and Roman and canon law at the University of Bologna. The business of the Church now demanded such systematic training: by the beginning of the thirteenth century, the Pope, and throughout Christendom lesser ecclesiastics such as bishops and abbots, were on an unprecedented scale dealing with issues affecting the lives, property, and salvation of important individuals and entire kingdoms.

During his pontificate, Innocent's actions touched all of Europe. He launched one crusade against heretics in southern France and another against the Moslems in the Middle East, called a council in Rome to which more than a thousand great churchmen came on business crucial to all Europe, and carried on politico-religious battles with the rulers of the Empire, England, and France, to mention only the more important. From the Papacy's viewpoint, what was at stake was the leadership of Christendom, and the principal weapon in Innocent's armory was the canon law, which formalized in a thousand specific ways the obligations of a good Christian. Since Scripture was one of the foundations of the canon law, the Pope spoke upon very great authority indeed when he launched one of his judgments, such as Novit Ille *(He [God] Knows), against a king.*

NOVIT ILLE*

Pope Innocent III

To the archbishops and bishops of France.

He, to whom nothing is unknown, who is the searcher of hearts and diviner of secrets, knows that 'out of a pure heart and of a pure conscience and of faith unfeigned' we love our dear son in Christ, Philip[1] illustrious king of the French, and that we greatly desire his honour, success, and increase regarding the exaltation of the French kingdom as the exaltation of the Apostolic See, because this kingdom, blessed by God, has always remained steadfast in devotion to Him and will never, we believe, depart from that devotion; for, though occasionally wicked angels make incursions from this quarter or that, we who know Satan's wiles will apply ourselves to outwit his artifices, confident that the king will not let himself be deceived by Satan's snares.

Let no man, therefore, imagine that we intend to diminish or disturb the king's jurisdiction and power, when he is obliged not to hinder or curb our jurisdiction and power. When we cannot fully discharge our own juris-

---

* *Selected Letters of Pope Innocent III*, trans. and ed. C. R. Cheyney and W. H. Semple (Edinburgh and London: Thomas Nelson & Sons, Ltd., New York: Oxford University Press, 1953), pp. 63–68.
[1]Philip Augustus of France (ruled 1180–1220), the great medieval king whose military activities against England, diplomatic success in Flanders, and administrative innovations within France did so much to establish France as a sound and successful kingdom in the early thirteenth century.

diction, why should we wish to usurp another's? But because the Lord says in the Gospel, 'If thy brother shall trespass against thee, go and rebuke him between thee and him alone; if he shall hear thee, thou hast gained thy brother. But if he will not hear thee, then take with thee one or two more, that in the mouth of two or three witnesses every word may be established. And if he shall neglect to hear them, tell it unto the church. But if he neglect to hear the church let him be unto thee as an heathen man and a publican'; and because the king of England[2] is ready (as he alleges) to produce ample evidence that the king of the French is trespassing against him and that he has himself proceeded by the Gospel rule in rebuking him; and because, having so far achieved nothing, he is now telling it to the church: how can we, who have been called by divine decree to govern the universal church—how can we obey the Lord's command except by proceeding as it appoints, unless King Philip, appearing before us or our delegate, shews sufficient reason to the contrary? For we do not intend to judge concerning a fief, judgment on which belongs to him, except where the application of the common law is limited by special privilege or contrary custom—but concerning sin, a judgment which unquestionably belongs to us, and which we can and should exercise against anyone.

His Majesty, therefore, should not think it damaging if he submits in this matter to the apostolic judgment; for we read that the renowned Emperor Valentinian[3] said to the suffragans of the church of Milan: 'Take care to place in the episcopal see a man to whom even we who govern the Empire may unfeignedly bow our head, one whose admonishments when as a man we have sinned we may unquestioningly accept like a physician's medicines.' There is also the decree of the Emperor Theodosius, reissued by Charles, from whose line King Philip is himself descended: 'If any man who has received leave to bring a suit into court shall at any stage in the proceedings (when he is making his plaint either at the beginning of the case or after some lapse of time, or when the case is being closed, or when the judge has already begun to deliver sentence) choose to be tried by the pontiff of the Most Holy See, then immediately, without question, and in spite of objections from the other side, he is to be sent, with the statements of the litigants, to the bishops' court'; but in humility we pass this over, for we depend not on any human decree but on the divine law, our authority being not of man but of God. There is no man of sound mind but knows that it belongs to our office to rebuke any Christian for any mortal sin and to coerce him by ecclesiastical penalty if he has spurned our reproof; and that we have the duty and power to rebuke is evident from both the Old and New Testaments, for the Lord proclaims by the prophet, 'Cry aloud, spare not, lift up thy voice like a trumpet, and shew my people their transgressions,' and also in the Old Testament he adds, 'If thou speakest not to the wicked man of his wicked way, he shall die in the iniquity which he has wrought, but his blood will I require at thine hand.' The Apostle also warns us 'to rebuke them that are unruly,' and elsewhere he adds, 'Reprove, rebuke, exhort with all longsuffering and doctrine.'

[2] John (ruled 1199–1216), who was later to be excommunicated by Innocent in a dispute over the appointment of bishops in England.

[3] Roman emperor (ruled 365–375) who continued the imperial concern for Christian doctrinal controversy that Constantine had initiated two generations earlier.

That we have also the power and duty to coerce is evident from what the Lord says to the prophet who was of the priests that were in Anathoth, 'See, I have this day set thee over the nations and over the kingdoms, to root out, and to pull down and to destroy, and to throw down, to build and to plant': obviously, all mortal sin must be rooted out, destroyed and thrown down. Furthermore, when the Lord gave the keys of the kingdom of Heaven to St Peter, he said to him, 'Whatsoever thou shalt bind on earth, shall be bound also in heaven: and whatsoever thou shalt loose on earth, shall be loosed also in heaven.' Now, no man doubts but that everyone who commits mortal sin is bound before God: therefore, that Peter may copy the divine judgment, he should bind on earth those who are undeniably bound in heaven.

But perhaps it will be said that kings should be treated differently from other men: but we know that it is written in the law of God, 'Thou shalt judge the great in the same way as the small: thou shalt not respect persons in judgment.' This respect of persons St James declares to occur if one says to a man clothed in goodly apparel, 'Sit thou here in a good place'; but to the poor man, 'Stand thou there, or sit here under my footstool.'

Though we are empowered to proceed thus in respect of any criminal sin so that we may recall the sinner from error to truth and from vice to virtue, yet we are specially so empowered when it is a sin against peace,— peace, which is the bond of love and about which Christ specially directed the apostles, 'Into whatsoever house ye enter, first say 'Peace be to this house'; and if the son of peace be there, your peace will rest on him'; and again, 'Whosoever will not receive you nor hear your words, when ye depart thence shake off the dust from your feet for a testimony against them.' For the apostles to depart from such people, what is it but to deny them apostolic communion? And to shake off the dust from their feet, what is it but to apply ecclesiastical punishment? For this is the dust which, when Moses sprinkled ashes from the furnace, became a plague of ulcers on all the land of Egypt. The heavy sentence and penalty which at the Last Judgment will smite those who do not receive the messengers of peace nor hear their words is shewn immediately afterwards by the Truth when it declares, not simply, but with a forceful emphasis, 'Verily, I say unto you, it shall be more tolerable for the land of Sodom and Gomorrha in the day of judgment than for that city'—by city meaning citizens, from whose number it does not exclude kings.

Moreover, since (according to the rules of law)[4] any right which one man has established against another may be used by another man against the first, and since the wise Cato[5] declares, 'Submit to the law you have made,' and since in time of war the king of the French availed himself of our office and good-will against Richard[6] of renowned memory, formerly king of the English, who was not of inferior status to himself (with all respect to King Philip be it spoken, for we say it not to shame him but to justify ourselves), how will he refuse to allow on King John's behalf against himself what he once

[4] This is in accord with the laws of procedure in classical Roman law.

[5] A Roman moralist whose treatise *On Customs* was very popular throughout the Middle Ages.

[6] Here Innocent III was referring to the truce of 1198 arranged by the papal legate between Philip and Richard I at a moment when the war between the two kings was going in favor of the English.

allowed on his own behalf against King Richard? Ought there to be in our court 'divers weights and divers measures, both of which are alike abomination to the Lord'? And lastly, when a treaty of peace was made between the kings and confirmed on both sides by an oath and yet was not kept for its full duration, how can we fail to take cognizance of a sworn obligation (which unquestionably belongs to the Church's jurisdiction) so that the broken treaty of peace may be remade?

Wherefore, that we may not seem by apathy to encourage so serious a breach, or to ignore the destruction of religious houses, or disregard the slaughter of Christian people, we have ordered our beloved son, the abbot of Casamari,[7] that—unless King Philip either remakes a stable peace with King John, or concludes a suitable truce, or at least humbly allows the said abbot and our venerable brother the archbishop of Bourges informally to ascertain whether the complaint, which the king of the English has lodged against him before the Church, is a just one or whether the exception which King Philip has chosen to state against King John in his letter to us is a lawful one,—he is to proceed in accordance with the instructions we have given him. And so, by apostolic letter we command you all and strictly charge you in virtue of your obedience, that, when the abbot has discharged the apostolic mandate in this matter, you should humbly receive his, or rather our, sentence, and observe it yourselves and see that it is observed by others; and know that, if you act otherwise, we will punish your disobedience.

About a century after Innocent III was able successfully to interfere in the affairs of the King of France and almost simultaneously subject John of England to his feudal lordship, another series of issues and incidents divided the pope and the Kings of England and France. In the 1290's, their countries at war, Philip IV of France and Edward I of England sought to tax their clergy and draw them into a national effort. Pope Boniface VIII, a tough old legist and administrator, responded by belligerently asserting papal authority in the strongest terms: he forbade taxation of the clergy by the secular authority save with papal approval. But more than revenues were involved; many believed that Boniface was asserting direct papal sovereignty over the nascent kingdoms. Indeed, such claims had been made by extreme papalists, many of them canon lawyers, in the course of the thirteenth century. Yet that very century had witnessed the construction not only of effective royal institutions such as courts, armies, and parliaments, but also of theories that exalted the dignity of the monarchy, equated king and emperor, and granted the king almost unlimited executive authority in matters affecting the public welfare.

The power of royal institutions was quickly revealed: Edward I denied the protection of royal justice and police power to the English clergy; Philip IV stopped the flow of revenue from France to Rome, and in many ways disturbed the normal function of the Church in France. By 1301, the old Pope was bitterly angry. Also, because of the great affection showed him by the

---

[7] The Abbot of Casamari was a trusted legate of the Pope who was to transmit to the French bishops the Pope's instructions for applying religious pressure upon Philip. The Abbot moved between John and Philip, attemping to arrange a peace.

thousands of pilgrims who visited Rome in the Jubilee year of 1300, he believed he could prevail over his royal adversaries. In 1301, he summoned the French clergy to Rome to plan the reorganization of the Church in France. And the next year, he issued Unam Sanctam (One Holy [Church]), *which went beyond any statement of Innocent III in asserting papal powers.*

UNAM SANCTAM*

Pope Boniface VIII

We are compelled, our faith urging us, to believe and to hold—and we do firmly believe and simply confess—that there is one holy catholic and apostolic church, outside of which there is neither salvation nor remission of sins. . . . In this church there is one Lord, one faith and one baptism. There was one ark of Noah, indeed, at the time of the flood, symbolizing one church; and this being finished in one cubit had namely, one Noah as helmsman and commander. And, with the exception of his ark, all things existing upon the earth were, as we read, destroyed. This church, moreover, we venerate as the only one. . . . She is that seamless garment of the Lord which was not cut but which fell by lot. Therefore of this one and only church there is one body and one head—not two heads as if it were a monster:—Christ, namely, and the vicar of Christ, St. Peter, and the successor of Peter. For the Lord Himself said to Peter, Feed my sheep. My sheep, He said, using a general term, and not designating these or those particular sheep; from which it is plain that He committed to Him *all* His sheep. If, then, the Greeks or others say that they were not committed to the care of Peter and his successors, they necessarily confess that they are not of the sheep of Christ; for the Lord says, in John, that there is one fold, one shepherd and one only. We are told by the word of the gospel that in this His fold there are two swords,—a spiritual, namely, and a temporal. For when the apostles said "Behold here are two swords"—when namely, the apostles were speaking in the church—the Lord did not reply that this was too much, but enough. Surely he who denies that the temporal sword is in the power of Peter wrongly interprets the word of the Lord when He says: "Put up thy sword in its scabbard." Both swords, the spiritual and the material, therefore, are in the power of the church; the one, indeed, to be wielded for the church, the other by the church; the one by the hand of the priest, the other by the hand of kings and knights, but at the will and sufferance of the priest. One sword, moreover, ought to be under the other, and the temporal authority to be subjected to the spiritual. For when the apostle says "there is no power but of God, and the powers that are of God are ordained," they would not be ordained unless sword were under sword and the lesser one, as it were, were led by the other to great deeds. . . . Not therefore, according to the law of the universe, are all things reduced to order equally and immediately; but the lowest through the intermediate, the intermediate

---

*Reprinted from Ernest F. Henderson, *Select Historical Documents of the Middle Ages* (London: Goerge Bell & Sons, 1892), pp. 435–437.

through the higher. But that the spiritual exceeds any earthly power in dignity and nobility we ought the more openly to confess the more spiritual things excel temporal ones. This also is made plain to our eyes from the giving of tithes, and the benediction and the sanctification; from the acceptation of this same power, from the control over those same things. For, the truth bearing witness, the spiritual power has to establish the earthly power, and to judge if it be not good. Thus concerning the church and the ecclesiastical power is verified the prophecy of Jeremiah: "See, I have this day set thee over the nations and over the kingdoms," and the other things which follow. Therefore if the earthly power err it shall be judged by the spiritual power; but if the lesser spiritual power err, by the greater. But if the greatest, it can be judged by God alone, not by man, the apostle bearing witness. A spiritual man judges all things, but he himself is judged by no one. This authority, moreover, even though it is given to man and exercised through man, is not human but rather divine, being given by divine lips to Peter and founded on a rock for him and his successors through Christ himself whom he has confessed; the Lord himself saying to Peter: "Whatsoever thou shalt bind," etc. Whoever, therefore, resists this power thus ordained by God, resists the ordination of God. . . . Indeed we declare, announce and define, that it is altogether necessary to salvation for every human creature to be subject to the Roman pontiff. The Lateran, Nov. 14, in our 8th year. As a perpetual memorial of this matter.

In the period of more than a century that passed between the death of Innocent III and publication of the Defensor Pacis *(Defender of the Peace) of Marsilius of Padua (1270–1342), as the Church, and especially the Papacy, was growing more powerful as an institution, it became less influential as Christendom's actual moral guide. The popes commanded an ever more efficient bureaucracy and judiciary, they codified and formally promulgated several new collections of canon law, and one pope successfully launched a crusade against the Holy Roman Emperor. But national monarchs continued to claim sovereignty over churchmen as well as laymen in their kingdoms; agents of a king on one occasion manhandled the pope himself; and, thanks to the diligence of scholars, the* Ethics *and* Politics *of Aristotle with their secular and naturalistic values and theories were put into the hands of both princes and popes and their theorists.*

Marsilius first studied medicine in Padua and then physical science and theology at Paris. Eventually, he became involved in a dispute between Pope John XXII and the elected emperor, Louis the Bavarian, to whom John refused recognition. In 1323, the Pope made his approval of Louis' election contingent upon the Emperor's prior surrender of his authority. The Defensor Pacis *appeared in 1324 as a refutation of papal claims and constituted an aggressive philosophical attack upon the theoretical foundations of papal power. Indeed, Marsilius' ideas struck against the whole medieval concept of a unitary Christendom and gave new arguments to support those throughout western Europe who were attempting to find a rationale for the secular national states, and stand against the claim that Christendom must accept papal or ecclesiastical guidance and direction.*

DEFENSOR PACIS*

Marsilius of Padua

. . . Now there is a difficult question to be considered. For we said . . . that the human legislator[1] itself, either directly or through its ruling part, is the active cause of the institution of all the offices or parts of the state. But we also recall that we said . . . that the priesthood or sacerdotal office of the New Law was first instituted by Christ alone; and, as we have shown . . . , He renounced all secular rule and temporal lordship and was not the human legislator. . . . Consequently, someone may well wonder to whom, especially in what are now perfect communities of believers, the authority to institute the priesthood really belongs; for the things we have said on this point seem to be inconsistent with each other.

Let us, therefore, try to solve the apparent contradiction. . . . In so far as it involves the personal qualification which the teachers of the Holy Scripture call the priestly 'character,' the efficient cause of the priesthood, immediately and as its maker, is God, Who imprints this character on the soul through the ministry of a previous and, as it were, preparatory human act. In the New Law, this began with Christ. For He, Who was true God and true Man, as a human priest performed the ministry which subsequent priests now perform and as God imprinted the character on the souls of those whom He instituted priests. And in this way He first instituted the apostles as His immediate successors and thus also, consequently, all other priests, through the ministry of the apostles and their successors in this office. For when the apostles or other priests lay their hands on other men and offer the proper words and prayers, Christ as God imprints the sacerdotal quality or character on those who worthily desire to receive it.

This applies likewise to the conferring of other orders in which a certain character is imprinted on the soul of the recipient. This sacerdotal character . . . is the power through which the priest is able to consecrate from bread and wine the blessed body and blood of Christ, by pronouncing certain words, and to administer the other sacraments of the church, and also that through which he can bind and loose men from their sins. . . .

Now it seems probable to me that this sacerdotal character . . . (which we shall hereafter call the authority *essential to* or *inseparable from* a priest as such) is the same in species in all priests, and that neither the bishop of Rome nor any other has it more fully than a simple priest. . . .

And, to show this more evidently, we should not conceal the fact that the words priest (*presbyter*) and bishop (*episcopus*) were synonymous in the early church, although they connoted different characteristics. For the word *presbyter* referred to age, meaning 'elder'; *episcopus,* meaning 'overseer,' to dignity or charge over others. . . .

---

* Reprinted from Ewart Lewis, *Medieval Political Ideas* (New York: Alfred A. Knopf, Inc., 1954), pp. 598–606.

[1] By *humanus legislator,* or sometimes simply *legislator,* Marsilius meant " . . . the prime and proper effective cause of law, the *populus* or body of citizens, or the dominant portion thereof, through its choice or will expressed verbally in a general assembly of the citizens. . . ."

But after the time of the apostles, when the number of priests had grown considerably, in order to avoid scandal and schism the priests chose one of themselves to direct and ordain the others in regard to the performance of the ecclesiastical office and service, and the distribution of the offerings made to the church, and the disposition of other matters in the more suitable way, lest the affairs and service of the temples be confused by a diversity of wishes, as they would be if everyone were acting at his own pleasure and whenever it suited him. And he who, according to this later custom, was chosen to rule the other priests kept for himself alone the name of bishop, or overseer, since he was overseer not only of the faithful people (for which reason all priests in the primitive church were called bishops) but also of the rest of his fellow priests. . . .

But this human election or institution conferred on the priest so chosen no more of essential merit, or sacerdotal authority, or the power first described above, but only a certain power of managerial rule in the house or temple of God, of ordaining others to be priests, deacons, and the rest of the officers, and of regulating the terms on which power was given to the monks of those times. It involved, I assert, no coercive authority whatever, except in so far as such power might have been granted by the human legislator, . . . nor any other intrinsic dignity or power. . . . It follows that the bishop of Rome has no more of essential sacerdotal authority than any other priest, even as the blessed Peter had no more than the other apostles. For all received this authority from Christ equally and immediately. . . .

Now certain matters and institutions of sacerdotal offices are not essential. This is true of the choice already discussed by which one of the priests is designated to the ordaining and governing of the others in regard to things pertaining to divine worship; and this is also true of the choice and institution of certain others to teach and instruct and administer the sacraments of the New Law to a particular people and in a specified place, greater or smaller, likewise also to administer, for themselves or for the poor, certain temporals appointed and ordained by the legislator or by individual persons for the sustenance of those poor clergy who teach the gospel in a certain province or community and also for the sustenance of other poor people . . . from whatever surplus remains after providing for those who teach the gospel. Which temporals, thus established, are in modern usage called ecclesiastical benefices. . . . For these temporals are entrusted to the ministers of the temples for the aforesaid uses: to the ministers, I say, who have been appointed, chosen, and ordained to certain provinces; for through their sacerdotal authority, in which they are successors of the apostles, they are assigned to teach and administer the sacraments of the New Law no more to any one place or people than to any other, even as the apostles were not so assigned. For it says in the last chapter of Matthew [28:19]. 'Go ye into all the world and teach all peoples.' Thus Christ did not assign them to specific places, but they themselves afterwards divided among themselves the peoples and provinces in which they would preach the word of God and the law of the gospel, which they had received by divine revelation. Whence also it was said in Galatians [11:9], 'They gave to me and to Barnabas the right hand of fellowship . . . that I should go to the gentiles, he to the circumcized.'

Thus, therefore, it is apparent from what we have said who is the efficient cause[2] of the institution of the priesthood in so far as it involves a quality or character of the soul, and of the other holy orders, since they are derived immediately from God, or Christ, although by way of a certain previous and, as it were, preparatory human ministry: namely, the laying on of hands and the pronunciation of certain words, which perhaps have no effect in this matter but precede it by a certain agreement or ordinance of God. It also appears from the aforesaid that there is a certain human institution by which one of the priests is set over the others, and by which priests are appointed to teach and instruct specific provinces and peoples in the divine law, and to administer the sacraments there, and to dispense the temporals which we have called ecclesiastical benefices. . . .

. . . Although . . . each successor of the blessed Peter may in a certain way appear more reverend than the successors of the other apostles, yet no necessity of Holy Scripture requires that the successors of the other apostles be regarded as subject to the successors of Peter in regard to any of the powers we have mentioned. Even if we grant that the apostles were unequal in authority, it does not follow that the blessed Peter or any other apostle had, by virtue of the words of the Scripture, the power of institution or deposition over others, either in regard to essential sacerdotal dignity, or in regard to the interpretation of the Scripture or of the catholic faith, or in regard to any coercive jurisdiction in this life; but rather the contrary. Whence we must necessarily conclude that neither does any successor of any one of the apostles have any of these powers over the successors of the others.[3]

. . . It seems clear that through the power or character by which a priest is instituted he has the power to minister anywhere at all and over any people, although, by divine revelation or human ordinance, certain priests are assigned to a certain place or people rather than to another, especially in these times. . . .

. . . I wish to show that after the time of the apostles and the early fathers who immediately succeeded them in office, and especially in what are now perfect communities of Christians, the immediate cause of the institution or assignment of a pastor (either a greater pastor, who is called a bishop, or a lesser, who is called a parish priest), and likewise of other minor clergy, is and ought to be the whole multitude of Christians of that place, through its choice or expressed will, or the person or persons to whom the said multitude has granted authority to make such institutions; and that it belongs to the authority of the same to remove any of the aforementioned officers or deprive him of his office, and also, if it seems expedient, to compel him to perform his office.

It must, however, be observed that, although any priest can extend his ministry by promoting any other willing Christian to the priesthood, he himself serving as an instrument while the essential priestly power or character is absolutely and immediately imprinted by God, yet I say that neither by divine law nor by human law ought he, in what are now perfect communities of

---

[2] On causation, see Aristotle, above, p. 80.
[3] See Gregory VII, above, pp. 197–203.

Christians, to confer this power on anyone at his pleasure, lest in conferring this power on one who is criminous or otherwise unqualified he sin lamentably against divine and human law. . . .

From these considerations, I wish further to draw the necessary inference that in already perfect communities of Christians it belongs only to the human legislator, or the multitude of Christians of the place over which the minister is to be established, to elect, determine, and present persons to be promoted to ecclesiastical orders; and that no priest or bishop singly, nor any single college thereof, is permitted to confer such orders without the permission of the human legislator or of the ruler who bears its authority. Moreover, I shall first demonstrate this by Holy Scripture and then confirm it by probable reason.

By the authority of Scripture this is evident from Acts 6:[1–6]. For the holy apostles, needing deacons to minister for themselves and for the people, summoned the multitude of Christians as that body whose it was to choose and determine such persons. Thus we read in this passage: 'Moreover the twelve, calling together the multitude of disciples (that is, of Christians . . .) said, "It is not right that we should leave the word of God in order to minister at tables. Choose therefore, brethren, seven men of good repute from among yourselves, full of the Holy Spirit and of wisdom, whom we may put in charge of this work. We, however, shall be constant in prayer and in the ministry of the word." And this speech pleased the whole multitude. And they chose Stephen, a man full of the Holy Spirit and of faith, and Philip,' and the rest likewise. But if, in the presence of the apostles, such an election was entrusted to a less perfect multitude, that the best qualified should be more certainly chosen (since a whole multitude may know something, especially of the morals and life of a man, of which a very learned man is often ignorant), how much more ought the election of priests, who have more need of virtue and wisdom than deacons, in the absence of such prelates as the apostles, and in a perfect community of Christians, to be entrusted to the whole body, that fuller and more certain knowledge of the candidate may be secured. . . .

Now, moreover, I wish to show by probable reason . . . that the election and approval of a candidate for holy orders, in already perfect communities of Christians, belongs to . . . the decision of the human legislator; as does his secondary institution, by which he is made bishop or parish priest over some Christian people in a specific place . . . ; also his removal from or deprivation of his office; and, if necessary, compelling him to perform his office. Then I shall show to whom belongs the allotment of ecclesiastical temporals, called benefices.

And the first can be proved by arguments like those with which we proved, in chs. 12, 13, and 14 of *dictio* 1, that legislation and the institution of rulers belong to the body of citizens, changing only the minor premise of the proof: that is, substituting for the term 'law' or 'ruler' the election or approval of a candidate for holy orders, and his institution or appointment to the charge of a certain people or province, and his deprivation of or removal from the same on account of delinquency or some other rational cause.

Moreover, in these arguments the necessity of doing these things through the legislator or body of citizens is more evident in proportion as error in regard to a candidate for the priesthood or some other ecclesiastical rank and for the pastoral office is more perilous than an error in regard to human law or a ruler instituted in accordance therewith. For if a man who is morally perverse or ignorant or otherwise deficient is promoted to the priesthood and is thus given the care and direction of a Christian people, the peril of eternal death and of many civil disadvantages thereby threatens the people. . . . And the Christian people has, and reasonably ought to have, the power of discretion or caution, for otherwise it could not avoid this evil. . . .

. . . Thus also, because of the peril [of eternal death] the ecclesiastical minister ought to be forced, and reasonably can be forced, through the human legislator or the prince, to administer the sacraments which are necessary for salvation, for instance, baptism, if he should perversely refuse to do this. . . .

Nor is there any obstacle in the argument that priests or a college of priests will know better how to judge concerning the qualifications of candidates for the priesthood or for the pastoral office or for other minor offices. . . . Because, even if we grant that priests have fuller and more certain judgment of such matters than have the rest of the multitude of citizens—which, however, is often not the case nowadays—yet it cannot be inferred from this premise that a college of priests alone has more certain judgment of these matters than has the whole multitude of which the priests are a part. Therefore when the rest of the multitude is joined to the college of priests, a more certain and secure judgment can be obtained than from the college of priests alone. For 'the whole is greater than any of its parts.'

Yet, of course, it ought to be maintained, and a law properly framed in accordance with divine law ought to decree, that in this matter the ruler should have confidence in the judgment of priests or doctors of divine law and other worthy men, even as he ought to use the judgment of experts and the findings of examiners on training and morals in regard to candidates for promotion in other disciplines. . . .

Therefore, candidates for ecclesiastical orders ought to be approved or rejected by the opinion or judgment . . . of the legislator or the ruler who bears its[4] authority; likewise instituted in or removed from a greater or lesser pastorate, or prohibited from exercising it, or even, if they wickedly cease to perform the duties of their offices, compelled to perform them lest by their perversity the peril of eternal death should threaten the people. . . . And this, of course, is to be understood as applying to already perfect communities of Christians. For in any place where the legislator and the ruler who bore its authority were infidels, as was the case in most and nearly all communities in the time of the primitive church, the authority to approve or reject candidates for ecclesiastical orders, with the rest of the institutions aforesaid and the exercise of offices, would belong to the priest or bishop together with the wiser part of the Christian group there, or to the priest or bishop alone if he was alone, without the consent or knowledge of the ruler. . . . This is what the apostles did at the beginning of the church of Christ, and in default of a legislator they were obliged, and by divine law would be obliged, to choose their own successors. . . .

---

[4] The antecedant of "its" is "legislator" which, in Marsilius' political theory, is the immediate cause of any political action, and which reflects, in any type of state be it monarchy or democracy, "the minds and will of men"—that is, of the citizens of a state.

Now, concerning the distribution of temporals, which are usually called ecclesiastical benefices, it must first be recognized that such temporals were ordained for the sustenance of ministers of the gospel and of other poor persons either by the legislator . . . or by some individual person or college. If such temporals were thus appropriated by the gift and ordinance of the legislator I say that legally, according to divine law, it can entrust to whom it wishes, when it wishes, the authority to allot them; and when it wishes it can, for cause, revoke this authority from the person or persons to whom it had entrusted it, whether a single individual or a college. . . . It can also sell or otherwise alienate them, if a rational cause has supervened, because they belong to the legislator and are by right always in its power, except in the case in which it had transferred the thing itself, either absolutely or by infeudation, to the power of another college or individual; with the qualification, however, that in any event the Christian people is bound by divine law to sustain the ministers of the gospel, if it can, with food and proper clothing: with which they ought to be content. . . . If, however, such temporals were designated for pious uses by the gift or bequest of an individual or individuals, I say that they ought to be kept, guarded, and allotted in accordance with the intention of the donor or testator. But if there appears any fault needing correction in those who allot such temporals, such an error ought to be corrected by the human legislator or the prince who bears its authority, in accordance with the intention of the donor or testator. . . .

Further, I wish to show that assertions made by the authority of the catholic kings of France concerning the institution of ecclesiastical ministers and the assignment or grant of temporals or benefices ought not to be despised but rather heeded. For they assert that by right, as up to the present time they have willed and caused to be observed in fact, the authority to institute and to allot some ecclesiastical offices and temporals or benefices belongs to them, and that they did not derive this authority from any individual or college of mortals of any sort. For the legislator or prince is not prohibited by divine law from instituting, granting, or assigning such things; on the contrary, in perfect communities of believers this authority, if it is legitimate and not surreptitiously usurped by individual priests or colleges of priests, is derived from the legislators. . . .

On the basis of the foregoing principles we must also add that, so long as there remains an adequate residue for the ministers of the gospel, the human legislator or the prince who bears its authority can in accordance with divine and human law legally take talliages and taxes from ecclesiastical temporals, especially from the proceeds of the immovables which we have called benefices, for the defence of the country, the ransom of those taken prisoner in the service of the faith, the support of public expenses, or any other reasonable cause according to the determination of the Christian legislator. For he who by legacy or gift established such temporals for pious causes and entrusted them to some person or persons for allotment could not grant them to any college or individual with greater immunity than he had when they were in his power. But they were never before immune from public burdens; therefore they are not immune after being transferred by a donor or testator to the power of anyone else.

2. What Is a Political Society and What Is Its Just Governance?

The career of John of Salisbury (c. 1115–1180) touched almost all the major constructive movements of the twelfth century. As a young student, he heard the great teacher Peter Abelard[1] lecture and worked with other great teachers at Paris and at the Cathedral School of Chartres. He studied law to prepare himself for an administrative career, but also logic, and especially ancient (pagan) literature. Most of his life was spent in the administrative service of the Church, both in England and in Rome as advisor and confidant to the English pope, Hadrian IV. But although two churchmen, Archbishops Theobald and Becket, were his actual superiors, John worked through them for the well-being of his king and country, until a violent quarrel broke out between Becket and Henry II of England. His migratory career, the sort that many able ecclesiastics followed throughout the Middle Ages, now in the employ of pope or bishop, now in the service of king or city council, came to rest when he became Bishop of Chartres.

He was a great Latinist by the standards of any age, and his surviving works all show a concern for style based upon wide reading in the ancient authors. The Policraticus, from which the following selections are taken, is usually translated as The Statesman's Handbook. *It is probably the most complete exposition we have of the best twelfth-century views on law, society, government, and justice, but like many great medieval works, it derives many of its fundamental questions and answers from classical models.*

POLICRATICUS*

John of Salisbury

A commonwealth, according to Plutarch,[1] is a certain body which is endowed with life by the benefit of divine favour, which acts at the prompting of the highest equity, and is ruled by what may be called the moderating power of reason. Those things which establish and implant in us the practice of religion, and transmit to us the worship of God . . . fill the place of the soul in the body of the commonwealth. And therefore those who preside over the practice of religion should be looked up to and venerated as the soul of the body. For who doubts that the ministers of God's holiness are His representa-

---

[1] Abelard (1079–1142) was one of the great teachers whose activities were fudamental to the revival of intellectual life in the twelfth century. His work in philosophy and theology drew thousands of students to the region of Paris and made it the center of higher learning in northern Europe. Abelard's most famous books were the *Sic et Non*, a treatment of conflicting theological passages that stimulated disputation, and the *History of My Misfortunes*, the most celebrated autobiography of the Middle Ages.

* From *The Statesman's Book of John of Salisbury*, trans. John Dickinson, pp. 64–65, 3–9, 198–200. Copyright 1927 by Alfred A. Knopf, Inc. Reprinted by permission of Appleton-Century-Crofts.

[1] A Roman biographer of the early Empire whose *Lives* was very popular during both Antiquity and the Middle Ages as history and moral guide.

tives? Furthermore, since the soul is, as it were, the prince of the body, and has rulership over the whole thereof, so those whom our author calls the prefects of religion preside over the entire body. . . . The place of the head in the body of the commonwealth is filled by the prince, who is subject only to God and to those who exercise His office and represent Him on earth, even as in the human body the head is quickened and governed by the soul. The place of the heart is filled by the senate, from which proceeds the initiation of good works and ill. The duties of eyes, ears, and tongue are claimed by the judges and the governors of provinces. Officials and soldiers correspond to the hands. Those who always attend upon the prince are likened to the sides. Financial officers and keepers . . . may be compared with the stomach and intestines. . . . The husbandmen correspond to the feet, which always cleave to the soil, and need the more especially the care and foresight of the head, since while they walk upon the earth doing service with their bodies, they meet the more often with stones of stumbling, and therefore deserve aid and protection all the more justly since it is they who raise, sustain, and move forward the weight of the entire body. . . .

Then and then only will the health of the commonwealth be sound and flourishing, when the higher members shield the lower, and the lower respond faithfully and fully in like measure to the just demands of their superiors, so that each and all are as it were members one of another by a sort of reciprocity, and each regards his own interest as best served by that which he knows to be most advantageous for the others.

* * *

OF THE DIFFERENCE BETWEEN A PRINCE AND A TYRANT AND OF WHAT IS MEANT BY A PRINCE

Between a tyrant and a prince there is this single or chief difference, that the latter obeys the law and rules the people by its dictates, accounting himself as but their servant.[2] It is by virtue of the law that he makes good his claim to the foremost and chief place in the management of the affairs of the commonwealth and in the bearing of its burdens; and his elevation over others consists in this, that whereas private men are held responsible only for their private affairs, on the prince fall the burdens of the whole community. Wherefore deservedly there is conferred on him, and gathered together in his hands, the power of all his subjects, to the end that he may be sufficient unto himself in seeking and bringing about the advantage of each individually, and of all; and to the end that the state of the human commonwealth may be ordered in the best possible manner, seeing that each and all are members one of another. Wherein we indeed but follow nature, the best guide of life; for nature has gathered together all the senses of her microcosm or little world, which is man, into the head, and has subjected all the members in obedience to it in such wise that they will all function properly so long as they follow the guidance of the head, and the head remains sane. Therefore the prince stands on

---

[2] Compare this with Aristotle's discussion of the forms of government, above, p. 120.

a pinnacle which is exalted and made splendid with all the great and high privileges which he deems necessary for himself. And rightly so, because nothing is more advantageous to the people than that the needs of the prince should be fully satisfied; since it is impossible that his will should be found opposed to justice. Therefore, according to the usual definition, the prince is the public power, and a kind of likeness on earth of the divine majesty. Beyond doubt a large share of the divine power is shown to be in princes by the fact that at their nod men bow their necks and for the most part offer up their heads to the axe to be struck off, and, as by a divine impulse, the prince is feared by each of those over whom he is set as an object of fear. And this I do not think could be, except as a result of the will of God. For all power is from the Lord God, and has been with Him always, and is from everlasting. The power which the prince has is therefore from God, for the power of God is never lost, nor severed from Him, but He merely exercises it through a subordinate hand, making all things teach His mercy or justice. "Who, therefore, resists the ruling power, resists the ordinance of God," in whose hand is the authority of conferring that power, and when He so desires, of withdrawing it again, or diminishing it. For it is not the ruler's own act when his will is turned to cruelty against his subjects, but it is rather the dispensation of God for His good pleasure to punish or chasten them. Thus during the Hunnish persecution, Attila, on being asked by the reverend bishop of a certain city who he was, replied, "I am Attila, the scourge of God." Whereupon it is written that the bishop adored him as representing the divine majesty. "Welcome," he said, "is the minister of God," and "Blessed is he that cometh in the name of the Lord," and with sighs and groans he unfastened the barred doors of the church, and admitted the persecutor through whom he attained straightway to the palm of martyrdom. For he dared not shut out the scourge of God, knowing that His beloved Son was scourged, and that the power of this scourge which had come upon himself was as nought except it came from God. If good men thus regard power as worthy of veneration even when it comes as a plague upon the elect, who should not venerate that power which is instituted by God for the punishment of evil-doers and for the reward of good men, and which is promptest in devotion and obedience to the laws? To quote the words of the Emperor,[3] "it is indeed a saying worthy of the majesty of royalty that the prince acknowledges himself bound by the Laws." For the authority of the prince depends upon the authority of justice and law; and truly it is a greater thing than imperial power for the prince to place his government under the laws, so as to deem himself entitled to do nought which is at variance with the equity of justice.

What the Law Is; and That Although the Prince Is Not Bound by the Law, He Is Nevertheless the Servant of the Law and of Equity, and Bears the Public Person, and Sheds Blood Blamelessly

Princes should not deem that it detracts from their princely dignity to believe that the enactments of their own justice are not to be preferred to the justice

---

[3] Justinian (ruled 527–565), who codified Roman law.

of God, whose justice is an everlasting justice, and His law is equity. Now equity, as the learned jurists define it, is a certain fitness of things which compares all things rationally, and seeks to apply like rules of right and wrong to like cases, being impartially disposed toward all persons, and allotting to each that which belongs to him. Of this equity the interpreter is the law, to which the will and intention of equity and justice are known. Therefore Crisippus[4] asserted that the power of the law extends over all things, both divine and human, and that it accordingly presides over all goods and ills, and is the ruler and guide of material things as well as of human beings. To which Papinian, a man most learned in the law, and Demosthenes,[5] the great orator, seem to assent, subjecting all men to its obedience because all law is, as it were, a discovery, and a gift from God, a precept of wise men, the corrector of excesses of the will, the bond which knits together the fabric of the state, and the banisher of crime; and it is therefore fitting that all men should live according to it who lead their lives in a corporate political body. All are accordingly bound by the necessity of keeping the law, unless perchance there is any who can be thought to have been given the license of wrong-doing. However, it is said that the prince is absolved from the obligations of the law; but this is not true in the sense that it is lawful for him to do unjust acts, but only in the sense that his character should be such as to cause him to practice equity not through fear of the penalties of the law but through love of justice; and should also be such as to cause him from the same motive to promote the advantage of the commonwealth, and in all things to prefer the good of others before his own private will. Who, indeed, in respect of public matters can properly speak of the will of the prince at all, since therein he may not lawfully have any will of his own apart from that which the law or equity enjoins, or the calculation of the common interest requires? For in these matters his will is to have the force of a judgment; and most properly that which pleases him therein has the force of law,[6] because his decision may not be at variance with the intention of equity. "From thy countenance," says the Lord, "let my judgment go forth, let thine eyes look upon equity"; for the uncorrupted judge is one whose decision, from assiduous contemplation of equity, is the very likeness thereof. The prince accordingly is the minister of the common interest and the bond-servant of equity, and he bears the public person in the sense that he punishes the wrongs and injuries of all, and all crimes, with even-handed equity. His rod and staff also, administered with wise moderation, restore irregularities and false departures to the straight path of equity, so that deservedly may the Spirit congratulate the power of the prince with the words, "Thy rod and thy staff, they have comforted me." His shield, too, is strong, but it is a shield for the protection of the weak, and

---

[4] Greek philosopher of the third century B.C., who argued against the Platonists and did much to systematize Stoic thought.

[5] Papinian was a great Roman jurist (d. 212) whose opinions are preserved in the *Code* and *Digest* of Justinian. Demosthenes is commonly considered the greatest of the Greek orators. In a famous series of orations called the *Philippics*, he warned his fellow Athenians of the growing military power of Macedon under Philip.

[6] The reference here is to C. 1.14.4, the famous *Digna vox* (*Worthy voice*), a passage from the *Code* which served as the basis for much medieval commentary on the issue of the responsibility of a ruler to the law.

one which wards off powerfully the darts of the wicked from the innocent. Those who derive the greatest advantage from his performance of the duties of his office are those who can do least for themselves, and his power is chiefly exercised against those who desire to do harm. Therefore not without reason he bears a sword, wherewith he sheds blood blamelessly, without becoming thereby a man of blood, and frequently puts men to death without incurring the name or guilt of homicide. For if we believe the great Augustine, David was called a man of blood not because of his wars, but because of Uria.[7] And Samuel is nowhere described as a man of blood or a homicide, although he slew Agag, the fat king of Amalech. Truly the sword of princely power is as the sword of a dove, which contends without gall, smites without wrath, and when it fights, yet conceives no bitterness at all. For as the law pursues guilt without any hatred of persons, so the prince most justly punishes offenders from no motive of wrath but at the behest, and in accordance with the decision, of the passionless law. For although we see that the prince has lictors of his own, we must yet think of him as in reality himself the sole or chief lictor,[8] to whom is granted by the law the privilege of striking by a subordinate hand. If we adopt the opinion of the Stoics, who diligently trace down the reason for particular words, "lictor" means "legis ictor," or "hammer of the law," because the duty of his office is to strike those who the law adjudges shall be struck. Wherefore anciently, when the sword hung over the head of the convicted criminal, the command was wont to be given to the officials by whose hand the judge punishes evil-doers. "Execute the sentence of the law," or "Obey the law," to the end that the misery of the victim might be mitigated by the calm reasonableness of the words.

That the Prince Is the Minister of the Priests and Inferior to Them; and of What Amounts to Faithful Performance of the Prince's Ministry

This sword, then, the prince receives from the hand of the Church, although she herself has no sword of blood at all. Nevertheless she has this sword, but she uses it by the hand of the prince, upon whom she confers the power of bodily coercion, retaining to herself authority over spiritual things in the person of the pontiffs. The prince is, then, as it were, a minister of the priestly power, and one who exercises that side of the sacred offices which seems unworthy of the hands of the priesthood. For every office existing under, and concerned with the execution of, the sacred laws is really a religious office, but that is inferior which consists in punishing crimes, and which therefore seems to be typified in the person of the hangman. Wherefore Constantine, most faithful emperor of the Romans, when he had convoked the council of priests at Nicaea, neither dared to take the chief place for himself nor even to sit among the presbyters, but chose the hindmost seat. Moreover, the decrees which he heard approved by them he reverenced as if he had

---

[7] In II Samuel, King David, lusting after the beautiful Bathsheba, sends her husband into battle to die, and thus gains the woman for himself.

[8] The guard, in ancient Rome, who bore the *fasces,* the symbol of governmental authority, before the magistrate.

seen them emanate from the judgment-seat of the divine majesty. Even the rolls of petitions containing accusations against priests which they brought to him in a steady stream he took and placed in his bosom without opening them. And after recalling them to charity and harmony, he said that it was not permissible for him, as a man, and one who was subject to the judgment of priests, to examine cases touching gods. . . .[9]

That the Soldiery of Arms Is Necessarily Bound to Religion Like That Which Is Consecrated to Membership in the Clergy and the Service of God; and That the Name of Soldier Is One of Honor and Toil

Turn over in your mind the words of the oath itself, and you will find that the soldiery of arms not less than the spiritual soldiery is bound by the requirements of its official duties to the sacred service and worship of God; for they owe obedience to the prince and ever-watchful service to the commonwealth, loyally and according to God. Wherefore, as I have said above, those who are neither selected nor sworn, although they may be reckoned as soldiers in name, are in reality no more soldiers than men are priests and clerics whom the Church has never called into orders. For the name of soldier is one of honor, as it is one of toil. And no man can take honor upon himself, but one who is called of God glories in the honor which is conferred upon him.

Moyses and the leaders of the faithful people, whenever it became needful to fight the enemy, selected men who were brave and well-trained to war. For these qualities are conditions prerequisite to selection. But the man who without being selected yet forces his way into the service, provokes against himself the sword which he usurps by his own rashness. For he runs against the everlasting decree that he who takes up the sword shall perish by the sword. Indeed if we accept the authority of Cicero regarding such a man, he is rightly called not a soldier but an assassin. For in the writings of the ancients men are called assassins and brigands who follow the profession of arms without a commission from the law. For the arms which the law does not itself use, can only be used against the law.

The sacred Gospel narrative bears witness that two swords are enough for the Christian *imperium;* all others belong to those who with swords and cudgels draw nigh to take Christ captive and seek to destroy His name. For wherein do they partake of the character of the true soldier who, although they may have been called, yet do not obey the law according to their oath, but deem the glory of their military service to consist in bringing contempt upon the priesthood, in cheapening the authority of the Church, in so extending the kingdom of man as to narrow the empire of Christ, and in proclaiming their own praises and flattering and extolling themselves with false commendations, thus imitating the braggart soldier to the amusement of all who hear them? Their valor shines forth chiefly in stabbing with swords or tongues the clergy and the unarmed soldiery. But what is the office of the duly ordained soldiery? To defend the Church, to assail infidelity, to venerate the priest-

---

[9] Compare this passage with Gregory VII's letter, above, pp. 197–203.

hood, to protect the poor from injuries, to pacify the province, to pour out their blood for their brothers (as the formula of their oaths instructs them), and, if need be, to lay down their lives.[10] The high praises of God are in their throat, and two-edged swords are in their hands to execute punishment on the nations and rebuke upon the peoples, and to bind their kings in chains and their nobles in links of iron. But to what end? To the end that they may serve madness, vanity, avarice, or their own private self-will? By no means. Rather to the end that they may execute the judgment that is committed to them to execute; wherein each follows not his own will but the deliberate decision of God, the angels, and men, in accordance with equity and the public utility. I say "to the end that they may *execute"*; for as it is for judges to pronounce judgment, so it is for these to perform their office by executing it. Verily, "This honor have all His saints." For soldiers that do these things are "saints," and are the more loyal to their prince in proportion as they more zealously keep the faith of God; and they advance the more successfully the honor of their own valor as they seek the more faithfully in all things the glory of their God.

3. To What Extent Did the Church Actually Shape Men's Behavior?

Historians have frequently speculated as to just how closely men in the Middle Ages adhered to contemporary high moral precepts and expectations. To put their question another way: To what extent did the Church, which necessarily had a view upon every issue involving human conduct, actually shape men's behavior? Some have denied that there was any substantial correspondence between ethical theory and action. For those who have insisted on the actuality of such a relation, the life of Louis IX of France has always been favorite evidence.

Louis IX, or St. Louis, ruled France from 1224 to 1270, and eventually became the most admired of Europe's kings. So careful was he to respect a man's rights, whether he was dealing with one of his own subjects or a fellow king, that his judgment was sought by men everywhere. Indeed, Henry III of England submitted a border dispute with Louis to Louis himself, and promised to accept the decision. At home, Louis' careful and equitable administration elevated respect for the monarchy. Abroad, his two crusades brought him renown, but also, among realists wise in affairs, the reputation for being a little deficient in worldly wisdom. Louis' first crusade (1248–1254) aimed at the reconquest of Jerusalem by destroying the center of Moslem power in Egypt. Louis was captured, thousands of knights lost their lives in battle or horrible prison camps, and the king returned home on payment of an enormous ransom only after several years in the Levant. His second crusade, in 1270, was another disaster. Louis died before Tunis, and with him most "sensible" men buried the whole crusading passion.

---

[10] A feudal oath was a bond of mutual allegiance and reciprocal aid. Hence, the good knight was expected to give his life for his lord, while for his part, the lord was to honor his principal obligation to his vassal, that of protection.

Jean, Sire de Joinville, Louis' biographer and close companion, was a distinguished warrior from Champagne. His book is not only one of the greatest literary works of the Middle Ages and one of the most vivid biographies of all time, it is also an unintended commentary on the whole code of feudal and chivalric conduct as embodied in the highest suzerain (feudal lord) of France, the king himself.

HISTORY OF ST. LOUIS*

Sire de Joinville

The governance of his land was such that every day he heard his Hours with music, and a Requiem Mass without music, and then the Mass of the day or the holy day, if there fell one, with music. Every day he rested, after meat, on his bed; and when he had slept and rested, the office of the dead was said privately in his chamber between him and one of his chaplains, before he heard vespers. At night he heard compline.

A friar came to him at the Castle of Hyères, where we landed from sea; and to instruct the King, said in his sermon that he had read the Bible and the books which speak of heathen princes; and he said that he had found, among believers and unbelievers alike, that never was a kingdom lost or changed from one lordship to another, but by failure of justice. 'Therefore let the King, who goeth hence to France, have a care,' said he, 'that he do right and speedy justice to his people, wherefore Our Lord will suffer his kingdom to remain in peace all the days of his life.'

They said that this worthy man, who thus taught the King, lieth at Marseilles where Our Lord doth many a fair miracle for him. And he would never tarry with the King, beseech he as he might, but one day.

The king forgat not this instruction, but governed his land loyally and by the law of God, as ye shall hear hereafter. He had his work so ordered that my lord of Nesle and the good Count of Soissons, and the rest of us who attended him, when we had heard Mass, used to go to hear pleas at the gate, which they now call Petitions.[1]

And when he came out of church, he would send for us, and seat himself at the foot of his bed and make us sit round him, and ask us if there were any suits to be dispatched that could not be dispatched without him; and we would name them to him, and he would send for the suitors, and ask them 'Why do ye not take what our people offer?' And they would answer: 'Sir, because they offer little.' And he would speak to them in this wise: 'Ye would do well to take what they wish.' And so the saintly man used to labour according to his power to set them on the right and reasonable path.

Many times it befell that in summer he would go and sit in the wood of Vincennes after Mass, and lean against a tree, and make us sit round him.

---

* Joinville, *The History of St. Louis*, trans. Joan Evans (Oxford: Oxford University Press, 1938), pp. 16–20, 210–215.

[1] Joinville's account is full of references to important nobles at the royal court. Their identification would add nothing to the understanding of the work.

All those that had business came there to speak to him, without disturbance of ushers or others. And then he would ask them of his own mouth: 'Is there any here that hath a suit?' And those that had suits would stand up. Then would he say: 'Be silent all, and your cases shall be settled one after the other.' And then he would call my lord Peter of Fontaines and my lord Geoffrey of Villette and say to one of them: 'Settle this case for me.'

And when he saw something to amend in the sayings of those that spake for him, or in the speech of those that spake for another, he would amend it out of his own mouth.

On a time I saw him in summer, when to do his people's business he came to the garden in Paris, dressed in a coat of camlet, a sleeveless surcoat of linsey-woolsey, a mantle of black silk about his neck, well combed and capless, and a coronal of white peacock's feathers on his head. And he had carpets spread for us to sit on round about him; and all the people who had business to do before him were round him standing. And then he settled their cases, after the manner I have told you of before, as he did in the wood of Vincennes.

On another time I saw him again in Paris, where all the prelates of France had sent him word that they wished to speak with him, and the King went to the Palace to hearken to them. And there was Bishop Guy of Auxerre, . . . and he spake to the King on behalf of all the bishops after this manner:

'Sir, these lords here present, archbishops and bishops, have bade me tell you that Christendom, which should be defended by you, is perishing in your hands.' The King crossed himself when he heard this saying, and answered: 'Now tell me how these things be.'

'Sir,' said he, "it is because in these days men hold excommunication so lightly that they allow themselves to die excommunicate without absolution and have no mind to make restitution to the Church. We would earnestly require you, Sir, for God's sake and your duty's, to command your judges and magistrates that all those that lie under excommunication for a year and a day should be constrained to seek absolution by the confiscation of their goods.'

To this the King answered that he would order it willingly for all those whom they could prove to him had done wrong. And the bishops said that they would on no account act thus, for so they would owe him jurisdiction over their suits. Then the King said he would not do otherwise; for it would be against God and against reason if he forced men to seek absolution when the clergy had done them wrong. 'And of this,' said the King, 'will I give you an ensample in the Count of Brittany, who for seven years, although excommunicate, was at law with the bishops of Brittany, and so laboured that the Apostolic See condemned them all. So that, had I constrained the Count of Brittany after the first year to seek absolution from them, I should have done wrong towards God and to him.' And then the prelates forbore; nor ever after did I hear of their asking for the aforesaid things.

The peace which he made with the King of England did he make against the will of his council, who said to him: 'Sir, it appeareth to us that ye cast away the land that ye give to the King of England, since he hath no right to it; for his father lost it by decree.' Whereto the King answered that he well knew that the King of England had no right to it; but there was a reason wherefor he did well to give it him. 'For we twain have two sisters to wife, and our children are cousins german; wherefore is it fitting that there should be peace. I have come to much honour in the peace that I make with the King of England, since now he is my liegeman, the which he was not heretofore.'

The uprightness of the King may be seen by the tale of my lord Renaud of Trie, who brought the saint a charter, declaring that the King had given the county of Dammartin in Gouelle to the heirs of the Countess of Boulogne, that was lately dead. The seal of the charter was broken, so that naught remained but the half of the legs of the figure on the King's seal, and the stool on which the King set his feet. And he showed it to all of us who were in his council that we might help him to give judgment.

Forthwith we said with one accord that he was in no wise holden to put the charter into deed. Then he told John Sarrasin, his chamberlain, to give him the charter that he had asked for. When he had this charter, he said unto us, 'My lords, see here the seal that I was wont to use before I went beyond the seas, and a man may see clearly by this that the impression of the broken seal is like unto the whole seal; wherefore I would not dare to keep that county with a clear conscience.' Then he summoned my lord Renaud of Trie and said to him; 'I give you the county back.'

*　　*　　*

He asked me if I were wont to wash the feet of the poor on Maundy Thursday, and I answered him nay, that it seemed not good to me. And he told me that I should not hold it in despite, for God had done it. 'Very loath would ye be to do what the King of England doth, that washeth the feet of lepers and kisseth them.'

Before he went to bed, he was wont to have his children come before him, and used to recount to them the deeds of good kings and good emperors, and to tell them that from such men should they take example. And he used to recount to them likewise the deeds of evil rich men who by their lusts and by their robberies and by their avarice had lost their realms. 'And these things', he used to say, 'I bring to your mind, that ye may keep yourselves therefrom, that God be not wroth with you therefor.' He made them learn the Hours of Our Lady, and had them say before him the Hours of the day, to accustom them to hear their Hours when they should hold their own lands.

The King was so great an almsgiver, that wheresoever he went in his realm he had gifts made to poor churches, to lazar-houses, to almshouses, to hospitals, and to poor gentlemen and gentlewomen. Every day he gave meat to a great number of poor folk, without counting those that ate in his chamber; and many a time I saw that he himself cut their bread and gave them to drink.

In his time were built many abbeys: that is to say, Royaumont, the Abbey of St. Anthony near Paris, the Abbey of the Lily, the Abbey of Maubuisson, and many another religious house of Friars Preachers and Grey Friars. He built the Hospital at Pontoise, the Hospital at Vernon, the Hospital for the Blind in Paris, and the nunnery of Grey Sisters of Saint-Cloud, that his sister my lady Isabel founded by his grant.[2]

As any benefice in Holy Church fell in to the King, before he gave it he took counsel with good men of religion and others; and when he had taken counsel, he would give the benefices of Holy Church in good faith, loyally and according to the will of God. Nor would he give any benefice to any clerk, except he renounced the other benefices of churches that he held. In all the towns of his kingdom where he had never been before, he used to go to the Friars Preachers and the Grey Friars, if any were there, to ask them for their prayers.

After that King Louis was come back to France from beyond the seas, he bare himself very devoutly towards Our Lord, and very righteously towards his subjects; and considered and bethought himself that it were a very fair thing and good to amend the realm of France. First, he established a general ordinance over his subjects throughout the realm of France, in the manner that followeth:

'We, Louis, by the grace of God King of France, ordain that all our judges, castellans, provosts,[3] mayors, and all others, in whatsoever business it be, or in whatsoever office they be, shall take oath that so long as they are in office or in authority they shall do justice to all, without exception of persons, as well to the poor as to the rich, and to the stranger as to the citizen, and they shall keep the usages and customs that are good and proved.[4]

'And if it befall that the judges or the castellans or others, as officers or rangers,[5] do aught contrary to their oath, and are attainted therefor, our will is that they shall be punished in their property, and in their persons if the misdeed require it; and the judges shall be punished by us, and the others by the judges.

'Henceforth the other provosts, the judges, and the officers shall swear that they will loyally keep our revenues and our rights, nor suffer our rights to be filched or taken away or minished; and therewith shall they swear that they will not take or receive on their own behalf or on another's, gold or silver or indirect benefits, nor aught else, unless it be fruit, or bread, or wine, or other present up to the sum of a shilling, and that the said sum shall not be exceeded.

'And therewith shall they swear that they will not take or have taken any gift, whatsoever it be, for their wives, or their children, or their brothers, or their sisters, or any other person that be of their family; and so soon as they know that such gifts have been received, they shall have them given back as soon as they can. And therewith shall they swear that they will receive no gift, whatsoever it be, from a man that is of their bailiwick, nor from any other that hath a suit or that pleadeth before them.

'Henceforth they shall swear that they will neither give nor send a gift to any man that is of our Council, nor to their wives, nor to their children, nor

---

[2] The Friars Preachers, or Dominicans, the Grey Friars, or Franciscans, and the Grey Sisters, the women's Franciscan order, were religious orders of the thirteenth century active in the Church's effort to reach the needy of the towns.

[3] Castellans were governors of castles. Provosts were officials of justice and administration.

[4] See John of Salisbury's description of the prince, above, pp. 221–222.

[5] Rangers were royal foresters.

to any soul that belongeth unto them, nor to any that receive their accounts on our behalf, nor to any inquisitors that we may send into their bailiwicks or into their jurisdictions, to make inquisition into their deeds. And therewith shall they swear that they will take no part in any sale that may be made of our revenues, our jurisdiction, or our mint, or of aught else that pertaineth to us.

'And they shall swear and promise that if they know that any official, officer, or provost that is under them be disloyal, robber, usurer, or full of other vices wherefore they should lose our service, that they will not sustain them for gift, or for promise, or for love, or for aught else, but will punish them and judge them in good faith. Henceforth our provosts, our castellans, our mayors, our rangers, and our other officers on foot or on horse, shall swear that they will give not gifts to their lords, nor to their wives, nor to the children that belong to them.

'And since we would that these oaths should be firmly stablished, our will is that they be taken in full assize,[6] before all men, by both clerks and laymen, knights and men-at-arms, albeit that they may already have sworn them before us; so that they may fear to incur the vice of perjury, not only for the fear of God and of us, but also for shame before the world.

'We desire and decree that all our provosts and our judges shall forbear from swearing any word that tendeth to the despite of God, or of Our Lady, or of all the saints, and shall keep themselves from dicing and taverns. Our will is that the fashioning of dice be forbidden throughout our realm, and that wanton women be turned out of houses; and whosoever shall rent a house to a wanton woman, shall pay back to the provost or magistrate a year's rent of the house.

'Next we forbid that our judges should purchase for themselves or for others undue possessions or lands that are in their bailiwicks, or in another's, so long as they are in our service, without our leave; and if such purchases be made, our will is that they be and remain in our hands.

'We forbid our judges that so long as they are in our service they make marriages for sons and daughters that they may have, or for other persons that belong to them, to any other person of their bailiwick, without a special leave; and therewith, that they put them into a religious house in their bailiwick, or get them benefices in Holy Church, or other occupation; and therewith, that they get their living or take any procuration in a religious house, or near one, at the expense of the religious. This injunction against making marriages and acquiring possessions, in the manner we have said, we would not extend to provosts, nor to mayors, nor to others in lesser offices.

'We ordain that neither judge nor provost nor any other should keep too great abundance of sergeants and bedels,[7] that the people be not oppressed thereby; and our will is that the bedels be nominated in full assize, or else be not held to be bedels. When our officers are sent to any distant place or to a

---

[6] The King wants the oath to be taken before a full assembly of all the notables of the district in which the official is to serve, even though the oath may already have been taken before the King.

[7] Bedels were ceremonial officials whose presence dignified the presiding official but added little if anything to the pursuit of justice.

strange land, our will is that trust be not put in them without letters from their sovereign lord.

'We order that judges or provosts that hold office under us oppress not our good people with their judgments beyond what is justice; nor that any of those that are under us be put in prison for debts that they owe unless it be for debts to ourselves.

'We ordain that none of our judges shall enforce a fine for a debt that our subjects owe, nor for ill doing, unless it be in open court, or that the fine be tried and assessed, and by counsel of good men and true, even when it hath been already distrained before them.

'And if it hap that he that be accused of aught is not of a mind to await the judgement of the court that is offered him, but offer a certain sum of money for the fine, such as hath commonly been received, our will is that the court receive the sum of money if it be reasonable and convenient; or if not, our will is that the fine be assessed, in the manner that is told above, although the culprit leave it to the will of the court. We forbid that the judges, or mayors, or provosts, constrain our subjects by threat, by fear, or by any pettifogging, to pay a fine in secret or in public, and that they accuse them without reasonable cause.

'And we ordain that they that hold provostships, castellanies, or other jurisdictions, that they may not sell them to another without our leave; and if several together buy the offices above named, our will is that one of the buyers fill the office on behalf of all the others, and make use of the exemption that pertaineth to posting-horses, to taxes, and to common charges, as the custom is.

'And we forbid that they sell the said offices to brothers, to nephews, and to cousins after they shall have bought them from us; and that they shall demand any debt that is owed them on their own behalf, unless it be debts that pertain to their office; but their own debts shall they demand by the authority of the judge as if they were not in our service.

'We forbid that judge or provost vex our subjects in suits that they have brought before them, by moving from one place to another; but hear the business that they have before them, in the place where they are wont to hear it, so that they let not their justice be sought by labour or expense.

'Henceforth, we command that they dispossess no man of seisin that he hold without taking cognizance of cause, or without special commandment from us; and that they oppress not our people by new exactions and taxes or new tolls; nor summon them to ride to arms to have their money; for our will is that no man that oweth service be summoned to the host without needful cause; and they that are of a mind to go to the host in their own person, be not constrained to redeem their going for money.

'Next, we forbid that judges or provosts ban the taking of corn or wine or other merchandise out of our realm, without needful cause; and when it behoveth that prohibition be made, our will is that it be made in common in the Council of sheriffs and without suspicion of fraud or deceit.

'Next, our will is that all former magistrates, castellans, provosts, and mayors, after they are out of office, be for forty days in the country wherein they have held office, in their own persons or by procuration, so that they may make answer to the new officers for aught wherein they may have done ill against those that would bring complaint against them.

'In all these things which we have ordained for the profit of our subjects and of our realm, we retain for ourselves the rights of explanation, emendation, adjustment, and minishing, according as our counsel may be.'

By this ordinance did he greatly better the realm of France, as many wise elders testify.

4. To What Laws Are Men Bound?

The new learning of the twelfth century brought with it some suspicion of the increased role of scholarship within the Church. As Aristotle's works were made available through translation into Latin, some Christian scholars immediately saw dangers in them: in his Physics, *for example, he attempted to explain phenomena in terms of laws of nature; in his* Ethics, *he relied not upon revealed truth but experience in this world. Others saw how different his theory of knowledge was from that of St. Augustine, which, with its assumptions about the soul and its theory of illumination and dependence upon God, had become the unofficial but dominant Christian theory. The opposition to Aristotle was powerful enough to force papal prohibition of his works at the University of Paris and the creation of a board to examine them. But Aristotle had systematized most of the best of Greek speculative thought and empirical investigation up to his time over the whole spectrum of human thought. No amount of opposition could divert scholars from the exploration of the wealth of substantial understanding and methods of orderly thought which his work offered.*

Two Dominican scholars, St. Albert the Great (1206–1280) and his pupil St. Thomas Aquinas (1225–1274), not only defended Aristotle but turned his work to the service of medieval intellectual needs and, temporarily at least, to the support of Catholic orthodoxy. St. Thomas, a native of Italy, studied at the Universities of Naples and Paris, and at Cologne, where he established and taught in a theological school. The last years of his life were spent in monasteries in France and Italy. The greatest effort to synthesize the corpus of Aristotelian writing with the traditional teaching of the Church was embodied in St. Thomas' Summa Theologica *and in his* Summa Contra Gentiles.

At the time St. Thomas was writing, the systematic study of ancient Roman law and more recent canon law was already a hundred and fifty years old. Bologna was still the center of legal studies, and from it and lesser universities thousands of jurists had gone into the service of kings, princes, and bishops. To the traditional religious concern for law and justice was thus added a secular interest. The combined weight of Church and university so influenced rulers that, almost without exception, they swore in their coronation oaths to preserve the law, and in more theoretical statements recognized that the very object of government was justice.

But what were law and justice? On such questions, the Bible had much to say, as did Christian tradition and some of the ancient fathers of the Church. And so, too, did such pre-Christian philosophers as Cicero and Aristotle, whose wisdom medieval men had come to revere. But since about justice, as about all matters, there could only be one truth, it fell to philosophers, like Aquinas, to find ways of harmonizing the views on justice and law that they found in the Roman law, in the writings of admired heathens of antiquity, and in Holy Writ.

SUMMA THEOLOGICA*

St. Thomas Aquinas

OF THE ESSENCE OF LAW

. . . Law is a rule and measure of acts whereby man is induced to act or is restrained from acting; for *lex* (law) is derived from *ligare* (to bind), because it binds one to act. Now the rule and measure of human acts is the reason, which is the first principle of human acts . . . since it belongs to the reason to direct to the end, which is the first principle in all matters of action, according to the Philosopher . . .[1]

Reason has its power of moving from the will, . . . for it is due to the fact that one wills the end that the reason issues its commands as regards things ordained to the end. But in order that the volition of what is commanded may have the nature of law, it needs to be in accord with some rule of reason. And in this sense is to be understood the saying that the will of the sovereign has the force of law; otherwise the sovereign's will would savor of lawlessness rather than of law.

QUESTION 91: OF THE VARIOUS KINDS OF LAW (IN SIX ARTICLES)

We must now consider the various kinds of law, under which head there are six points of inquiry (1) Whether there is an eternal law? (2) Whether there is a natural law? (3) Whether there is a human law? (4) Whether there is a divine law? (5) Whether there is one divine law or several? (6) Whether there is a law of sin?

First Article: Whether There Is an Eternal Law?

We proceed thus to the First Article:

Objection 1. It would seem that there is no eternal law. Because every law is imposed on someone. But there was not someone from eternity on whom a law could be imposed, since God alone was from eternity. Therefore no law is eternal.

Obj. 2. Further, promulgation is essential to law. But promulgation

---

* St. Thomas Aquinas, *Summa Theologica*, I–II, qq. 90–91, trans. The Dominican Fathers of the English Province (New York: Benziger Brothers, Inc., London: Burns, Oates, and Washburne, Ltd., 1920), pp. 7–8, 9–23.

[1] In Aquinas' writings, the "Philosopher" is always Aristotle, whose authority was so great that there was no need to cite him by name.

could not be from eternity, because there was no one to whom it could be promulgated from eternity. Therefore no law can be eternal.

Obj. 3. Further, a law implies order to an end. But nothing ordained to an end is eternal, for the last end alone is eternal. Therefore no law is eternal.

On the contrary, Augustine says: "That Law which is the Supreme Reason cannot be understood to be otherwise than unchangeable and eternal."

I answer that . . . a law is nothing else but a dictate of practical reason emanating from the ruler who governs a perfect community. Now it is evident, granted that the world is ruled by divine providence . . . that the whole community of the universe is governed by divine reason. Wherefore the very Idea of the government of things in God the Ruler of the universe has the nature of a law. And since the divine reason's conception of things is not subject to time but is eternal, according to Proverbs viii. 23, therefore it is that this kind of law must be called eternal.

Reply Obj. 1. Those things that are not in themselves exist with God, inasmuch as they are foreknown and preordained by Him, according to Romans iv. 17, "Who calls those things that are not, as those that are." Accordingly the eternal concept of the divine law bears the character of an eternal law in so far as it is ordained by God to the government of things foreknown by Him.

Reply Obj. 2. Promulgation is made by word of mouth or in writing; and in both ways the eternal law is promulgated, because both the divine word and the writing of the Book of Life are eternal. But the promulgation cannot be from eternity on the part of the creature that hears or reads.

Reply Obj. 3. The law implies order to the end actively, in so far as it directs certain things to the end, but not passively—that is to say, the law itself is not ordained to the end—except accidentally, in a governor whose end is extrinsic to him, and to which end his law must needs be ordained. But the end of the divine government is God Himself, and His law is not distinct from Himself. Wherefore the eternal law is not ordained to another end.

Second Article: Whether There Is in Us a Natural Law?

We proceed thus to the Second Article:

Objection 1. It would seem that there is no natural law in us. Because man is governed sufficiently by the eternal law; for Augustine says that "the eternal law is that by which it is right that all things should be most orderly." But nature does not abound in superfluities, as neither does she fail in necessaries. Therefore no law is natural to man.

Obj. 2. Further, by the law man is directed in his acts to the end. . . . But the directing of human acts to their end is not a function of nature, as is the case in irrational creatures, which act for an end solely by their natural appetite; whereas man acts for an end by his reason and will. Therefore no law is natural to man.

Obj. 3. Further, the more a man is free, the less is he under the law. But man is freer than all the animals, on account of his free will, with which he is endowed above all other animals. Since therefore other animals are not subject to a natural law, neither is man subject to a natural law.

On the contrary, A gloss on Romans ii. 14: "When the Gentiles, who have not the law, do by nature those things that are of the law," comments as follows: "Although they have no written law, yet they have a natural law, whereby each one knows, and is conscious of, what is good and what is evil."

I answer that, . . . law, being a rule and measure, can be in a person in two ways: in one way, as in him that rules and measures; in another way, as in that which is ruled and measured, since a thing is ruled and measured in so far as it partakes of the rule or measure. . . . Wherefore, since all things subject to divine providence are ruled and measured by the eternal law, . . . it is evident that all things partake somewhat of the eternal law, in so far as, namely, from its being imprinted on them, they derive their respective inclinations to their proper acts and ends. Now among all others the rational creature is subject to divine providence in the most excellent way, in so far as it partakes of a share of providence, by being provident both for itself and for others. Wherefore it has a share of the eternal reason, whereby it has a natural inclination to its proper act and end: and this participation of the eternal law in the rational creature is called the natural law. Hence the Psalmist after saying: "Offer up the sacrifice of justice," as though someone asked what the works of justice are, adds: "Many say, Who showeth us good things?" in answer to which question he says: "The light of Thy countenance, O Lord, is signed upon us"; thus implying that the light of natural reason, whereby we discern what is good and what is evil, which is the function of the natural law, is nothing else than an imprint on us of the divine light. It is therefore evident that the natural law is nothing else than the rational creature's participation of the eternal law.

Reply Obj. 1. This argument would hold if the natural law were something different from the eternal law, whereas it is nothing but a participation thereof, as stated above.

Reply Obj. 2. Every act of reason and will in us is based on that which is according to nature, as stated above; for every act of reasoning is based on principles that are known naturally, and every act of appetite in respect of the means is derived from the natural appetite in respect of the last end. Accordingly the first direction of our acts to their end must needs be in virtue of the natural law.

Reply Obj. 3. Even irrational animals partake in their own way of the eternal reason, just as the rational creature does. But because the rational creature partakes thereof in an intellectual and rational manner, therefore the participation of the eternal law in the rational creature is properly called a law, since a law is something pertaining to reason. . . . Irrational creatures, however, do not partake thereof in a rational manner, wherefore there is no participation of the eternal law in them, except by way of similitude.

Third Article: Whether There Is a Human Law?

We proceed thus to the Third Article:

Objection 1. It would seem that there is not a human law. For the natural law is a participation of the eternal law. . . . Now through the eternal law "all thing are most orderly," as Augustine states. Therefore the natural law suffices for the ordering of all human affairs. Consequently there is no need for a human law.

Obj. 2. Further, a law bears the character of a measure. . . . But human reason is not a measure of things, but vice versa, as stated in *Metaphysics* x. text. 5. Therefore no law can emanate from human reason.

Obj. 3. Further, a measure should be most certain, as stated in *Metaphysics* x. text. 3. But the dictates of human reason in matters of conduct are uncertain, according to Wisdom ix. 14: "The thoughts of mortal men are fearful, and our counsels uncertain." Therefore no law can emanate from human reason.

On the contrary, Augustine distinguishes two kinds of law—the one eternal; the other temporal which he calls human.

I answer that, . . . A law is a dictate of the practical reason. Now it is to be observed that the same procedure takes place in the practical and in the speculative reason, for each proceeds from principles to conclusions. . . . Accordingly we conclude that just as, in the speculative reason, from naturally known indemonstrable principles we draw the conclusions of the various sciences, the knowledge of which is not imparted to us by nature, but acquired by the efforts of reason; so, too, it is from the precepts of the natural law, as from general and indemonstrable principles, that the human reason needs to proceed to the more particular determination of certain matters. These particular determinations, devised by human reason, are called human laws, provided the other essential conditions of law be observed. . . . Wherefore Cicero says in his *Rhetoric* that "justice has its source in nature; thence certain things came into custom by reason of their utility; afterward these things which emanated from nature and were approved by custom were sanctioned by fear and reverence for the law."

Reply Obj. 1. The human reason cannot have a full participation of the dictate of the divine reason but according to its own mode, and imperfectly. Consequently, as on the part of the speculative reason, by a natural participation of divine wisdom, there is in us the knowledge of certain general principles, but not proper knowledge of each single truth, such as that contained in the divine wisdom; so, too, on the part of the practical reason man has a natural participation of the eternal law, according to certain general principles, but not as regards the particular determinations of individual cases, which are, however, contained in the eternal law. [Hence the necessity that human reason proceed to certain particular sanctions of law.]

Reply Obj. 2. Human reason is not of itself the rule of things, but the principles impressed on it by nature are general rules and measures of all things relating to human conduct, whereof the natural reason is the rule and measure, although it is not the measure of things that are from nature.

Reply Obj. 3. The practical reason is concerned with practical matters, which are singular and contingent, but not with necessary things, with which the speculative reason is concerned. Wherefore human laws cannot have that inerrancy that belongs to the demonstrated conclusions of sciences. Nor is it necessary for every measure to be altogether unerring and certain, but according as it is possible in its own particular genus.

Fourth Article: Whether There Was Any Need for a Divine Law?

We proceed thus to the Fourth Article:

Objection 1. It would seem that there was no need for a divine law. Because . . . the natural law is a participation in us of the eternal law. But the eternal law is a divine law . . . . Therefore there is no need for a divine law in addition to the natural law and human laws derived therefrom.

Obj. 2. Further, it is written that "God left man in the hand of his own counsel." Now counsel is an act of reason, as stated above. Therefore man was left to the direction of his reason. But a dictate of human reason is a human law , . . . Therefore there is no need for man to be governed also by a divine law .

Obj. 3. Further, human nature is more self-sufficing than irrational creatures. But irrational creatures have no divine law besides the natural inclination impressed on them. Much less, therefore, should the rational creature have a divine law in addition to the natural law.

On the contrary, David prayed God to set His law before him, saying: "Set before me for a law the way of Thy justifications, O Lord."

I answer that, Besides the natural and human law it was necessary for the directing of human conduct to have a divine law. And this for four reasons. First, because it is by law that man is directed how to perform his proper acts in view of his last end. And indeed, if man were ordained to no other end than that which is proportionate to his natural faculty, there would be no need for man to have any further direction on the part of his reason besides the natural law and human law which is derived from it. But since man is ordained to an end of eternal happiness which is inproportionate to man's natural faculty, . . . therefore it was necessary that, besides the natural and the human law, man should be directed to his end by a law given by God.

Secondly, because, on account of the uncertainty of human judgment, especially on contingent and particular matters, different people form different judgments on human acts; whence also different and contrary laws result. In order, therefore, that man may know without any doubt what he ought to do and what he ought to avoid, it was necessary for man to be directed in his proper acts by a law given by God, for it is certain that such a law cannot err.

Thirdly, because man can make laws in those matters of which he is competent to judge. But man is not competent to judge of interior movements that are hidden, but only of exterior acts which appear; and yet for the perfection of virtue it is necessary for man to conduct himself aright in both kinds of acts. Consequently human law could not sufficiently curb and direct interior acts, and it was necessary for this purpose that a divine law should supervene.

Fourthly, because, as Augustine says, human law cannot punish or forbid all evil deeds; since while aiming at doing away with all evils, it would do away with many good things, and would hinder the advance of the common good, which is necessary for human intercourse. In order, therefore, that no evil might remain unforbidden and unpunished, it was necessary for the divine law to supervene, whereby all sins are forbidden.

And these four causes are touched upon in Psalm cxviii. 8, where it is said: "The law of the Lord is unspotted," i.e., allowing no foulness of sin; "converting souls," because it directs not only exterior but also interior acts; "the testimony of the Lord is faithful," because of the certainty of what is true and right; "giving wisdom to little ones," by directing man to an end supernatural and divine.

Reply Obj. 1. By natural law the eternal law is participated in proportionately to the capacity of human nature. But to his supernatural end man needs to be directed in a yet higher way. Hence the additional law given by God, whereby man shares more perfectly in the eternal law.

Reply Obj. 2. Counsel is a kind of inquiry; hence it must proceed from some principles. Nor is it enough for it to proceed from principles imparted by nature, which are the precepts of the natural law, for the reasons given above; but there is need for certain additional principles, namely, the precepts of the divine law.

Reply Obj. 3. Irrational creatures are not ordained to an end higher than that which is proportionate to their natural powers; consequently the comparison fails.

Fifth Article: Whether There Is But One Divine Law?

We proceed thus to the Fifth Article:

Objection 1. It would seem that there is but one divine law. Because where there is one king in one kingdom there is but one law. Now the whole of mankind is compared to God as to one king, according to Psalm xlvi. 8: "God is the King of all the earth." Therefore there is but one divine law.

Obj. 2. Further, every law is directed to the end which the lawgiver intends for those for whom he makes the law. But God intends one and the same thing for all men; since, according to I Timothy ii. 4, "He will have all men to be saved, and to come to the knowledge of the truth." Therefore there is but one divine law.

Obj. 3. Further, the divine law seems to be more akin to the eternal law, which is one, than the natural law, according as the revelation of grace is of a higher order than natural knowledge. Therefore much more is the divine law but one.

On the contrary, The Apostle says: "The priesthood being translated, it is necessary that a translation also be made of the law." But the priesthood is twofold, as stated in the same passage, viz., the levitical priesthood and the priesthood of Christ. Therefore the divine law is twofold, namely, the Old Law and the New Law.

I answer that, . . . distinction is the cause of number. Now things may be distinguished in two ways. First, as those things that are altogether specifically different, e.g., a horse and an ox. Secondly, as perfect and imperfect in the same species, e.g., a boy and a man; and in this way the divine law is divided into Old and New. Hence the Apostle compares the state of man under the Old Law to that of a child "under a pedagogue"; but the state under the New Law to that of a full-grown man who is "no longer under a pedagogue."

Now the perfection and imperfection of these two laws is to be taken in connection with the three conditions pertaining to law, as stated above.

For, in the first place, it belongs to law to be directed to the common good as to its end. . . . This good may be twofold. It may be a sensible and earthly good; and to this, man was directly ordained by the Old Law; wherefore, at the very outset of the law, the people were invited to the earthly kingdom of the Chananaeans. Again it may be an intelligible and heavenly good; and to this man is ordained by the New Law. Wherefore, at the very beginning of His preaching, Christ invited men to the kingdom of heaven, saying: "Do penance, for the kingdom of heaven is at hand." Hence Augustine says that "promises of temporal goods are contained in the Old Testament, for which reason it is called old; but the promise of eternal life belongs to the New Testament."

Secondly, it belongs to the law to direct human acts according to the order of righteousness . . . , wherein also the New Law surpasses the Old Law, since it directs our internal acts, according to Matthew v. 20: "Unless your justice abound more than that of the Scribes and Pharisees, you shall not enter into the kingdom of heaven." Hence the saying that "the Old Law restrains the hand, but the New Law controls the mind."

Thirdly, it belongs to the law to induce men to observe its commandments. This the Old Law did by fear of punishment; but the New Law, by love, which is poured into our hearts by the grace of Christ, bestowed in the New Law, but foreshadowed in the Old. Hence Augustine says that "there is little difference between the Law and the Gospel—fear and love."

Reply Obj. 1. As the father of a family issues different commands to the children and to the adults, so also the one King, God, in His one kingdom, gave one law to men while they were yet imperfect, and another more perfect law when, by the preceding law, they had been led to a greater capacity for divine things.

Reply Obj. 2. The salvation of man could not be achieved otherwise than through Christ, according to Acts iv. 12: "There is no other name . . . given to men, whereby we must be saved." Consequently the law that brings all to salvation could not be given until after the coming of Christ. But before His coming it was necessary to give to the people of whom Christ was to be born a law containing certain rudiments of righteousness unto salvation in order to prepare them to receive Him.

Reply Obj. 3. The natural law directs man by way of certain general precepts, common to both the perfect and the imperfect; wherefore it is one and the same for all. But the divine law directs man also in certain particular matters to which the perfect and imperfect do not stand in the same relation. Hence the necessity for the divine law to be twofold, as already explained.

Sixth Article: Whether There Is a Law in the Fomes[2] *of Sin?*

We proceed thus to the Sixth Article:

Objection 1. It would seem that there is no law of the "fomes" of sin. For Isidore says that the "law is based on reason." But the "fomes" of sin is not based on reason, but deviates from it. Therefore the "fomes" has not the nature of a law.

---

[2] See below, p. 241, for Aquinas' definition of "fomes."

Obj. 2. Further, every law is binding, so that those who do not obey it are called transgressors. But man is not called a transgressor from not following the instigations of the "fomes," but rather from his following them. Therefore the "fomes" has not the nature of a law.

Obj. 3. Further, the law is ordained to the common good. . . . But the "fomes" inclines us, not to the common, but to our own private good. [Therefore the "fomes" does not have the nature of a law.]

On the contrary, The Apostle says: "I see another law in my members, fighting against the law of my mind."

I answer that, . . . the law, as to its essence, resides in him that rules and measures; but, by way of participation, in that which is ruled and measured, so that every inclination or ordination which may be found in things subject to the law is called a law by participation. . . . Now those who are subject to a law may receive a twofold inclination from the lawgiver. First, in so far as he directly inclines his subjects to something, sometimes indeed different subjects to different acts; in this way we may say that there is a military law and a mercantile law. Secondly, indirectly; thus by the very fact that a lawgiver deprives a subject of some dignity, the latter passes into another order, so as to be under another law, as it were: thus if a knight is dropped from chivalry, he becomes a subject of rural or mercantile legislation.

Accordingly under the divine lawgiver various creatures have various natural inclinations, so that what is, as it were, a law for one is against the law for another: thus I might say that fierceness is, in a way, the law of a dog, but against the law of a sheep or another meek animal. And so the law of man, which, by the divine ordinance, is allotted to him according to his proper natural condition, is that he should act in accordance with reason; and this law was so effective in the primitive state that nothing either beside or against reason could take man unawares. But when man turned his back on God, he fell under the influence of his sensual impulses—in fact this happens to each one individually the more he deviates from the path of reason—so that, after a fashion, he is likened to the beasts that are led by the impulse of sensuality, according to Psalm xlviii. 21: "Man, when he was in honour, did not understand: he hath been compared to senseless beasts, and made like to them."

So, then, this very inclination of sensuality which is called the "fomes," in other animals has simply the nature of a law (yet only in so far as a law may be said to be in such things), by reason of a direct inclination. But in man, it has not the nature of law in this way, rather is it a deviation from the law of reason. But since, by the just sentence of God, man is destitute of original justice and his reason bereft of its vigor, this impulse of sensuality whereby he is led, in so far as it is a penalty following from the divine law depriving man of his proper dignity, has the nature of a law.

Reply Obj. 1. This argument considers the "fomes" in itself, as an incentive to evil. It is not thus that it has the nature of a law, as stated above, but according as it results from the justice of the divine law: [it is as though one were to say that it is legal to authorize that a nobleman, because of his transgressions, be made to perform the tasks of a slave].

Reply Obj. 2. This argument considers law in the light of a rule or measure, for it is in this sense that those who deviate from the law become transgressors. But the "fomes" is not a law in this respect, but by a kind of participation, as stated above.

Reply Obj. 3. This argument considers the "fomes" as to its proper inclination, and not as to its origin. And yet if the inclination of sensuality be considered as it is in other animals, thus it is ordained to the common good, namely, to the preservation of nature in the species or in the individual. And this is in man also, in so far as sensuality is subject to reason. But it is called the "fomes" in so far as it strays from the order of reason.

5. What Are the Nature, the Basis, and the Substance of Men's Rights?

Medieval political theory exalted kingship as the ideal form of government. Ecclesiastics cited Old Testament precedent, and, by the twelfth century, students of the classical Roman law were able to quote the weighty texts of imperial Rome in favor of both emperor and national monarch. Moreover, the old Germanic tradition also favored rule by a single warrior, one from a special family selected first, in the tribal days, by a pagan deity, and later, in Christian days, by the Church.

But the exercise of unlimited executive and judicial authority was another matter. From about the year 1100, able kings in France and England attempted to create nonfeudal institutions of centralized government that were amenable to their will alone. But, by that same date, throughout feudal Europe, much of local government had been in the hands of the local nobility for hundreds of years. Thus, according to feudal law, a large part of justice and administration properly pertained to the feudal lords by right of usage over time, and these lords regarded the fruits of administration and justice as their private property. As such, confirmed by customary law, and supported by another Roman law tradition holding that the king was bound to respect property rights, those fruits were not to be seized by an aggressive king. Kings always knew that too radical an approach to feudal liberties would rouse universal sympathy for the aggrieved. They knew, too, that in war—which always cost the monarchy not only money but also new grants of jurisdiction and privilege in return for support—military technology favored the defense.

The result was always something of a tense balance. Royal vassals were usually willing to perform their proper duties in the army and council chambers and to grant the King established revenues. But they were ever on the lookout for the growth of royal claims and of officialdom. In specific disputes, both groups had right on their side, but there was no recognized institution with the responsibility and authority to judge. The closest thing to such an institution was some form of royal council, where the issues were talked over and a compromise reached. Such agreements were embodied in charters, legally binding documents issued by the ruler to those he wanted to or had to conciliate. Such charters thus provided part of the substance—and a very important part—of medieval law. They were, in effect, fragments of the constitutions of medieval political societies.

Into the construction of these agreements entered the law recognized by both parties as applicable and binding, whatever documentary evidence was available, and the actual political and military conditions of the moment. When Henry I of England issued his coronation charter, he was concerned to gain the support of the nobility. Only three days before, King William II, his brother, had been killed while hunting, and upon receipt of the news, Henry rode not to his brother's body but rather to his treasury. Wishing the acclaim and support of the nobility, he was prepared to be generous. Later, throughout his reign, he confirmed the towns in their ancient rights of self-government and granted them new ones—for a fee. Profiting from Europe's new prosperity, the towns, like Newcastle, were prepared to pay for charters; for his part Henry was quite willing to provide them to gain urban support and wealth.

Magna Carta resulted from a breakdown of ordinary political process. For more than a decade before 1215, John's relations with the great men who should have been his loyal generals and trusted advisors had deteriorated. He was overcrafty and an unsuccessful warrior. His taxes were high and his collectors efficient. His law courts were grasping for new cases. Also, because of his contest with Pope Innocent III, England had only recently (1213) been freed from the interdict, but at the price of John's homage to the Pope. Then, in 1214, John suffered a military disaster in his war with the French king. His promises of good government were no longer acceptable to the barons, who, with military might, exacted from the King redress of their specific grievances and forced him to acknowledge that the monarchy was no despotism above the law. A hundred years later, the French nobility, self-organized into regional leagues, imposed their conditions upon Louis X. Under Philip the Fair, who had died in 1314, the French monarchy had much enlarged its central administrative, its tax, and its judicial bureaus. Big government seems to have made for abuses, if the petitions to Philip are to be believed, and even before his death, leagues were forming in opposition to royal policy. This source cluster illustrates the tensions between rulers and magnates in the Middle Ages and the attempts to cope with them. It also in some measure prefigures and in some measure exemplifies subsequent and more general tensions between the rulers and the ruled.

THE CORONATION CHARTER OF KING HENRY I[*]

Henry, king of the English, to Samson the bishop, and Urse of Abbetot, and to all his barons and faithful vassals, both French and English, in Worcestershire, greeting.

1. Know that by the mercy of God and by the common counsel of the barons of the whole kingdom of England I have been crowned king of this realm. And because the kingdom has been oppressed by unjust exactions, I now, being moved by reverence towards God and by the love I bear you all, make free the Church of God; so that I will neither sell nor lease its property;

---

[*] From *English Historical Documents*, Vol. II, *1042–1189*, trans. D. C. Douglas and G. W. Greenaway (New York: Oxford University Press, 1953), pp. 400–402. Reprinted by permission.

nor on the death of an archbishop or a bishop or an abbot will I take anything from the demesne of the Church or from its vassals during the period which elapses before a successor is installed. I abolish all the evil customs by which the kingdom of England has been unjustly oppressed. Some of those evil customs are here set forth.

2. If any of my barons or of my earls or of any other of my tenants shall die his heir shall not redeem his land as he was wont to do in the time of my brother, but he shall henceforth redeem it by means of a just and lawful 'relief.' Similarly the men of my barons shall redeem their lands from their lords by means of a just and lawful 'relief.'

3. If any of my barons or of my tenants shall wish to give in marriage his daughter or his sister or his niece or his cousin, he shall consult me about the matter; but I will neither seek payment for my consent, nor will I refuse my permission, unless he wishes to give her in marriage to one of my enemies. And if, on the death of one of my barons or of one of my tenants, a daughter should be his heir, I will dispose of her in marriage and of her lands according to the counsel given me by my barons. And if the wife of one of my tenants shall survive her husband and be without children, she shall have her dower and her marriage portion, and I will not give her in marriage unless she herself consents.

4. If a widow survives with children under age, she shall have her dower and her marriage portion, so long as she keeps her body chaste; and I will not give her in marriage except with her consent. And the guardian of the land, and of the children, shall be either the widow or another of their relations, as may seem more proper. And I order that my barons shall act likewise towards the sons and daughters and widows of their men.

5. I utterly forbid that the common mintage,[1] which has been taken from the towns and shires, shall henceforth be levied, since it was not so levied in the time of King Edward. If any moneyer or other person be taken with false money in his possession, let true justice be visited upon him.

6. I forgive all pleas and all debts which were owing to my brother, except my own proper dues, and except those things which were agreed to belong to the inheritance of others, or to concern the property which justly belonged to others. And if anyone had promised anything for his heritage, I remit it, and I also remit all 'reliefs' which were promised for direct inheritance.

7. If any of my barons or of my men, being ill, shall give away or bequeath his movable property, I will allow that it shall be bestowed according to his desires. But if, prevented either by violence or through sickness, he shall die intestate as far as concerns his movable property, his widow or his children or his relatives or one of his true men shall make such division for the sake of his soul, as may seem best to them.

8. If any of my barons or of my men shall incur a forfeit, he shall not be compelled to pledge his movable property to an unlimited amount, as was done in the time of my father and my brother; but he shall only make payment according to the extent of his legal forfeiture, as was done before the time of my father and in the time of my earlier predecessors. Nevertheless, if he be

---

[1] *monetagium:* mintage is here apparently used in the sense of a forced levy to prevent loss to the king from depreciation of the coinage. [Translator's note.]

convicted of breach of faith or of crime, he shall suffer such penalty as is just.

9. I remit all murder-fines which were incurred before the day on which I was crowned king; and such murder-fines as shall now be incurred shall be paid justly according to the law of King Edward.

10. By the common counsel of my barons I have retained the forests in my own hands as my father did before me.

11. The knights, who in return for their estates perform military service equipped with a hauberk of mail, shall hold their demesne lands quit of all gelds and all work; I make this concession as my own free gift in order that, being thus relieved of so great a burden, they may furnish themselves so well with horses and arms that they may be properly equipped and prepared to discharge my service and to defend my kingdom.

12. I establish a firm peace in all my kingdom, and I order that this peace shall henceforth be kept.

13. I restore to you the law of King Edward together with such emendations to it as my father made with the counsel of his barons.

14. If since the death of my brother, King William, anyone shall have seized any of my property, or the property of any other man, let him speedily return the whole of it. If he does this no penalty will be exacted, but if he retains any part of it he shall, when discovered, pay a heavy penalty to me.

Witness: Maurice, bishop of London; William, bishop-elect of Winchester; Gerard, bishop of Hereford; Henry the earl; Simon the earl; Walter Giffard; Robert of Montfort-sur-Risle; Roger Bigot; Eudo the steward; Robert, son of Haimo; and Robert Malet.

At London when I was crowned. Farewell.

THE CUSTOMS OF NEWCASTLE-UPON-TYNE*

These are the laws and customs which the burgesses of Newcastle-upon-Tyne had in the time of Henry, king of England, and which they still have by right:

The burgesses may distrain foreigners within their market and without, and within their homes and without, and within their borough and without, and they may do this without the permission of the reeve,[1] unless the courts are being held within the borough, or unless they are in the field on army service, or are doing castle-guard. But a burgess may not distrain on another burgess without the permission of the reeve.

If a burgess shall lend anything in the borough to someone dwelling outside, the debtor shall pay back the debt if he admit it, or otherwise do right in the court of the borough.

Pleas which arise in the borough shall there be held and concluded except those which belong to the king's crown.

If a burgess shall be sued in respect of any plaint he shall not plead outside the borough except for defect of court; nor need he answer, except at

* From *English Historical Documents*, Vol. II, *1042-1189*, ed. D. C. Douglas and G. W. Greenaway (New York: Oxford University Press, 1953), pp. 970-971. Reprinted by permission.
[1] Chief magistrate; he was a royal official.

a stated time and place, unless he has already made a foolish answer, or unless the case concerns matters pertaining to the crown.

If a ship comes to the Tyne and wishes to unload, it shall be permitted to the burgesses to purchase what they please. And if a dispute arises between a burgess and a merchant, it shall be settled before the third tide.

Whatever merchandise a ship brings by sea must be brought to the land; except salt and herring which must be sold on board ship.

If anyone has held land in burgage for a year and a day justly and without challenge, he need not answer any claimant, unless the claimant is outside the kingdom of England, or unless he be a boy not having the power of pleading.

If a burgess have a son in his house and at his table, his son shall have the same liberty as his father.

If a villein come to reside in the borough, and shall remain as a burgess in the borough for a year and a day, he shall thereafter always remain there, unless there was a previous agreement between him and his lord for him to remain there for a certain time.

If a burgess sues anyone concerning anything, he cannot force the burgess to trial by battle, but the burgess must defend himself by his oath, except in a charge of treason when the burgess must defend himself by battle. Nor shall a burgess offer battle against a villein unless he has first quitted his burgage.

No merchant except a burgess can buy wool or hides or other merchandise outside the town, nor shall he buy them within the town except from burgesses.

If a burgess incurs forfeiture he shall give 6 oras[2] to the reeve.

In the borough there is no 'merchet' nor 'heriot' nor 'bloodwite' nor 'stengesdint.'[3]

Any burgess may have his own oven and handmill if he wishes, saving always the rights of the king's oven.

If a woman incur a forfeiture concerning bread or ale, none shall concern himself with it except the reeve. If she offend twice she shall be punished by the forfeiture. If she offend thrice justice shall take its course.

No one except a burgess may buy cloth for dyeing or make or cut it.

A burgess can give or sell his land as he wishes, and go where he will, freely and quietly unless his claim to the land is challenged.

MAGNA CARTA*

John, by the Grace of God, King of England, Lord of Ireland, Duke of Normandy, Aquitaine, and Count of Anjou, to his Archbishops, Bishops,

---

[2] A money of account introduced by the Danes into England. In the Domesday Book of 1086, its value was about 20 pennies of silver—not a small amount.

[3] In feudal law, "merchet" was the fine paid to a superior for the privilege of marrying off one's daughter. "Heriot" was the feudal duty owed to a lord on the death of a vassal. It often consisted of the arms or horse of the deceased, or both. "Bloodwite" was the fine imposed for drawing blood, "stengesdint" a fine for striking another.

* *Magna Charta, or the Great Charter of King John* (Boston: Directors of the Old South Work, 1896), pp. 1–12.

Abbots, Earls, Barons, Justiciaries, Foresters, Sheriffs, Governors, Officers, and to all Bailiffs, and his faithful subjects, greeting. Know ye, that we, in the presence of God, and for the salvation of our soul, and the souls of all our ancestors and heirs, and unto the honour of God and the advancement of Holy Church, and amendment of our Realm, by advice of our venerable Fathers, Stephen, Archbishop of Canterbury, Primate of all England and Cardinal of the Holy Roman Church; Henry, Archbishop of Dublin; William, of London; Peter, of Winchester; Jocelin, of Bath and Glastonbury; Hugh, of Lincoln; Walter, of Worcester; William, of Coventry; Benedict, of Rochester—Bishops: of Master Pandulph, Sub-Deacon and Familiar of our Lord the Pope; Brother Aymeric, Master of the Knights-Templars in England; and of the noble Persons, William Marescall, Earl of Pembroke; William, Earl of Salisbury; William, Earl of Warren; William, Earl of Arundel; Alan de Galloway, Constable of Scotland; Warin FitzGerald, Peter FitzHerbert, and Hubert de Burgh, Seneschal of Poitou; Hugh de Neville, Matthew FitzHerbert, Thomas Basset, Alan Basset, Philip of Albiney, Robert de Roppell, John Mareschal, John Fitz-Hugh, and others, our liegemen, have, in the first place, granted to God, and by this our present Charter confirmed, for us and our heirs for ever:—

1. That the Church of England shall be free, and have her whole rights, and her liberties inviolable; and we will have them so observed, that it may appear thence that the freedom of elections, which is reckoned chief and indispensable to the English Church, and which we granted and confirmed by our Charter, and obtained the confirmation of the same from our Lord the Pope Innocent III., before the discord between us and our barons, was granted of mere free will; which Charter we shall observe, and we do will it to be faithfully observed by our heirs for ever.

2. We also have granted to all the freemen of our kingdom, for us and for our heirs for ever, all the underwritten liberties, to be had and holden by them and their heirs, of us and our heirs for ever: If any of our earls, or baron, or others, who hold of us in chief by military service, shall die, and at the time of his death his heir shall be of full age, and owe a relief, he shall have his inheritance by the ancient relief—that is to say, the heir or heirs of an earl, for a whole earldom, by a hundred pounds; the heir or heirs of a baron, for a whole barony, by a hundred pounds; the heir or heirs of a knight, for a whole knight's fee, by a hundred shillings at most; and whoever oweth less shall give less, according to the ancient custom of fees.

3. But if the heir of any such shall be under age, and shall be in ward, when he comes of age he shall have his inheritance without relief and without fine.

4. The keeper of the land of such an heir being under age, shall take of the land of the heir none but reasonable issues, reasonable customs, and reasonable services, and that without destruction and waste of his men and his goods; and if we commit the custody of any such lands to the sheriff, or any other who is answerable to us for the issues of the land, and he shall make destruction and waste of the lands which he hath in custody, we will take of him amends, and the land shall be committed to two lawful and discreet men of that fee, who shall answer for the issues to us, or to him to whom we shall assign them; and if we sell or give to any one the custody of such lands, and

he therein make destruction or waste, he shall lose the same custody, which shall be committed to two lawful and discreet men of that fee, who shall in like manner answer to us as aforesaid.

5. But the keeper, so long as he shall have the custody of the land, shall keep up the houses, parks, warrens, ponds, mills, and other things pertaining to the land, out of the issues of the same land; and shall deliver to the heir, when he comes of full age, his whole land, stocked with ploughs and carriages, according as the time of wainage shall require, and the issues of the land can reasonably bear.

6. Heirs shall be married without disparagement, and so that before matrimony shall be contracted, those who are near in blood to the heir shall have notice.

7. A widow, after the death of her husband, shall forthwith and without difficulty have her marriage and inheritance; nor shall she give anything for her dower, or her marriage, or her inheritance, which her husband and she held at the day of his death; and she may remain in the mansion house of her husband forty days after his death, within which time her dower shall be assigned.

8. No widow shall be distrained to marry herself, so long as she has a mind to live without a husband; but yet she shall give security that she will not marry without our assent, if she hold of us; or without the consent of the lord of whom she holds, if she hold of another.

9. Neither we nor our bailiffs shall seize any land or rent for any debt so long as the chattels of the debtor are sufficient to pay the debt; nor shall the sureties of the debtor be distrained so long as the principal debtor has sufficient to pay the debt; and if the principal debtor shall fail in the payment of the debt, not having wherewithal to pay it, then the sureties shall answer the debt; and if they will they shall have the lands and rents of the debtor, until they shall be satisfied for the debt which they paid for him, unless the principal debtor can show himself acquitted thereof against the said sureties.

10. If any one have borrowed anything of the Jews, more or less, and die before the debt be satisfied, there shall be no interest paid for that debt, so long as the heir is under age, of whomsoever he may hold; and if the debt falls into our hands, we will only take the chattel mentioned in the deed.

11. And if any one shall die indebted to the Jews, his wife shall have her dower and pay nothing of that debt; and if the deceased left children under age, they shall have necessaries provided for them, according to the tenement[1] of the deceased; and out of the residue the debt shall be paid, saving, however, the service due to the lords, and in like manner shall it be done touching debts due to others than the Jews.

12. No scutage[2] or aid shall be imposed in our kingdom, unless by the general council of our kingdom; except for ransoming our person, making our eldest son a knight, and once for marrying our eldest daughter; and for these there shall be paid no more than a reasonable aid. In like manner it shall be concerning the aids of the City of London.

13. And the City of London shall have all its ancient liberties and free

---

[1] Feudal holding, fief.

[2] A tax levied on a knight in place of military service.

customs, as well by land as by water: furthermore, we will and grant that all other cities and boroughs, and towns and ports, shall have all their liberties and free customs.

14. And for holding the general council of the kingdom concerning the assessment of aids, except in the three cases aforesaid, and for the assessing of scutages, we shall cause to be summoned the archbishops, bishops, abbots, earls, and greater barons of the realm, singly by our letter. And furthermore, we shall cause to be summoned generally, by our sheriffs and bailiffs,[3] all others who hold of us in chief, for a certain day, that is to say, forty days before their meeting at least, and to a certain place; and in all letters of such summons we will declare the cause of such summons. And summons being thus made, the business shall proceed on the day appointed, according to the advice of such as shall be present, although all that were summoned come not.

15. We will not for the future grant to any one that he may take aid of his own free tenants, unless to ransom his body, and to make his eldest son a knight, and once to marry his eldest daughter; and for this there shall be only paid a reasonable aid.

16. No man shall be distrained to perform more service for a knight's fee, or other free tenement, than is due from thence.

17. Common pleas shall not follow our court, but shall be holden in some place certain.

18. Trials upon the Writs of Novel Disseisin, and of Mort d'ancestor, and of Darrein Presentment,[4] shall not be taken but in their proper counties, and after this manner: We, or if we should be out of the realm, our chief justiciary, will send two justiciaries through every county four times a year, who, with four knights of each county, chosen by the county, shall hold the said assizes in the county, on the day, and at the place appointed.

19. And if any matters cannot be determined on the day appointed for holding the assizes in each county, so many of the knights and freeholders as have been at the assizes aforesaid shall stay to decide them as is necessary, according as there is more or less business.

20. A freeman shall not be amerced for a small offence, but only according to the degree of the offence; and for a great crime according to the heinousness of it, saving to him his contenement; and after the same manner a merchant, saving to him his merchandise. And a villein shall be amerced after the same manner, saving to him his wainage, if he falls under our mercy; and none of the aforesaid amerciaments shall be assessed but by the oath of honest men in the neighborhood.

21. Earls and barons shall not be amerced but by their peers, and after the degree of the offence.

22. No ecclesiastical person shall be amerced for his lay tenement, but according to the proportion of the others aforesaid, and not according to the value of his ecclesiastical benefice.

23. Neither a town nor any tenant shall be distrained to make bridges

---

[3] Both royal officers. Sheriffs were the chief officials of shires or counties; bailiffs collected revenues and administered justice.
[4] "Disseisin" is dispossession. "Mort d'ancestor" is "death of the ancestor," i.e., in cases of disputed possession of land. "Darrein presentment" is the last presentation of a benefice.

or embankments, unless that anciently and of right they are bound to do it.

24. No sheriff, constable, coroner, or other our bailiffs, shall hold "Pleas of the Crown."[5]

25. All counties, hundreds, wapentakes, and trethings, shall stand at the old rents, without any increase, except in our demesne manors.

26. If any one holding of us a lay fee die, and the sheriff, or our bailiffs, show our letters patent of summons for debt which the dead man did owe to us, it shall be lawful for the sheriff or our bailiff to attach and register the chattels of the dead, found upon his lay fee, to the amount of the debt, by the view of lawful men, so as nothing be removed until our whole clear debt be paid; and the rest shall be left to the executors to fulfil the testament of the dead; and if there be nothing due from him to us, all the chattels shall go to the use of the dead, saving to his wife and children their reasonable shares.

27. If any freeman shall die intestate, his chattels shall be distributed by the hands of his nearest relations and friends, by view of the Church, saving to every one his debts which the deceased owed to him.

28. No constable or bailiff of ours shall take corn or other chattels of any man unless he presently give him money for it, or hath respite of payment by the good-will of the seller.

29. No constable shall distrain any knight to give money for castle-guard, if he himself will do it in his person, or by another able man, in case he cannot do it through any reasonable cause. And if we have carried or sent him into the army, he shall be free from such guard for the time he shall be in the army by our command.

30. No sheriff or bailiff of ours, or any other, shall take horses or carts of any freeman for carriage, without the assent of the said freeman.

31. Neither shall we nor our bailiffs take any man's timber for our castles or other uses, unless by the consent of the owner of the timber.

32. We will retain the lands of those convicted of felony only one year and a day, and then they shall be delivered to the lord of the fee.

33. All kydells [weirs] for the time to come shall be put down in the rivers of Thames and Medway, and throughout all England, except upon the sea-coast.

34. The writ which is called *præcipe,* for the future, shall not be made out to any one, of any tenement, whereby a freeman may lose his court.

35. There shall be one measure of wine and one of ale through our whole realm; and one measure of corn, that is to say, the London quarter; and one breadth of dyed cloth, and russets, and haberjeets, that is to say, two ells within the lists; and it shall be of weights as it is of measures.

36. Nothing from henceforth shall be given or taken for a writ of inquisition of life or limb, but it shall be granted freely, and not denied.

37. If any do hold of us by fee-farm, or by socage, or by burgage, and he hold also lands of any other by knight's service, we will not have the custody of the heir or land, which is holden of another man's fee by reason of that fee-farm, socage, or burgage; neither will we have the custody of the fee-farm, or socage, or burgage, unless knight's service was due to us out of

---

[5] "Pleas of the Crown" were criminal suits conducted in the name of the Crown.

the same fee-farm. We will not have the custody of an heir, nor of any land which he holds of another by knight's service, by reason of any petty serjeanty by which he holds of us, by the service of paying a knife, an arrow, or the like.

38. No bailiff from henceforth shall put any man to his law upon his own bare saying, without credible witnesses to prove it.

39. No freeman shall be taken or imprisoned, or disseised, or outlawed, or banished, or any ways destroyed, nor will we pass upon him, nor will we send upon him, unless by the lawful judgment of his peers, or by the law of the land.

40. We will sell to no man, we will not deny to any man, either justice or right.

41. All merchants shall have safe and secure conduct, to go out of, and to come into England, and to stay there and to pass as well by land as by water, for buying and selling by the ancient and allowed customs, without any unjust tolls; except in time of war, or when they are of any nation at war with us. And if there be found any such in our land, in the beginning of the war, they shall be attached, without damage to their bodies or goods, until it be known unto us, or our chief justiciary, how our merchants be treated in the nation at war with us; and if ours be safe there, the others shall be safe in our dominions.

42. It shall be lawful, for the time to come, for any one to go out of our kingdom, and return safely and securely by land or by water, saving his allegiance to us; unless in time of war, by some short space, for the common benefit of the realm, except prisoners and outlaws, according to the law of the land, and people in war with us, and merchants who shall be treated as is above mentioned.

43. If any man hold of any escheat, as of the honour of Wallingford, Nottingham, Boulogne, Lancaster, or of other escheats which be in our hands, and are baronies, and die, his heir shall give no other relief, and perform no other service to us than he would to the baron, if it were in the baron's hand; and we will hold it after the same manner as the baron held it.

44. Those men who dwell without the forest from henceforth shall not come before our justiciaries of the forest, upon common summons, but such as are impleaded, or are sureties for any that are attached for something concerning the forest.

45. We will not make any justices, constables, sheriffs, or bailiffs, but of such as know the law of the realm and mean duly to observe it.

46. All barons who have founded abbeys, which they hold by charter from the kings of England, or by ancient tenure, shall have the keeping of them, when vacant, as they ought to have.

47. All forests that have been made forests in our time shall forthwith be disforested; and the same shall be done with the water-banks that have been fenced in by us in our time.

48. All evil customs concerning forests, warrens, foresters, and warreners, sheriffs and their officers, water-banks and their keepers, shall forthwith be inquired into in each county, by twelve sworn knights of the same county, chosen by creditable persons of the same county; and within forty days after the said inquest be utterly abolished, so as never to be restored: so as we are

first acquainted therewith, or our justiciary, if we should not be in England.

49. We will immediately give up all hostages and charters delivered unto us by our English subjects, as securities for their keeping the peace, and yielding us faithful service.

50. We will entirely remove from their bailiwicks the relations of Gerard de Atheyes, so that for the future they shall have no bailiwick in England; we will also remove Engelard de Cygony, Andrew, Peter, and Gyon, from the Chancery; Gyon de Cygony, Geoffrey de Martyn, and his brothers; Philip Mark, and his brothers, and his nephew, Geoffrey, and their whole retinue.

51. As soon as peace is restored, we will send out of the kingdom all foreign knights, cross-bowmen, and stipendiaries, who are come with horses and arms to the molestation of our people.

52. If any one has been dispossessed or deprived by us, without the lawful judgment of his peers, of his lands, castles, liberties, or right, we will forthwith restore them to him; and if any dispute arise upon this head, let the matter be decided by the five-and-twenty barons hereafter mentioned, for the preservation of the peace. And for all those things of which any person has, without the lawful judgment of his peers, been dispossessed or deprived, either by our father King Henry, or our brother King Richard, and which we have in our hands, or are possessed by others, and we are bound to warrant and make good, we shall have a respite till the term usually allowed the crusaders; excepting those things about which there is a plea depending, or whereof an inquest hath been made, by our order before we undertook the crusade; but as soon as we return from our expedition, or if perchance we tarry at home and do not make our expedition, we will immediately cause full justice to be administered therein.

53. The same respite we shall have, and in the same manner, about administering justice, disafforesting or letting continue the forests, which Henry our father, and our brother Richard, have afforested; and the same concerning the wardship of the lands which are in another's fee, but the wardship of which we have hitherto had, by reason of a fee held of us by knight's service; and for the abbeys founded in any other fee than our own, in which the lord of the fee says he has a right; and when we return from our expedition, or if we tarry at home, and do not make our expedition, we will immediately do full justice to all the complainants in this behalf.

54. No man shall be taken or imprisoned upon the appeal of a woman, for the death of any other than her husband.

55. All unjust and illegal fines made by us, and all amerciaments imposed unjustly and contrary to the law of the land, shall be entirely given up, or else be left to the decision of the five-and-twenty barons hereafter mentioned for the preservation of the peace, or of the major part of them, together with the aforesaid Stephen, Archbishop of Canterbury, if he can be present, and others whom he shall think fit to invite; and if he cannot be present, the business shall notwithstanding go on without him; but so that if one or more of the aforesaid five-and-twenty barons be plaintiffs in the same cause, they shall be set aside as to what concerns this particular affair, and others be chosen in their room, out of the said five-and-twenty, and sworn by the rest to decide the matter.

56. If we have disseised or dispossessed the Welsh of any lands, liberties, or other things, without the legal judgment of their peers, either in England or in Wales, they shall be immediately restored to them; and if any dispute arise upon this head, the matter shall be determined in the Marches by the judgment of their peers; for tenements in England according to the law of England, for tenements in Wales according to the law of Wales, for tenements of the Marches according to the law of the Marches: the same shall the Welsh do to us and our subjects.

57. As for all those things of which a Welshman hath, without the lawful judgment of his peers, been disseised or deprived of by King Henry our father, or our brother King Richard, and which we either have in our hands or others are possessed of, and we are obliged to warrant it, we shall have a respite till the time generally allowed the crusaders; excepting those things about which a suit is depending, or whereof an inquest has been made by our order, before we undertook the crusade: but when we return, or if we stay at home without performing our expedition, we will immediately do them full justice, according to the laws of the Welsh and of the parts before mentioned.

58. We will without delay dismiss the son of Llewellin, and all the Welsh hostages, and release them from the engagements they have entered into with us for the preservation of the peace.

59. We will treat with Alexander, King of Scots, concerning the restoring his sisters and hostages, and his right and liberties, in the same form and manner as we shall do to the rest of our barons of England; unless by the charters which we have from his father, William, late King of Scots, it ought to be otherwise; and this shall be left to the determination of his peers in our court.

60. All the aforesaid customs and liberties, which we have granted to be holden in our kingdom, as much as it belongs to us, all people of our kingdom, as well clergy as laity, shall observe, as far as they are concerned, towards their dependents.

61. And whereas, for the honour of God and the amendment of our kingdom, and for the better quieting the discord that has arisen between us and our barons, we have granted all these things aforesaid; willing to render them firm and lasting, we do give and grant our subjects the underwritten security, namely that the barons may choose five-and-twenty barons of the kingdom, whom they think convenient; who shall take care, with all their might, to hold and observe, and cause to be observed, the peace and liberties we have granted them, and by this our present Charter confirmed in this manner; that is to say, that if we, our justiciary, our bailiffs, or any of our officers, shall in any circumstance have failed in the performance of them towards any person, or shall have broken through any of these articles of peace and security, and the offence be notified to four barons chosen out of the five-and-twenty before mentioned, the said four barons shall repair to us, or our justiciary, if we are out of the realm, and, laying open the grievance, shall petition to have it redressed without delay: and if it be not redressed by us, or if we should chance to be out of the realm, if it should not be redressed by our judiciary within forty days, reckoning from the time it has been notified to us, or to our justiciary (if we should be out of the realm), the four barons

aforesaid shall lay the cause before the rest of the five-and-twenty barons; and the said five-and-twenty barons, together with the community of the whole kingdom, shall distrain and distress us in all the ways in which they shall be able, by seizing our castles, lands, possessions, and in any other manner they can, till the grievance is redressed, according to their pleasure; saving harmless our own person, and the persons of our Queen and children; and when it is redressed, they shall behave to us as before. And any person whatsoever in the kingdom may swear that he will obey the orders of the five-and-twenty barons aforesaid in the execution of the premises, and will distress us, jointly with them, to the utmost of his power; and we give public and free liberty to any one that shall please to swear to this, and never will hinder any person from taking the same oath.

62. As for all those of our subjects who will not, of their own accord, swear to join the five-and-twenty barons in distraining and distressing us, we will issue orders to make them take the same oath as aforesaid. And if any one of the five-and-twenty barons dies, or goes out of the kingdom, or is hindered any other way from carrying the things aforesaid into execution, the rest of the said five-and twenty barons may choose another in his room, at their discretion, who shall be sworn in like manner as the rest. In all things that are committed to the execution of these five-and-twenty barons, if, when they are all assembled together, they should happen to disagree about any matter, and some of them, when summoned, will not or cannot come, whatever is agreed upon, or enjoined, by the major part of those that are present shall be reputed as firm and valid as if all the five-and-twenty had given their consent; and the aforesaid five-and-twenty shall swear that all the premises they shall faithfully observe, and cause with all their power to be observed. And we will procure nothing from any one, by ourselves nor by another, whereby any of these concessions and liberties may be revoked or lessened; and if any such thing shall have been obtained, let it be null and void; neither will we ever make use of it either by ourselves or any other. And all the ill-will, indignations, and rancours that have arisen between us and our subjects, of the clergy and laity, from the first breaking out of the dissensions between us, we do fully remit and forgive: moreover, all trespasses occasioned by the said dissensions, from Easter in the sixteenth year of our reign till the restoration of peace and tranquillity, we hereby entirely remit to all, both clergy and laity, and as far as in us lies do fully forgive. We have, moreover, caused to be made for them the letters patent testimonial of Stephen, Lord Archbishop of Canterbury, Henry, Lord Archbishop of Dublin, and the bishops aforesaid, as also of Master Pandulph, for the security and concessions aforesaid.

63. Wherefore we will and firmly enjoin, that the Church of England be free, and that all men in our kingdom have and hold all the aforesaid liberties, rights, and concessions, truly and peaceably, freely and quietly, fully and wholly to themselves and their heirs, of us and our heirs, in all things and places, for ever, as is aforesaid. It is also sworn, as well on our part as on the part of the barons, that all the things aforesaid shall be observed in good faith, and without evil subtilty. Given under our hand, in the presence of the witnesses above named, and many others, in the meadow called Runingmede,

between Windsor and Staines, the 15th day of June, in the 17th year of our reign.

STATUTE OF KING LOUIS X*

Louis, by the grace of God . . . King of France and Navarre. Let it be known to all . . . that we desire and are bound to desire the peace and tranquility of our loyal subjects . . . and that we wish to establish in what ways they may be kept from harm, oppression, and undue grief, and maintained and protected in their legitimate and approved liberties, franchises, and customs, those they have enjoyed in times past, without prejudice to us and our realm.[1]

And as the nobles of our bailiwicks of Amiens and Vermandois have again complained that from the days of St. Louis, our lord, they have been much burdened and improperly treated by the officials of our predecessors and still are every day . . . by our own officials, contrary to the old customs and usages . . . they had enjoyed in times past . . . they humbly petition for just redress. And on the basis of the aforesaid petitions and the articles presented to us, in the presence of our very loyal and dear friends, brothers, uncles, and prelates of our realm and of our barons and our council, having deliberated and seen and known the truth on the basis of the registers of St. Louis, our lord, as well as the good usages and customs of the past which we have known to have been used formerly in the said bailiwicks, we declare to the said nobles. . . .

1. First, Given the complaint, we order that, by reason of usage and the customary practices of the said bailiwicks, our sergeants shall neither do justice nor take away cases in the land of the lord who has the right of justice, unless the sergeant has a commission granted by ourselves to hear specific cases or judge in specific territories. And if the sergeants do otherwise, they are to be taken and punished. And our sergeants, without commission and on their own authority, are bound to summon the cases of another, those cases that properly belong to the lords, and they are bound to arrange the return of the cases and persons involved. . . . And if those subject to judgment do not appear, in proportion to their responsibility to the court, one is to try to levy fines of default according to the aforesaid usage or custom. We wish and order that this be done and that the aforementioned custom and usage be preserved. He who acts to the contrary shall be punished. And if new pleas concerning estates and castles be instituted, we order that the jurisdic-

---

* Reprinted from André Artonne, *Le mouvement de 1314 et les chartes provinciales de 1315* (Paris, 1912), pp. 171–175, trans. Peter Riesenberg.

[1] A single footnote will describe the royal officials mentioned in this statute. Bailiffs were appointed officials whose duty it was to handle, at first, matters of justice, and eventually matters of finance and administration in a given geographical area, the bailiwick. In contrast, provosts were officials of justice and administration who purchased their offices from the king, and who, therefore, were frequently faced with the temptation to exploit the office. Sergeants were lesser officials who might handle any military or administrative concern for the king; on occasion they might also hold court. Castellans were officials responsible for the management and performance of a royal castle; they too might have delegated judicial as well as military responsibilities.

tion over such cases not be taken away from the lords wrongly and without cause.

II. If new evidence is proposed against either the lord or his subject, either directly or indirectly, we order that the jurisdiction of the case be granted to the lord.

III. Item. We wish and decree that if any lord has taken someone subject to his jurisdiction and imprisoned him with the intent to try him . . . that the provosts may not take the prisoner from the lord unless the prisoner is detained in a case of *recroiance*.[2] And if the lord does not wish to do justice in that case, we shall be forced to make him free the individual on bail.

IV. Item. We and our bailiffs have by usage the right of appointing sergeants at the provosts' courts and castle courts of the said bailiwicks [of Amiens and Vermandois], and of presenting them, and having them take an oath before the people. And one is to obey them at the aforesaid courts. And although there are already more sergeants than there should be according to our statutes, our provosts shall try to appoint more of them and shall again endeavor to strike off a goodly number of such persons who are of small value and whom we should not trust. . . .[3]

V. Item. We wish and decree that, when our bailiffs, provosts, castellans, and other judges have summoned their men to their feudal court, if these men leave before the judgment, the judgments pronounced against them be delivered.

VI. Item. As the nobles demand that we appoint good men to our provostships and not sell these offices, and that if any be sold we sell them for three years at most, and that at the end of three years these offices not be sold again to those who have held them before, we order that an early inquest be made with regard to the provostships by one good and upright man commissioned by us who will work with two other good and upright men of the county; for when the officials have held their provostships for their three years and have done considerable evil, they keep their provostships, as matters now stand, if respectable subjects do not dare to complain about them. We order that the investigation be made generally against those who have held the provostships and [other] offices. And we wish and decree that this be done unless we should choose to sell our provostships; and if we sell them, matters will be kept as the nobles have asked.

VII. Item. If any bailiff, provost, or castellan, or sergeant of any court imprisons or causes to be imprisoned any person in order to take his property, or out of hate, we order that the judge or sergeant who has committed this crime because of such malice, if he be found guilty, make restitution and pay the court and legal damages of the person he has imprisoned; and he shall be punished according to the magnitude of the offense.

VIII. Item. The nobles demand that any man be able to petition and plead as plaintiff as well as defendant without the services of an attorney, since the law has given him this right up to now. We will preserve to the nobles the established custom.

---

[2] That is, freedom from prison under bail.
[3] This is the sense of an obviously corrupt text.

IX. Item. When the provosts perform their duties, their expenses are too great, and the nobles demand that the rates be fixed for them and for the sergeants as well, and for the expenses of those who undertake judicial inquests. We order the commissioners whom we will send into the county . . . to see this done.

XI. Item. As the said nobles petitioned us that the good old coins minted in our kingdom by our predecessors be accepted along with new mintings without being seized, we order that those who have assayed our monies and our grants or those of our predecessors be reproved for their excesses, for the people are thereby greatly burdened. . . .

XIII. Item. We wish and decree that if anyone holds up letters from us or from our court, where there is a question of jurisdiction, such orders shall not be executed until [proper] jurisdiction is established; and once it is, execution of the said letters shall be made as reason dictates.

XIV. Item. We wish and decree that no one be summoned . . . outside the place where he goes to bed and wakes up; rather he shall be arraigned in the place where he goes to bed and wakes up. . . .

And all the above matters, and each of them, in the form and manner written . . . , for us and our successors and for the nobles mentioned and their successors, the churches and the clergy, and for all the common folk of the said bailiwicks, we order and firmly command that they be strictly held, preserved, and put into effect, point by point, henceforth, without corruption in all or part. And we order and specifically enjoin our bailiffs of Amiens and Vermandois and all our provosts and other officials in these areas for now and all time to observe and carry into effect all the above without opposition. Let them so do, and each time they take office let them swear before the commonality that they will care for all these matters and accomplish them, and cause these things to be kept and observed by those whose responsibility it is to do so, under penalty of paying all the costs, damages, and interest of those who rightly would make complaint.

And that this matter may be settled and established for all time, we have closed these letters with our own seal, excepting in all other things our right, and in all things the right of any other.

Done in Paris the year of our Lord 1315, in the month of May.

6. What Is the Relationship of Truths Discovered by Human Reason to Those Revealed by God?

What made Aristotle so attractive to men of orderly mind was that his answers to the technical questions of philosophy were interdependent. His views of nature depended on his theory of knowledge, for example, and even his ethics and politics were related to his logic and general theory of science. Thomas Aquinas (see page 233, above) saw the strength of such systematic thinking applied to the infinity of problems about men and nature that the New Testament implied. He attempted to synthesize pagan Aristotelianism with Christian thought in a system now called Thomism.

One fundamental issue faced by every Christian philosopher who tried to reconcile pagan thought with his own religious beliefs was that of the relationship between the truths discovered by human reason and those revealed by God. In the following passage taken from the Summa contra Gentiles, *Thomas dealt with this problem. His solution made the pursuit of science religiously acceptable, and therefore possible for the Middle Ages.*

SUMMA CONTRA GENTILES*

St. Thomas Aquinas

IN WHAT WAY IT IS POSSIBLE TO MAKE KNOWN THE DIVINE TRUTH

Since . . . not every truth is to be made known in the same way, *and it is the part of an educated man to seek for conviction in each subject, only so far as the nature of the subject allows,* as the Philosopher most rightly observes as quoted by Boethius,[1] it is necessary to show first of all in what way it is possible to make known the aforesaid truth.

Now in those things which we hold about God there is truth in two ways. For certain things that are true about God wholly surpass the capability of human reason, for instance that God is three and one: while there are certain things to which even natural reason can attain, for instance that God is, that God is one, and others like these, which even the philosophers proved demonstratively of God, being guided by the light of natural reason.

That certain divine truths wholly surpass the capability of human reason, is most clearly evident. For since the principle of all the knowledge which the reason acquires about a thing, is the understanding of that thing's essence, because according to the Philosopher's teaching the principle of a demonstration is *what a thing is,* it follows that our knowledge about a thing will be in proportion to our understanding of its essence. Wherefore, if the human intellect comprehends the essence of a particular thing, for instance a stone or a triangle, no truth about that thing will surpass the capability of human reason. But this does not happen to us in relation to God, because the human intellect is incapable by its natural power of attaining to the comprehension of His essence: since our intellect's knowledge, according to the mode of the present life, originates from the senses: so that things which are not objects of sense cannot be comprehended by the human intellect, except in so far as knowledge of them is gathered from sensibles. Now sensibles cannot lead our intellect to see in them what God is, because they are effects unequal to the power of their cause. And yet our intellect is led by sensibles to the divine knowledge so as to know about God that He is, and other such truths, which need to be ascribed to the first principle. Accordingly some divine truths are attainable by human reason, while others altogether surpass the power of human reason.[2]

---

* St. Thomas Aquinas, *Summa contra Gentiles,* trans. The Dominican Fathers of the English Province (New York: Benziger Brothers, Inc., London: Burns, Oates, and Washburne, Ltd., 1924), pp. 292–297, 299–300.

[1] Roman philosopher (A.D. 475–525) who was one of the greatest influences upon medieval philosophical development. His textbooks transmitted much of what medieval thinkers before the thirteenth century knew of ancient thought, and his *Consolation of Philosophy* was much read as an inspirational piece.

[2] Compare this paragraph with Plato, above, pp. 57–59 and 73–74.

Again. The same is easy to see from the degrees of intellects. For if one of two men perceives a thing with his intellect with greater subtlety, the one whose intellect is of a higher degree understands many things which the other is altogether unable to grasp; as instanced in a yokel who is utterly incapable of grasping the subtleties of philosophy. Now the angelic intellect surpasses the human intellect more than the intellect of the cleverest philosopher surpasses that of the most uncultured. For an angel knows God through a more excellent effect than does man, for as much as the angel's essence, through which he is led to know God by natural knowledge, is more excellent than sensible things, even than the soul itself, by which the human intellect mounts to the knowledge of God. And the divine intellect surpasses the angelic intellect much more than the angelic intellect surpasses the human. For the divine intellect by its capacity equals the divine essence, wherefore God perfectly understands of Himself what He is, and He knows all things that can be understood about Him: whereas the angel knows not what God is by his natural knowledge, because the angel's essence, by which he is led to the knowledge of God, is an effect unequal to the power of its cause. Consequently an angel is unable by his natural knowledge to grasp all that God understands about Himself: nor again is human reason capable of grasping all that an angel understands by his natural power. Accordingly just as a man would show himself to be a most insane fool if he declared the assertions of a philosopher to be false because he was unable to understand them, so, and much more, a man would be exceedingly foolish, were he to suspect of falsehood the things revealed by God through the ministry of His angels, because they cannot be the object of reason's investigations.

Furthermore. The same is made abundantly clear by the deficiency which every day we experience in our knowledge of things. For we are ignorant of many of the properties of sensible things, and in many cases we are unable to discover the nature of those properties which we perceive by our senses. Much less therefore is human reason capable of investigating all the truths about that most sublime essence.

With this the saying of the Philosopher is in accord (2 *Metaph.*) where he says that *our intellect in relation to those primary things which are most evident in nature is like the eye of a bat in relation to the sun.*

To this truth Holy Writ also bears witness. For it is written (Job xi, 7): *Peradventure thou wilt comprehend the steps of God and wilt find out the Almighty perfectly?* and (xxxvi, 26): *Behold God is great, exceeding our knowledge,* and (1 Cor. xiii, 9): *We know in part.*

Therefore all that is said about God, though it cannot be investigated by reason, must not be forthwith rejected as false, as the Manicheans and many unbelievers have thought.

That the Truth about Divine Things Which Is Attainable by Reason is Fittingly Proposed to Man as an Object of Belief

While then the truth of the intelligible things of God is twofold, one to which the inquiry of reason can attain, the other which surpasses the whole range of human reason, both are fittingly proposed by God to man as an object of belief. We must first show this with regard to that truth which is attainable by the inquiry of reason, lest it appears to some, that since it can be attained by reason, it was useless to make it an object of faith by supernatural inspiration. Now three disadvantages would result if this truth were left solely to the inquiry of reason. One is that few men would have knowledge of God: because very many are hindered from gathering the fruit of diligent inquiry, which is the discovery of truth, for three reasons. Some indeed on account of an indisposition of temperament, by reason of which many are naturally indisposed to knowledge; so that no efforts of theirs would enable them to reach to the attainment of the highest degree of human knowledge, which consists in knowing God. Some are hindered by the needs of household affairs. For there must needs be among men some that devote themselves to the conduct of temporal affairs, who would be unable to devote so much time to the leisure of contemplative research as to reach the summit of human inquiry, namely the knowledge of God. And some are hindered by laziness. For in order to acquire the knowledge of God in those things which reason is able to investigate, it is necessary to have a previous knowledge of many things: since almost the entire consideration of philosophy is directed to the knowledge of God: for which reason metaphysics, which is about divine things, is the last of the parts of philosophy to be studied. Wherefore it is not possible to arrive at the inquiry about the aforesaid truth except after a most laborious study: and few are willing to take upon themselves this labour for the love of a knowledge, the natural desire for which has nevertheless been instilled into the mind of man by God.

The second disadvantage is that those who would arrive at the discovery of the aforesaid truth would scarcely succeed in doing so after a long time. First, because this truth is so profound, that it is only after long practice that the human intellect is enabled to grasp it by means of reason. Secondly, because many things are required beforehand, as stated above. Thirdly, because at the time of youth, the mind, when tossed about by the various movements of the passions, is not fit for the knowledge of so sublime a truth, whereas *calm gives prudence and knowledge,* as stated in 7 *Phys.* Hence mankind would remain in the deepest darkness of ignorance, if the path of reason were the only available way to the knowledge of God: because the knowledge of God which especially makes men perfect and good, would be acquired only by the few, and by these only after a long time.

The third disadvantage is that much falsehood is mingled with the investigations of human reason, on account of the weakness of our intellect in forming its judgments, and by reason of the admixture of phantasms. Consequently many would remain in doubt about those things even which are most truly demonstrated, through ignoring the force of the demonstration: especially when they perceive that different things are taught by the various men who are called wise. Moreover among the many demonstrated truths, there is sometimes a mixture of falsehood that is not demonstrated, but assumed for some probable or sophistical reason which at times is mistaken for a demonstration. Therefore it was necessary that definite certainty and pure truth about divine things should be offered to man by way of faith.

Accordingly the divine clemency has made this salutary commandment, that even some things which reason is able to investigate must be held by faith: so that all may share in the knowledge of God easily, and without doubt or error.

Hence it is written (Eph. iv, 17, 18): That *henceforward you walk not as also the Gentiles walk in the vanity of their mind, having their understanding darkened:* and (Isa. liv, 13): *All thy children shall be taught of the Lord.*

That Those Things Which Cannot Be Investigated by Reason Are Fittingly Proposed to Man as an Object of Faith

It may appear to some that those things which cannot be investigated by reason ought not to be proposed to man as an object of faith: because divine wisdom provides for each thing according to the mode of its nature. We must therefore prove that it is necessary also for those things which surpass reason to be proposed by God to man as an object of faith.

For no man tends to do a thing by his desire and endeavour unless it be previously known to him. Wherefore since man is directed by divine providence to a higher good than human frailty can attain in the present life, as we shall show in the sequel, it was necessary for his mind to be bidden to something higher than those things to which our reason can reach in the present life, so that he might learn to aspire, and by his endeavours to tend to something surpassing the whole state of the present life. And this is especially competent to the Christian religion, which alone promises goods spiritual and eternal: for which reason it proposes many things surpassing the thought of man: whereas the old law which contained promises of temporal things, proposed few things that are above human inquiry. It was with this motive that the philosophers, in order to wean men from sensible pleasures to virtue, took care to show that there are other goods of greater account than those which appeal to the senses, the taste of which things affords much greater delight to those who devote themselves to active or contemplative virtues.

Again is is necessary for this truth to be proposed to man as an object of faith in order that he may have truer knowledge of God. For then alone do we know God truly, when we believe that He is far above all that man can possibly think of God, because the divine essence surpasses man's natural knowledge, as stated above. Hence by the fact that certain things about God are proposed to man, which surpass his reason, he is strengthened in his opinion that God is far above what he is able to think.

There results also another advantage from this, namely, the checking of presumption which is the mother of error. For some there are who presume so far on their wits that they think themselves capable of measuring the whole nature of things by their intellect, in that they esteem all things true which they see, and false which they see not. Accordingly, in order that man's mind might be freed from this presumption, and seek the truth humbly, it was necessary that certain things far surpassing his intellect should be proposed to man by God.

Yet another advantage is made apparent by the words of the Philosopher (*10 Ethic.*). For when a certain Simonides maintained that man should neglect the knowledge of God, and apply his mind to human affairs, and declared that *a man ought to relish human things, and a mortal, mortal things:* the Philosopher contradicted him, saying that *a man ought to devote himself to immortal and divine things as much as he can.* Hence he says (*11 De Animal.*) that though it is but little that we perceive of higher substances, yet that little is more loved and desired than all the knowledge we have of lower substances. He says also (*2 De Caelo et Mundo*) that when questions about the heavenly bodies can be answered by a short and probable solution, it happens that the hearer is very much rejoiced. All this shows that however imperfect the knowledge of the highest things may be, it bestows very great perfection on the soul: and consequently, although human reason is unable to grasp fully things that are above reason, it nevertheless acquires much perfection, if at least it hold things, in any way whatever, by faith.

Wherefore it is written. . . . *Many things are shown to thee above the understanding of men,* and (I Cor. ii, 10, 11): *The things . . . that are of God no man knoweth, but the Spirit of God: but to us God hath revealed them by His Spirit.*

* * *

That the Truth of Reason Is Not in Opposition to the Truth of the Christian Faith

Now though the aforesaid truth of the Christian faith surpasses the ability of human reason, nevertheless those things which are naturally instilled in human reason cannot be opposed to this truth. For it is clear that those things which are implanted in reason by nature, are most true, so much so that it is impossible to think them to be false. Nor is it lawful to deem false that which is held by faith, since it is so evidently confirmed by God. Seeing then that the false alone is opposed to the true, as evidently appears if we examine their definitions, it is impossible for the aforesaid truth of faith to be contrary to those principles which reason knows naturally.

Again. The same thing which the disciple's mind receives from its teacher is contained in the knowledge of the teacher, unless he teach insincerely, which it were wicked to say of God. Now the knowledge of naturally known principles is instilled into us by God, since God Himself is the author of our nature. Therefore the divine Wisdom also contains these principles. Consequently whatever is contrary to these principles, is contrary to the divine Wisdom; wherefore it cannot be from God. Therefore those things which are received by faith from divine revelation cannot be contrary to our natural knowledge.

Moreover. Our intellect is stayed by contrary arguments, so that it cannot advance to the knowledge of truth. Wherefore if conflicting knowledges were instilled into us by God, our intellect would thereby be hindered from knowing the truth. And this cannot be ascribed to God.

Furthemore. Things that are natural are unchangeable so long as nature remains. Now contrary opinions cannot be together in the same subject. Therefore God does not instil into man any opinion or belief contrary to natural knowledge.

Hence the Apostle says (Rom. x, 8): *The word is nigh thee even in thy heart and in thy mouth. This is the word of faith which we preach.* Yet because it surpasses reason some look upon it as though it were contrary thereto; which is impossible.

This is confirmed also by the authority of Augustine who says *(Gen. ad. lit.* ii): *That which truth shall make known can nowise be in opposition to the holy books whether of the Old or of the New Testament.*

From this we may evidently conclude that whatever arguments are alleged against the teachings of faith, they do not rightly proceed from the first self-evident principles instilled by nature. Wherefore they lack the force of demonstration, and are either probable or sophistical arguments, and consequently it is possible to solve them.

In What Relation Human Reason Stands to the Truth of Faith

It would also seem well to observe that sensible things from which human reason derives the source of its knowledge, retain a certain trace of likeness to God, but so imperfect that it proves altogether inadequate to manifest the substance itself of God. For effects resemble their causes according to their own mode, since like action proceeds from like agent; and yet the effect does not always reach to a perfect likeness to the agent. Accordingly human reason is adapted to the knowledge of the truth of faith, which can be known in the highest degree only by those who see the divine substance, in so far as it is able to put together certain probable arguments in support thereof, which nevertheless are insufficient to enable us to understand the aforesaid truth as though it were demonstrated to us or understood by us in itself. And yet however weak these arguments may be, it is useful for the human mind to be practised therein, so long as it does not pride itself on having comprehended or demonstrated; since although our view of the sublimest things is limited and weak, it is most pleasant to be able to catch but a glimpse of them, as appears from what has been said.

The authority of Hilary is in agreement with this statement: for he says *(De Trin.)* while while speaking of this same truth: *Begin by believing these things, advance and persevere; and though I know thou wilt not arrive, I shall rejoice at thy advance. For he who devoutly follows in pursuit of the infinite, though he never come up with it, will always advance by setting forth. Yet pry not into that secret, and meddle not in the mystery of the birth of the infinite, nor presume to grasp that which is the summit of understanding: but understand that there are things thou canst not grasp.*

7. What Is the Nature of Motion?

Although Albert the Great and Thomas Aquinas established a philosophical foundation for the pursuit of science, interest in the natural world long antedated them. In the generation preceding the year 1000, Gerbert, who later became Pope Sylvester II, went to Spain to study ancient and Arabic mathematics and astronomy. In the twelfth century, scholars at the Cathedral School of Chartres studied Plato's Timaeus *and the Arabs, the better to understand Genesis. The twelfth century also saw a great number of trans-lations from Greek and Arabic into Latin, as scholars went to Sicily, Spain, and Constantinople to use books not available in Latin in western Europe. By the early thirteenth century, more than two hundred of the most significant Greek works in logic, physics, medicine, astronomy, and mathematics had become accessible in Latin to scholars at the universities. At Paris and Oxford, men picked up where the ancients had left off, and after a thousand years of relative inactivity, Western scholars launched an assault upon the secrets of nature.*

This attempt to understand the natural world—one of the greatest achievements in Western history—was not limited to the study of ancient books. Although many scholars wrote commentaries on Aristotle's Physics, *some also did original work. In the thirteenth century, Peter of Maricourt ex-perimented and wrote a book on magnetism; at about the same time, Dietrich of Freiburg successfully developed a scientifically sound theory of the rainbow.*

While such men were examining nature, they were also examining their own scientific procedures. Probably the greatest medieval study of what we today would call "scientific method" was that of the English bishop Robert Grosseteste. Beyond empiricism and critical self-examination, medieval scientists developed something else—mathematics. By the thirteenth century, Arabic numerals were in fairly general use, and calculation thus became easier. In the same century, especially at Paris, Oxford, and Cambridge, scholars were at-tempting to deal with the observed facts of nature in mathematical terms.

John Buridan (c. 1296–c. 1366) was one of these early mathematical physicists. The difficult selection that follows is Buridan's discussion of some traditional concerns of ancient and medieval physics: the problem of motion. Aristotle had raised the questions, and subsequent scientists had either agreed with his answers (the usual case), or developed new theories in opposition. Buridan disagreed with Aristotle, and his treatment of the problems pointed the way to Newton, who gave the answers in mathematical formulae four centuries later.

QUESTIONS ON THE EIGHT BOOKS OF THE PHYSICS OF ARISTOTLE*

John Buridan

1. BOOK VIII, QUESTION 12. It is sought whether a projectile after leav-ing the hand of the projector is moved by the air, or by what it is moved.

It is argued that it is not moved by the air, because the air seems rather to resist, since it is necessary that it be divided. Furthermore, if you say that the projector in the beginning moved the projectile and the ambient air along with it, and then that air, having been moved, moves the projectile furth-er to such and such a distance, the doubt will return as to by what the air

* Reprinted with permission of the copyright owner, Marshall Clagett, from Marshall Clagett, *The Science of Mechanics in the Middle Ages* (Madison: University of Wisconsin Press, 1959), pp. 532–538.

is moved after the projector ceases to move. For there is just as much difficulty regarding this (the air) as there is regarding the stone which is thrown.

Aristotle takes the opposite position in the [fourth book] of this work (the *Physics*) thus: "Projectiles are moved further after the projectors are no longer in contact with them, either by antiperistasis, as some say, or by the fact that the air having been pushed, pushes with a movement swifter than the movement of impulsion by which it (the body) is carried towards its own [natural] place." He determines the same thing in the seventh and eighth [books] of this work (the *Physics*) and in the third [book] of the *De caelo* [*On the Heavens*].

2. This question I judge to be very difficult because Aristotle, as it seems to me, has not solved it well. For he touches on two opinions. The first one, which he calls "antiperistasis," holds that the projectile swiftly leaves the place in which it was, and nature, not permitting a vacuum, rapidly sends air in behind to fill up the vacuum. The air moved swiftly in this way and impinging upon the projectile impels it along further. This is repeated continually up to a certain distance. . . . But such a solution notwithstanding, it seems to me that this method of proceeding was without value because of many experiences.

The first experience concerns the top and the smith's mill (i.e., wheel) which are moved for a long time and yet do not leave their places. Hence, it is not necessary for the air to follow along to fill up the place of departure of a top of this kind and a smith's mill. So it cannot be said [that the top and the smith's mill are moved by the air] in this manner.

The second experience is this: A lance having a conical posterior as sharp as its anterior would be moved after projection just as swiftly as it would be without a sharp conical posterior. But surely the air following could not push a sharp end in this way, because the air would be easily divided by the sharpness.

The third experience is this: a ship drawn swiftly in the river even against the flow of the river, after the drawing has ceased, cannot be stopped quickly, but continues to move for a long time. And yet a sailor on deck does not feel any air from behind pushing him. He feels only the air from the front resisting [him]. Again, suppose that the said ship were loaded with grain or wood and a man were situated to the rear of the cargo. Then if the air were such an impetus that it could push the ship along so strongly, the man would be pressed very violently between that cargo and the air following it. Experience shows this to be false. Or, at least, if the ship were loaded with grain or straw, the air following and pushing would fold over the stalks which were in the rear. This is all false.

3. Another opinion, which Aristotle seems to approve, is that the projector moves the air adjacent to the projectile [simultaneously] with the projectile and that air moved swiftly has the power of moving the projectile. He does not mean by this that the same air is moved from the place of projection to the place where the projectile stops, but rather that the air joined to the projector is moved by the projector and that air having been moved moves another part of the air next to it, and that [part] moves another (i.e., the next) up to a certain distance. Hence the first air moves the projectile into the second

air, and the second [air moves it] into the third air, and so on. Aristotle says, therefore, that there is not one mover but many in turn. Hence he also concludes that the movement is not continuous but consists of succeeding or contiguous entities.

But this opinion and method certainly seems to me equally as impossible as the opinion and method of the preceding view. For this method cannot solve the problem of how the top or smith's mill is turned after the hand [which sets them in motion] has been removed. Because, if you cut off the air on all sides near the smith's mill by a cloth the mill does not on this account stop but continues to move for a long time. Therefore it is not moved by the air.

Also a ship drawn swiftly is moved a long time after the haulers have stopped pulling it. The surrounding air does not move it, because if it were covered by a cloth and the cloth with the ambient air were withdrawn, the ship would not stop its motion on this account. And even if the ship were loaded with grain or straw and were moved by the ambient air, then that air ought to blow exterior stalks toward the front. But the contrary is evident, for the stalks are blown rather to the rear because of the resisting ambient air.

Again, the air, regardless of how fast it moves, is easily divisible. Hence it is not evident as to how it would sustain a stone of weight of one thousand pounds projected in a sling or in a machine.

Furthermore, you could, by pushing your hand, move the adjacent air, if there is nothing in your hand, just as fast or faster than if you were holding in your hand a stone which you wish to project. If, therefore, that air by reason of the velocity of its motion is of a great enough impetus to move the stone swiftly, it seems that if I were to impel air toward you equally as fast, the air ought to push you impetuously and with sensible strength. [Yet] we would not perceive this.

Also, it follows that you would throw a feather farther than a stone and something less heavy farther than something heavier, assuming equal magnitudes and shapes. Experience shows this to be false. The consequence is manifest, for the air having been moved ought to sustain or carry or move a feather more easily than something heavier. . . .

4. Thus we can and ought to say that in the stone or other projectile there is impressed something which is the motive force of that projectile. And this is evidently better than falling back on the statement that the air continues to move that projectile. For the air appears rather to resist. Therefore, it seems to me that it ought to be said that the motor in moving a moving body impresses in it a certain impetus or a certain motive force of the moving body, [which impetus acts] in the direction toward which the mover was moving the moving body, either up or down, or laterally, or circularly. *And by the amount the motor moves that moving body more swiftly, by the same amount it will impress in it a stronger impetus.*[1] It is by that impetus that the stone is moved after the projector ceases to move. But that impetus is continually decreased by the resisting air and by the gravity of the stone, which inclines it in a direction contrary to that in which the impetus was naturally

---

[1] The italics here and elsewhere are those of the translator.

predisposed to move it. Thus the movement of the stone continually becomes slower, and finally that impetus is so diminished or corrupted that the gravity of the stone wins out over it and moves the stone down to its natural place.

This method, it appears to me, ought to be supported because the other methods do not appear to be true and also because all the appearances are in harmony with this method.

5. For if anyone seeks why I project a stone farther than a feather, and iron or lead fitted to my hand farther than just as much wood, I answer that the cause of this is that the reception of all forms and natural dispositions is in matter and by reason of matter. *Hence by the amount more there is of matter, by that amount can the body receive more of that impetus and more intensely. Now in a dense and heavy body, other things being equal, there is more of prime matter than in a rare and light one. Hence a dense and heavy body receives more of that impetus and more intensely, just as iron can receive more calidity than wood or water of the same quantity.* Moreover, a feather receives such an impetus so weakly that such an impetus is immediately destroyed by the resisting air. *And so also if light wood and heavy iron of the same volume and of the same shape are moved equally fast by a projector, the iron will be moved farther because there is impressed in it a more intense impetus, which is not so quickly corrupted as the lesser impetus would be corrupted. This also is the reason why it is more difficult to bring to rest a large smith's mill which is moving swiftly than a small one, evidently because in the large one, other things being equal, there is more impetus.* And for this reason you could throw a stone of one-half or one pound weight farther than you could a thousandth part of it. For the impetus in that thousandth part is so small that it is overcome immediately by the resisting air.

6. From this theory also appears the cause of why the natural motion of a heavy body downward is continually accelerated. For from the beginning only the gravity was moving it. Therefore, it moved more slowly, but in moving it impressed in the heavy body an impetus. This impetus now [acting] together with its gravity moves it. Therefore, the motion becomes faster; and by the amount it is faster, so the impetus becomes more intense. Therefore, the movement evidently becomes continually faster.

[The impetus then also explains why] one who wishes to jump a long distance drops back a way in order to run faster, so that by running he might acquire an impetus which would carry him a longer distance in the jump. Whence the person so running and jumping does not feel the air moving him, but [rather] feels the air in front strongly resisting him.

Also, since the Bible does not state that appropriate intelligences move the celestial bodies, it could be said that it does not appear necessary to posit intelligences of this kind, because it would be answered that God, when He created the world, moved each of the celestial orbs as He pleased, and in moving them He impressed in them impetuses which moved them without his having to move them any more except by the method of general influence whereby he concurs as a co-agent in all things which take place; "for thus on the seventh day He rested from all work which He had executed by committing to others the actions and the passions in turn." And these impetuses which He impressed in the celestial bodies were not decreased nor corrupted afterwards, because there was no inclination of the celestial bodies for other movements. Nor was there resistance which would be corruptive or repressive of that impetus. But this I do not say assertively, but [rather tentatively] so that I might seek from the theological masters what they might teach me in these matters as to how these things take place.

* * *

. . . In the same way that a luminant generating light generates light reflexively because of an obstacle, so that impetus because of an obstacle acts reflexively. It is true, however, that other causes aptly concur with that impetus for greater or longer reflection. For example, the ball which we bounce with the palm in falling to earth is reflected higher than a stone, although the stone falls more swiftly and more impetuously to the earth. This is because many things are curvable or intracompressible by violence which are innately disposed to return swiftly and by themselves to their correct position or to the disposition natural to them. In thus returning, they can impetuously push or draw something conjunct to them, as is evident in the case of the bow. Hence in this way the ball thrown to the hard ground is compressed into itself by the impetus of its motion; and immediately after striking, it returns swiftly to its sphericity by elevating itself upwards. From this elevation it acquires to itself an impetus which moves it upward a long distance.

Also, it is this way with a cither cord which, put under strong tension and percussion, remains a long time in a certain vibration from which its sound continues a notable time. And this takes place as follows: As a result of striking [the chord] swiftly, it is bent violently in one direction, and so it returns swiftly toward its normal straight position. But on account of the impetus, it crosses beyond the normal straight position in the contrary direction and then again returns. It does this many times. For a similar reason a bell, after the ringer ceases to draw [the chord], is moved a long time, first in one direction, now in another. And it cannot be easily and quickly brought to rest.

This, then, is the exposition of the question. I would be delighted if someone would discover a more probable way of answering it. And this is the end.

8. What Do Merchants Do and Is What They Do in Accordance with God's Law?

Sometime during the half-century before 1100, the economic and social organization of western Europe began to change significantly, especially in central and northern Italy, the Rhineland, and Flanders. The vast majority of people still lived in the country, but now every generation saw the rebirth of old, and growth of new, cities and towns. If the number of townsmen remained relatively small, their power and influence grew large, based as it was upon their increasing wealth. What is striking about this wealth is that it was of a size and origin unknown in the Western world since the collapse of the economy of the western part of the Roman Empire. It came from the manufacture of goods and their merchandising in international as well as local markets, from insurance and from commercial banking activities that included Moslem as well as Christians, from the long-distance transport of foodstuffs to the urban populations of western Europe, and from relations between private finance and public authority on a grand scale. To be sure, most wealthy men derived their income exclusively from the land, but the number and importance of those whose fortunes were made in trade and manufacture grew significantly every generation.

Out of this new activity came many of the techniques and institutional arrangements of the modern business world: forms of business organization, credit instruments for the transfer of monies, commercial law, double-entry bookkeeping, and rational production procedures. In effect, an international business community existed, whose members led a daily life quite different from that of the parochially oriented great majority. Moreover, they acted, as many of them well knew, not altogether in keeping with the long-standing tradition of the Christian West that regarded money and material success with suspicion.

The three documents that follow illustrate several aspects of medieval commercial and moral development. The first is a letter from the head office of a company of merchant-bankers in Siena to the company agent at the Fairs of Champagne, which were something of a year-round market for money and goods. Analysis of many such letters has given us a vivid picture of how business was actually carried on. The second selection is from the Summa Theologica *of St. Thomas Aquinas. The final selection is taken from one of the few books written by a merchant about the mercantile life. Benedetto Cotrugli wrote* On Commerce and the Perfect Merchant *in Naples in the 1450's. Long before Cotrugli wrote his apology, or defense, more speculative thinkers had asked the question: What value was to be accorded the wealthy in society now that money came abundantly from trade and banking? The question was asked against the background of a thousand years' distrust of the rich, who might grind down the poor in time of greatest need, and against the background, too, of popular familiarity with Christ's condemnation of the wealthy as reported in the Gospels. St. Thomas gave one answer to the questions. Before and after him, moralists have had to face the issue as one of the most crucial in their area of concern.*

*A LETTER FROM MERCHANT-BANKERS**

[Siena], July 5, 1260

In the name of the Lord, amen. Reply to the letters from France [brought] by the first messenger of the May fair of Provins, year 1260.
[Dear] Giacomo di Guido Cacciaconti:

Giacomo and Giovanni di [Gregorio, Vincente di Aldobrandino Vincenti?], and the other partners send you greetings. And we are informing you that we have safely received the letters which you sent us by the messenger

---

* *Medieval Trade in the Mediterranean World*, trans. and ed. R. S. Lopez and I. Raymond (New York: Columbia University Press, 1955), pp. 388–391.

of the gild merchant from the May fair of Provins of this year. And through these letters we perfectly understand what were your instructions, and we shall get busy on what will be our business here. Therefore we beg you to be on the alert and to make it your concern to work and get busy on what you have to do. And especially we beg you to be careful in investing and in lending what you have in your hands and what you will have in the future to good and reliable payers, so that we can have it back at any time we may need it or we may want it back. And to do this we ask from God our Lord mercy, that He grant you the grace to do it so that honor may come to you personally and that the partnership may come out in good standing. Amen.

You ought to know, Giacomo, that we shall write accurately [all] that we have to write, and especially what you will instruct us by your letters, such as your receipts, your payments, and the loans you will make. Just as you will instruct us by your letters at each fair, so at each fair shall we write and enter it in our book. The receipts we shall post to your receipts, the payments we shall post to your payments, and the loans we shall write to the loans, just as we have always done up to the present time. Therefore, any money which you collect or which comes into your hands, when you have instructed us once by letter about it, do not repeat it any more; for as soon as you have instructed us about it, we post it at once—whatever you tell us are receipts among receipts, and we post the payments to the payments, and the loans to the loans. And we do so for every letter. Therefore, if you should instruct us through more than one letter, you see that it would not be a good thing to do; for just as many times as you instruct us, so many times we shall post it in the book in our customary way. Therefore do take care. And we mention this in connection with the £ 3 Provisine, which Testa Tebaldi takes and Tederigo Lei gives. For you received out of them 34 soldi less 4 deniers, and you have sent me instructions about this through several letters.[1] For if we had not remembered that we had posted them once to your receipts, we certainly would have posted them a second time. Therefore take care—do not instruct us about it more than once.

And just as we instructed you in the other letter, so we repeat in this that you must not be astonished that we have sold and are selling Provisines; for you ought to know, Giacomo, that we are under great expense and extremely busy because of the war we are having against Florence. And you ought to know that we have to have money to spend and to make war; on account of this, we see that we cannot raise money from any source more advantageous for us than by selling Provisines. And should you say that we ought to obtain a loan here, it would do us no good: for you ought to know that money costs from 5 to 6 deniers a pound from one merchant to another, and it costs those who are not merchants from 10 to 12 deniers a pound in *corsa,*[2]

---

[1] Although medieval coinage was a very complicated system, the following generalizations may be made: 1 £ = 20 solidi (shillings) = 240 denarii (pennies). Over time, certain governments gained a reputation for minting coins of honest weight, and their money was widely used. Here the reference is to the coinage of Provins, one of the towns in which the Counts of Champagne held their international fairs.

[2] In this kind of contract, the interest was specified in advance; thus, the lender knew what his return was going to be, and that it was not subject to fluctuations in rates of exchange.

although it is in the same state. Now you see what [the conditions of] lending are here. Therefore do not feel too badly that we are selling Provisines, since we had rather be in debt in France than be in debt here or sell sterling. For it is worth far more to us so long as we can get Provisines at the price they cost you today than it would be to sell the sterling or to borrow here; because we draw greater interest in England than we would in France, and in order to raise a loan here today we should have to pay a price greater than would be any profit that we could get in France. Therefore be satisfied with what we are doing, and do not be astonished at all about it. And you ought to know, Giacomo, that if in the country of France one could profit more than one can profit there today, we should do well, since you would have a great many Provisines, so that you would well get whatever arrangement you may wish, and we would certainly get our share of whatever profit might be made in that land; and about that be of good cheer.

And we understand from you through your letter that you have gone, both without and with Tolomeo Pelacane, to see the dean of Saint Etienne of Troyes about the business of Lyons-on-the-Rhone, and that you spoke and argued a good deal with the procurator of that archbishop of Lyons-on-the-Rhone, and you could not persuade him to come to any conclusion or agreement that was good for us; nor could you persuade him unless we sent you a letter from the papal Curia against him. In this matter you ought to know that we have had and are still having a great deal of trouble, because of the war and making expeditions and cavalry raids, so that we have not been able to devote our attention to obtaining the letter. Therefore you ought to know that as soon as we have a [breathing] spell to devote our attention to it we shall do so, and we shall see to it that you get the said letter against them. . . .

And we also understand from you through a note of yours that we are expected to beg Orlando Bonsignore that he should instruct his partners over there that whenever you wish to borrow from his partners they should consent to it, for that would be a great boon to us. In this regard we tell you that the said Orlando Bonsignore was not in Siena when this letter was written, but he was with the army at Montepulciano. Therefore, when he returns, we shall get in touch with him and remind him about it; and we definitely believe that he will do what we wish about it. . . .

And also we let you know that we have sold £106 Provisine to Giacomo Ubertini, changer, to be paid at the fair of Saint John, year [12]60; and we sold them at the rate of s.33 a dozen, and we have been paid. Therefore you shall pay them at his order to Rimbotto Buonaiuti at the latter's pleasure; and when you make the payment to him, have a record made of it in the book of the Officials of the Merchants, as is customary to do. . . .

On the other hand, we want to let you know about the developments in Tuscany. For you ought to know, Giacomo, that we are today under great expense and extremely busy because of the war we are having against Florence. And you ought to know that it will take plenty out of our pocket; but we shall lick Florence so [badly] that we shall never have to guard ourselves from her any more, if God protects from evil the lord King Manfred, to whom may God grant long life, amen. . . .

SUMMA THEOLOGICA*

St. Thomas Aquinas

WHETHER, IN TRADING, IT IS LAWFUL TO SELL A THING AT A HIGHER PRICE THAN WHAT WAS PAID FOR IT?

We proceed thus to the Fourth Article:—

Objection 1. It would seem that it is not lawful, in trading, to sell a thing for a higher price than we paid for it. For Chrysostom[1] says on Matth. xxi. 12: *He that buys a thing in order that he may sell it, entire and unchanged, at a profit, is the trader who is cast out of God's temple.* Cassiodorus speaks in the same sense in his commentary on Ps. lxx. 15, *Because I have not known learning,* or *trading* according to another version:[2] *What is trade,* says he, *but buying at a cheap price with the purpose of retailing at a higher price?* and he adds: *Such were the tradesmen whom Our Lord cast out of the temple.* Now no man is cast out of the temple except for a sin. Therefore suchlike trading is sinful.

Obj. 2. Further, It is contrary to justice to sell goods at a higher price than their worth, or to buy them for less then their value. . . .[3] Now if you sell a thing for a higher price than you paid for it, you must either have bought it for less than its value, or sell it for more than its value. Therefore this cannot be done without sin.

Obj. 3. Further, Jerome says *(Ep. ad Nepot.* lii.*): Shun, as you would the plague, a cleric who from being poor has become wealthy, or who, from being a nobody has become a celebrity.* Now trading would not seem to be forbidden to clerics except on account of its sinfulness. Therefore it is a sin in trading, to buy at a low price and to sell at a higher price.

On the contrary, Augustine commenting on Ps. lxx. 15, . . . says: *The greedy tradesman blasphemes over his losses: he lies and perjures himself over the price of his wares. But these are vices of the man, not of the craft, which can be exercised without these vices.* Therefore trading is not in itself unlawful.

I answer that, A tradesman is one whose business consists in the exchange of things. According to the Philosopher *(Polit.* i. 3), exchange of things is twofold; one, natural as it were, and necessary, whereby one commodity is exchanged for another, or money taken in exchange for a commodity, in order to satisfy the needs of life. Suchlike trading, properly

---

* St. Thomas Aquinas, *Summa Theologica*, Q.77. Art. 4, trans. The Dominican Fathers of the English Province (New York: Benziger Brothers, Inc., London: Burns, Oates, and Washburne, Ltd., 1929), pp. 326–328.

[1] St. John Chrysostom (*c.* 345–407), Patriarch (bishop) of Constantinople famed for his eloquence.

[2] Sixth-century Roman statesman and writer. He founded several monasteries whose monks he had translate Greek works into Latin.

[3] The student should always keep in mind the interrelatedness of Thomas' arguments.

speaking, does not belong to tradesmen, but rather to housekeepers or civil servants who have to provide the household or the state with the necessaries of life. The other kind of exchange is either that of money for money, or of any commodity for money, not on account of the necessities of life, but for profit, and this kind of exchange, properly speaking, regards tradesmen, according to the Philosopher (*Polit.* i. 3). The former kind of exchange is commendable because it supplies a natural need: but the latter is justly deserving of blame, because, considered in itself, it satisfies the greed for gain, which knows no limit and tends to infinity. Hence trading, considered in itself, has a certain debasement attaching thereto, in so far as, by its very nature, it does not imply a virtuous or necessary end. Nevertheless gain which is the end of trading, though not implying, by its nature, anything virtuous or necessary, does not, in itself, connote anything sinful or contrary to virtue: wherefore nothing prevents gain from being directed to some necessary or even virtuous end, and thus trading becomes lawful. Thus, for instance, a man may intend the moderate gain which he seeks to acquire by trading for the upkeep of his household, or for the assistance of the needy: or again, a man may take to trade for some public advantage, for instance, lest his country lack the necessaries of life, and seek gain, not as an end, but as payment for his labour.

Reply Obj. 1. The saying of Chrysostom refers to the trading which seeks gain as a last end. This is especially the case where a man sells something at a higher price without its undergoing any change. For if he sells at a higher price something that has changed for the the better, he would seem to receive the reward of his labour. Nevertheless the gain itself may be lawfully intended, not as a last end, but for the sake of some other end which is necessary or virtuous, as stated above.

Reply Obj. 2. Not everyone that sells at a higher price than he bought is a tradesman, but only he who buys that he may sell at a profit. If, on the contrary, he buys not for sale but for possession, and afterwards, for some reason wishes to sell, it is not a trade transaction even if he sell at a profit. For he may lawfully do this, either because he has bettered the thing, or because the value of the thing has changed with the change of place or time, or on account of the danger he incurs in tranferring the thing from one place to another, or again in having it carried by another. In this sense neither buying nor selling is unjust.

Reply Obj. 3. Clerics should abstain not only from things that are evil in themselves, but even from those that have an appearance of evil. This happens in trading, both because it is directed to worldly gain, which clerics should despise, and because trading is open to so many vices, since *a merchant is hardly free from sins of the lips.* (Ecclus. xxvi. 28). There is also another reason, because trading engages the mind too much with worldly cares, and consequently withdraws it from spiritual cares; wherefore the Apostle says (2 Tim. ii. 4): *No man being a soldier to God entangleth himself with secular businesses.* Nevertheless it is lawful for clerics to engage in the first mentioned kind of exchange, which is directed to supply the necessaries of life, either by buying or by selling.

ON THE DIGNITY AND OFFICE OF MERCHANTS*

Benedetto Cotrugli

The dignity and office of merchants is great and exalted in many respects, and most particularly in four. First, with respect to the common weal. For the advancement of public welfare is a very honorable [purpose], as Cicero states, and one ought [to be willing] even to die [for it]. . . . The advancement, the comfort, and the health of republics to a large extent proceed from merchants; we are always speaking, of course, not of plebeian and vulgar merchants but of the glorious merchant of whom we treat [and who is] lauded in this work of ours. And with respect to mercantile business and activity [we may say] this: Through trade, that ornament and advancement [of republics], sterile countries are provided with food and supplies and also enjoy many strange things which are imported from places where [other] commodities are lacking. [Merchants] also bring about an abundance of money, jewels, gold, silver, and all kinds of metals. They bring about an abundance of gilds of various crafts. Hence, cities and countries are driven to cultivate the land, to enlarge the herds, and to exploit the incomes and rents. And [merchants] through their activity enable the poor to live; through their initiative in tax farming they promote the activity of administrators; through their exports and imports of merchandise they cause the customs and excises of the lords and republics to expand, and consequently they enlarge the public and common treasury.

Secondly, I exalt the dignity and office of merchants with respect to the useful and honorable management of their private properties and goods. As a matter of fact, a sparing, temperate, solid, and upright merchant increases and augments his wealth. This is why we observe that merchants abound in movable and immovable property, in the wealth of their homes and furniture, in the ornaments and clothing of their families, in the dowering of their sons and daughters, and consequently in the continuous improvement of their condition through intermarriage with ever higher [families]. . . . And quite the reverse happens to those who do not have this glorious initiative. That is why the proverb was popular and commonplace with our elders: Sad is the house which [never] engaged in trade. For [whenever] a farmer or a gentleman lives on his income without supplementing it through commercial initiative, [the income], large though it may be, is worth much less than it would be in the hands of a merchant. . . . If he wants to marry off his daughters, he has to sell real estate and to take bread from his own mouth. As for what is left after the death of a farmer who during his life was unable to enlarge his estate through trade and initiative . . . his goods must be divided among his children according to the share which is going [to each of them]. And if his sons do not end in an almshouse, his grandsons or great-grandsons will, and the house will continue to decline. . . .

Third, the dignity of merchants is to be esteemed and appreciated with

* Reprinted from *Medieval Trade in the Mediterranean World,* trans. and ed. R. S. Lopez and I. Raymond (New York: Columbia University Press, 1955), pp. 416–418.

respect to association, both private and public. Private [association] means at home, where [the merchant] associates with an honorable family in continuous and virtuous activity. For you have to consider that where silver, gold, money, and other things of similar value are handled, there is no room for rogues, retainers, henchmen of all sorts, partisans, thieves, runaways, and gamblers such as are wont to live at the courts of princes, magnates, and lords. . . . Outside their homes, merchants associate with artisans, gentlemen, lords, princes, and prelates of every rank, all of whom flock [to see] the merchants since they always need them. And very frequently great scholars come to visit merchants in their homes. . . . For no professional [man] understands or has ever understood the monarchies of this world and the states in regard to man-agement of money—upon which all human states depend—as does a good and learned merchant. . . .

We have left for the fourth [place] the dignity of merchants with respect to [good] faith. . . . It is generally said that today [good] faith abides with merchants and men-at-arms. . . . Neither kings nor princes nor any [other] rank of men enjoy as much reputation or credit as a good merchant. Hence, a merchant's [reputation and credit] serve him readily for cash, while those of others do not: and if they [i.e., the credit and reputation of others] are given in payment, they carry a much higher interest [charge than the merchants']. And whereas a simple and plain receipt of a merchant is valid even without witnesses, the rulers and any other people are not believed without an instru-ment and strong cautions. Hence, and for the reasons [already] given, mer-chants ought to take pride in their outstanding dignity.

And to proceed according to our design we shall state that in order to maintain this dignity it is necessary for a merchant to remove from himself any undignified ornament both of the soul and of the body. And merchants must not have the fierce manners of husky men-at-arms, nor must they have the soft manners of jesters and comedians, but they must be serious in speak-ing, in walking, and in all actions, maintaining as much as possible their dignity. . . .

9. How Can Men Best Serve God?

One of the great inspirational figures of the Middle Ages is St. Francis of Assisi. Born in 1182 to a merchant father who indulged his young son, Francis deeply experienced "conversion." He renounced worldly luxury to lead a beggar's life of poverty and an active life of love for his fellow man and all of God's creation. In the early thirteenth century, the Church looked with suspi-cion upon men whose way of life, preaching, and attractiveness to followers constituted a de facto criticism of ecclesiastical institutions; during the very years of Francis' initial activities, Pope Innocent III preached a crusade against heresy in southern France. But Francis' orthodoxy was proved, and in 1215 his group, with its special emphasis upon poverty, love, and help to brother Chris-tians, was formally recognized. Although heresy and anticlericalism eventually developed within the order, throughout the Middle Ages and beyond, the Franciscan ideals of charity and love strengthened the Church at moments of crisis.

DEVOTIONAL WRITINGS*

St. Francis of Assisi

LETTER TO A MINISTER

To Brother N . . . , Minister. May God bless you.

This is my advice with regard to the state of your soul. As I see it, you should consider everything that makes it difficult for you to love God as a special favour, even if other persons, whether friars or not, are responsible for it, or even if they go so far as to do you physical violence. This is the way you should want it to be, and you can take this as a command from God and from me. I am convinced that this is true obedience. You must love those who behave like this towards you, and you should want nothing else from them, except what God permits to happen to you. You can show your love for them by wishing that they should be better Christians. This should be of greater benefit to you than the solitude of a hermitage.

I should like you to prove that you love God and me, his servant and yours, in the following way. There should be no friar in the whole world who has fallen into sin, no matter how far he has fallen, who will ever fail to find your forgiveness for the asking, if he will only look into your eyes. And if he does not ask forgiveness, you should ask him if he wants it. And should he appear before you again a thousand times, you should love him more than you love me, so that you may draw him to God; you should always have pity on such friars. Tell the guardians, too, that this is your policy.

At the Pentecost Chapter,[1] with God's help and the advice of the friars, we shall make one chapter out of all the chapters in the Rule that speak of mortal sin. It will go like this:

> If a friar is tempted and falls into mortal sin, he is bound by obedience to have recourse to his guardian. The other friars who know that he has sinned should not embarrass him by speaking about it. They should have the greatest sympathy for him and keep their brother's fall a secret. *It is not the healthy who need a physician, but they who are sick* (Mt. 9: 12). They are obliged by obedience to send him to their superior, in the company of another friar. The superior, in his turn, is bound to provide compassionately for him, just as he would wish provision to be made for him if he were in a similar position. A friar who falls into venial sin should confess to a confrère who is a priest; if there is no priest present, he should confess to another friar, until he meets a priest who can absolve him sacramentally, as has been said. The other friars have no authority to impose a penance, but must be content with the advice, *Go thy way, and from now on sin no more* (Jn 8: 11).

---

* Reprinted from Benen Fahy, O.F.M., and Placid Hermann, O.F.M., *The Writings of St. Francis of Assisi* (Chicago: Franciscan Herald Press, 1964), pp. 110–111, 125–126, 130–131.
[1] Meeting of the members of the Franciscan order.

Keep this letter until Pentecost, so that it may be more faithfully observed. You will attend the chapter with your friars. With the help of God, you will see that these and other points not provided for in the Rule are fulfilled.

Praises of God

You are holy, Lord, the only God,
    and your deeds are wonderful.
You are strong.
        You are great.
        You are the Most High,
        You are almighty.
        You, holy Father, are
        King of heaven and earth.
You are Three and One,
        Lord God, all good.
        You are Good, all Good, supreme Good,
        Lord God, living and true.
You are love,
        You are wisdom.
        You are humility,
        You are endurance.
        You are rest,
        You are peace.
        You are joy and gladness.
        You are justice and moderation.
        You are all our riches,
        And you suffice for us.
You are beauty.
        You are gentleness.
        You are our protector,
        You are our guardian and defender.
        You are courage.
        You are our haven and our hope.
You are our faith,
        Our great consolation.
        You are our eternal life,
        Great and wonderful Lord,
        God almighty,
        Merciful Saviour.

The Blessing for Brother Leo

God bless you and keep you.
    May God smile on you, and be merciful to you;
May God turn his regard towards you
    and give you peace.

May God bless you, Brother Leo.

THE CANTICLE OF BROTHER SUN

Most high, all-powerful, all good, Lord!
    All praise is yours, all glory, all honour
    And all blessing.
To you, alone, Most High, do they belong.
    No mortal lips are worthy
    To pronounce your name.
All praise be yours, my Lord, through all that you have made,
    And first my lord Brother Sun,
    Who brings the day; and light you give us through him.
How beautiful is he, how radiant in all his splendour!
    Of you, Most High, he bears the likeness.
All praise be yours, my Lord, through Sister Moon and Stars;
    In the heavens you have made them, bright
    And precious and fair.
All praise be yours, my Lord, through Brothers Wind and Air,
    And fair and stormy, all the weather's moods,
    By which you cherish all that you have made.
All praise be yours, my Lord, through Sister Water,
    So useful, lowly, precious and pure.
All praise be yours, my Lord, through Brother Fire,
    Through whom you brighten up the night.
    How beautiful is he, how gay! Full of power and strength.
All praise be yours, my Lord, through Sister Earth, our mother,
    Who feeds us in her sovereignty and produces
    Various fruits with coloured flowers and herbs.
All praise be yours, my Lord, through those who grant pardon
    For love of you; through those who endure
    Sickness and trial.
Happy those who endure in peace,
    By you, Most High, they will be crowned.
All praise be yours, my Lord, through Sister Death,
    From whose embrace no mortal can escape.
Woe to those who die in mortal sin!
    Happy those She finds doing your will!
    The second death can do no harm to them.
Praise and bless my Lord, and give him thanks,
    And serve him with great humility.

10. What Was the Nature of Medieval Social Justice?

The author of Piers Plowman *was probably one man, William Lang-land, who lived from about 1332 to about 1400, and not, as some scholars have believed, a mythical author whose work was written by five different men. The son of a minor landowner, Langland was educated at the monastery of Great Malvern in England, and then entered minor orders. Not ordained,*

unbeneficed, he was a member of what has been described as a "clerical pro-
letariat." In the course of his life, he knew the poor of London as well as of
the countryside, and in London he supported his family by celebrating religious
offices for the wealthy.

Piers Plowman is a great poem, and not the least of its virtues is the
range of its vision. It is often compared with Chaucer's Canterbury Tales for
the vividness with which it depicts men and women of all classes and evaluates
their performance of their tasks in relation to traditional values and expecta-
tions. That the poem was popular in its own day suggests that Langland's
attacks on social abuses were well received. Well over a century before the
Reformation, he voiced criticisms of the Church that bit deep both because of
their poetic power and because they came from such a deeply religious soul.
But even if the poem expresses sympathy for the weak and hatred for their op-
pressors, it is not a revolutionary document. Langland wanted something very
different from an upheaval of the social order.

PIERS PLOWMAN*

William Langland

Prologue

In a summer season   when soft was the sun,
I clothed myself in a cloak   as I shepherd were,
Habit like a hermit's   unholy in works,
And went wide in the world   wonders to hear.
But on a May morning   on Malvern hills,
A marvel befell me   of fairy, methought.
I was weary with wandering   and went me to rest
Under a broad bank   by a brook's side,
And as I lay and leaned over   and looked into the waters
I fell into a sleep   for it sounded so merry.
   Then began I to dream   a marvellous dream,
That I was in a wilderness   wist I not where.
As I looked to the east   right into the sun,
I saw a tower on a toft   worthily built;
A deep dale beneath   a dungeon therein,
With deep ditches and dark   and dreadful of sight.
A fair field full of folk   found I between,
Of all manner of men   the rich and the poor,
Working and wandering   as the world asketh.
Some put them to plow   and played little enough,

---

* William Langland, *The Book Concerning Piers the Plowman*, trans. into Modern English by Donald and Rachel Attwater ("Everyman's Library Edition," London: J. M. Dent & Sons; New York: E. P. Dutton & Co., 1957), pp. 1–3, 137–139, 141–143. Reprinted by permission of E. P. Dutton & Co., Inc., and J. M. Dent & Sons, Ltd.

At setting and sowing   they sweated right hard
And won that which wasters   by gluttony destroy.
    Some put them to pride   and apparalled themselves so
In a display of clothing   they came disguised.
    To prayer and penance   put themselves many,
All for love of our Lord   living hard lives,
In hope for to have   heavenly bliss.
Such as anchorites and hermits   that kept them in their cells,
And desired not the country   around to roam;
Nor with luxurious living   their body to please.
    And some chose trade   they fared the better,
As it seemeth to our sight   that such men thrive.
And some to make mirth   as minstrels know how,
And get gold with their glees   guiltlessly, I hold.
But jesters and janglers   children of Judas,
Feigning their fancies   and making folk fools,
They have wit at will   to work, if they would;
Paul preacheth of them   I'll not prove it here—
Qui turpiloquium loquitur[1]   is Lucifer's hind.
    Tramps and beggars   went quickly about,
Their bellies and their bags   with bread well crammed;
Cadging for their food   fighting at ale;
In gluttony, God knows   going to bed,
And getting up with ribaldry   the thieving knaves!
Sleep and sorry sloth   ever pursue them.
    Pilgrims and palmers   pledged them together
To seek Saint James   and saints in Rome.
They went forth on their way   with many wise tales,
And had leave to lie   all their life after—
I saw some that said   they had sought saints:
Yet in each tale that they told   their tongue turned to lies
More than to tell truth   it seemed by their speech.
    Hermits, a heap of them   with hooked staves,
Were going to Walsingham   and their wenches too;
Big loafers and tall   that loth were to work,
Dressed up in capes   to be known from others;
And so clad as hermits   their ease to have.
    I found there friars   of all the four orders,
Preaching to the people   for profit to themselves,
Explaining the Gospel   just as they liked,
To get clothes for themselves   they construed it as they would.
Many of these master friars   may dress as they will,
For money and their preaching   both go together.
For since charity hath been chapman   and chief to shrive lords,
Many miracles have happened   within a few years.
Except Holy Church and they   agree better together,

---

[1] "Who speaks filth."

Great mischief on earth   is mounting up fast.
    There preached a pardoner   as if he priest were:
He brought forth a brief   with bishops' seals thereon,
And said that himself might   absolve them all
From falseness in fasting   and of broken vows.
    Laymen believed him   welcomed his words,
And came up on their knees   to kiss his seals;
He cozened them with his brevet   dimmed their eyes,
And with his parchment   got his rings and brooches:
Thus they gave their gold   gluttons to keep.
And lent it to such louts   as follow lechery.
If the bishop were holy   and worth both his ears,
His seal should not be sent   to deceive the people.
But a word 'gainst bishop   the knave never preacheth.
Parish priest and pardoner   share all the silver
That the parish poor would have   if he were not there.
    Parsons and parish priests   complained to the bishop
That their parishes were poor   since the pestilence time,[2]
And asked leave and licence   in London to dwell
And sing *requiems* for stipends   for silver is sweet.[3]
    Bishops and bachelors   both masters and doctors,
That have charge under Christ   and the tonsure as token
And sign that they should   shrive their parishioners,
Preach and pray for them   and feed the poor,
These lodge in London in Lent   and at other times too.[4]
Some serve the king   and his silver count
In Chequer and Chancery courts[5]   making claim for his debts
Of wards and of wardmotes   waifs and estrays.
And some serve as servants   to lords and ladies,
And instead of stewards   sit in session to judge.
Their mass and their matins   their canonical hours,
Are said undevoutly   I fear at the last
Lest Christ in his council   accurse will full many.
I perceived of the power   that Peter had to keep,
To bind and to unbind   as the Book telleth,
How he left it with love   as our Lord ordained,
Amongst four virtues   the best of all virtues,
That cardinal are called   for they hinge the gates
Where Christ is in glory   to close and to shut
And to open it to them   and show heavenly bliss.
But of cardinals at Rome   that receiveth that name
And power presumed in them   a pope to make,

---

[2] Reference is to the great (bubonic) plague of 1348 that devastated life throughout Europe.
[3] Towns were usually frequented by wandering priests who said a private mass for a fee.
[4] Compare St. Gregory, *Pastoral Care*, above, pp. 169–175.
[5] Here Langland was referring to two branches of the royal government located in London: the Exchequer handled taxation; the Chancery issued royal documents, letters, privileges, etc.

That they have Peter's power   deny it I will not;
For to love and learning   that election belongeth,
Therefore I can, and yet cannot   of that court speak more.

*At this point in the poem, the poet, who is seeking salvation, dreams of
a meeting with Anima. Anima has many names, and in this creature are
united the higher spiritual and intellectual powers—Mind, Soul, Life. In this
passage, Anima tells Piers what charity is and launches into a discussion of the
responsibilities and performance of the priesthood.*

'What is Charity?' quoth I then   'a childlike thing,' he said;
   'Nisi efficiamini sicut parvuli, non intrabitis in regnum caelorum;[6]
Without childishness or folly   a free liberal will.'
'Where should men find such a friend   with so free a heart?
I have lived in the land,' quoth I   'my name is Long Will,
And found I never full charity   before nor behind!
Men be merciful   to mendicants and to poor,
And will lend where they believe   honestly to be payed.
'But charity that Paul praiseth best   and most pleasant to our Saviour,
   As, *non inflatur, non est ambitiosa, non quaerit quae sua sunt,*[7]
I saw never such a man   so me God help,
That would not ask after his own   and other whiles covet
Things that he needed not   and take if he might!
Clerks teach me that Christ   is in all places;
But I saw him never truly   but as myself in a mirror,
   Ita in aenigmate, tunc facie ad faciem.[8]
And so I trow truly   by what men telleth of charity,
It is not champions' contest   nor trade, as I think.'
'Charity,' quoth he, 'chaffereth not   nor challengeth, nor craveth.
As proud of a penny   as of a pound of gold,
And is as glad of a gown   of a gray wool
As of a tunic of Tharsian silk   or of choice scarlet.
He is glad with all the glad   and good to all wicked,
And believeth and loveth all   that our Lord made.
Curseth he no creature   nor can he bear wrath,
Nor no liking hath to lie   nor laugh men to scorn.
All that men saith, he hold it true   and in peace taketh,
And in all manner of mischiefs   in mildness he suffereth;
Coveteth he no earthly good   but bliss of heaven's kingdom.'
'Hath he any rents or riches   or any rich friends?'
'Of rents nor of riches   recketh he never.
For a friend findeth him   that faileth him never at need;
Fiat-voluntas-tua[9]   finds him evermore.

---

[6] "For unless you become as little children, you shall not enter into the Kingdom of
Heaven." Matt. 18:3.
[7] "vaunteth not itself, is not puffed up, and seeketh not her own." I Cor. 13:4–5.
[8] "For now we see through a glass darkly, but then face to face." I Cor. 13:12.
[9] "Thy-will-be-done." Matt. 6:10.

And if he suppeth, he eats but a sop   of *spera-in-Deo*.[10]
He can portray well the *pater noster*[11]   and paint it with *aves*,
And otherwhiles is his wont   to wend in pilgrimage,
Where poor men and prisoners lie   their pardon to have.
Though he bear them no bread   he beareth them sweeter livelihood,
Loveth them as our Lord biddeth   and looketh how they fare.
    'And when he is weary of that work   then will he sometimes
Labour in a laundry   well the length of a mile,
And go to youth   and eagerly address
Pride with all its appurtenances   and pack them together,
And soak them in his breast   and beat them clean,
And labour on them long   with *laboravi-in-gemitu-meo*,[12]
And with warm water at his eyes   wash them after.
And then he singeth when he doth so   and sometimes saith weeping,
    Cor contritum et humiliatum, Deus, non despicies.'[13]
    'By Christ, I would that I knew him,' quoth I   'no creature rather!'
'Without help of Piers Plowman,' quoth he   'his person seest thou never.'
'Do clerks know him,' quoth I   'that keep holy church?'
    'Clerks have no knowing,' quoth he   'but by works and by words.
But Piers the Plowman   perceiveth more deeper
What is the will and wherefore   that many wights suffer,
    Et vidit Deus cogitationes eorum.[14]
For there are full proud-hearted men   patient of tongue,
And polite as of bearing   to burgesses and to lords,
And to poor people   have pepper in the nose,
And as a lion he looketh   where men blame their works.
    'For there are beggars and bidders   beadsmen as it were,
Looketh as lambs   and seem life-holy,
But it is more to have their meat   with such an easy manner,
Than for penance and perfectness   the poverty that such have.
Therefore by sight nor by clergy   know shalt thou him never,
Neither through words nor works   but through will alone.
And that knoweth no clerk   nor creature on earth,
But Piers the Plowman   *Petrus, id est, Christus.*[15]
For he is not among rascals   nor vagabond hermits,
Nor among anchorites, where a box hangeth   all such they deceive.
Fie on deceivers   and *in fautores suos!*[16]
For charity is God's champion   and as a good child mild,
And the merriest of mouth   at meat where he sitteth.
The love that lieth in his heart   maketh him light of speech,

---

[10] "Trust-in-the-Lord." Ps. 37:3.
[11] The Lord's Prayer, from the first two words in the Latin.
[12] "I-am-weary-with-my-groaning." Ps. 6:6.
[13] "A broken and contrite heart, O God, shalt thou not despise." Ps. 51:17.
[14] "And God sees their thoughts."
[15] "Peter, that is, Christ."
[16] "upon their supporters."

And is companionable and cheerful   as Christ himself bids,
 Nolite fieri sicut hypocritae, tristes, etc.[17]
For I have seen him in silk   and sometimes in russet.
Both in grey and in fur   and in gilt armour,
And as gladly he gave   to people that needed.
Edmund and Edward   both were kings,[18]
And saints considered   when charity them followed.
I have seen charity also   sing and read,
Ride and run   in ragged weeds,
But bidding as beggars   beheld I him never.
But in rich robes   soonest he walketh,
Capped and annointed   and his crown shaved,
And cleanly clothed   in lawn and in silk of Tartary.
And in a friar's frock   he was found once,
But it is far agone   in St. Francis' time;
In that sect since   too seldom hath he been known.
Rich men he recommendeth   and of their robes taketh,
That without guile   lead their lives,
 Beatus est dives, qui, etc.[19]
In king's court he cometh oft   where the counsel is true,
But if covetousness be of the counsel   he will not come therein.
In court among jesters   he cometh but seldom,
For brawling and back-biting   and bearing of false witness.
In the consistory before the commissary   he cometh not full oft,
For their law lasteth over-long   unless they take silver;
And matrimony for money   make and unmake,
And what Conscience and Christ   have knit fast,
They undo it unworthily   those doctors of law.
Amongst archbishops and other bishops   and prelates of holy church,
To dwell among them   his wont was some time,
And Christ's patrimony to the poor   deal out in portions.
But Avarice hath the keys now   and keepeth for his kinsmen,
And for his executors and his servants   and some for their children.

*   *   *

Who performeth this prophesy   of the people that now live,
 Dispersit, dedit pauperibus, etc.?[20]
If any people perform that text   it is these poor friars!
For what they beg around   in building they spend,
And on themselves some   and such as be their labourers,

---

[17] "Be not, as the hypocrites, of a sad countenance." Matt. 6:16.

[18] King of the English (ruled 993–1016), Edmund was famous for his defense of England against the Danes. However, upon his death, the Dane Canute became king. Edward the Confessor (ruled 1042–1066) struggled to maintain the authority of the English monarchy against the power of the magnates and various foreign threats. His piety was famous, and he was canonized in 1161.

[19] "Blessed is the rich man that is found without blemish, and hath not gone after gold."

[20] "He hath dispersed abroad and given to the poor." II Cor. 9:9.

And from them that have they take   and give them that have not.
  'But clerks and knights   and commoners that be rich,
Many of you fareth   as if I a forest had,
That were full of fair trees   and I considered and thought
How I might more therein   amongst them set.
Right so, ye rich   ye robbeth those that be rich,
To help them that help you   and give where no need is.
As whoso filled a cask   from a fresh river,
And went forth with that water   to wet with the Thames.
Right so, ye rich   ye robbeth and feedeth
Them that have as ye have;   them ye make at ease.
  'But religious that rich be   should rather feast beggars
Than burgesses that rich be   as the book teacheth;
       Quia sacrilegium est res pauperum non pauperibus dare.
       Item: peccatoribus dare, est daemonibus immolare.
       Item: monache, si indiges et accipis, potius das quam accipis;
          si autem non eges, et accipis, rapis.
       Porro non indiget monachus, si habeat quod naturae sufficit.[21]
Therefore I counsel all Christians   to conform them to charity;
For charity without demanding   unchargeth the soul,
And many a prisoner from purgatory   through his prayers he delivereth.
But there is a fault in the folk   that the faith keep;
Wherefore folk are the feebler   and not firm of belief.
As in counterfeit is an evil alloy   and yet looketh it like sterling,
The mark of that money is good   but the metal is feeble;
So it fareth by some folk now   they have fair speech,
Crown and christening   the king's mark of heaven,
But the metal, that is man's soul   with sin is foul alloyed;
Both lettered and unlearned   be now alloyed with sin,
That no man loveth the other   nor our Lord, as it seemeth.
For through war and wicked works   and weathers unreasonable,
Weather-wise shipmen   and wise clerks also
Have no belief in the sky   nor the lore of philosophers.
  'Astronomers all days   in their art fail,
That whilom warned before   what should befall after.
Shipmen and shepherds   that with ship and sheep went,
Wist by the welkin   what should betide;
As of weathers and winds   they warned men oft.
Tillers that tilled the earth   told their masters,
By the seed that they sowed   what they sell might,
And what to lend and what to live by   the land was so true.
Now faileth the folk of the flood   and of the land both,
Shepherds and shipmen   and so do these tillers;
Neither they see nor know   one course before another.

---

[21] "If you do not give to the poor what belongs to them, you commit sacrilege; and similarly, if you give to sinners, you are sacrificing to demons. And when a needy monk receives alms, he should give away more than he gets, and it is a theft for him to accept more than he needs. Indeed, a monk never wants if he has enough to satisfy nature."

Astronomers also   are at their wits' end;
Of that was calculated by the elements   the contrary they find.[22]
Grammar, the ground of all   beguileth now children;
There is none of these new clerks   whoso taketh heed,
That can versify fair   nor formally write;
Nor not one among a hundred   that an author can construe,
Nor read a letter in any language   but in Latin or in English.
Go now to any degree   and unless Guile be master,
And Flatterer his fellow   under him to work,
Much wonder methinketh   amongst us all.
Doctors of decrees   and of divinity masters,
That should learn and know   all kinds of knowledge,
And answers to arguments   and also to a *quodlibet*[23]
(I dare not say it for shame)   if such were opposed,
They would fail in their philosophy   and in physic both.
Wherefore I am afeared   of folk of holy church,
Lest they skip over as others do   in offices and in hours;
But if they skip over, as I hope not   our belief sufficeth;
As clerks at Corpus Christi feast   sing and read,
That *sola fides sufficit*[24]   to save with unlearned people.

---

[22] Actually, it is astrologers who forecast the future from the positions of the planets in the heavens.

[23] A form of disputation or written statement of a philosophical position in use at the medieval universities.

[24] "Faith alone suffices."